Studies in Historical Linguistics

Vol. 7

Edited by

Dr Graeme Davis, Karl A. Bernhardt & Dr Mark Garner

PETER LANG

Oxford · Bern · Berlin · Bruxelles · Frankfurt am Main · New York · Wien

Tomonori Matsushita, A.V.C. Schmidt
and David Wallace (eds)

From *Beowulf* to Caxton

Studies in Medieval Languages and
Literature, Texts and Manuscripts

PETER LANG

Oxford · Bern · Berlin · Bruxelles · Frankfurt am Main · New York · Wien

Bibliographic information published by Die Deutsche Nationalbibliothek
Die Deutsche Nationalbibliothek lists this publication in the Deutsche National-
bibliografie; detailed bibliographic data is available on the Internet
at http://dnb.d-nb.de.

A catalogue record for this book is available from the British Library.

Library of Congress Cataloguing-in-Publication Data:

From Beowulf to Caxton : studies in medieval languages and literature,
texts and manuscripts / Tomonori Matsushita, A.V.C. Schmidt and David
Wallace (eds).
    p. cm. -- (Studies in historical linguistics; 7)
  Includes bibliographical references and index.
  ISBN 978-3-0343-0104-6 (alk. paper)
  1. Language and languages--Early works to 1800. 2. Literature,
Medieval--Classical influences. 3. Literature, Medieval--History and
criticism. 4. Classical literature--History and criticism. 5.
Linguistics--History. I. Matsushita, Tomonori. II. Schmidt, A. V. C.
(Aubrey Vincent Carlyle) III. Wallace, David, 1954-
  P101.F76 2011
  809'.02--dc22

                           2011012141

ISSN 1661-4704
ISBN 978-3-0343-0104-6

© Peter Lang AG, International Academic Publishers, Bern 2011
Hochfeldstrasse 32, CH-3012 Bern, Switzerland
info@peterlang.com, www.peterlang.com, www.peterlang.net

Printed in Germany

To Helen Cooper

Helen Cooper

Contents

List of Tables and Figures

Tables

Figures

Acknowledgements

We have benefited from the help of many scholars who read our articles and made suggestions that improved the finished volume, in particular Linne Mooney.

The editors thank our research assistants – Miwako Honaga, Ryohei Mita and Yuta Okajima – who helped check references in the early stages of the work. All of the contributors have benefited from the patience and expertise of the staff at Peter Lang Ltd. Nick Reynolds was generous in responding to the editors' enquiries and greatly improved the volume.

The editors gratefully acknowledge the permission granted to reproduce the following copyrighted material in this volume.

The following five articles originally appeared in the journal of our project: *Universals and Variation in Language (UVL)*, vols 2–4 (2007–9). Copyright © The Center for Language and Culture, Institute for Social Intelligence, Senshu University:

Kazutomo Karasawa, 'Hrothgar and the Germanic Context in *Beowulf*', *UVL*, vol. 3 (2008): 73–85.

A.V.C. Schmidt, 'The Four Elements as a Structural Idea in *Piers Plowman*', *UVL*, vol. 2 (2007): 37–49.

Yoshiyuki Nakao, 'Textual Variations in *Troilus and Criseyde* and the Rise of Ambiguity', *UVL*, vol. 2 (2007): 119–42.

Sylvia Huot, 'Senshu University Manuscripts 2 and 3 and the *Roman de la Rose* Manuscript Tradition', *UVL*, vol. 4 (2009): 9–21.

Patrick P. O'Neill, 'The Senshu Psalter', *UVL*, vol. 3 (2008): 45–58.

Graham D. Caie, 'A Case of Double Vision: Denmark in *Beowulf* and *Beowulf* in England', *SIMELL* 16 (2001): 21–36. Copyright © The Japan Society for Medieval English Studies.

Mitsu Ide, 'The Old English Equivalents for *Factum Esse* and the Salisbury Psalter', *The Journal of Social Sciences and Humanities (Jinbun Gakuho)* 321 (2001): 371–408. Copyright © The Faculty of Social Sciences and Humanities, Tokyo Metropolitan University.

Figure 6–1. The double prism structure. From Yoshiyuki Nakao, *Chaucer no aimaisei no kozo* (*The Structure of Chaucer's Ambiguity*). Tokyo: Shohakusha, 2004.

Figure 6–2. The stemma of *Troilus and Criseyde*. From R.K. Root, *The Textual Tradition of Chaucer's Troilus*. London: Kegan Paul, Trench, Trübner & Co., Ltd, 1916. Copyright © Kegan Paul, Trench, Trübner & Co., Ltd.

Appendix 7–1. List of external fonts adopted from Cambridge, Parker Library, CCC MS 61. © The Corpus Christi Parker Library, Cambridge.

The editors thank Senshu University Library for permission to reproduce images from the *Le Roman de la Rose* (MS 3 and MS 3) and the Northern England Psalter (MS 8).

Every effort has been made to trace copyright holders and to obtain their permission for the use of copyright material. The publisher apologizes for any errors or omissions in the above list and would be grateful for notification of any corrections that should be incorporated in future reprints or editions of this book.

The publication of this book was partly supported by the 'Open Research Center' Project for Private Universities, matching the funds provided by MEXT (Ministry of Education, Culture, Sports, Science and Technology), 2005–9.

— TOMONORI MATSUSHITA
January 2011

TOMONORI MATSUSHITA

Introduction

In establishing their kingdom of England in the ninth and tenth centuries, the Anglo-Saxons created their own literature in their own language.[1] R.D. Fulk and Christopher M. Cain (2003: 2) pointed out that, for literary purposes, the defining characteristic of Anglo-Saxon culture lies in its fusion of two differing strains: the military culture of the Germanic peoples who invaded Britain in the fifth century and the Mediterranean learning introduced by Christian missionaries from the end of the sixth. Germanic legend proved vital to the Anglo-Saxons for several centuries in establishing a distinctively Germanic cultural identity in their new land.[2] The material of Germanic legend was transmitted in the form of short narrative songs, or 'lays'.[3] 'The verse form used for vernacular poetry throughout the Anglo-Saxon period', observed Donald G. Scragg,

> was that common to all the Germanic peoples, and was carried to England by the migrating tribes of the fifth century ... Heroic poetry in Old English tells of the professional minstrel at the court of kings, singing traditional legends from the Germanic past, and occasionally adding Christian stories to his repertoire ....[4]

---

1   Patrick Wormald, 'Anglo-Saxon Society and its Literature', in M. Godden and M. Lapidge eds., *The Cambridge Companion to Old English Literature* (Cambridge: Cambridge University Press, 1991): 1.

2   R.D. Fulk and Christopher M. Cain, *A History of Old English Literature* (Oxford and Berlin: Blackwell, 2003): 2.

3   Roberta Frank, 'Germanic Legend in Old English Literature', in *The Cambridge Companion to Old English Literature* (1991): 90.

4   Donald G. Scragg, 'The Nature of Old English Verse', in *The Cambridge Companion to Old English Literature* (1991): 55.

Medieval English literature in the post-Conquest period is generally considered as a fruit growing to maturity under the ripening influence of Classical and medieval Latin, medieval French and Italian early Renaissance literature. Medieval English writers were particularly drawn to the writings of Virgil and Ovid in Latin, works such as the *Roman de la Rose* in Old French, and Italian works such as Dante's *Divina Commedia* and Boccaccio's *Il Filostrato* and *Il Teseida*. As Helen Cooper put it, 'medieval writers were very conscious of living in the shadow of the classical world, its literature, and its learning. "The Philosopher" meant Aristotle; Virgil and Ovid were the greatest poets.'[5]

Piero Boitani particularly acknowledged the great and fortunate influence of the Italian Trecento on the greatest poet of medieval English literature:

> The Trecento is the first 'golden' century in Italian culture after Augustus, Trajan and Constantine, and a century in which the Middle Ages, classical antiquity and the roots of modern European culture met. It was indeed fortunate that Chaucer visited Italy and read Italian literature in the second half of this century.[6]

Speaking of the impact of classical writers, Christopher Baswell observed,

> The second half of the fourteenth century witnessed a revival of interest in classical story and particularly in the *Aeneid* ... Geoffrey Chaucer began to write his own Troy poems, including two works that specifically claimed to represent the Virgilian story of Aeneas and Dido.[7]

5   Helen Cooper, 'The Classical Background', in Steve Ellis (ed.), *Chaucer: An Oxford Guide* (Oxford: Oxford University Press, 2005): 255.
6   Piero Boitani (ed.), *Chaucer and the Italian Trecento* (Cambridge: Cambridge University Press, 1983): 1.
7   Christopher Baswell, *Virgil in Medieval England* (Cambridge: Cambridge University Press, 1995): 220.

And as Cooper noted,

> A number of Chaucer's works are set in the classical, pagan world, foremost among them being *Troilus and Criseyde* and the 'Knight's Tale'. ... The setting matters because in these poems he makes a striking attempt to re-create the mindset of pre-Christian characters.[8]

> With *Troilus*, English poetry takes its place in the great tradition of European literature derived from the classics.[9]

C.S. Lewis famously argued '[that] the process which *Il Filostrato* underwent at Chaucer's hands was first and foremost a process of *medievalization*.'[10] David Wallace, speaking of Chaucer's relations with Italy, reminded us that

> When Chaucer travelled to Florence on a trade mission in the spring of 1373 he probably heard Boccaccio spoken of as Dante's most distinguished disciple .... And on 23 October 1373 [Boccaccio] gave the first of his celebrated Dante lectures at the Florentine church of Santo Stefano di Badia.[11]

Boitani found much common ground between Dante and Chaucer, his most diligent fourteenth-century pupil:

> They both loved the classics, in particular Virgil and Statius; they were both steeped in medieval philosophy and literature; they were both interested in science. There are important parallels in their formative years as poets and men: both started as love poets; for both the *Roman de la Rose* seems to have had a fundamental, though different, importance; for both the reading of Boethius was a key experience.[12]

---

8   Cooper, 'The Classical Background': 261.
9   Cooper, 'The Classical Background': 269.
10 C.S. Lewis, 'What Chaucer Really Did to *Il Filostrato*', in Stephen A. Barney (ed.), *Geoffrey Chaucer: Troilus and Criseyde* (New York and London: W.W. Norton, 2006): 56.
11 David Wallace, *Chaucer and the Early Writings of Boccaccio*, Chaucer Studies XII (Cambridge: D.S. Brewer, 1985): 5.
12 Piero Boitani (ed.), *Chaucer and the Italian Trecento* (Cambridge: Cambridge University Press, 1983): 115.

In relation to the great French allegory Boitani mentions here, Helen Phillips pointed out,

> The influence of the *Roman de la Rose* appears throughout Chaucer's work. Its phrases and themes became part of his own language; his use of proverbs and mythological allusions often echoes the *Roman's*. ... Guillaume's elegant allegory of a young man falling in love, presented as the entry into a walled 'garden of delight', representing courtly society as well as the pursuit of heterosexual desire, was the seminal influence on the great medieval tradition of amorous dream-literature.[13]

She continued:

> Chaucer's writing encompasses philosophical inquiry, moral debate, and a sympathy with sensual experience and emotional psychology that he shares with Ovid. He shows that a great poet joins a great tradition by being new.[14]

In speaking of *Piers Plowman*, the work of Chaucer's great contemporary, William Langland, T.P. Dunning observed:

> In treating of human activity in terms of man's final end, Langland made use of the positive dogmatic system promulgated by the Church and accepted by the consciences of the faithful. For the medievals, this system constituted a complete interpretation of human life and destiny. 'Christianity was presented through the Church,' as Powicke (1935: 21, 13) observes, 'as an interpretation of the Universe'; the Church's 'secret was not merely part of life, it gave meaning to life, and was the spring of that knowledge of the Universe of which the Church was the vehicle.'[15]

Medieval English culture had developed from its ancient Germanic base to produce a new stage through a gradual process of interpenetration between ancient Germanic cultures and newly introduced Romance influences. Chaucer and Langland achieved remarkably distinctive forms of creativity in Middle English literature. The former enjoyed consuming Classical

---

13   Helen Phillips, 'The French Background', in Steve Ellis (ed.), *Chaucer: An Oxford Guide* (Oxford: Oxford University Press, 2005): 309.

14   Phillips, 'The French Background': 311.

15   T.P. Dunning, '*Piers Plowman*: An Interpretation of the A Text', in Edward Vasta (ed.) *Interpretations of* Piers Plowman (Notre Dame, IN and London: University of Notre Dame Press, 1968): 87.

Latin, Italian Renaissance and Old French literatures and expressing his humour by translating continental masterpieces and composing his original works. The latter expressed himself through dream visions and allegories of a highly individual character, availing himself of continental influences in more occulted ways. Insular authors thus achieved writerly identity by fashioning works in English that drew abundantly from the continental and classical influences.

The Senshu Project 'The Development of the Anglo-Saxon Language and Linguistic Universals' organized national and international conferences on Medieval English literature; from these, a collection of papers was selected. The present volume consists of four parts. The first is devoted to topics relating to the Old and Middle English alliterative poems *Beowulf*, *Piers Plowman* and *Pierce the Ploughman's Creed*: Graham D. Caie, 'A Case of Double Vision: Denmark in *Beowulf* and *Beowulf* in England'; Kazutomo Karasawa, 'Hrothgar in the Germanic Context of *Beowulf*'; A.V.C. Schmidt, 'The Four Elements as a Structural Idea in *Piers Plowman*'; and Helen Barr, 'The Place of the Poor in "the *Piers Plowman* Tradition"'.

The second part consists of three articles dedicated to Chaucer, especially *Troilus and Criseyde*: Masatoshi Kawasaki, '"My Wyl Is This" (*Canterbury Tales*. I [A] 1845): Chaucer's Sense of Power in *The Knight's Tale* and *The Clerk's Tale*'; Yoshiyuki Nakao, 'Textual Variations in *Troilus and Criseyde* and the Rise of Ambiguity': and Yoshiyuki Nakao and Masatsugu Matsuo, 'A Comprehensive Textual Comparison of *Troilus and Criseyde*: Corpus Christi College, Cambridge, MS 61 and B.A. Windeatt's Edition of *Troilus and Criseyde* (1990)'.

The third part concerns philological aspects of Old and Middle English, including Robert Henryson's rhymes and Caxton's word pairs and doublets: Mitsu Ide, 'The Old English Equivalents for *Factum Esse* and the Salisbury Psalter'; Akiyuki Jimura: 'On the Decline of the Prefix *y-* of Past Participles'; Hiroshi Yonekura, 'Compound Nouns in Late Middle English: Their Morphological, Syntactic and Semantic Description'; Masa Ikegami, 'Robert Henryson's Rhymes between 'Etymological −$\bar{e}$ and −$\bar{\imath}$' and the Special Development of Unstressed /i/'; and Akinobu Tani, 'Word Pairs or Doublets in Caxton's *History of Reynard the Fox*: Rampant and Tedious?'

The last part is devoted to three manuscripts that are now happily found at Senshu University Library: Sylvia Huot, 'Senshu Manuscripts 2 and 3 and the *Roman de la Rose* Manuscript Tradition', and Patrick P. O'Neill, 'The Senshu Psalter'.

References

Barney, Stephen A., ed. *Geoffrey Chaucer: Troilus and Criseyde*. New York and London: W.W. Norton, 2002.

Baswell, Christopher. *Virgil in Medieval England*. Cambridge: Cambridge University Press, 1995.

Boitani, Piero, ed. *Chaucer and the Italian Trecento*. Cambridge: Cambridge University Press, 1983.

Cooper, Helen. 'The Classical Background', in Steve Ellis, ed., *Chaucer: An Oxford Guide*. Oxford: Oxford University Press, 2005: 255–71.

Donaldson, E. Talbot. 'The Ending of *Troilus*', in Stephen A. Barney, ed., *Geoffrey Chaucer: Troilus and Criseyde*. New York and London: W.W. Norton, 2002: 475–87.

Dunning, T.P. '*Piers Plowman*: An Interpretation of the A Text', in Edward Vasta, ed., *Interpretations of* Piers Plowman. Notre Dame, IN, and London: University of Notre Dame Press, 1968: 87–114.

Ellis, Steve, ed. *Chaucer: An Oxford Guide*. Oxford: Oxford University Press, 2005.

Frank, Roberta. 'Germanic Legend in Old English Literature', in Malcolm Godden and Michael Lapidge, eds., *The Cambridge Companion to Old English Literature*. Cambridge: Cambridge University Press, 1991: 88–106.

Fulk, R.D., and Christopher M. Cain. *A History of Old English Literature*. Oxford and Berlin: Blackwell, 2003.

Godden, Malcolm, and Michael Lapidge, eds. *The Cambridge Companion to Old English Literature*. Cambridge: Cambridge University Press, 1991.

Lewis, C.S. 'What Chaucer Really Did to *Il Filostrato*', in Stephen A. Barney, ed., *Geoffrey Chaucer: Troilus and Criseyde*. New York and London: W.W. Norton, 2006: 451–64.

Mann, Jill. 'From Feminizing Chaucer', in Stephen A. Barney, ed., *Geoffrey Chaucer: Troilus and Criseyde*. New York and London: W.W. Norton, 2002: 606–22.

Phillips, Helen. 'The French Background', in Steve Ellis, ed., *Chaucer: An Oxford Guide*. Oxford: Oxford University Press, 2005: 292–312.

Powicke, F.M. *The Christian Life in the Middle Ages and Other Essays*. Oxford: Clarendon Press, 1935.

Scragg, Donald G. 'The Nature of Old English Verse', in Malcolm Godden and Michael Lapidge, eds., *The Cambridge Companion to Old English Literature*. Cambridge: Cambridge University Press, 1991: 55–70.

Vasta, Edward, ed. *Interpretations of* Piers Plowman. Notre Dame, IN, and London: University of Notre Dame Press, 1968.

Wallace, David. *Chaucer and the Early Writings of Boccaccio*, Chaucer Studies XII. Cambridge: D.S. Brewer, 1985.

Wormald, Patrick. 'Anglo-Saxon Society and its Literature', in Malcolm Godden and Michael Lapidge, eds., *The Cambridge Companion to Old English Literature*. Cambridge: Cambridge University Press, 1991: 1–22.

GRAHAM D. CAIE

1   A Case of Double Vision: Denmark in *Beowulf* and *Beowulf* in England

1.0. Introduction

A study of the reception of any literary work in a specific period tells us much about the culture and attitudes of that period. Why is an author or a literary period popular in one age and not another? One might ask why the English poet who composed *Beowulf* chose a Danish hero when his country was besieged by the Danes or why this English epic was so popular in early nineteenth-century Denmark which was at war with England.

Beowulf has recently been brought to public attention by the excellent translation by Seamus Heaney, who for decades has had a particular interest in Denmark and its ancient history.[1] He sees parallels in the myths and beliefs of the early peoples of Denmark and Ireland, and in the Introduction to this work he states that using choice Irish words in translation is 'one way for an Irish poet to come to terms with the complex history of conquest and colony, absorption and resistance, integrity and antagonism'.[2] For him, then, *Beowulf* is not simply a distant relic, difficult to access through remote language and customs, but a living work that informs our own times. Heaney has done much to dispel the myth that this work is little more than an obstacle at the door of English Literature studies at universities, a monster to be vanquished before the delights of accessible post-medieval literature can be sampled.

---

1   Seamus Heaney, *Beowulf: A New Translation* (London: Faber and Faber, 1999).
2   *Ibid.*, xxx.

At the other extreme is Valentine Cunningham, who considers Anglo-Saxon a dinosauric museum piece 'which should be excluded from the English curriculum'.[3] He quotes Philip Larkin who calls it 'ape's bum fodder' and Cunningham claims that 'Latin is more integral to the English language than Old English.' This argument at Oxford has lasted for over a decade with a passion that makes one wonder if *Beowulf* can be the same poem that is described by Heaney as 'a work of the greatest imaginative vitality, a masterpiece ... a work of art [that] lives in its own continuous present, equal to our knowledge of reality in the present time'.[4]

1.1. Modern Danish Translations and Attitudes to *Beowulf*

Heaney's refreshing approach to *Beowulf* is akin to that found in Denmark today. There have been many modern Danish translations of the poem and one of the two that appeared in 1984 was by Professor Andreas Haarder. On the cover of the translation, *Sangen om Bjovulf*,[5] he states, in Danish, that this is a heroic tale which survived in Old English, but which concerns our own mythical history. One meets King Skjold, Roar and Helge, Rolf Krake and Weland the Smith and all these well-known figures are included in one unified tale, he explains. In his Introduction he writes [here translated] that 'a poem of this kind breaks down boundaries in time and space; it is a "gamle-nye tekst", "an old-new text". No one is foreign in *Beowulf*, and the poem is common property to England and Denmark'.[6] Haarder uses a simile by N.F.S. Grundtvig, whom I shall discuss later, to describe *Beowulf*, namely as the phoenix which forever changes, dies and re-appears, yet keeps its essential spirit.

3   *The Times*, 8 July 1991.
4   *Op. cit.*
5   Andreas Haarder, *Sangen om Bjovulf; I dansk gengivelse* (Copenhagen: G.E.C. Gad, 1984).
6   My translation.

For Andreas Haarder, *Beowulf* is highly relevant to people of all edu-
cational backgrounds and interests in modern Denmark; but can one say
the same thing today about the UK or any other English-speaking country
that might well be forgiven for taking this work as the oldest and arguably
the greatest epic poem in their language? Haarder seems sure that the figures of Skjold and Roar, the Scyld Scefing and Hrothgar of *Beowulf*, are
central to the mythical origins of his country, but who would the modern
British person claim to be the heroes of pre-historic Britain? I am sure the
name of King Arthur would emerge in any popular survey, as the Arthurian
myth still grips the imagination of the general public. A slate inscription
at the Tintagel site a few years ago that was supposed to have the name of
Arthur inscribed on it received front-page coverage in the national press,
but I doubt if there would have been any interest if it had contained the
name of Scyld, Grendel or Beowulf. There are illustrated children's books
in the UK on the Beowulf myth, which continues to catch the attention
of the young with the story of dragon fights and monsters; but few in the
streets could tell you the 'plot' of *Beowulf* and even fewer would think that
the poem contributed to an understanding of English cultural history. So
let's begin at the beginning to see where and why the English lost the plot,
as it were, and the Danes retained it.

1.2. *Beowulf:* Its History and Manuscript

In *Beowulf* we have a collection of myths interwoven into historical facts
that are also found in Gregory of Tours's sixth-century *History of the Franks*
and in the eighth-century *Gesta Francorum* that mention Chochilaicus
or Hugletus who is the Hygelac of the poem. References to characters
such as Eormenric can be traced back to the fourth century,[7] while many

---

7   See the *Rerum Gestarum Libri* and the other references in G.N. Garmonsway,
     J. Simpson and Hilda Ellis Davidson, *Beowulf and its Analogues* (London: J.M.
     Dent, 1980).

others such as Sigemund, Hrothgar, Weland, Helga, Hrothulf, Offa and Ingeld would indeed have been well-known long before the poem was composed. All these characters, along with commonly known incidents and wars amongst the Swedes and Frisians from the mists of myth and history, were combined in the epic story that centred on a fictional hero, Beowulf. The events are almost certainly from the sixth century, but the only other known date is the late tenth or early eleventh century, when the one and only manuscript witness of the poem's text was captured. When and how the poem itself was composed is still a mystery, although much scholarly debate has centred on its date of composition.[8] Did it evolve orally over the centuries, slowly gathering tales and developing plot until captured by an imaginative *scop* at the end of the Anglo-Saxon period, the time when nearly all the preserved Old English poetic manuscripts were written, or was it a fresh composition by a poetic genius at around the date of the manuscript? The debate still continues, but any one date is not vital to my argument, which centres on the reception of the poem once it was written.

We have no contemporary evidence of the work; that is, there are no mentions of the poem or manuscript until the 18th century. Grendel, the monster, appears in some topographical names in the *Anglo-Saxon Chronicle* of the eighth and ninth centuries, but it is possible that this was a common name for a monster. And so the poem begins its history in the famous manuscript, London, British Library, Cotton Vitellius A. xv; and it is only by chance that we have it today, as it was badly damaged in the 1731 fire in which many manuscripts in the possession of Sir Robert Cotton perished. Even so, many folios are badly scorched and letters indecipherable. Luckily there were transcriptions made of the manuscript a short time after the fire by G.J. Thorkelin, an Icelandic scholar who worked in Denmark, when more of the charred edges were decipherable than today,

---

8   See the arguments for a late date of composition in Kevin Kiernan's *Beowulf and the Beowulf Manuscript* (Ann Arbor, MI: University of Michigan Press, 1996); Colin Chase (ed.), *The Dating of Beowulf* (Toronto Old English series 6, Toronto, 1981); R.M. Liuzza, 'On the Dating of *Beowulf*', in Peter S. Baker (ed.), *Beowulf: Basic Readings* (New York: Garland Publishing, 1995): 281–302.

and the Beowulf Project initiated by Kevin Kiernan has done much to reclaim readings lost in the fire and by later damage.[9]

Beowulf suffered the same fate as most Old English texts in the centuries that followed the Norman Conquest. The language quickly became obscure and had to be glossed by the twelfth century. It was undoubtedly in the following five centuries that most of the writings in Old English were lost and today we have only around 30,000 lines of poetry left. The famous manuscript of the Exeter Book, which contains all the best-known poetry such as the elegies, was used as a carving board, while others had their expensive bindings torn off for the jewels and gold and the texts were lost. Scraps of Old English are still occasionally found in the bindings of later volumes, as the vellum was considered a good means of preserving printed works; an example is the fifty-six strips of an Ælfrician homily found in the spine of a series of Dutch books now in the National Archives of Copenhagen.[10] Anglo-Saxon came to represent the evil barbaric times, the Dark Ages in England, and Tudor kings claimed Arthur not Alfred as their ancestor. The popular literature and myths were of King Arthur and Robin Hood, not of great Anglo-Saxon heroes like Alfred and Athelstan of Wessex.

1.3. The Myths Surrounding Anglo-Saxon England

Nicholas Howe in *Migration and Mythmaking in Anglo-Saxon England* states that society constantly needs to revise its origins. He suggests that cultural identity is dependent on remembered history and myth and that 'the Anglo-Saxons could conceive of themselves as a common people because

9   See the Electronic *Beowulf* Project at <http://www.uky.edu/ArtsSciences/English/Beowulf/>.
10   E. Fausbøll (ed.), *Fifty-Six Ælfric Fragments: The newly-found Copenhagen fragments of Ælfric's 'Catholic Homilies'*, Publications of the Department of English, University of Copenhagen, vol. 14 (Copenhagen, 1986).

of the ancestral migration ... they could gather a sense of unity from their continental origins as these were memorialised in the central works of the culture.'[11] He continues: 'In the absence of the political cohesiveness offered by nationhood, a myth of origin provides a people with some means for determining its organic status as a group'.[12] A migration myth of the past with common Germanic heroes and values was interwoven with the biblical story of the Exodus of the Chosen People to the Promised Land and evolved, giving identity and common purpose. This is reflected in *The Battle of Brunanburh*, a poem about how King Athelstan of Wessex, grandson of Alfred, defeated a combined army of Scots, Strathclyde Britons and Vikings from Dublin, and thereby secured the supremacy of West Saxon England. It is a poem that is deliberately archaic in vocabulary and style, with many Biblical formulas and themes, as its aim is to compare this great victory in 937 with that of the first Germanic invaders. 'This was the greatest of slaughters, according to what the books tell us', the poet states, 'since the time when from the east the Angles and Saxons arrived to seek the land of Britain across the broad sea, the proud war-smiths, keen for glory, they gained this land.'[13] Athelstan is then called 'King of the English and the Danes', as Cnut was to be called slightly later.

It is significant that the great heroic poems such as *Beowulf*, *The Battle of Maldon* and *Brunanburh* are all very late in the Anglo-Saxon period and that we have no earlier works extant about the victories at the migration period when the events in *Beowulf* took place. All three poems convey a sense of nostalgia and a hazy, distant remembrance of a great heroic past. It reminds one of the popular, albeit questionable, belief today of the Victorian period having solid, fixed values and high moral standards, a myth which allows us to criticize and judge our own times. Roberta Frank succinctly sums up this misty, half-remembered view:

11   Nicholas Howe, *Migration and Mythmaking in Anglo-Saxon England* (New Haven, CT: Yale University Press, 1989): 6.

12   *Ibid.*, 179.

13   *The Battle of Brunanburh*, ll. 65–73. See also Howe, 30–2 and Graham D. Caie, 'The Shorter Heroic Verse', in Henk Aertsen and Rolf H. Bremmer (eds.), *Companion to Old English Poetry* (Amsterdam: VU University Press, 1994): 85–8.

> The imagination of the Anglo-Saxons was stirred by this tradition, vague and unformed, of something majestic out of the distant past, of a golden age in which men were taller, bolder, freer and more glorious. And Old English poets were moved to find and make some drama played by these great kings and heroes, cutting them loose from history and setting them free to perform their collective magic on a stage larger than their own lives and history ... Poets of Germanic legend, too, conjured up for their contemporaries a magnificent, aristocratic descent, a proud history embodying current hopes and fears, a pleasant dream transmuting the desert of daily existence into a landscape rare and strange.[14]

But it was more than escapism; it was an attempt to create a proud, national identity out of fragments, an identity that was necessary if the English were to see themselves as a nation.

Alexander Murray demonstrates that the genealogical introduction in *Beowulf*, starting with Scyld Scefing and continuing through Hrothgar, was not based on legend but on official royal genealogy of the ninth and tenth century West-Saxon kings and was intended as dynastic flattery. Roberta Frank sums up the dynastic argument as follows:

> A pedigree going back to Geat apparently had propaganda value for the English kings around 800 ... The genealogy of King Alfred's father Athelwulf ... gives Geat a number of northern ancestors, among which five – Scyld, Scef, Beaw, Heremod and Hwala – appear as legendary figures in Old English poetry.[15]

'A Danish background', states Murray,

> gave [the West-Saxon kings] prestige and leverage among the petty and disunited Scandinavian kings and earls of northern England and supported the claim of West-Saxon sovereignty over the North. The heroic North attracted them and their interest in it permitted them to establish a common background for contemporary political and ethnic relations.[16]

---

14   Roberta Frank, 'Germanic Legend in Old English Literature', in Malcolm Godden and Michael Lapidge (eds.), *The Cambridge Companion to Old English Literature* (Cambridge: Cambridge University Press, 1991): 104. See also Caie, 'The Shorter Heroic Verse': 79–80 and 93–4.

15   Roberta Frank, 'Germanic Legend': 95.

16   A.C. Murray, '*Beowulf*, the Danish Invasions and Royal Genealogy', in Colin Chase (ed.), *The Dating of Beowulf* (Toronto: Toronto University Press): 101–12.

It is therefore not a vague, mythical introduction in *Beowulf*, but a concrete foundation on which to build a national myth.

So what is emerging is the fact that the West-Saxons differentiated between the petty, marauding Danes of the Danelaw and the great Germanic and mythic heroes in the 'old country', Denmark. Alfred was fascinated with Scandinavian geography and trade, as witnessed by the prominence he gave the Nordic voyages of Ohthere and Wulfstan inserted in the Old English Orosius. Much later, at the end of the Anglo-Saxon period, Archbishop Wulfstan of York chastises the English in his sermons, as he claims that their evil and feeble faith caused God to send the Danes as a punishment, while he still supported the Scandinavians in their bid to preserve northern independence.

There are also many other signs of peaceful co-existence between Danes and English throughout the Danelaw period, such as the adoption of so many Scandinavian words into Old English, the blending of both the traditions in the design of art and weapons, the adoption of Scandinavian dress and even Danish personal names by the Anglo-Saxons, and a similar success story of co-operation and interdependence can be found in the laws of the Northumbrians (even the word 'law') and in place-names on the east coast. *Beowulf* then might be another example of this blending of cultures and the need to find a common heritage and national identity at a time when England was finally becoming united and strong within Europe.

The *Beowulf* poet gives the feeling of historical and geographic veracity and this contributes to the sense of common origins, myths and values. He takes it for granted that all his readers know about Weland the Smith, Sigemund, Ingeld, Eormanric and the Danish royal lineage. Critics, however, have marvelled at the fact that the country of England's major enemy is chosen as the setting for *Beowulf*. Yet it is a Denmark of yester-year and it is obvious that the poet is attempting, like a good historical novelist or the saga writers, to give his story a solid historical and geographic base on which to spin his fiction. Beowulf is not a Dane, but a fictional, archetypal Scandinavian, a Waymunding. He is larger than life, a James Bond figure, a mythical sea-god who fights sea monsters in full armour underwater, yet he has all the virtues of humility, humanity, gentleness and modesty that are more Christian than heroic. Of course the sixth-century Beowulf must have been heathen, and indeed he has a pagan burial; his soul seeks the fate of the faithful (*sothfæstra dom*), as he is raised to religious neutrality or, as a critic has put it, into a theological vacuum.

Beowulf, I would argue, fits into this romanticized history of origins which the late Anglo-Saxons share with their northern cousins. But what happened to this myth of origins? It would be a gross exaggeration to lay all the blame on 1066, but after the Conquest the political focus naturally changed and, in spite of the Normans' own Scandinavian origins, Anglo-Norman eyes looked south to the Mediterranean and not east to Denmark in the desire to find origins. Geoffrey of Monmouth in his twelfth-century *History of the Kings of Britain* turned English attention to Romano-British roots and further back to Troy and the Mediterranean. Brutus, sailing from the ruins of Troy, becomes the founder of England, and the Romano-British troops, headed by the ubiquitous Arthur and his noble army, are said to have fought the invading Germanic tribes and Germanic heroes, such as Hengest and Horsa, who were now the enemy. The nationalistic literature of post-Conquest England, for example, La3amon's *Brut* and the growing wealth of Arthurian material reflect this. The bulk of literature took its inspiration now from France and eventually Italy, and the Anglo-Saxon language was rapidly becoming unintelligible.

It was not until the Reformation that Anglo-Saxon came into its own again in England and it was for political and theological, not literary, reasons.[17] Defenders of the new Anglican faith wished to show that the Church *in* England had a long and noble history and was descended from Paul not Peter. Anglo-Saxon theology showed that transubstantiation was not a necessary belief, that married clergy had been tolerated, and that the Bible (or parts of it) had been read in English. Matthew Parker, Master of Corpus Christi College, Cambridge and Archbishop of Canterbury from 1559–75, collected as many Anglo-Saxon manuscripts as he could, and his legacy is the fine collection in the Parker Library at Corpus. His views

---

17   For a more detailed description of Matthew Parker's interest in Anglo-Saxon see A.J. Frantzen, *Desire for Origins: New Language, Old English, and Teaching the Tradition* (New Brunswick, NJ: Rutgers University Press, 1990).

are clearly expressed in *A Testimonie of Antiquitie* (1567) in which he uses
Anglo-Saxon sources, in particular Ælfric, to justify the independence
of the national church from the papacy. To read the material he taught
himself Anglo-Saxon, demanded that all Anglo-Saxon manuscripts be
'lent' to him and then annotated the useful passages in characteristic red
crayon. But *Beowulf* and the other poetic texts still remained dormant, like
the dragon in the poem; and if he had seen the manuscript, it would have
been of little use in his political agenda.

A similar, political use of Anglo-Saxon scholarship is seen in America by Thomas Jefferson, himself an Anglo-Saxon scholar, who strongly
believed in explaining to his fellow Americans the origins of English society,
social organization and the beginnings of democracy. He had plans to have
Hengest and Horsa on the Great Seal of America, introduced the subject
into the curriculum of the University of Virginia and even advocated the
teaching of Old English in primary schools. Allen Frantzen states that:

> Their own disputes [were] anticipated and acted out in Anglo-Saxon texts, which
> thereby became extensions of their horizons, of their views ... Thomas Jefferson saw
> his ambitions for democracy foreshadowed in Anglo-Saxon laws and chronicles.
> Their Anglo-Saxon studies were narratives of their origins.[18]

Once more, the subject is privileged for political and social reasons, not as
a dead language, but one that explains historical origins.

The political interest in Anglo-Saxon is seen in the Victorian period.
John Kemble, whom we will meet again later as the first editor of *Beowulf*,
dedicated his work, *The Saxons in England*, to Queen Victoria, herself
descended from the German royal family and married to a German prince,
Albert. He claimed that Saxon principles were at the basis of the great
empire and that Anglo-Saxon history is 'the history of the childhood of
our own age, – the explanation of its manhood'.[19]

Another reason why the study of Anglo-Saxon increased in the eighteenth century was the growing interest in historical linguistics, in particular the Germanic languages. George Hickes at the end of the seventeenth

18   *Ibid.*, 22. See also 15–16.
19   *Ibid.*, 35.

century aided the study of the language by publishing *Institutiones grammaticae Anglo-Saxonicae* and Humphrey Wanley produced a catalogue of Anglo-Saxon manuscripts. Later Elizabeth Elstob wrote a grammar of Anglo-Saxon in 1715, while in the following century Germanic philology flourished in Germany and to a lesser extent in England. Indeed there were seven times as many Anglo-Saxon scholars in Germany than in England, a fact that led Henry Sweet to complain about the 'Germanizing' of the subject.

The eighteenth century was an age when writers, such as Jonathan Swift, attempted to 'fix' the English language, to standardize it and stop the 'corruption' of constant change. Swift called Anglo-Saxon 'that vulgar tongue, so barren and so barbarous.'[20] Even Anglo-Saxon scholars such as Sharon Turner write of 'the barren and peculiar state of Anglo-Saxon poetry'.[21] There was a condescending indulgence towards the language and literature of the Anglo-Saxons: it was crude, unsophisticated, undeveloped, but it still was the ancestor of their own, fine language and so tolerated. So Anglo-Saxon studies emerged into the nineteenth century as a difficult, compulsory subject for students, a 'disciplining rod', and the literature a stomping ground for philologists looking for sound changes. Indo-Germanic philology, as it was called before it was renamed Indo-European, was also felt in the UK to be too closely related to German methodology and nationalism. In multi-cultural countries such as the UK and USA it was increasingly distasteful to talk about 'our' Anglo-Saxon origins as if all came from one race, and Anglo-Saxon philology was associated with the growing German nationalism in the late nineteenth century and first half of the twentieth. However, even in contemporary Danish works on their history, authors use the first-person plural pronoun when writing about early history; there is still a sense there of continuity and association with their forefathers in the time of Roarr and Helge. We can see a major reason for this sustained interest in mythical and early Danish history by examining the earliest historiography.

20   *Ibid.*, 53.
21   *Ibid.*, 33.

1.4. Myths of Denmark's Origins

Most European countries were creating their own mythical histories in the twelfth and thirteenth centuries, and Denmark was not to be left behind. Rome, Greece, France and eventually Britain with Geoffrey of Monmouth had established strong, nationalistic beliefs in their noble origins, no matter how fabulous. Denmark in the twelfth century was becoming a strong nation state and under Valdemar I was making inroads into the Baltic states, while his foster brother Archbishop Absolon (1128–201) in the name of our Lord and with a formidable axe was hacking down nations with great success. Absolon commissioned his secretary, Saxo Grammaticus, to write a great Latin history of Denmark, the *Gesta Danorum* (written in the 1220s) that would rival the fictionalized mythologies of Geoffrey of Monmouth, Gregory of Tours or Paul the Deacon. He may have looked to southern Europe for his Latin literary style,[22] but he based his characters on the orally transmitted legends of Denmark and Iceland. He began with the brothers Dan and Angul who lived twenty generations before Christ; then came Skjold, Halvdan, Ro, Helge, Rolf Krake, not forgetting Prince Amled. So Saxo helped consolidate Danish origins, gave the Danish monarchy power and legitimacy, and made a history to equal those of the great southern nations. Skjold became the great warrior and law-giver, while Rolf Krake was the Arthur-figure, with his Camelot at Lethra or Lejre.

Saxo had another aim: he wanted to stress the Anglo-Danish relationship, as there was a threat from the south, and Schleswig, as ever, was hotly disputed. The Anglo-Danish period, a time when Denmark, Norway, England and parts of Sweden were all under Cnut, is therefore glorified. The marriage of Cnut's daughter Gunnilda to the Holy Roman Emperor Henry, according to Saxo, was a major coup for Henry and not vice-versa. And so Saxo gripped the Danish imagination and his work was embraced by generations of monarchs for obvious, political reasons; and it is still closely studied today by Danes. Saxo gave the nation the oldest continuous monarchy in

---

22   See *Dansk Litteratur Historie: ca.800–1480*, Bind 1, ed., Søren Kaspersen, *et al.* (Copenhagen: Gyldendal, 1984): 328–30.

Europe, the oldest European flag, and stressed the fact that they once ruled most of northern Europe, thanks to the Anglo connection.

The Danish gaze from then on – and some might say even today – continued westward to England, while the English at the time of Saxo, now with their strong Norman influence, looked south for their literary and cultural inspiration, and the language, myths, literature and versification of the Saxons were largely forgotten. Had there been no Norman Conquest, England – and possibly Scotland too – might today still honour the great Anglo-Saxon and Germanic heroes such as Alfred and Cnut instead of inventing ones such as Arthur and Robin Hood.

But the poem *Beowulf*, like the treasure in that poem that the dragon protected, lay hidden, dormant, unknown in both England and Denmark from the time it was written until the late eighteenth century. Historically, few would credit that this was the time when the great English epic caught the imagination of the Danes, as Britain at this time was at war with Denmark during the Napoleonic period. Thorkelin, the poem's first editor, had all his papers for his edition of *Beowulf* destroyed when his house, the nearby university and cathedral were all bombed and burned by the British in 1807 during the Battle of Copenhagen.

The rediscovery of *Beowulf* in Denmark arose from strong nationalistic reasons. It was therefore with keen interest that a Dane, Jakob Langebek, read in Humphrey Wanley's catalogue of Anglo-Saxon manuscripts of 1705 that there was a poem about 'Beowulf the Dane', an error that had fortunate consequences. This was the first time the poem had ever been catalogued, although others, such as Francis Junius, had known about its existence. Jakob Langebek encouraged Grimur Jonsson Thorkelin (1752–1829), an Icelandic civil servant working in Copenhagen, to travel to London to copy this manuscript which he thought might uncover more facts about early Danish history. Thorkelin had two transcripts of the Cotton manuscript made, one by himself and another by a copyist, and these are kept in the Royal Library, Copenhagen. They are still of great value, as they were made when the manuscript, which had been in the Cotton fire some fifty years earlier, was much more legible than it is now. Indeed it is thought that some 2,000 letters now illegible were noted by Thorkelin. But all his work (both edition and Latin translation) was burned, ironically, as a result of British military action, and it was not until 1815 that his edition appeared.

Thorkelin called his edition, echoing Saxo, *De Danorum Rebus Gestis [seculi 3 & 4] Poema danicum dialecto anglosaxonica* ('On the deeds of the Danes in the third and fourth centuries: a Danish poem in the Anglo-Saxon dialect'). Thorkelin's view that the poem was originally written in Danish was shared by his contemporary Danes in early reviews, who saw it as an adaptation of an Old Norse original but with the pious reflective passages added by the Christian Anglo-Saxons.[23] He claimed in his Preface that the language of the Anglo-Saxons is really that of the Danes preserved in its purest form by the Icelanders. *Beowulf* was 'a song that poured forth from the Danish bard ... the language spoken by the English before William I had been common to three peoples of the north – all called by one name, "Danes" – who spoke slightly different dialects of the same tongue. This fact is as clear as the light of the day.'[24] Both descend from West Danish, he insisted. Thorkelin also stressed 'the intimate friendship that exists between us and the English', while pouring scorn on the Frisians and Germans. Although most of Thorkelin's contemporaries and critics did not think that *Beowulf* was originally a Danish poem, there were many who wished to use the work to cement the political links between the two nations at a time when the powers to the south threatened.

The Danish edition and Latin translation that Thorkelin prepared received positive reviews from most, as it confirmed the nationalistic notion that the Danes ruled the world in earlier ages. One reviewer, Nicholai Outzen from Schleswig, seems convinced that *Beowulf* takes place in Schleswig and that the poem 'is a most invaluable source of information about the very great age of our fatherland. What is of importance to the Anglo-Saxons is important to us. The Anglo-Saxon language sheds light on ours.'[25] All this has roots in nationalism and has political significance.

23   See Andreas Haarder, *Beowulf, The Appeal of the Poem* (Viborg: Akademisk Forlag, 1975): 14–16.

24   Quoted by Robert E. Bjork, 'Nineteenth-Century Scandinavia and the Birth of Anglo-Saxon Studies', in Allen J. Frantzen and John D. Niles (eds.), *Anglo-Saxonism and the Construction of Social Identity* (Florida, FL: University Press of Florida, 1998): 118.

25   I am grateful to Professor Andreas Haarder for permission to use his unpublished translation of material from the Grundtvig Archive in Copenhagen.

The main character responsible for the *Beowulf* revival in Denmark, however, was Nikolai Frederik Severin Grundtvig, a name known to all Danes today and arguably the most influential person ever in Danish education. Bishop Grundtvig was a statesman, cleric, founder of a political party, scholar, poet, author of many of the hymns in the Danish hymnary today, founder of the Danish Folk High Schools – a one-man institution. He was a large and imposing man, who married three times and had many children, and it is interesting that he claims Beowulf's only flaw is that he had 'a hermit-like relationship with the fair sex which betrays his English descent'!

Grundtvig states in the introduction to his translation, called *Beowulfs Drape* ('Beowulf's Heroic Poem') that it is a Gothic heroic poem which he translates from Anglo-Saxon to Danish. He was deeply concerned that classical works were better known than Nordic myths and intended his translation of *Beowulf* to be read by all Danes, including farmers and children. It is intended as a 'Læsebog for alle vore Børn', a reading book for all our children.[26] He could not understand how the British did not share his admiration for this great epic.

> The Isle of the Angles [as he called Britain] neglects this pearl [*Beowulf*], and this treasure is regarded as a dung-hill there .... Anglo-Saxon poetry is nowhere more neglected through the civilised world than in England. Far from being the dull stupid trash, that some English writers of no small name have chosen to suppose, it deserves the attention and admiration of cultivated minds ... The English neglect, and are unkind to their high-born kinsman.[27]

He made frequent visits to England to find a scholar who would undertake the editing of *Beowulf* into English. His first choice as editor was Richard Price, but he died. Then he found John Kemble, 'an idle young Englishman'; however, as he states in *Mands Minde 1788–1838*, 'he has much more poetical awareness than is normally found with philologists',[28] and Kemble finally produced his edition of the poem in 1831. Grundtvig's dislike of

---

26   Haarder, *Beowulf: The Appeal of the Poem* (Viborg: Akademisk Forlag, 1975): 65.
27   Translation by Andreas Haarder.
28   Translation by Andreas Haarder.

academic philologists ('under whom we grow mouldy like the ancient treasure in *Beowulf*') reflects his attitude to Copenhagen University and what he considered arid philological research; for he saw *Beowulf* as being of central political, cultural and spiritual significance to Danes and British alike – if only they would read it.

Grundtvig, significantly, saw *Beowulf* as 'the missing link' between past and present, and between England and Denmark. His great disappointment all his life was the fact that the English did not share his brotherly views, but he always wrote about 'our common history, our common mythology'. The poem for him gave answers to moral, political, economic and nationalistic views that he passionately held. First, it created a link with England and the mythic past that, he always felt, united the two countries. The English, he says, are 'our foster brothers who already in the cradle mixed their blood'. The language of the poem was not Danish – and here he strongly criticized Thorkelin – but 'Angul-dansk' [Anglo-Danish] and 'we were all Angul-dansk before the migration', a belief that we have already seen in the Old English poem, *Brunanburh*. His reasons for Nordic and North Sea co-operation were the same as Saxo's, namely a fear of the southern neighbour:

> *Beowulf* will aid our awareness of basic interdependence that will stimulate ancient kinship amongst these three small nations, that they may vie without envy in knowing the spirit of the north and ward off foreign rule ... Grendel the troll with his mother is the most apposite picture one could wish of the Germans in Denmark, if they can only be put to shame, like Grendel and his mother.[29]

On another occasion he states: 'Denmark is the female element in the North Sea and, when cheerful, Dana joins the North as a shield maiden, but when captured by the evil troll who tricks her into being a German slave, she is no longer beneficial to the north'.

Grundtvig's 1820 Danish translation, then, was intended to revive a national appreciation of the great myths and moral truths of the past by awakening 'the heroic spirit of the north through the release of the power

---

29   *Ibid.*, 80–1. Quoted by Haarder from 'Trolden Grændel og hans Moder i Danmark', *Danskeren* III (1850): 227.

of the spoken word, hidden in ancient myths.' He describes the art of the translator as that of one who melts down the gold of the original and rec-reates a new golden object: 'the original letters have gone, but the spirit of the spoken word is released anew'. In his Introduction to his translation of *Beowulf* he creates his own Anglo-Saxon poem in which he states in typically hyperbolic fashion: 'Let Dan and Angul [here referring to Saxo] in mid-ocean shake their brotherly hands. Let ships carry the matchless song betwix the ocean'. But in spite of what he said about scholars, he was a researcher of considerable stature and made many important discoveries of a philological and historical nature. He identified Hygelac with Hugletus, and his notes and emendations to Thorkelin's edition were standard for a long time and in fact are still adopted.

Grundtvig's final reason for promoting *Beowulf* was moral: it gave 'insights into humanity, ideals of human fellowship and the reflection of a civilised community striving for peace.' Beowulf is the perfect, moral hero, 'a mirror to all in all generations: courageous, mild, patient, prudent, loyal'. Anglo-Saxon learning, claims Grundtvig, was of such high quality that 'it is therefore to England that we must look for the source of humanising influence'.

1.5. Conclusion

And so the poem was seen as the vital clue, the missing link, that showed, firstly, the unity between Britain and Denmark – and such a link was useful for political and economic reasons – and secondly added to the important, albeit harsh, heroic tales of the North a humanizing and Christian element that was so important to the great bishop. *Beowulf* was indeed far from being a stuffy, academic piece; it was of vital importance to the develop-ment of the health of the nation, and the results of this moral, political and cultural movement, generally called Grundtvigian, can still today be seen in many aspects of Danish culture and outlook.

So a study of the scholarship surrounding a work can say much about national identity and the way that a literary work can have political and social importance. Allen Frantzen in *Desire for Origins* urges us to 'study all that has grown up around the text and that filters the text and conditions its reception'. He continues:

> The search for origins is never disinterested; those wishing to trace an idea or tradition to its historical, linguistic, and textual beginnings have always done so with a thesis in mind ... My thesis – thus my own reason for seeking the origin of Anglo-Saxon studies – is that engagement with political controversy has always been a distinctive and indeed an essential motive ... for studying Anglo-Saxon.[30]

Frantzen quotes Edward W. Said who defines an origin as 'divine, mythical, privileged' and a beginning as 'secular, humanly produced and ceaselessly re-examined', 'designated in order to indicate, clarify, or define *a later* time, place, or action'.[31] There seems to be, then, in Danish folk memory a continuity of these mythic characters from the Middle Ages to today, a direct link that does not exist in Britain. And the reason, according to Frantzen, is that we have 'effaced the myth of origin'.[32]

I hope to have shown that a study of the reception of a medieval work, its perceptions and uses in any specific period, can tell us much about the times and culture of that period – and thereby about ourselves.

1.6. References

Bjork, Robert E. 'Nineteenth-Century Scandinavia and the Birth of Anglo-Saxon Studies', in Allen J. Frantzen and John D. Niles, eds., *Anglo-Saxonism and the Construction of Social Identity*. Florida, FL: University Press of Florida, 1998: 111–13.

30   Frantzen, xii–xiii.
31   *Ibid.*, 23.
32   *Ibid.*, 26.

Caie, Graham D. 'The Shorter Heroic Verse', in Henk Aertsen and Rolf H. Bremmer, eds., *Companion to Old English Poetry*. Amsterdam: VU University Press, 1994: 79–94.

Chase, Colin, ed. *The Dating of Beowulf*. Toronto Old English series 6. Toronto: Toronto University Press, 1981.

Fausbøll, E., ed. *Fifty-Six Ælfric Fragments: The newly-found Copenhagen fragments of Ælfric's Homilies*. Publications of the Department of English vol. 14. Copenhagen: University of Copenhagen, 1986.

Frank, Roberta. 'Germanic Legend in Old English Literature', in Malcolm Godden and Michael Lapidge, eds., *The Cambridge Companion to Old English Literature*. Cambridge: Cambridge University Press, 1991: 88–106.

Frantzen, Allen. J. *Desire for Origins: New Language, Old English, and Teaching the Tradition*. New Brunswick, NJ: Rutgers University Press, 1990.

Garmonsway, G.N., J. Simpson and Hilda Ellis Davidson. *Beowulf and its Analogues*. London: J.M. Dent, 1980.

Haarder, Andreas. *Beowulf: The Appeal of the Poem*. Viborg: Akademisk Forlag, 1975.

——. *Sangen om Bjovulf; I dansk gengivelse*. Copenhagen: G.E.C. Gad, 1984.

Heaney, Seamus. *Beowulf: A New Translation*. London: Faber and Faber, 1999.

Howe, Nicholas. *Migration and Mythmaking in Anglo-Saxon England*. New Haven, CT: Yale University Press, 1989.

Kaspersen, Søren *et al.* eds., *Dansk Litteratur Historie: ca. 800–1480*, Bind 1. Copenhagen: Gyldendal, 1984.

Kiernan, Kevin. *Beowulf and the Beowulf Manuscript*. Ann Arbor, MI: University of Michigan Press, 1996.

Liuzza, R.M. 'On the Dating of *Beowulf*', in Peter S. Baker ed., *Beowulf: Basic Readings*. New York: Garland Publishing, 1995: 281–302.

Murray, Alexander C. '*Beowulf*, the Danish Invasions and Royal Genealogy', in *The Dating of Beowulf*. Toronto Old English Series 6. Toronto: Toronto University Press, 1981: 101–12.

The Electronic *Beowulf* Project at:
<http://www.uky.edu/ArtsSciences/English/Beowulf/>

KAZUTOMO KARASAWA

2   Hrothgar in the Germanic Context of *Beowulf*[1]

2.0.   Introduction

The so-called Unferth Intermezzo (ll. 499–661) and Hrothgar's Sermon (1700–84) are two scenes in the first half of *Beowulf* so impressive as often to be referred to by their own titles. This is why each has been examined fairly closely and a great variety of readings has been suggested. However, they have rarely been discussed together as two interrelated elements of the poem. They are related in that they both have their settings in the Danish court featuring the two major characters representing it: Unferth and Hrothgar, respectively. It is true that they are depicted quite differently. Hrothgar is a benign, wise and old king, as seen reflected in his 'sermon', whereas Unferth is rather aggressive and seemingly malignant, as is especially the case with the flyting he urges against Beowulf. As I shall argue in the first section, however, it is most reasonable to consider that in the Unferth episode, they are not antagonistic in nature but represent fundamentally the same ethos. Otherwise, it is hard to imagine how wise and benign Hrothgar can trust openly malignant Unferth as a very important retainer. Hrothgar is often viewed as a (quasi-)Christian character, and his 'sermon' is often interpreted from this perspective as a homily on avarice and pride in Christian terms. As we shall see in the second section, however, the context of the sermon itself suggests that it reflects rather the secular, traditional/Germanic ethos. This reading is also quite natural considering the pre-Christian Germanic setting of the poem. In the Unferth episode,

---

1   This is a slightly modified version of the article 'Hrothgar and the Germanic Context in *Beowulf*', published in *Universals and Variation in Language* 3 (2008): 73–85.

not only Beowulf and Unferth but also Hrothgar seem to be characterized as deeply rooted in the Germanic warrior society. Hrothgar's 'sermon' should also be interpreted along these lines in the Germanic context, if we are to recognize a reasonable unity in the character of Hrothgar and in the poem itself. In this essay, I shall focus on words and deeds of Hrothgar in the first half of the poem and suggest that they should be understood in the context of Germanic warrior society rather than in a Christian context.

2.1. Hrothgar and the Unferth Intermezzo

The character of Unferth, together with the origin of the name Unferth and his title *þyle*, have often been considered enigmatic and problematic,[2] so that a great variety of interpretations has been suggested. Thus he is suggested to be an evil, treacherous retainer,[3] a pagan

---

2   In *Klaeber's Beowulf*, ed. R.D. Fulk, R.E. Bjork, and J.D. Niles (eds.), *Klaeber's Beowulf and the Fight at Finnsburg*. 4th edn. (Toronto: University of Toronto Press, 2008), Unferth is said still to be 'a somewhat enigmatic figure' (Fulk, Bjork and Niles, 149).

3   E.g., A. Olrik, *The Heroic Legends of Denmark*, trans. L.M. Hollander (New York: The American-Scandinavian Foundation, 1919): 56; Morton W. Bloomfield, '*Beowulf* and Christian Allegory: An Interpretation of Unferth', *Traditio* 7 (1949–51): 410–15; Frederick Klaeber (ed.), *Beowulf and the Fight at Finnsburg*. 3rd edn (Boston, MA: D.C. Heath, 1950): 148–50; A.G. Brodeur, *The Art of Beowulf* (Berkeley, CA: University of California Press, 1959): 153–4; R.W. Chambers, *Beowulf: An Introduction to the Study of the Poem with a Discussion of the Stories of Offa and Finn*. 3rd edn. (Cambridge: Cambridge University Press, 1959): 27; J.L. Rosier, 'Design for Treachery: The Unferth Intrigue', *PMLA* 77 (1962): 1–7; G. Hughes, '*Beowulf*, Unferth and Hrunting: An Interpretation', *English Studies* 58 (1977): 385–95; W.F. Bolton, *Alcuin and Beowulf: An Eighth-Century View* (New Brunswick, NJ: Rutgers University Press, 1978): 117–22; P.A. Jorgensen, 'The Gift of the Useless Weapon in *Beowulf* and the Icelandic Sagas', *Arkiv för Nordisk Filologi* 94 (1979): 82–90; D. Williams, *Cain and Beowulf: A Study in Secular Allegory* (Toronto: University of Toronto Press, 1982): 87–8; A.A. Lee, *Gold-Hall and Earth-Dragon: Beowulf as Metaphor* (Toronto: University of Toronto Press, 1998): 215–16.

priest,[4] a poet,[5] a spokesman of the Danes,[6] a public prosecutor,[7] a challenger to a hero often mentioned in folktales and legends,[8] the most reputed and/or the most important retainer,[9] a court jester,[10] an allegorical figure representing *Discordia*,[11] etc.

4   B.S. Phillpotts, *The Elder Edda and Ancient Scandinavian Drama* (Cambridge: Cambridge University Press, 1920): 181–5; H. Munro Chadwick and N.K. Chadwick, *The Growth of Literature I: The Ancient Literature of Europe* (Cambridge: Cambridge University Press, 1932): 618ff.; A. Hardy, 'The Christian Hero Beowulf and Unferð Þyle', *Neophilologus* 53 (1969): 55–69 and 'Historical Perspective and the *Beowulf*-Poet', *Neophilologus* 63 (1979): 430–49; J.L. Baird, 'Unferth the Þyle', *Medium Ævum* 39 (1970): 1–12; and I.M. Hollowell, 'Unferth the þyle in *Beowulf*', *Studies in Philology* 73 (1976): 239–65.

5   N.E. Eliason, 'The Þyle and Scop in *Beowulf*', *Speculum* 38 (1963): 267–84.

6   E.B. Irving, Jr., *Introduction to Beowulf* (Englewood Cliffs, NJ: Prentice-Hall, 1969): 68–9; M.M. Brennan, 'Hrothgar's Government'; K. Smits, 'Die "Stimmen" des schweigenden Königs: ein Erzählmotiv im *Beowulf*, im *Nibelungenlied* und im *Parzival*', *Literaturwissenschaftliches Jahrbuch* 27 (1986): 23–45; P.S. Baker, 'Beowulf the Orator', *Journal of English Linguistics* 21 (1988): 3–23; E.B. Irving, Jr., *Rereading Beowulf* (Philadelphia, PA: University of Pennsylvania Press, 1989): 38–40; G. Clark, *Beowulf* (Boston, MA: Twayne, 1990): 62.

7   C.J. Clover, 'The Germanic Context of the Unferth Episode', *Speculum* 55 (1980): 444–68; Brennan, 'Hrothgar's Government'; and B. Daldorph, 'Mar-Peace, Ally: Hunferð in *Beowulf*', *Massachusetts Studies in English* 10 (1986): 143–60.

8   T.A. Shippey, 'The Fairy-Tale Structure of *Beowulf*', *N&Q* n.s. 16 (1969): 2–11; Daniel R. Barnes, 'Folktale Morphology and the Structure of *Beowulf*', *Speculum* 45 (1970): 416–34; T.P. Feldman, 'The Taunter in Ancient Epic: The *Iliad, Odyssey, Aeneid*, and *Beowulf*', *Papers on Language and Literature* 15 (1979): 3–16; and K.Gould, '*Beowulf* and Folktale Morphology: God as Magical Donor', *Folklore* 96 (1985): 98–103.

9   W.W. Lawrence, *Beowulf and Epic Tradition* (Cambridge, MA: Harvard University Press, 1930): 153; D.E. Martin-Clarke, 'The Office of Thyle in *Beowulf*', *RES* 12 (1936): 61–6; J.D.A. Ogilvy, 'Unferth: Foil to Beowulf?', *PMLA* 79 (1964): 370–5; R.S. Gingher, 'The Unferth Perplex', *Thoth* 14 (1974): 19–28; G. Hughes, 'Beowulf, Unferth and Hrunting: An Interpretation' and M.J. Enright, 'The Warband Context of the Unferth Episode', *Speculum* 73 (1998): 297–337.

10 J.L. Rosier, 'Design for Treachery: The Unferth Intrigue'; and F.C. Robinson, 'Personal Names in Medieval Narrative and the Name of Unferth in *Beowulf*', in H. Creed (ed.), *Essays in Honor of Richebourg Gaillard McWilliams* (Birmingham, AL: Birmingham – Southern College, 1970): 43–8.

11 Bloomfield, '*Beowulf* and Christian Allegory: An Interpretation of Unferth': 410–15.

On the other hand, the episode has rarely been examined in terms of its relationship with Hrothgar. It is true that the flyting takes place exclusively between Unferth and Beowulf and Hrothgar plays no role in it. As we shall see, however, the way Hrothgar commits himself in the debate furnishes us with a key to conceiving an aspect of the nature of the flyting and the character of its inciter Unferth. In this section, we shall examine what role Hrothgar plays in terms of the flyting, which is closely related to how we should understand the debate and the character of Unferth.

When meeting Hrothgar, Beowulf greets him (407a), briefly introduces his pedigree and status (407b-8a), explains why he has come to meet him (409b-18), boasts about his bravery and physical strength (408b–9a, 415–24a), shows his unshakable resolution to fight with Grendel (424b–6a), and asks him to let him undertake the venture (426b–32). Before meeting Beowulf, when his sudden visit is announced, Hrothgar finds gratification in the news and, regarding him as a God-sent benefactor, expects him to deliver them from the affliction caused by Grendel (381b–9a). However, when Beowulf actually asks permission of him to do this, Hrothgar, strangely enough, neither gives any clear-cut response nor openly expresses his pleasure at hearing this. Instead, he first refers to a special favour he once bestowed upon Beowulf's father Ecgtheow (459–72) and then to their current critical situation (480–8).

It has often been suggested that the reason why Hrothgar does not give any direct answer here is that he wants to insinuate that, owing to his favour to Beowulf's father, he has a good claim to be helped by Beowulf now. In other words, he means that this is the repayment of the past favour and so does not accumulate a debt on his side.[12] This may well be so, but it

12 See Johannes Hoops, *Beowulfstudien*. Anglistische Forschungen 74 (Heidelberg: Carl Winter, 1932): 97–8; Johannes Hoops, *Kommentar zum Beowulf*. 2nd edn (Heidelberg: Carl Winter, 1965): 71–2; A. Bonjour, *The Digressions in Beowulf*. Medium Ævum Monographs V (1950. [Reprinted Oxford: Basil Blackwell, 1965]): 15–17; Brennan, 'Hrothgar's Government': 8–9; 苅部恒徳「Beowulfの栄光の陰画としてのデネ王国の衰亡」忍足欣四郎他編*Philologia Anglica: Essays Presented to Professor Yoshio Terasawa on the Occasion of His Sixtieth Birthday* (東京：研究社、1988) [Karibe, Tsunenori. 'Beowulf's Glory and the Decline of the

only reveals their relationship and the situation they are in, and is too vague and subtle as an answer to the petition. As we shall see, in fact, Hrothgar's permission is granted much later, and it is very reasonable to consider that the issue remains still pending at this point.

Without giving any definite answer, Hrothgar concludes his words as follows:

> Site nu to symle   ond onsæl meoto,
> sigehreð secgum,   swa þin sefa hwette.[13]

(*Beowulf* 489–90)
[Join in the feast and express your thoughts (and) glories of victory to people as your mind urges you.]

Bonjour considers that Beowulf is officially accepted as a protector of the hall by these words,[14] but being invited to a feast as a guest and being accepted as an official guard are two different things and cannot be identified. As Hrothgar himself says later when he finally grants his permission, to commit one's own hall to someone else is highly exceptional and, indeed, it has never occurred in his fifty years' reign (655–7). His invitation to the feast is too simple, conventional and vague for a declaration of such a significant decision.

Danish Kingdom.' K. Oshitari, et al. eds., *Philologia Anglica: Essays Presented to Professor Yoshio Terasawa on the Occasion of His Sixtieth Birthday* (Tokyo: Kenkyusha, 1988)]: 330; and J.M. Hill, *The Cultural World in Beowulf* (Toronto: University of Toronto Press, 1995): 76.

13 All the quotations from *Beowulf* are based on Klaeber, *Beowulf*. Translations are mine.

14 Bonjour, *The Digressions in Beowulf*: 22. Similarly, Ogilvy and Baker also consider that Beowulf has officially been accepted by the end of these words by Hrothgar, but without any basis (J.D.A. Ogilvy and D.C. Baker, *Reading Beowulf: An Introduction to the Poem, Its Background, and Its Style* (Norman, OK: University of Oklahoma Press, 1983): 50).

On hearing these words, the Danish people are said to provide seats for Beowulf and his men and they all begin to enjoy the feast (491–8). On the other hand, Beowulf does not begin to talk about his thoughts (*meoto*) and the glories (*sigehreð*) he achieved despite Hrothgar's words, but instead Unferth starts immediately to taunt him. Judging from this, unless Unferth ignores what his lord says, (as does not seem to be the case), it is reasonable to consider that Hrothgar does not mean Beowulf immediately to begin to boast and everyone else to listen to him quietly. Literally, his words are directed to Beowulf, but as tellingly reflected in the fact that people begin immediately to proffer the Geats seats and cups, the words virtually function as directions for everyone present. In other words, here Hrothgar declares the commencement of a Danish-Geatish feast, in which Beowulf's past achievements and future prospects are especially to be proclaimed.

Unferth duly follows these words and begins to talk about some negative aspects of Beowulf's exploits, suspecting that he lacks both *sapientia* and *fortitudo* (506–24),[15] and further expresses his own, negative view of the coming fight of Beowulf with Grendel (525–8). It is true that his words sound so aggressive and malicious that they might well seem to be intended to arouse the hostility of the Geats and ruin the feast and the friendship that may otherwise be nurtured.[16] However, it is also true that his words deal only with the topics Hrothgar has directed to be discussed at the feast, and not just mere pointless insults. Thus, though Unferth certainly is annoyed at Beowulf's visit (499–505), something that explains his open hostility, still he faithfully follows his lord's words. As far as this episode is concerned, he is certainly not a treacherous but a loyal retainer.

15   See Arthur G. Brodeur, *The Art of Beowulf* (Berkeley, CA: University of California Press, 1959): 142–50; and R.E. Kaske, '*Sapientia et Fortitudo* as the Controlling Theme of *Beowulf*', in L.E. Nicholson (ed.), *An Anthology of Beowulf Criticism* (Notre Dame, IN: University of Notre Dame Press, 1963): 278–9.

16   Because of this, earlier scholars often considered that *Unferð* (though always spelt *Hunferð* in the MS) consists of the negative *un-* and *ferð* (< *frið*), intended allegorically to mean 'mar-peace, unpeace.' As we shall see below, this is wide off the mark and outdated at the same time. As regards the name Unferth and its interpretations, see R.D. Fulk, 'Unferth and His Name', *Modern Philology* 85 (1987): 113–27.

The following passage describing Hrothgar's psychology just after the flyting clearly reveals that Unferth has not neglected but duly followed Hrothgar's words quoted above:

> Þa wæs on salum   sinces brytta
> gamolfeax ond guðrof;   geoce gelyfde
> brego Beorht-Dena;   gehyrde on Beowulfe
> folces hyrde   fæstrædne geþoht.
> (*Beowulf* 607–10)

[At that moment, the distributor of treasure, grey-haired and brave in battle, was in joy, the chief of the Bright-Danes believed in (Beowulf's) help; the protector of people heard a firmly-resolved thought from Beowulf.]

Responding to Unferth's taunting words, Beowulf begins to correct what is inaccurately claimed (530–81a), blames Unferth for his fratricide and coward-ice (581b–94), and openly points out the incapacity of the Danes (including Hrothgar) for self-defense, sometimes sounding almost insulting, claiming that, now that the Danes have proved incapable of getting rid of Grendel from their own hall, the mighty and brave Geats will face the enemy (595–606). Brennan suggests that, when Hrothgar talks about Ecgtheow's indebted-ness to himself and avoids announcing his verdict on Beowulf's petition, he implies it will be granted only if the proposed fight is construed as the discharge of Beowulf's indebtedness (through his father) to Hrothgar, and not as the glorification of the Geats.[17] If this is the case, Hrothgar may well feel bitter and even be enraged by Beowulf's words contrasting the ineffectual Danes and the potent Geats without a single reference to his indebtedness to Hrothgar. In actual fact, however, Hrothgar is said to feel happy, and this proves that what has been expressed in the aggressive verbal exchange is exactly what he expected at the beginning of the feast. In other words, the *meoto* (489b) and *sigehreð* (490a) that he expects Beowulf to express are exactly what he has heard, i.e. *fæstrædne geþoht* (610b). Thus Unferth can be seen as a retainer who, exchanging words with Beowulf on the very topic appointed, duly follows his lord's words and, consequently, achieves what his lord wants. It is no wonder that Hrothgar never blames Unferth for what might seem his highly rude attitude toward the honoured guest.

17 Brennan, 'Hrothgar's Government': 8–9.

When Hrothgar feels happy, it is said, people in the hall are laughing joyfully and talking together, and Hrothgar's wife Wealhtheow is said to begin to act as cupbearer (611–28a). Wealhtheow can be seen as playing the part of a *freoðuwebbe* 'peace-weaver', a part performed by a noble woman especially at a feast with occasional diplomatic/political speeches and gift-giving.[18] Thus the context proves that the aggressive verbal exchange affects nobody in a negative way, but instead seems even to help them establish and promote the peace between those two tribes, which is most symbolically expressed by Wealhtheow's role as a *freoðuwebbe*.

Some consider that it is curious that no violence is caused by the aggressive quarrel. For instance, etymologizing the name *Unferð* (but actually consistently *Hunferð* in the manuscript) as the negative *un-* plus *ferð* (< *frið*) 'peace' and seeing some allegorical meaning behind such nomenclature,[19] Klaeber claims that the 'absence of battle challenge and defiance ... is an obvious, inherent defect of our poem.'[20] Needless to say, however, we must try to understand the original as it stands before questioning its adequacy; and in this case, we need not see any defect in the poem itself.

On the other hand, Robinson interprets the name as 'nonsense', etymologizing it as the negative *un-* plus *fer(h)ð* 'mind, intellect', and claims that Unferth is a court jester and this is why people never take seriously what he says.[21] This is implausible when we take into consideration other

18   See L.J. Sklute, '*Freoðuwebbe* in Old English Poetry', in H. Damico and A.H. Olsen (eds.), *New Readings on Women in Old English Literature* (Bloomington, IN: Indiana University Press, 1990): 204–10; and J. Chance, 'The Structural Unity of *Beowulf*: The Problem of Grendel's Mother', in H. Damico and A.H. Olsen (eds.), *New Readings on Women in Old English Literature* (Bloomington, IN: Indiana University Press, 1990): 250.

19   Klaeber, *Beowulf*, 147–50.

20   Klaeber, *Beowulf*, lvi. In Fulk, Bjork and Niles (lxxxviii), this statement is modified as 'The absence of battle challenge and defiance ... is an apparent effect of the deployment of monsters as the hero's chief adversaries.'

21   Fred C. Robinson, 'Personal Names in Medieval Narrative and the Name of Unferth in *Beowulf*', in H. Creed (ed.), *Essays in Honor of Richebourg Gaillard McWilliams* (Birmingham, AL: Birmingham-Southern College, 1970): 43–8. The same article is reprinted in his *The Tomb of Beowulf*, 219–23, at the end of which he adds a note reading 'This and other studies on this subject should be re-examined in the light of

descriptions of Unferth in the poem. For instance, when Unferth lends his highly reputed sword Hrunting to Beowulf, who is going to fight with Grendel's mother, Beowulf resolutely declares that he would either win the battle using the sword or die (1490b–1). It seems unlikely that a court jester would have a great sword to lend, and it sounds even stranger that a hero would believe in a sword lent by a court jester, and make such a brave and resolute declaration. Even after the battle, when the sword has turned out to be useless (at least against Grendel's mother), Beowulf blames neither Unferth nor his sword but very politely pays his respects to Unferth (1659–60, 1807–12), something that is also unlikely as a response to a court jester who lent a useless sword. Thus Robinson's interpretation of Unferth's name scarcely applies to other parts of the poem and is not tenable.

Since Clover's detailed article, it has widely been accepted that the verbal exchange between Unferth and Beowulf can be seen as an example of Germanic flyting, and in this case, especially as a 'hostile investigation into the reputation of a newcomer by a man who stands in a delegate relation to the king and is explicitly known as a man of word.'[22] It is not unusual for this sort of flyting to be directed against a newcomer, nor does it necessarily cause a violent outcome, and this reading may well let the episode fit the context, where no one seems to be disturbed by the apparently violent quarrel.

It should be noted here again not only that this sort of flyting is not an unusual event during a feast but that this particular one is induced (and accordingly expected) by Hrothgar himself for the purpose of decision-making. As we have seen above, without giving any clear-cut verdict on Beowulf's petition, Hrothgar opens a feast in which he expects Beowulf to express his ardent thoughts in his conversation with the Danish people. In this circumstance, where no decision has yet been made, the feast is reasonably interpreted as an occasion on which to make a decision, for which Beowulf's words and the people's reactions will be the chief test. In such a feast, it is quite natural for Unferth or any Danish retainer to interrogate him to see whether he is promising enough.

Carol Clover, 'The Germanic context of the Unferþ episode,' *Speculum*, 55 (1980): 444–68.

22 Clover, 'The Germanic context of the Unferþ episode': 488.

As observed in Hrothgar's reaction, the joyful atmosphere of the people, and Wealhtheow's function as a *freoðuwebbe*, the flyting (and especially Beowulf's words in it), however aggressive and peace-breaking it may sound to the modern ear, works as the core of the process of the peace and decision making, and this must be exactly what Hrothgar expects when declaring the opening of the feast. Hrothgar gives no clear-cut answer to Beowulf's request before the necessary decision-making process, at the end of which he formally accepts Beowulf as an official guard of Heorot (655–61). Thus, opening a decision-making feast which may well include aggressive verbal exchanges, Hrothgar is the formal inducer of the flyting while, though spurred on by jealousy and intoxication, Unferth, the actual initiator of it, behaves according to, or at least within the limits of, his lord's expectation and consequently achieves what is expected.

One of the reasons why earlier scholars tended to view Unferth as a peace-breaker, believing in the folk-etymological meaning of his name, 'mar-peace', may be that his words sound so aggressive and malicious when directed at a potentially beneficent visitor. But it should have also been noted that Beowulf is more skilful than Unferth in insulting and condemning[23] and fights back with equally provocative condemnatory utterances to Unferth and the Danes in general, despite his merciful and heroic purpose in visiting them. It is obvious that by those words Beowulf does not mean to stir up discord but tries to gain credence and eventually permission, and this reveals that words very offensive to our modern ears are not always taken as such in the Germanic world depicted in *Beowulf*.

In the same way, it is fair to say that Unferth's words cannot be taken at face value; they are not always conceived simply as what symbolizes or causes *Discordia*.[24] What is more, as the inducer of the flyting who utilizes

---

23   As regards the superiority of Beowulf's words to those of Unferth, see, for instance, S.B. Greenfield, *The Interpretation of Old English Poems* (London: Routledge and Kegan Paul, 1972): 130–1, and P. Silber, 'Rhetoric as Prowess in the Unferth Episode', *Texas Studies in Literature and Language* 23 (1981): 471–83.

24   Attacking Jusserand's reading that Beowulf's words to Unferth can be summarized as 'liar, drunkard, coward, murderer!', Tolkien comments that anything 'that any character says or does in a poem written in Anglo-Saxon is just a picture of "Anglo-Saxon

it as a main test in the decision-making, Hrothgar himself is depicted as a man deeply rooted in this 'savage' Germanic ethos.

2.2. Hrothgar's Sermon revisited

As reflected in the use of the term 'sermon', Hrothgar's warning on avarice and pride sounds homiletic, abounding in expressions and motifs seemingly of Christian origin,[25] and many scholars actually interpret it as a Christian sermon. For instance, in his edition Magoun calls lines 1724b–84 'On the Deadly Sins of Pride, Sloth, and Covetousness', and indicates in the margin the names of the deadly sins – i.e. 'Accidia', 'Avaritia', and 'Superbia' – where he considers they are mentioned.[26] Stanley says 'The densest concentration in *Beowulf* of pious thoughts, "Christian elements", is to be found in Hrothgar's so-called "sermon", ... Divine worship as well as homiletic matter are suitably expressed by Hrothgar.'[27] Goldsmith even claims that Hrothgar's

---

behaviour"', and that 'the Jusserandian method of criticizing such a passage would reduce all poetry to vulgarity; and its employment can proceed only from malice, or from an ignorance and an insensibility to an ancient mode, which is in one presuming to criticize almost as criminal' (J.R.R. Tolkien, *Beowulf and the Critics*, in M.D.C. Drout (ed.) (Tempe, AZ: Arizona Center for Medieval and Renaissance Studies, 2002): 94). Naturally this is also applicable to Unferth's 'vulgar' remarks. As regards Jusserand's view, see J.J. Jusserand, *A Literary History of the English People from the Origins to the Renaissance*. vol. 1, (1895. [Reprinted New York: Benjamin Blom, 1968]): 55.

25 Because of this, Müllenhoff, at a very early stage of *Beowulf* scholarship, claimed that the 'sermon' must be a Christian interpolation, and recently Orchard has written on the use of homiletic, Christian language in the 'sermon'. See Karl Müllenhoff, *Beovulf: Untersuchungen über das angelsächsischen Epos und die älteste Geschichte der germanischen Seevölker* (Berlin: Weidmannsche, 1889): 130–1; and Andy Orchard, *A Critical Companion to Beowulf* (Woodbridge, Cambridge: D.S. Brewer, 2003): 158–62.

26 F.P. Magoun, Jr. (ed.), *Beowulf and Judith* (Cambridge, MA: Department of English, Harvard University, 1959): 49.

27 Eric G. Stanley, *In the Foreground: Beowulf* (Cambridge: D.S. Brewer, 1994): 240.

sermon has much to do with the second part of the poem, in which she claims that Beowulf becomes proud and eventually dies because of his failing to follow the sermon by Hrothgar (or, indirectly, by the Church fathers).[28] According to her, Hrothgar comes to realize his arrogance in consequence of the affliction caused by Grendel, and his thoughts turn 'from their complacent dwelling upon his success and wealth towards *ece rædas* (1760a)', which she interprets as 'attitudes, decisions, or acts which will profit the soul in the perspective of eternity.'[29]

It is true that the 'sermon' includes various expressions and motifs probably of Christian origin. It does not, however, necessarily follow that it is actually meant to be a Christian sermon. Introducing Christian motifs and expressions does not necessarily entail the introduction of Christian ideas and values. This is obvious when we consider that the Old English poetic vocabulary and motifs are mostly of pre-Christian origin but Cædmon, or whoever composed the first OE Christian poem, made full use of them in order to express Christian ideas creating Christian contexts.[30] If vocabulary and motifs of heathen origin can be used to express Christian ideas, Christian expressions and motifs might also be used to create non-Christian contexts even without any pious or profound religious meanings. When we try to understand the nature of Hrothgar's sermon, therefore, we need closely to follow the context rather than decide from the outset that it is Christian in character just because of the expressions and motifs used in it.

Let us begin with considering the reading of the following words:

28   M.E. Goldsmith, *The Mode and Meaning of Beowulf* (London: Athlone Press, 1970): 183–209.

29   Goldsmith, *Mode and Meaning*: 207 and 205, respectively. Bosse and Wyatt advance a somewhat similar view, regarding Hrothgar's sermon as a manifestation of his penance for the sin of pride. See R.B. Bosse and J.L. Wyatt, 'Hrothgar and Nebuchadnezzar: Conversion in Old English Verse', *Papers on Language and Literature* 23/3 (1987): 257–71.

30   See W. Whallon, *Formula, Character, and Context: Studies in Homeric, Old English, and Old Testament Poetry* (Washington, D.C.: Center for Hellenic Studies, 1969): 117–38. See also Fred C. Robinson, *Beowulf and the Appositive Style* (Knoxville, TN: University of Tennessee Press, 1985): 32–5.

Bebeorh þe ðone bealonið   Beowulf leofa,
secg betsta,   ond þe þæt selre geceos,
ece rædas;   oferhyda ne gym,
mære cempa!
(*Beowulf* 1758–61a)

[Guard yourself against the wickedness, dear Beowulf, the best of men, and follow the better (way), the long-lasting counsels. Do not care for pride, reputed warrior!]

This is the core of the admonition and its effect should naturally be deduced from what has been claimed up to this point. Placed just after the passage in which the process of a prosperous man's becoming avaricious and arrogant up to his downfall is narrated (1740–57), the term *ðone bealonið* 'the pernicious enmity' or 'the wickedness' (with the demonstrative) refers not to wickedness in general[31] but to what is denoted by *egesan* (1757b) 'dreadful thing',[32] which represents the source of avarice and pride, namely, a diabolic assault (1743b–4), or more precisely, the sharp arrow (*biteran stræle* (1745a)), which is equated with perverse, mysterious commands of an evil spirit (*wom wundorbebodum wergan gastes* (1747)). Compared or contrasted with *ðone bealonið*,[33] *þæt selre* 'the better (way)' in the next line is intended to mean protecting himself from the *bealonið* and not following

---

31   Cf. *beorgað him bealoniþ* in *Guthlac A* (809a), where the word is used in the same collocation but without the demonstrative. Here it represents wickedness in general.

32   The word *egesa* here has often been considered to mean either fear in general or anxiety about losing wealth through generous treasure-distribution. (See, for instance, Hoops, *Kommentar*, 192). However, both readings seem debatable. Taking into account the context up to this part and the fact that *egesa* can also mean 'something dreadful', it seems more plausible that it means '(the) dreadful thing', referring to the source of avarice and pride mentioned just before the passage. For details, see K. Karasawa, 'A Note on *egesan ne gymeð* in *Beowulf* Line 1757', *Modern Philology* 106/1 (2008): 101–8.

33   Klaeber claims that the counterpart of *þæt selre* 'the better (way)' is not mentioned, but I do not know why the negative *þone bealonið* (or following it) cannot be meant to stand in comparison with 'the better (way)' placed side by side with it. See Frederick Klaeber, 'Die christlichen Elemente im *Beowulf*', *Anglia* 35 (1911): 479 and *The Christian Elements in Beowulf*. Trans. P. Battles. Old English News Letter, Subsidia 24 (Kalamazoo, MI: West Michigan University, 1996): 50.

the same way as the anonymous proud lord (as well as Heremod) is said to do, shot by the *bona* (1743b), controlled by *wom wundorbebodum wergan gastes* (1747) and leading himself to self-destruction. Appositive with *þæt selre* 'the better (way)', moreover, the phrase *ece rædas* means 'long-lasting counsels', which enable him to be prosperous for a long time without being interrupted by pride.[34] Hrothgar's admonition itself is an example of such counsels; another one is also found in lines 20–5.

The phrase *ece rædas* has often been understood from the Christian point of view as 'eternal salvation, eternal gain, eternal counsel, etc.' closely connected to eternal life after death,[35] partly, it seems, because of the phrase *ece ræd* (but always in the singular form)[36] used for eternal divine and/or heavenly benefit. Goldsmith, for instance, notes that 'If he chooses the better way, he will place the observance of God's law above every other consideration, directing his life towards *ece rædas*, not to *eorðan dreamas*.'[37] Considering the context, however, this sort of reading must be said to be rather awkward. Hrothgar takes Heremod as an example of an arrogant lord, who used to be highly prosperous but destroyed himself because of his pride:

34   See M.A. Parker, *Beowulf and Christianity* (New York: Peter Lang, 1987): 43–5.
     Mitchell and Robinson interpret it in a similar fashion as '"lasting gains", "enduring
     benefit" (in contrast with the short-term satisfaction of arrogance and miserliness).'
     See Bruce Mitchell and Fred C. Robinson (eds.), *Beowulf: An Edition with Relevant
     Shorter Texts* (Oxford: Blackwell, 1998): 106.
35   See Klaeber, *Beowulf*, 457–8; Johannes Hoops, *Kommentar zum Beowulf* 2nd edn.
     (Heidelberg: Carl Winter, 1965): 192; and Goldsmith, *The Mode and Meaning of
     Beowulf*: 204–5. See also Michael Swanton (ed. and trans.). *Beowulf*, revised edn
     (Manchester: Manchester University Press, 1997): 119; and R.M. Liuzza, (trans.).
     Beowulf: A New Verse Translation (Peterborough, Ont.: Broadview, 2000): 106.
36   The phrase in this meaning always appears in its singular form, i.e. in *Beowulf* 1201,
     Daniel 30, and *Metres of Boethius* metre 20 line 224. In *Heliand*, moreover, a phrase
     similar in its meaning, *langsamoron rad* (1202a) is also used in the singular form.
     In *Exodus* 516, on the other hand, plural *ece rædas* refers to words by Moses and not
     something directly related to a divine or heavenly benefit.
37   Goldsmith, *Mode and Meaning of Beowulf*: 204.

```
        Ne wearð Heremod swa
eaforum Ecgwelan,        Ar-Scyldingum;
ne geweox he him to willan,        ac to wælfealle
ond to deaðcwalum        Deniga leodum;
breat bolgenmod        beodgeneatas,
eaxlgesteallan,        oþ þæt he ana hwearf,
mære þeoden        mondreamum from,
ðeah þe hine mihtig God        mægenes wynnum,
eafeþum stepte,        ofer ealle men
forð gefremede,        Hwæþere him on ferhþe greow
breosthord blodreow;        nallas beagas geaf
Denum æfter dome;        dreamleas gebad,
þæt he þæs gewinnes        weorc þrowade,
leodbealo longsum.        Ðu þe lær be þon,
gumcyste ongit!
(Beowulf 1709b–23a)
```

[Heremod was not like that, the son of Ecgwela, to the glorious Scyldings. He became not their delight but the slayer and destroyer of the Danish people. Enraged, he killed his table-companions, shoulder-companions, so that the reputed lord left the joy of men alone, although Mighty God had exalted him by the joy of power and strength, advanced (him) ahead of all men. However, in his breast grew a bloodthirsty mind. He never gave rings to the Danes in pursuit of glory. He lived without the joy (of human society), so that he suffered distress of strifes, long affliction. Teach yourself by this and know a virtue of man.]

Here Hrothgar does not mention anything about Heremod's death and his misery in hell nor does he make any contrast between glory in heaven and misery in hell. Instead, he explains how, afflicted by arrogant pride, Heremod lost his prosperity and lived a miserable life *in this world*. In this context, it is most natural to consider that *gumcyst* (1723a), a lesson that is to be learned from Heremod's example, should refer to a virtue as a lord, and not a Christian virtue necessary for one to be granted an 'eternal gain.' Hrothgar reveals how Heremod lost his *mondream* (1715b) and became *dreamleas* (1720b) in this world, because he failed to behave as befits a lord, respect his retainers, and nurture a good lord-retainer relationship.

Despite Goldsmith's argument, thus, all that is told about Heremod here is his loss of worldly *dream*, i.e., joy enjoyed in a prosperous human society,[38] rather than his pursuit of it.[39] The lesson to be learnt from this example, therefore, is that, in order to maintain one's prosperity as a lord and live in *dream*, he needs to be generous and conduct himself as befits a lord. God is mentioned merely as a dispenser of great talents, which can be a source of avarice and pride, and nothing about eternal salvation or benefit can be learned from this.

The same thing as mentioned in relation to Heremod is repeated in regard to the anonymous fallen lord in the following passage:

> þinceð him to lytel,   þæt he lange heold,
> gytsað gromhydig,   nallas on gylp seleð
> fætte beagas,   ond he þa forðgesceaft
> forgyteð ond forgymeð,   þæs þe him ær God sealde,
> wuldres Waldend,   weorðmynda dæl.
> (*Beowulf* 1748–52)

[What he has possessed for a long time seems him too little, and he becomes avaricious, and never distributes ornamented rings gloriously, and he forgets and neglects his future state, because God, the Ruler of glory, gave him a great portion of honour.]

Thus, just as in the case of Heremod, he meets his downfall and dies, and what happens after this is:

38 As indicated in the parentheses in the quotation above, the word *dream*, when used for some joy in this world, bears a strong connotation of ideal human society. In this use, accordingly, *dreamleas* more or less means to be without prosperity, having no family and friends helping each other to prosper together. For details, see K. Karasawa, 'An Aspect of OE Joy Term *Dream* in Comparison with *Wynn*', *Soundings* 24 (1999): 9–26 and K. Karasawa, 'Christian Influence on OE *dream*: Pre-Christian and Christian Meanings', *Neophilologus* 87/2 (2003): 307–22.

39 In fact, Heremod is said, in the quoted passage, never to have given any treasures to his retainers in pursuit of glory (as a lord). Needless to say, distribution of treasures is one of the chief sources of the ideal lord-retainer relationship causing *dream*, as also implied in this passage. Goldsmith neglects the actual context, when unfavourably referring to Beowulf's potential pursuit of *eorðan dreamas*.

> fehð oþer to,
> se þe unmurnlice   madmas dæleþ,
> eorles ærgestreon,   egesan ne gymeð.
> (*Beowulf* 1755b–7)

[Another one takes over, who happily distributes treasures, the man's ancient treasure, and does not care for the dreadful deception (of the devil).][40]

A better lord is said to take over, and here again, treasure-giving is mentioned as a typical example of lordly conduct, whereas nothing about his Christian faith, pious attitudes, eternal salvation, etc. is mentioned or even implied. As regards the fallen lord, his death is briefly mentioned (1753–5a) but no attention is paid to his afterlife, clearly reflecting its insignificance here. Instead of his afterlife, moreover, what is narrated here is what happens *in this world* after his death. Indeed, in his 'sermon', Hrothgar is exclusively concerned with matters in this world and nothing posthumous. Thus he narrates up to the man's downfall or at the furthest up to his death but never mentions anything that happens to him after death.

After these examples of Heremod and the anonymous arrogant lord comes the core passage of the admonition quoted above. Without a single mention or even implication of posthumous life, eternal gain or salvation in the foregoing part of the sermon, it is implausible for Hrothgar to conclude his admonition suddenly saying that Beowulf should worship God as a humble and pious Christian in order to attain eternal salvation rather than pursuing transient worldly joy. Nowhere does he make any contrast between a humble and pious Christian lord going to heaven and an arrogant, profane lord going to hell. Instead of doing this, he gives two examples of an arrogantly proud lord for Beowulf not to make the same mistake. Thus he is admonishing Beowulf not to stray from the right path as a secular lord because of arrogant pride and become *dreamleas* as did Heremod. This also works as advice indicating how to maintain for long an ideal state of his lordship and court society filled with *dream*, which Beowulf has actually been enjoying as he is called *dreamhealdende* (1227b) 'one having *dream*' by Wealhtheow, Hrothgar's wife.

40 Regarding the interpretation of the last half-line, see note 32 above.

Just after the core passage in the admonition, Hrothgar continues as follows:

> Nu is þines mægnes blæd
> ane hwile;   eft sona bið
> þæt þec adl oððe ecg   eafoþes getwæfeð,
> oððe fyres feng,   oððe flodes wylm,
> oððe gripe meces,   oððe gares fliht,
> oððe atol yldo;   oððe eagena bearhtm
> forsiteð ond forsworceð;   semninga bið,
> þæt ðec, dryhtguma,   deað oferswyðeð.
> (*Beowulf* 1761b–8)

[Now the glory of thy power lasts only a while. Soon after, it happens that disease or sword deprives thee of thy strength, or embrace of fire, or a surge of flood, or the edge of sword, or spear's flight, or horrible old age; or brightness of the eyes diminishes and becomes dark. It is not long before death destroys thee, warrior.]

This correlates with the following passage in an earlier part of the sermon describing a prosperous lord's psychology, which leads shortly to arrogant pride:

> Wunað he on wiste;   no hine with dweleð
> adl ne yldo,   ne him inwitsorh
> on sefa(n) sweorceð,   ne gesacu ohwær
> ecghete eoweð, ...
> (*Beowulf* 1735–8a)

[He dwells in prosperity and neither disease nor old age afflicts him, no sorrow makes him dark in his mind, and no enmity, sword-war occurs anywhere.]

Basically the same state of mind of a proud lord is repeated briefly as: *ond he þa forðgesceaft / forgyteð ond forgymeð* (1750b–51a) 'and he forgets and neglects his future state.' Thus, Hrothgar says it is important always to be aware of potential future difficulties and be prepared for them, no matter how greatly one is thriving at a certain moment. Various causes of decline of one's power, emphatically enumerated in the former passage, function to deter the development of the dangerous state of mind mentioned in the latter passage. The interrelation between these two passages may well be reflected in some shared words and elements such as *adl, yldo, ecg, sweorcan*. Thus, just after admonishing Beowulf not to be occupied by arrogant thoughts, Hrothgar, in highly dismal words in the former quotation, warns Beowulf always to be aware of and prepared for the difficulties that sooner or later will befall him in the future.

Thus, the essence of the admonition concerns almost exclusively secular issues based on traditional values handed down from the pre-Christian past. God is mentioned as a distributor of prosperity and a ruler of everything (1724b–7), but this is certainly not the main point of the admonition. At the same time, however, it is noteworthy that near the end of the poem, the dying Beowulf thanks God for giving him the victory over the fire-dragon and allowing him to win the treasures (2794–8). By the standard of Hrothgar's 'sermon', this might well indicate that Beowulf remains untroubled by pernicious pride until his very last moments, since he is aware that God is the ultimate source of power and wealth, something which, according to Hrothgar, is forgotten by proud people.

Just before and after the fight with the fire-dragon, in addition, Beowulf is referred to as a generous lord (*goldwine* 'gold-friend, generous prince'),[41] as actually witnessed to by Wiglaf and other retainers (2633ff.), and this also suggests that he is not avaricious and proud, unlike Heremod and the anonymous lord in the 'sermon.' Since Hrothgar repeatedly mentions liberality as a test of ideal lords that proud and arrogant lords fail, Beowulf's generosity suggests that he remains free from avarice and pride throughout his life, at least by Hrothgar's standard.[42] Thus Beowulf is depicted as a lord righteous until the end of his life, as he is actually praised by his people at the very end of the poem (3180–2). His reign continues as long as Hrothgar's without any major difficulties, a fact that may well be regarded as another manifestation of his following the lesson.

41 See Klaeber, *Beowulf*: 346, under *goldwine*.
42 His righteousness as a young lord is clearly contrasted with Heremod's arrogance in lines 2177–83a. See Klaeber, *Beowulf*: 207; Hoops, *Kommentar*: 238.

Those who assert Beowulf's disregard of Hrothgar's admonition and
his growing arrogance and pride in his later years seem to ignore all these
correlative statements and the other clues, quite apart from interpreting
the 'sermon' in purely Christian terms irrespective of the actual context
in which it is given.

2.3. Conclusion

It is interesting to compare the treatment of boasting and flyting in the
Unferth Intermezzo in *Beowulf* and that in the Old English poem *Vain-glory*. In the former, the flyting between Unferth and Beowulf functions
as an important activity during a peace- and decision-making process. In
the latter, equally boastful and aggressive verbal exchanges at a feast are
regarded as manifestations of pernicious pride, and boasters and taunters
are called *feondes bearn* (*Vainglory* 47b) 'devil's child.' By the standard of
Vainglory, therefore, Beowulf and Unferth may well be regarded as vicious
characters stained with vainglorious, arrogant and proud thoughts.[43] In
fact, Unferth has often been regarded as an evil character, whereas those
who propose hyper-Christian interpretations sometimes conceive even
Beowulf as growing proud and arrogant in the latter half of the poem. On
the other hand, the peaceable Hrothgar never participates in the aggressive
verbal exchange itself, but as inducer of the flyting uses it as a major test

43   Cf. Alcuin's words on pride in 'De superbia' in his *Liber de virtutibus et vitiis* (ch.
      23): 'Superbi cupiunt in se praedicari quod non faciunt: humiles refugiunt, quidquid
      boni operantur, agnosci. Non elevetur homo in bono suo, nec laudem sibi quaerat,
      quamvis aliquid boni faciat: sed Deum laudare [Ms., laudari] cupiat in donis suis,
      quia nihil boni facit [Ms. fecit], nisi quod Deus donavit ei facere'. (This passage is
      quoted from *Patrologia Latina* 101.) Thus, a boastful hero in heroic poems like *Beowulf*
      might well be regarded as a typical example of a man suffering from pernicious pride.
      Alcuin's famous words 'Quid Hinieldus cum Christo?' criticising people's preference
      for heroic poems might well have much to do with this issue.

of Beowulf's capability and credibility. Hence, fundamentally the king shares the same mentality as his *þyle*. This explains why Hrothgar neither denounces Unferth for his openly hostile remarks to Beowulf nor is enraged by Beowulf's equally provocative and sometimes insulting words, but highly esteems these very words by Beowulf. Thus Hrothgar's indirect but important commitment and his reaction to the flyting clearly reveal that he is as deeply permeated by the Germanic ethos as Beowulf, Unferth and others in the poem.

Whereas Hrothgar's character reflected in the Unferth episode has been almost neglected, it has tended to be judged rather on the basis of the 'sermon' he addresses to Beowulf. He is generally depicted as a wise, old, peaceable, noncombatant king often invoking God, and he has often been regarded as a nearly or completely Christian character. His 'sermon' has also often been compared with various patristic writings and interpreted in Christian terms. In this way, the general impression of both Hrothgar and his sermon have together promoted the Christian understanding of both.

However, Hrothgar's sermon in its context concerns not theological/Christian issues but much more practical and secular ones. He warns Beowulf not to be so self-confident as to underestimate his retainers, since in the long run they are the source of his long-lasting prosperity. This is a piece of traditional wisdom, as also reflected in lines 20–5; Hrothgar advises Beowulf to follow the traditionally cultivated way of a lord and to avoid the pitfall of self-destruction into which a prosperous lord like him tends to fall. Thus Hrothgar's 'sermon' is to be understood as a lesson on a secular issue for a secular lord by an equally secular lord. This reading agrees with his character as discernible in the Unferth episode. Despite various readings that see him as a Christian ruler giving a Christian sermon, Hrothgar's words and deeds reveal that the poet does not treat him as a spokesman of the Church thinly disguised as a pagan king but as a king deeply rooted in the Germanic culture.

2.4. References

2.4.1. Primary sources

Fulk, R.D., R.E. Bjork, and J.D. Niles, eds. *Klaeber's Beowulf and the Fight at Finnsburg*.
4th edn with a foreword by Helen Damico, with first and second supplements
of *Beowulf and the Fight at Finnsburg*, ed. Fr. Klaeber. Toronto: University of
Toronto Press, 2008.
Klaeber, Frederick, ed. *Beowulf and the Fight at Finnsburg*. 3rd edn, with first and
second supplements. Boston, MA: D.C. Heath, 1950.
Magoun, Jr., F.P., ed. *Beowulf and Judith*. Cambridge, MA: Department of English,
Harvard University, 1959.
Mitchell, Bruce, and Fred C. Robinson, eds. *Beowulf: An Edition with Relevant Shorter
Texts*. Oxford: Blackwell, 1998.
Swanton, Michael, ed. and trans. *Beowulf*, rev. edn. Manchester: Manchester Uni-
versity Press, 1997.

2.4.2. Secondary sources

Baird, Joseph L. 'Unferth the Þyle', *Medium Ævum* 39 (1970): 1–12.
Baker, P.S. 'Beowulf the Orator', *Journal of English Linguistics* 21 (1988): 3–23.
Barnes, Daniel R. 'Folktale Morphology and the Structure of *Beowulf*', *Speculum* 45
(1970): 416–34.
Bloomfield, Morton W. '*Beowulf* and Christian Allegory: An Interpretation of
Unferth', *Traditio* 7 (1949–51): 410–15.
Bolton, W.F. *Alcuin and Beowulf: An Eighth-Century View*. New Brunswick, NJ:
Rutgers University Press, 1978.
Bonjour, Adrien. *The Digressions in Beowulf*. Medium Ævum Monographs V, 1950.
[Reprinted Oxford: Basil Blackwell, 1965.]
Bosse, R.B., and J.L. Wyatt. 'Hrothgar and Nebuchadnezzar: Conversion in Old
English Verse', *Papers on Language and Literature* 23/3 (1987): 257–71.
Brennan, M.M. 'Hrothgar's Government', *Journal of English and Germanic Philology*
84 (1985): 3–15.
Brodeur, Arthur G. *The Art of Beowulf*. Berkeley, CA: University of California Press,
1959.

Chadwick, H. Munro, and N.K. Chadwick. *The Growth of Literature I: The Ancient Literature of Europe*. Cambridge: Cambridge University Press, 1932.

Chambers, R.W. *Beowulf: An Introduction to the Study of the Poem with a Discussion of the Stories of Offa and Finn*. 3rd edn, with a supplement by C.L. Wrenn. Cambridge: Cambridge University Press, 1959.

Chance, Jane. 'The Structural Unity of *Beowulf*: The Problem of Grendel's Mother', in H. Damico and A.H. Olsen, eds. *New Readings on Women in Old English Literature*. Bloomington, IN: Indiana University Press, 1990. 248–61.

Clark, George. *Beowulf*. Boston, MA: Twayne, 1990.

Clover, C.J. 'The Germanic Context of the Unferth Episode', *Speculum* 55 (1980): 444–68.

Daldorph, B. 'Mar-Peace, Ally: Hunferð in *Beowulf*', *Massachusetts Studies in English* 10 (1986): 143–60.

Eliason, N.E. 'The Þyle and Scop in *Beowulf*', *Speculum* 38 (1963): 267–84.

Enright, M.J. 'The Warband Context of the Unferth Episode', *Speculum* 73 (1998): 297–337.

Feldman, T.P. 'The Taunter in Ancient Epic: The *Iliad, Odyssey, Aeneid*, and *Beowulf*', *Papers on Language and Literature* 15 (1979): 3–16.

Fulk, R.D. 'Unferth and His Name', *Modern Philology* 85 (1987): 113–27.

Gingher, R.S. 'The Unferth Perplex', *Thoth* 14 (1974): 19–28.

Goldsmith, Margaret. E. *The Mode and Meaning of Beowulf*. London: Athlone Press, 1970.

Gould, Kent. '*Beowulf* and Folktale Morphology: God as Magical Donor', *Folklore* 96 (1985): 98–103.

Greenfield, S.B. *The Interpretation of Old English Poems*. London: Routledge and Kegan Paul, 1972.

Hardy, Adelaide. 'The Christian Hero Beowulf and Unferð Þyle', *Neophilologus* 53 (1969): 55–69.

——. 'Historical Perspective and the *Beowulf*-Poet', *Neophilologus* 63 (1979): 430–49.

Hill, John. M. *The Cultural World in Beowulf*. Toronto: University of Toronto Press, 1995.

Hollowell, Ida Masters. 'Unferth the þyle in *Beowulf*', *Studies in Philology* 73 (1976): 239–65.

Hoops, Johannes. *Beowulfstudien*. Anglistische Forschungen 74. Heidelberg: Carl Winter, 1932.

——. *Kommentar zum Beowulf*. 2nd edn. Heidelberg: Carl Winter, 1965.

Hughes, Geoffrey. 'Beowulf, Unferth and Hrunting: An Interpretation', *ES* 58 (1977): 385–95.

Irving, Jr., Edward B. *Introduction to Beowulf.* Englewood Cliffs, NJ: Prentice-Hall, 1969.

———. *Rereading Beowulf.* Philadelphia, PA: University of Pennsylvania Press, 1989.

Jorgensen, Peter A. 'The Gift of the Useless Weapon in *Beowulf* and the Icelandic Sagas', *Arkiv för Nordisk Filologi* 94 (1979): 82–90.

Jusserand, J.J. *A Literary History of the English People from the Origins to the Renaissance.* vol. 1, 1895. [Reprinted New York: Benjamin Blom, 1968.]

Karasawa, Kazutomo. 'An Aspect of OE Joy Term *Dream* in Comparison with *Wynn*', *Soundings* 24 (1999): 9–26.

———. 'Christian Influence on OE *dream*: Pre-Christian and Christian Meanings', *Neophilologus* 87/2 (2003): 307–22.

———. 'Hrothgar and the Germanic Context in *Beowulf*', *Universals and Variation in Language* 3 (2008): 73–85.

———. 'A Note on *egesan ne gymeð* in *Beowulf* Line 1757', *Modern Philology* 106/1 (2008): 101–8.

Karibe, Tsunenori. See 苅部恒徳 below.

Kaske, R.E. '*Sapientia et Fortitudo* as the Controlling Theme of *Beowulf*', in L.E. Nicholson, ed. *An Anthology of Beowulf Criticism.* Notre Dame, IN: University of Notre Dame Press, 1963. 269–310.

Klaeber, Frederick. 'Die christlichen Elemente im *Beowulf*', *Anglia* 35 (1911): 111–36, 249–70, and 453–82.

———. *The Christian Elements in Beowulf.* Trans. P. Battles. Old English News Letter, Subsidia 24. Kalamazoo, MI: West Michigan University, 1996.

Lawrence, W.W. *Beowulf and Epic Tradition.* Cambridge, MA: Harvard University Press, 1930.

Lee, Alvin. A. *Gold-Hall and Earth-Dragon: Beowulf as Metaphor.* Toronto: University of Toronto Press, 1998.

Liuzza, R.M., trans. *Beowulf: A New Verse Translation.* Peterborough, Ont.: Broadview, 2000.

Martin-Clarke, D.E. 'The Office of Thyle in *Beowulf*', *RES* 12 (1936): 61–6.

Müllenhoff, Karl. *Beovulf: Untersuchungen über das angelsächsischen Epos und die älteste Geschichte der germanischen Seevölker.* Berlin: Weidmannsche, 1889.

Ogilvy, J.D.A. 'Unferth: Foil to Beowulf?', *PMLA* 79 (1964): 370–5.

Ogilvy, J.D.A., and D.C. Baker. *Reading Beowulf: An Introduction to the Poem, Its Background, and Its Style.* Norman, OK: University of Oklahoma Press, 1983.

Olrik, Axel. *The Heroic Legends of Denmark.* Trans. L.M. Hollander. New York: The American-Scandinavian Foundation, 1919.

Orchard, Andy. *A Critical Companion to Beowulf.* Woodbridge, Suffolk: D.S. Brewer, 2003.

Parker, M.A. *Beowulf and Christianity*. New York: Peter Lang, 1987.

Phillpotts, B.S. *The Elder Edda and Ancient Scandinavian Drama*. Cambridge: Cambridge University Press, 1920.

Robinson, Fred C. 'Personal Names in Medieval Narrative and the Name of Unferth in *Beowulf*', in H. Creed, ed. *Essays in Honor of Richebourg Gaillard McWilliams*. Birmingham, AL: Birmingham-Southern College, 1970. 43–8.

———. *Beowulf and the Appositive Style*. Knoxville, TN: University of Tennessee Press, 1985.

———. 'Personal Names in Medieval Narrative and the Name of Unferth in *Beowulf*', *The Tomb of Beowulf and Other Essays in Old English*. Oxford: Blackwell, 1993. 219–23.

Rosier, James L. 'Design for Treachery: The Unferth Intrigue', *PMLA* 77 (1962): 1–7.

Shippey, T.A. 'The Fairy-Tale Structure of *Beowulf*', *N&Q* n.s. 16 (1969): 2–11.

Silber, Patricia. 'Rhetoric as Prowess in the Unferth Episode', *Texas Studies in Literature and Language* 23 (1981): 471–83.

Sklute, L.J. '*Freoðuwebbe* in Old English Poetry', in H. Damico and A.H. Olsen, eds., *New Readings on Women in Old English Literature*. Bloomington, IN: Indiana University Press, 1990: 204–10.

Smits, K. 'Die "Stimmen" des schweigenden Königs: ein Erzählmotiv im *Beowulf*, im *Nibelungenlied* und im *Parzival*', *Literaturwissenschaftliches Jahrbuch* 27 (1986): 23–45.

Stanley, Eric G. *In the Foreground: Beowulf*. Cambridge: D.S. Brewer, 1994.

Tolkien, J.R.R. *Beowulf and the Critics*. M.D.C. Drout, ed. Tempe, AZ: Arizona Center for Medieval and Renaissance Studies, 2002.

Whallon, W. *Formula, Character, and Context: Studies in Homeric, Old English, and Old Testament Poetry*. Washington, D.C.: Center for Hellenic Studies, 1969.

Williams, David. *Cain and Beowulf: A Study in Secular Allegory*. Toronto: University of Toronto Press, 1982.

苅部恒徳 「Beowulf の栄光の陰画としてのデネ王国の衰亡」忍足欣四郎他編 *Philologia Anglica: Essays Presented to Professor Yoshio Terasawa on the Occasion of His Sixtieth Birthday*. 東京：研究社、1988: 328–35. [Karibe, Tsunenori, 'Beowulf's Glory and the Decline of the Danish Kingdom.' K. Oshitari, *et al.* eds., *Philologia Anglica: Essays Presented to Professor Yoshio Terasawa on the Occasion of His Sixtieth Birthday*. Tokyo: Kenkyusha, 1988: 328–35.]

A.V.C. SCHMIDT

3 The Four Elements as a Structural Idea in *Piers Plowman*

3.0. Introduction

It will not seem surprising that a major medieval poem dealing with a wide range of human experience should make some reference to the 'elements', this term signifying the fundamental substances and qualities that underlie our contact with physical reality. But any claim that the Elements form a 'structural idea' in *Piers Plowman* will obviously need to go beyond the straightforward assertion that this major medieval poem is in some sense 'about the world'. My argument in the present paper is based on seeing Langland as a religious poet who uses 'elemental' images in an essentially *symbolic* way, which I shall go on to define more specifically as 'sacramental', and which I shall argue is fundamental to the structure of his work.

3.1. The Four Elements

By way of introduction, a brief (and very elementary) sketch of how the Elements were understood in Langland's day may be helpful. Medieval physical theory saw the material world as made up of the four 'simple substances' or basic principles, which were designated 'elements': in ascending order of fineness, these were earth, water, air and fire. They were sometimes identified with, and sometimes distinguished from, the common material substances bearing the same names, which we directly experience in various forms. Existing below the sphere of the moon, these terrestrial substances, *as ideally conceived*, each possessed an 'elementary quality': earth was dry, water moist, air cold and fire hot. But *as experienced* the substances evidently combined these qualities in various proportions: earth could be both cold and wet, and air could become warm through the influence of the sun. The elements were also associated (somewhat arbitrarily, it seems) with the four orientations: earth with the west, water with the south, air with the north and fire with the east. Finally, they were believed to form the constitutive material not only of the universe (the 'great world' or macrocosm) but also of man (the 'little world' or microcosm):

> *Macrocosmos* constat ex *quatuor elementis*: igne, aere, aqua et terra. Sic et *microcosmos* id est homo constat ex *eisdem iiii elementis*: igne, aere, aqua et terra.[1]

> [The macrocosm and the microcosm (man) are both constituted of the four elements, fire, air, water and earth]

1 The text is found in a twelfth-century astronomical manuscript from Bavaria in the Austrian National Library, Vienna, reproduced by R. Lawlor, *Sacred Geometry* (London: Thames and Hudson, 1982): 24 (my italics). The *four orientations* appear in *Piers Plowman* in the 'Four Daughters of God' scene in B XVIII 110–70, where Mercy enters from the west, Truth from the east, Justice from the north and Peace from the south; but no particular connection with the elements seems here implied or intended, except for a mention of the 'nyppe of the north' (XVIII 163), whence Justice comes (alluding to 'air'). But in C I 111–24, contentment is associated, expectedly, with the warm south and misery with the cold north, whence Lucifer was traditionally held to have fallen (cf. also B II 5//); and at C I 132 the east (the source of the rising sun) is declared the direction of heaven. The *harmonious tempering* of the elements by Love is described in a well-known passage of Boethius's *De Consolatione Philosophiae*, Bk IV, metrum 6, ll. 19–24: *Haec Concordia temperat aequis / Elementa modis, ut pugnantia / Vivibus cedant umida siccis / Iungantque fidem frigora flammis / Pendulus ignis surgat in altum / Terraeque graues pondere sidant* (H.P. Stewart and E.K. Rand (eds.) [Boston, MA: Harvard University Press, 1962]: 354). ['This accordaunce atempryth by evenelyke maneres the elementz, that the moiste thingis, stryvynge with the drye thingis, yeven place by stoundes; and that the colde thingis joynen hem by feyth to the hote thingis; and that the lyghte fyr ariseth into heighte, and the hevy erthes avalen by her weyghtes' (Chaucer's *Boece*, in *The Riverside Chaucer*, ed. L.D. Benson [Boston, MA: Houghton Mifflin, 1987]: 454b–5a)].

Man, as Natura explains in Alan of Lille's *De Planctu Naturae*, is an 'exemplary likeness' (*exemplarem similitudinem*) or mirror (*speculum*) of the macrocosm (*mundanae machinae*); and it is through the 'complexions', the combinations that constitute his body, that man mediates between the contradictory qualities (*concors discordia*) of the elements, establishing peace between the 'humours'.[2]

In the Third Vision of *Piers Plowman*, Langland's personage Wit explains to the Dreamer how the soul (*Anima*) lives

> In a castel that Kynde made of foure kynnes thynges.
> Of erthe and eyr is it maad, medled togideres,
> With wynd and with water wittily enioyned
> (B IX 2–4)[3]

2 'Ego sum illa, quae ad exemplarem mundanae machinae similitudinem, hominis exemplavi naturam; ut in eo velut in speculo, ipsius mundi scripta natura appareat. Sicut enim *quatuor elementorum concors discordia*, unica pluralitas, consonantia dissonans, consensus dissentiens, mundialis regiae structuras conciliat, sic *quatuor complexionum* compar disparitas, inaequalis aequalitas, deformis conformitas, divisa identitas, aedificium corporis humani compaginat. Et *quae qualitates inter elementa mediatrices* convenient, hae eaedem *inter quatuor humores* pacis sanciunt firmitatem' (*Alani de Insulis Opera Omnia*, in *Patrologia Latina* (*PL*) 210:443; italics mine). ['I am the one who has modelled man's nature as an exemplary likeness of the structure of the world, so that in him, as in a mirror, the nature of that same world may appear inscribed. For just as the structures of the world's palace are assembled through the Four Elements' concordant discord, single plurality, dissonant harmony and dissenting agreement, so too is the edifice of the human body joined together through the similar unlikeness, the unequal equality, misshapen symmetry and divided sameness of the four complexions. And those same qualities that serve to mediate between the elements establish a durable peace between the four humours']. With these we may compare the passage on Nature's creation of man by 'dividing, collecting and commingling' the four elements in Alan's *Anticlaudianus* VII 1 (*PL* 210:549). On the microcosm and macrocosm, see B. Stock, *Myth and Science in the Twelfth Century* (Princeton, NJ: Princeton University Press, 1972): 14–19.

3 Citations of all versions of the poem are from my *Piers Plowman: A Parallel Text Edition* (London: Longman, 1995); the Middle English letters *thorn* and *yogh* have been modernized as in my Everyman edition of *The Vision of Piers Plowman* (London: Dent, 2nd edn, 1995).

This passage, oddly, makes no reference to the element 'fire'; but it is just possible that Langland's word *eyr* (apparently here contrasted with *wynd*) may be employed to signify the *spiritus* or breath that warms the living body. If so, it could be meant as a loose equivalent of Latin *aether*, perhaps through association with the so-called fifth element, 'ether'.[4] However, while Langland elsewhere speaks of the four terrestrial substances severally in a number of places, he never names a fifth element as such. The *ether*, called the 'quintessence' by Plato, was thought of in the Middle Ages as a 'shining fluid substance variously described as a kind of fire or air'; it had been considered by Aristotle a material element distinct from the other four, and was taken by Isidore of Seville to denote the 'upper parts' of the elements of fire and air.[5]

4   Cf. *Middle English Dictionary* (*MED*), eds. H. Kurath *et al.* (Ann Arbor, MI: University of Michigan, 1954–2001) s.v. *air* n. (1), sense 5, which notes that pure air was said to exist in the *caelum aethereum* 'ethereal heaven'. For an interesting and unusual illustration (Rheims, Municipal Library MS 672) of *Aer* (personified as a winged figure inscribed in a circle), see O. Von Simson, *The Gothic Cathedral* (London: Routledge and Kegan Paul, 1956): 42n and pl. 10.

5   Cf. *MED* s.v. *ether* n. 2(a). Three of the Elements (in the order wind, water, fire) occur in the Z-text lines on the powers of Truth (Z 6. 68–75), but earth is not mentioned by name there. What is probably the poet's most idiosyncratic variation on the customary four (this time, water, wind, *wit* and fire) appears in B VII 52–5 // ZAC. His surprising substitution of *wit* for the expected *erthe* here is ascribed by J.A.W. Bennett to 'the frequent association of the five wits with the four elements' (*Piers Plowman: The Prologue and Passus I–VII* [Oxford: Clarendon Press, 1972]: 219); and he is supported by Derek Pearsall, who in a note on IX 56 suggests *kynde witt* Pr 141 as the possible referent (*Piers Plowman: A New Annotated Edition of the C-Text* (Exeter: University of Exeter Press, 2008): 173. But Langland's 'wits' are elsewhere the *senses*, not 'intellect(ual) knowledge', and the argument here is rather (in Skeat's words) that 'Human intelligence is a gift of God, like three at least of the four elements [*sc.* excluding *earth*, which was *not* owned in common], and is therefore free for all men to profit by. Just as we should afford the free use of [these] to all men, so should we give ... advice and ... counsel *even* to those who cannot afford ... it' (W.W. Skeat, *Piers Plowman in Three Parallel Texts* [Oxford: Clarendon Press, 1886]:vol. II, 120–1). Langland's bold treatment of *wit* as an 'elemental' akin to a 'common' *tresor* thus makes possible a 'case by analogy' for making this faculty's *fruits* ('knowledge') freely available to all. And if such a notion of '*wit* got from others' (including, for

The word 'element' itself is not found in the earlier versions of the poem, Z and A, and only once in the B-text, in Passus XVIII. This is in the famous passage on the motif of the 'Witnessing Elements', which has been discussed by Robert Kaske in an important essay.[6] In the C-version, however, the word *element* does appear at an earlier stage of the poem, in a revision of some lines in Passus I. Holy Church has been telling the Dreamer that Truth (God), the creator of all, has given man five senses (*wittes*) with which to worship him during his life (BC I 15–16), and she goes on to explain that God commanded *the earth* to provide for his bodily necessities:

> And therfore he highte the erthe to helpe yow echone
> Of wollene, of lynnen, of lyflode at nede
> In mesurable manere to make yow at ese
>
> (B I 17–19)

These lines become in the C version:

> Wherfore he hette the *elementis* to helpe yow *alle tymes*
> And brynge forth youre bilyue, bothe lynnen and wollene,
> And in mesure, *thow muche were*, to make yow attese
>
> (C I 17–19; my italics)

The substantive revisions here involve small but important changes in sense; and for both early and modern readers familiar with the B-version these might have awakened 'intertextual' echoes of the 'Book' passage in B XVIII (which was itself retained unrevised in C). Langland's substitution of *elementis* for *erthe* has, I suggest, three main purposes. The first is

---

example, an attorney's arguments in a law-court) as constituting a more than 'purely personal' *catel* (cf. B XIII 151) seems quixotic, the modern democratic notion of state-provided legal aid for the indigent shows it, on the contrary, as prophetic.

6 'The Speech of "Book" in *Piers Plowman*', *Anglia* 77 (1959): 117–44. The topic is discussed *ad loc* in the note to C XX 245 in A.V.C. Schmidt (ed.), *William Langland: Piers Plowman: A Parallel-Text Edition of the A, B, C and Z Versions*, vol. 2 (Kalamazoo, MI: Medieval Institute Publications, 2008): 692.

didactic: to assert that *each* 'primary substance' (not just earth but also water, air and fire) contributes to the happiness of human life. The second is explanatory: to tighten the parallel between the substances and the senses (for although *five* are not specified, the substitution of the word *elementis* may imply their matching with the *fyue wittes* of B I 15).[7] The third purpose is homiletic: to remind us, through the phrases *alle tymes* and *thow much were*, how abundance (no less than dearth) demands that men should observe temperance (a cardinal virtue that will assume great importance at Passus XXII 23). For both plenty and scarcity, to the medieval mind, were not haphazard occurrences; they were natural conditions ordained by divine providence, and climatic events like drought and tempest were fraught with religious significance. Moreover, since the domain of nature was held to possess its correlative in the domain of morality, the notion that men should make 'temperate' use of the element of fire would most probably have been understood 'metonymically', as referring to the fuel from which fire is kindled (wood), a special need of the poor in the cold of winter.[8] But as my concern here is the symbolic meaning of the elements in the poem, I shall concentrate on locating the passage in the context not of medieval social history but of the scriptural and patristic sources on which it draws.

7   Conversely, the five wits could be collapsed conceptually into four because of the semantic overlap between the polysemes 'taste' and 'touch' of the lexeme *tasten* (*MED* s.v. 1 and 2); see especially B XVII 148, XVIII 84 and (? with pun on 'taste') B XIII 346. At B IX 20–4 the 'right uses' of the wits are personified by Langland as the sons of Inwit, commanded by Kynde to protect Anima.
8   No less immediately, modern readers conscious of the threat posed by global warming and industrial pollution to supplies of water, pure air and cultivable land, will readily grasp Langland's demand for moderation in using natural resources.

3.2. The Religious Meaning of the Elements

I wish first to examine the way in which Langland set out to deepen and refine his argument about the 'elements' by modifying, in his typically 'clerkly' manner, the Biblical account of creation that underlies Holy Church's words. In that account, found in Genesis chapter 1, God commands the earth to bring forth plants and fruit-bearing trees (verses 11–12), stating that they are meant for man's food (verse 29). The Bible specifically mentions only two of the elements, at the point where God divides the dry land from the waters (verse 10), calling them Earth and Sea (Air and Fire may, however, be obliquely implied in the preceding references to the dark void and to the light at verses 2–5). But in Langland's revised version of these lines at C I 17 it is the elements, tacitly personified, that receive a *command* from God to serve man; and on their only other appearance, they carry out this command in a special way at the behest of Christ, who was understood theologically as the New Man or second Adam. This event is described in Book's speech, where the elements are said to testify to Christ's divinity. The order of the four in this 'Witnessing Elements' passage is *air* (XVIII 237 = C XX 246), *water* (241 / 250), *fire* (245 / 254) and *earth* (247 / 256). This particular sequence seems to have no special significance; but what is interesting is how Langland has each element 'change' its given nature by behaving in a manner contrary to the expected one. Thus at the birth of Jesus (239), the upper air reveals a comet 'kindled' in the heavens; during his ministry (241), the water of the Sea of Galilee becomes like dry land when Jesus walks on it; as he dies, the sun is eclipsed, and the earth trembles like a living thing. What was dark becomes light, what was fluid turns solid, what was light grows dark, and what was solid breaks apart. The whole tone of the passage seems to me to foreshadow very suggestively the cataclysmic events that are expected to herald the Last Judgement and the creation of 'new heavens and a new earth ... in which justice dwelleth', as those events are described in the Second Epistle of St Peter (2 Pet 3:13).

That Langland did intend to evoke this 'apocalyptic' parallel seems to me indicated by his probable patristic sources for the lines on the 'Witnessing Elements': St Gregory's Epiphany sermon on Mt 2:1–12 (for the star at the birth of Jesus), and St Leo's sermon on the Passion, read at Matins on Good Friday (for the earthquake and eclipse at his death). These passages describe both Christ's coming 'into the lowe erthe' (XVIII 240) and his departure from it (XVIII 60). What looks on the face of it like the 'missing' feature in Langland is any explicit reference to the Judgement; but that event is, perhaps, hinted at by the echo of 2 Peter. Thus, given that 'alle the elements ... beren witnesse' at three key points during the First Advent of Christ that 'he was God that al wroghte' (236–7), it may be tacitly implied that they will behave similarly during his Second Advent, when *elementa ignis ardore tabescent* 'the elements will melt with the burning heat' (2 Pet 3:12). Textual support for such a supposition may be found in the immediately following account of the Harrowing of Hell. Langland's description here of how 'this lord and this light' (B XVIII 273) descends low into hell to rescue the patriarchs contains distinct echoes of Book's words describing the *stella comata* ('The light folwede the Lord into the lowe *erthe*' [B XVIII 240]). And in this scene, the poet's chosen symbol for Christ's divine dominion is *light*, the archetypal image for the Word used in St John's Gospel, 1:4–5. This symbolism is even more emphatic in the C revision, which repeats the word 'light' six times between XX 269–96, three times in conjunction with the divine title 'lord' as at B XVIII 240 / C XX 249 quoted above. It seems, therefore, very likely that we are being meant to associate the 'brihtnesse' that blinds the demons (C XX 284) with *two* discrete events: immediately, with the sun's loss of light at Christ's death (B XVIII 245 //), and more remotely, with the miraculous star's appearance at his birth (B XVIII 240). 'Light' as a symbol of 'lordship' thus occurs at the crucial beginning and end of the Saviour's life. This image of *lux vera quae illuminat omnem hominem* (Jn 1:9) is charged with its characteristic 'Johannine' signification as God's Truth graciously revealed to man: *Deus lux est* (I Jn 1:5), and *verum lumen iam lucet* (I Jn 2:8). It will acquire further meanings too in Langland, depending on the context in which it appears; but here it seems especially appropriate that when Christ's Soul manifests itself in hell it is as 'a *vois* loude in that light'. For what the *Verbum* that is also *Lumen Verum* does is to *speak*, with the authority of radiant Truth, where 'There is derknesse and drede and the deuel maister' (B XVI 85).

I should like to turn my attention now to that earlier 'elements' passage at C I 15–40, which remains substantially constant over the revision from Z to C. Its purpose is, I think, to convey an 'Alanian' sense of both the macrocosm and the microcosm as forming an intelligible unity. Man, for Langland, has his part in sustaining this unity, and from it he can learn what Alan of Lille calls 'a lesson about our life' (*nostrae vitae lectio*).[9] The structure of Holy Church's exposition reveals an interesting pattern of numerical 'descent and ascent': she moves from speaking of 'all' (14), to 'five wits' (15) and – by implication – 'five elements' (17); to 'three things' (20, the common necessaries); to *one* of these three (*likerous drynke* 25); and finally back to a second set of 'three things' (the enemies of the soul – *lycame, world* and *fend* 36–40). In order to make her lesson easier to comprehend (C I 22), she divides the sixteen things into four groups, two groups of five and two of three. These groups reveal no close mutual correspondence that I can discern, but each serves as a 'background' against which the item isolated for attention may be seen to stand out. Thus among the five *wits* this is taste; among the five *elements*, water; among the three *necessaries*, drink; and among the soul's three *enemies*, the flesh. In this way we are provided an 'intelligible circle' of ideas that may be easily remembered: the sense of taste; the water it needs; the wine it enjoys; and the flesh (of which the taste-organ is composed) that this enjoyment serves to weaken.

On an initial impression, Langland might seem to be suggesting that the body is bad, unless it is subjected by the soul to an austere régime, one somewhat like that evoked in Chaucer's poem 'The Former Age', when 'unkorven and ungrobbed lay the vyne' and men drank 'water of the colde welle'.[10] I think that closer inspection, however, proves this to be untrue;

9   In his poem *Omnis mundi creatura* (*PL* 210:579–80), inspired by Isaiah 40:6; this text is most readily accessible in *The Oxford Book of Medieval Latin Verse*, ed. F.J.E. Raby (Oxford: Clarendon Press, 1974): no. 242.

10 See L.D. Benson, ed., *The Riverside Chaucer* (Boston, MA: Houghton Mifflin, 1987): 650, and the discussion in A.V.C. Schmidt, 'Chaucer and the Golden Age', *Essays in Criticism* 26 (1976): 99–115. A sermon of *c.* 1360 in Worcester Cathedral Library, in answer to the question of what the people of the Golden Age drank, cites a poem identified as the famous lyric 'Maiden in the mor lay' in Oxford, Bodleian Library

for Langland is not urging upon the ordinary Christian 'necessitous depri-
vation'[11] but more 'rational temperance'. This is not to deny that he greatly
admires (as will be shown at the end of this paper) the heroic asceticism
of such desert saints as Anthony and Mary of Egypt, who lived on bread
and water, or Mary Magdalene, who lived on dew. But the *drede* of *del-
itable drynke* that Holy Church is here recommending is not to be construed as total avoidance; rather, it is salutary watchfulness against an
over-indulgence that may undermine man's resistance to all the pleasures
of the senses.[12] 'Fear' and 'desire' (*drede, yerne* 32–3) may be the weights
placed on either side of the moral see-saw; but 'moderation' (*mesure*) is
the fulcrum upon which they balance. Thus, not only does drink (as Holy
Church acknowledges at 24) 'do you good', but the small alteration to B I
25 *whan thow driest* acknowledges that beverages such as wine or ale, made
from what the 'elements' provide, nourish as well as giving *delite* 'pleasure'.
The elements (the 'greater world'), as the larger revision at C I 17–18 brings
out, have been commanded by the Creator of all to serve man's common
bodily needs, not only 'in common' but 'at all times'. And if at all times
(times of both plenty and dearth) the 'lesser world' of man must move in
correspondent 'measure', this is partly for the individual's own good, and
partly so that there will be enough for all. For to fail in *mesure* is to act
against the 'nature' shared in common by both the macrocosm and the
microcosm as, for example, Lot did in committing incest with his daughters after drinking too much wine.

MS Rawlinson D. 13; see S. Wenzel, 'The Moor Maiden – A Contemporary View',
Speculum 49 (1974): 69–74.

11   The phrase is J.A. Burrow's in *Langland's Fictions* (Oxford: Clarendon Press, 1993):
98.

12   The traditional association of drink with lechery is made in Chaucer's Wife of Bath's
Prologue, *CT* III 465–6; and cf. Alan's *De Planctu Naturae*, with its account of how
'diluviosi potus inundatio venenosum patrat incendium' [a deluge of drink produces
a deadly heat] and 'gulositas est quoddam Venereae exsecutionis prooemium' [glut-
tony is a sort of preface to the sexual act] (*PL* 210:460–1).

3.3. The Sacramental Meaning of the Elements

For Langland, God's initial command to the elements is thus connected with the goodness of the world that he has made for man to enjoy lawfully. Indeed, the memorable expression *Ertheliche honeste thynges* 'honourable things of the earth' (B XIX 94 = C XXI 94) boldly affirms what I take to be the poet's attitude. The 'things' that this phrase refers to are, admittedly, not quite so 'ordinary' as the food, drink and clothing that Holy Church speaks of. On the contrary, the incense, gold and myrrh brought by the Three Kings are both rich and rare. Moreover, these precious objects are understood as emblems respectively of reason, justice and mercy, the royal attributes appropriate to 'Our Lord Prince Jesu'. Finally, since the *Magi* possess 'al the wit of the world' (B XIX 82–4), they fittingly offer the King of both matter and spirit three gifts that possess deep spiritual significance under their material form. For this passage illustrates in an exemplary way what we might call a 'sacramental' view of the elemental world; and the Magi's gifts could be described as 'sacramental' in the sense that they are physical things with a spiritual meaning. They may not possess the full theological character of Christian sacraments as 'outward signs of inward *grace*' (even as an infant, Jesus, being divine, must be regarded as the *author* of the sacraments, not as their recipient). But the gifts do perhaps qualify as 'quasi-sacraments', in the manner of the adult Christ's Baptism in the waters of the Jordan. For this action is obviously not (for him) a necessary cleansing from Original Sin but rather a formal *semeion* 'sign' of his freely-willed identification with what Alan of Lille calls 'our state and fate' (see note 9 above): a sign pointing to a deep religious truth that would otherwise not be open to view. The Magi, for their part, acting from a wisdom that is the pagan equivalent of revelation, are able to recognize in Jesus the 'souereyn / Bothe of sond, sonne and see' (B XIX 77–8) and thereby offer him gifts appropriate to his sovereignty. And so it would seem no accident that Langland's lines interpreting their gifts' spiritual meaning should recall some famous words of St Thomas Aquinas about the Eucharist, the sacrament where 'faith must assist when the weak senses

fail' (*praestet fides supplementum / sensuum defectui*).[13] Further examples of
such 'allusively sacramental' writing occur in Langland's punning descriptions of the gift of Reason as *couered vnder sense* and in the gift of Mercy
as *apperynge by mirre* (B XIX 86, 92). Such instances of what I have elsewhere called 'lexical Platonism' (the positing of real affinities between
word-forms and their referents)[14] intimate how, in a 'mystical' way, the very
names of *incense* and *myrrh* serve to relate the Magi's material offerings to
their spiritual *significata*.[15]

Having said this, however, I would certainly not expect to find formal
discussion of sacramental theology in a poem with such intensely practical
religious preoccupations as *Piers Plowman*. So while the importance of
baptism and particularly confession is emphasized, and the Eucharist is a
major concern of his,[16] Langland does not use the term 'sacrament' itself in

13   From verse 5 of St Thomas's 'Pange Lingua', the hymn sung in procession on Maundy
      Thursday at the Mass of the Last Supper and also on the feast of Corpus Christi; for
      the text see *Daily Missal*, ed. G. Lefebvre (London: George Coldwell, 1934):1043.
      Langland quotes the last line of verse 4 (*Sola fides sufficit*) at B XV 389.

14   On 'lexical Platonism' see the discussion in A.V.C. Schmidt, *The Clerkly Maker*
      (Cambridge: D.S. Brewer, 1987): 89–93. My term is adapted from the 'grammatical
      Platonism' of Jean Jolivet, who examines 'Quelques cas de "platonisme grammatical"
      du VIIè au XIIè siècle' in P. Gallais and Y.-J. Riou, eds., *Mélanges offerts à René Crozet*
      (2 vols, Poitiers: Société d'Etudes Médiévales, 1966): 93–9. Alan of Lille refers to
      this common medieval notion in *De Planctu Naturae*: 'si nominis proprietas suam
      significationis germanitatem in voce retineat' [how a word's distinctive form preserves
      its semantic relationship in (a word of like) sound] (*PL* 210:463).

15   As well as the homophonic wordplay on 'sense' and 'incense', 'mercy' and 'myrrh',
      there may also be polysemantic wordplay in *apperynge* on two distinct lexemes (cf.
      MED s.v. *apperen* v. (1), sense 4(a) 'be revealed' and *apperen* v. (2) 'be the equal of',
      the latter of which is found in Langland only in its base form *peeren* at B XV 417
      and A XII 4.

16   See for example the notes to V 492 and XVII 95 in my Everyman edition of the B-text
      and those to C VII 133, XIX 90 in my *Piers Plowman: A Parallel-Text*, vol. II; my
      comments in *JEGP* 89 (1990): 214; and my '"Elementary" Images in the Samaritan
      Episode of *Piers Plowman*', in *Essays in Criticism* 56 (2006): 303–23. The central
      importance of the Eucharist for Langland is brought out by D. Aers, *Sanctifying Signs*
      (Notre Dame, IN: University of Notre Dame Press, 2004): 29–51 (I do not, however,

the poem. This word seems largely confined to fifteenth-century religious writings and is not found frequently in the other major Ricardian poets, in either its general sense (Chaucer uses it of marriage at *Canterbury Tales* IV 1319, as does Gower in 'In Praise of Peace', l. 309),[17] or (with the definite article) to denote the Eucharist.

It must thus remain a matter of interpretation whether Langland's nature-descriptions could be appropriately ascribed the sort of 'sacramental' significance found in Alan of Lille's description of the macrocosm as 'a trustworthy symbol [*fidele signaculum*] of our life, our death, our condition and our fate [*nostrae sortis*]'. At first glance, indeed, the nature scenes in *Piers Plowman* might seem purely conventional settings for a dream vision to take place in; examples are the prelude to the First Vision, with its May morning and running stream, or the more extended passage that introduces the Third Vision (B Pr 5–18; VIII 62–7). But in both instances the significant word *wildernesse* also occurs: in the *Visio* Prologue after the dream has begun, and in the Dowel Prologue with reference to the country Will traverses before the birdsong lulls him to sleep. In its second appearance, *wildernesse* need signify no more than 'wild, uninhabited or uncultivated territory' (*MED* s.v. n. (a)). But the first instance seems to me to carry some of the figurative meaning given to it by devotional and mystical writers of the period, that of 'human life and experience' or 'the world' (*MED* s.v. (e)). This meaning is found in the thirteenth-century *Ancrene Wisse* 4.17

---

share Aers's conclusions about Langland's view of this sacrament). It will be clear from my argument in this article that while I regard Langland as a great Middle English religious poet, I do not view him as a 'vernacular theologian' in the sense proposed in Nicholas Watson's 'Censorship and Cultural Change in Late-Medieval England: Vernacular Theology, the Oxford Translation Debate, and Arundel's Constitutions of 1409', *Speculum* 70 (1995): 822–64, which includes *Piers Plowman* in the list of 'vernacular theologies' on p. 861, and applied by him to 'The *Gawain*-Poet as a Vernacular Theologian', in Derek Brewer and Jonathan Gibson (eds.), *A Companion to the Gawain-Poet* (Cambridge: D.S. Brewer, 1997): 293–313. *Piers Plowman* is poetry, not *scientia*; and to judge from Study's words at B X 182–5, it is extremely improbable that Langland would have acknowledged Watson's description of it as 'theology'.

17   See G.C. Macaulay (ed.), *The English Works of John Gower*, vol. 2 (London: Oxford University Press for EETS, 1901): 490.

and is illustrated in a quotation from the early fourteenth-century *Psalter* of Richard Rolle: 'In erth we trauayle, wery, seke ... and slaw, bot he forsakes vs noght in this *wildirenes*'[18] Now the patently symbolic sense here presupposes the reader's awareness of how 'wilderness' is used in the Old and New Testament; specifically, it relates to the forty-year wandering of the Hebrews (Exodus 16) and its New Testament 'antitype', the forty-day fast of Jesus (Mt 1:13 and //), the Latin text using the word *desertus* (= Greek *eremos*) in reference to the wilderness of Judea. But that 'symbolic' meaning might be thought virtually to approach the 'sacramental' if we go on to draw a connection between these Biblical 'wilderness' periods and the forty-day liturgical fast of Lent, culminating in the Easter Eucharist that forms the climax of the B-text's Seventh Vision.

Nature, moreover, may in a more general way be interpreted as 'caught up' in the Incarnation of Jesus (taking that term now to cover his life, death and resurrected bodily existence). For Langland understands 'Incarnation' in the light of St Paul's teaching on the 'New Creation' in Christ (II Cor 5:14–21). Thus, just as Adam in Genesis is said to be made out of 'the slime of the earth' (Gen 2:7), so the descent from heaven of divine Love becoming incarnate is described in words strongly reminiscent of the creation of Man:

> For heuene myghte nat holden it, so was it heuy of hymselue,
> Til it hadde of the erthe eten his fille.
> And whan it hadde of this fold flesh and blood taken
> Was neuere leef vpon lynde lighter therafter ...
>   (B I 153–6)[19]

Of the Four Elements discussed in this paper, the relevant one here is obviously earth, out of which Adam was created as 'flesh and blood'; and this 'common' *ertheliche* origin of Man and of God-made-Man is to prove of

---

18   See *Ancrene Wisse*, ed. Bella Millett, EETS OS 326. 2 vols. (Oxford: Oxford University Press for EETS, 2005–6), Vol. I: 74; Richard Rolle, *The Psalter*, ed. H.R. Bramley (Oxford: Clarendon Press, 1884): 147.

19   The best discussion of this whole passage remains P.M. Kean, 'Langland on the Incarnation', *Review of English Studies* 15 (1965): 349–63.

great importance at the climax of the poem. For there it will justify Christ's saving action, when in his great speech to Lucifer in Hell he distinguishes the 'mercy' that he will show to man from the judgement he will exercise upon the fallen angels:

> Ac to be merciable to man thanne, my kynde it asketh,
> For we beth bretheren of blood ...
> (B XVIII 376–7 [*o bloed* C XX 418])

The same notion of shared *kynde* or nature also underlies Christ's tremendous promise of mercy to 'manye' of these brethren (XVIII 394):

> For blood may suffre blood bothe hungry and acale,
> Ac blood may noght see blood blede, but hym rewe
> (B XVIII 395–6)

For as the theologian Edward Schillebeeckx has expressed it, the Incarnation itself may be called the 'sacrament' of man's encounter with God.[20]

The poetry of *Piers Plowman* is, I would argue, implicitly 'sacramental' in its general stance towards reality and language. It is, however, unsurprising that when it becomes most *explicitly* sacramental, its subject should be the Eucharist, which even more than Baptism recalls the Passion and Death of Christ. A striking example of this occurs in Langland's idiosyncratic re-telling of the Samaritan Parable, when the Samaritan says of fallen Man that

> stalworthe worth he neuere
> Til he haue eten al the barn and his blood ydronke
> (B XVII 97–8)

This passage, so resonant of the rite of Holy Communion, also echoes Holy Church's quoted description of the Incarnation in terms of the divine Son as metaphorically 'eating' the *earth* in order to become flesh and blood. The

---

20   E. Schillebeeckx, *Christ the Sacrament of the Encounter with God* (London: Sheed and Ward, 1963).

Conception and the Passion of Jesus were closely connected in the medieval mind, partly because they were traditionally thought to have occurred on the same day of the year (25 March), but more generally because Christ's death was seen as completing that voluntary identification with *nostra sors* 'our lot' (as Alan of Lille calls it) that his birth began. Similarly, 'the sacrament of man's encounter with God' in Christ's initial and final self-giving were understood as being 'recapitulated' in the Eucharist, in which (according to orthodox teaching) the earthly substance of bread and wine becomes the true body and blood of Christ. And among the sacraments, the Eucharist is the one that restores man fully to the condition of original innocence, enables him, after baptism and confession, to 'stonde and steppe' as at his first creation, and makes him 'stalworthe' and 'stronge' (C XIX 89) through communion with his Creator.[21] Given that 'sacramental' significances seem virtually inescapable in such outwardly 'realistic' parables as that of the Good Samaritan, it would seem natural enough that other New Testament incidents in the poem should acquire such significances 'by association'. One of these is the allegorical character Book's description of how the sea obeyed Christ's command in 'witness[ing] that he was God' (B XVIII 241), an 'elemental' miracle whereby *aqua* obediently 'turned' its nature and behaved like *terra* under Christ's feet. The Gospel passage describing this incident (Mt 14:25–6), it seems to me, audibly echoes God's mastering of the primeval waters in the Bible (of which Book is a personification): 'And the spirit of God moved over the waters' (Gen 1:2).[22]

---

21   For examples of specific uses of this term in the sense 'The Communion elements, the Host' see *MED* s.v. *creatour* n. 2 (a). The *Pearl*-poet's view 'That in the fourme of bred and wyn / The preste vus shewez vch a daye' the sacrifice of the Lamb of God (*Pearl*, ed. E.V. Gordon [Oxford: Clarendon Press, 1953], ll. 1209–10) closely parallels Langland's; both poets are, of course, wholly traditional.

22   The association would have been all the easier for contemporary readers to make since in medieval iconography God the Creator is commonly shown with the features of Christ the Creating Word [Logos]. An example is the miniature in the Austrian National Library, Vienna (Codex 2554, fol. 1) reproduced in Von Simson, *Gothic Cathedral* pl. 6a (with discussion on p. 35, n. 37), and the motif is also seen in a well-known thirteenth-century *Bible Moralisée* illustration in Oxford, Bodleian Library, MS Bodleian 270B (Lawlor, *Sacred Geometry*: pl. 11). The textual source of this image

Even more densely fraught with sacramental meaning is the miracle at Cana as Conscience recounts it, where water does not behave like *another* of the elements but 'turns' into its most *honest* ('honourable') form, wine:

> In his iuuentee this Iesus at Iewene feeste
> Turnede water into wyn as Holy Writ telleth
>
> (B XIX 108–9)

This action too is presented as a 'divine' work, wrought by the youthful Jesus 'After the kynde that he cam of' (123). Initially, Conscience's words might seem to invite a tropological more than a sacramental interpretation, since the explicit parallelism in 'For wyn is *likned to* lawe and lif of holynesse' (B XIX 111) recalls his expository interpretation of the Magi's gifts ('Gold is *likned to* Leautee that laste shal euere' [B XIX 89]). But further reflection suggests that this 'turning' of the Mosaic Law is to be seen as more awesome than the making-good of a 'lack' or defect (B XIX 112). It is a *transformation*, a change not just in degree but in kind, whereby a new 'spiritual element' is introduced into the world of man. For Christ's counsel-and-command (113) is not just a 'law' of mercy replacing a law of strict justice, its summons 'to *louyen* oure enemys' embodies Christianity's new and unique ethical demand. Langland's version of the Miracle at Cana thus comes across as a *semeion* or 'sign-action' very much in the spirit of St John, the Evangelist whom Langland praises as 'passynge alle other' (XIX 268).

As the poet retails the event, the Miracle at Cana operates at three main levels of signification. At the explicit moral level, it signifies the move from Old Covenant justice to New Covenant mercy, a 'change' summarized in

---

may be Prov 8:27: *Quando certa lege et gyro vallabat abyssos* 'when with a certain law and compass [God] enclosed the depths', with which compare Job 26:10: *terminum circumdedit aquis, usque dum finiantur lux et tenebrae* '[God] has set bounds about the waters, till light and darkness come to an end' (*The Holy Bible. The Catholic Bible: Douay-Rheims Version* [New York: Benziger, 1941]). The RSV translation 'described a circle upon the face of the waters at the boundary between light and darkness' better suggests a terrestrial horizon marked out by the divine geometer.

the command to love one's enemies instead of seeking retribution.[23] At the sacramental level, the miracle points to two of the seven Christian 'mysteries'. By virtue of its context (being performed at a wedding feast), it raises an 'earthly thing', the natural institution of marriage (emblematized by water) to the status of an 'honest [honourable] thing', Christ's mystical union with his Church, which Christian marriage itself was held to symbolize (customarily emblematized by the wine used to celebrate marriage). Lastly, at a typological level, the miracle foreshadows the institution of the Eucharist, the sacrament that in its turn transforms this 'earthly honest thing' (wine) into a 'heavenly honest thing', the blood of Christ, and thereby effects the mystical union of the believer with Christ and with his Church.[24] These 'meanings' should not, I suggest, be sharply distinguished as hierarchical 'levels of signification' but rather seen as 'dimensions of significance'. Nor are the senses I have disengaged equally prominent, for only the first is explicit and overt. But part of the peculiar experience of *Piers Plowman* lies in the effort the reader must make to connect different parts of the work in a productive way. This is something that a brief glance at Langland's treatment of the Desert Saints and their miracles will bear out, and I shall consider this next in the final section of my paper.

---

23   As Alan of Lille wittily expresses it in his *Sententiae*, Christ in this miracle 'mutavit insipiditatem antiquae legis in saporem novae legis ... mutata poena in poenitentiam, austeritas in gratiam, miseria in misericordiam' [changed the tastelessness of the Old Law into the fine savour of the New Law ... (so that) water there underwent a three-fold transformation into wine, punishment becoming penitence, rigour becoming grace and misery becoming mercy] (*PL* 210:252).

24   See Bettina Bildhauer, *Medieval Blood* (Cardiff: University of Wales Press, 2006): 137–47, and A.V.C. Schmidt, 'The Sacramental significance of blood in *Piers Plowman*', in John A. Burrow and Hoyt N. Duggan (eds.), *Medieval Alliterative Poetry: Essays in Honour of Thorlac Turville-Petre* (Dublin: Four Courts Press, 2010): 212–24, especially 213–16.

3.4. Spiritual Food in the Desert

The Miracle at Cana has, to my knowledge, no exact parallel in the legends of the saints; but in a general way miracles of healing and feeding like those of Christ were believed to have been performed through the power of the Holy Spirit, first by the Apostles and then, over the course of history, by exceptionally holy men and women. Along with the martyrs, the saints that Langland especially admired were the ascetic solitaries, whose life of simplicity witnessed to perfect faith and total dependence upon God. In their case, the power of divine grace was manifest in its enabling them to overcome bodily wants, such as the need for food. This is well brought out by Langland's explanation of the nature of Charity, with specific reference to the requirement to love our enemies. In Passus XV of the B-text the allegorical character Anima, anticipating the counsel-command of XIX 114, declares how it was through imitating the divine sufferer Christ that the hermit saints schooled themselves to 'take no vengeaunce / Of oure foes that dooth vs falsnesse' (XV 261–2). And by way of proof he cites some who 'Woneden in wildernesse among wilde beestes' (XV 273), modelling their existence on Christ's sojourn in the desert. These saints include Antony and Paul the Hermit, who were provided bread by birds, and Giles [Egidius], who was given milk by a hind. All three figures have a strongly Old Testament quality, recalling most directly the prophet Elijah, who was fed by ravens in the wilderness (3 Kgs 17:4–6). But one particular 'ensample' contains a more conspicuous sacramental *lectio*; this is Mary Magdalene, who lived on roots and dew, 'Ac moost thorugh deuocion and mynde of God Almyghty' (XV 294–5). In making God himself her food, Mary is seen to have followed literally the words of her master Christ: 'I have meat to eat which you know not ... My meat is to do the will of him that sent me, that I may perfect his work' (Jn 4:32–4). The C-text version of B XV 295 ('Loue and lele byleue held lyf and soule togideres' [C XVII 22]) seems to me to elaborate the point even further; and though the revision still mentions roots and dew, the significance of these 'earthly things' is now more obviously symbolic.

This reading is strengthened, I believe, by the C text's added reference at this point to another desert solitary, Mary of Egypt, who 'eet in thritty winter / Bote thre little loues and loue was here souel' (C XVII 23–4). Here, at a semantic level, the phrase 'thritty winter' can be seen clearly to correspond to the 'thritty wynter' of Christ's earthly life (C XX 329), a life nourished on the will 'of him that sent me' (Jn 4:33; see above). But at a more 'Platonic' lexical level, the annominative wordplay on *loues* and *loue* wittily hints at the 'heavenly honest things' (love and faith) that the 'little loaves' stand for. It is true that neither passage speaks directly of the Eucharist, a sacrament that was not available to the two Marys in their wilderness existence. But directness is not needed; for the poet's re-iterated stress on 'love' implies that Mary of Egypt's loaves (like Mary Magdalene's roots and dew) are 'trewe tokenes' (C XVII 247)[25] of that sacrament, just as 'divine love' is what the Eucharist betokens.

The interpretation proposed here finds support in Langland's Latin source for the lives of these two saints, the *Legenda Aurea* of Jacobus a Voragine. Both of this text's accounts of Mary Magdalene's death (ch. XCVI) describe her ecstatic reception of the *corpus et sanguinem domini* as her last act before dying; similarly, its history of Mary of Egypt (ch. LVI) emphasizes the saint's longing for the *sacramenta dominica* and her profound reverence towards the priest who brings it to her.[26] Langland's citation of such 'verray ensamples' (B XV 268) could perhaps suggest (misleadingly) that he thought regular Communion to be of greater importance for the ordinary Christian (the traveller fallen among thieves of the Samaritan Parable) than for the saint, who has other consolations and is shown as asking for the Church's chief sacrament only at the point of death. But I think that if his reference to the hermit saints is examined closely in the context of the Latin source, it will emerge that Langland saw the *entire* existence of the two Marys as penitential: as an heroically prolonged 'amendment' for their previous sinful lives that forms an exemplary preparation for the viaticum.

25   See further Schmidt, 'Sacramental significance of blood': 222–4.
26   Jacobi a Voragine, *Legenda Aurea*, ed. T. Graesse (2nd edn, Leipzig: Librariae Arnoldianae, 1850): 414, 249.

3.5. Conclusion

By way of conclusion, I would wish to argue that in the course of *Piers Plowman* Langland expresses two main 'positions' on the question of man's use of the physical world and its resources, one voiced by Holy Church and one by Anima. These are to be understood not as mutually contradictory but as complementary. For the majority of people, as Holy Church explains, the 'three things' that God commanded the elements to provide are indeed 'needful' (C I 16–22); and this is because human beings have been given bodily senses 'to worshipe hym therwith the while [they] ben here' and to share God's material gifts 'in comune'. A just earthly society, therefore, will be a society modelled on the 'holy comune' of heaven (C V 186); and in such a society, living according to *mesure* will indeed be 'good to the goost' (B I 36). But as Anima demonstrates, for the exceptional few, even *mesure* might seem 'too much'. And this is not because temperance can (logically) ever be 'excessive' in itself, but because it may come to seem so if 'necessary sufficiency' is measured by the (limitless) sacrificial love that contemplatives feel towards their suffering Lord. Thus loaves that last thirty years, or bread brought by birds, function as purely symbolic concessions to the saints' bodily condition, while dramatically pointing beyond towards what truly holds their 'lyf and soule togyderes' (C XVII 22), that is 'loue and lele byleue'. In other words, the ascetics' example is not meant to make the poem's ordinary Christian readers spurn God's bounty; it is meant to inspire them to undertake penance and pursue holiness in whatever manner suits their state.

This last point may be best illustrated by the *ensample* of the titular 'hero' of the poem, whose penitential feelings (we recall) are awakened immediately after he receives the Pardon:

That loueth God lelly, his liflode is ful esy:
Fuerunt michi lacrime mee panes die ac nocte

[My tears have been my bread day and night (Ps 41:4)]
(B VII 124–4a)[27]

It is Piers Plowman himself, I suggest, who is offered by Langland as a model for the common Christian: and he lives what may be called a life of the 'four elements', a life regularly nourished by 'honest things' (the sacraments) provided through the ministry of the Church. The ascetic saints, by contrast, may be seen as scattered instances of the elusive 'fifth element', the fiery ether from heaven that witnesses even in the darkest night to the continual presence of the Spirit in the world. As such, they are realized instances of what 'elemental' humanity may at least hope, through the sacraments, to become.

3.6. References

3.6.1 Primary sources

Piers Plowman

Bennett, J.A.W., ed. *Piers Plowman: The Prologue and Passus I–VII of the B-Text.* Oxford: Clarendon Press, 1972.
Pearsall, Derek, ed. *Piers Plowman: A New Annotated Edition of the C-Text.* Exeter: University of Exeter Press, 2008.

27   The quotation is from Ps 41:4, which is sung at the blessing of the font on Holy Saturday (*Daily Missal*, 860). The preceding psalm-verse makes clear that the *fontes aquarum* longed for by the psalmist's soul symbolize spiritual life and strength, and that the way to them is by a 'diet' of tears, i.e. that God is to be found through heartfelt penitence.

Schmidt, A.V.C., ed. *William Langland: Piers Plowman, A Parallel-Text Edition of the A, B, C and Z Versions.* vol. I. London and New York: Longman, 1995.

———. *William Langland, The Vision of Piers Plowman: A Critical Edition of the B-Text Based on Trinity College Cambridge MS B. 15. 17.* 2nd edn. London: Dent, 1995.

———. *William Langland: Piers Plowman, A Parallel-Text Edition of the A, B, C and Z Versions.* vol. II. Kalamazoo, MI: Medieval Institute Publications, Western Michigan University, 2008.

Skeat, W.W., ed. *The Vision of William Concerning Piers Plowman in Three Parallel Texts.* Oxford: Clarendon Press, 1886.

Other texts

Benson, Larry D., ed. *The Riverside Chaucer.* Boston, MA: Houghton Mifflin, 1987.

Bramley, H.R., ed. Richard Rolle, *The Psalter.* Oxford: Clarendon Press, 1884.

Gordon, E.V., ed. *Pearl.* Oxford: Clarendon Press, 1953.

Graesse, T., ed. Jacobi a Voragine, *Legenda Aurea.* 2nd edn. Leipzig: Librariae Arnoldianae, 1850.

Lefebvre, Gaspar, ed. *Daily Missal.* London: George Coldwell, 1934.

Macaulay, G.C., ed. John Gower, *The English Works of John Gower.* 2 vols, EETS E.S. 81–2. London: Oxford University Press, 1900–01.

Migne, Jacques-Paul, ed. Alan of Lille, *Anticlaudianus* and *De Planctu Naturae.* In *Alani de Insulis Opera Omnia* in *Patrologia Latina (PL).* Paris, 1855: 210.

Millett, Bella, ed. *Ancrene Wisse.* 2 vols. EETS O.S. 325–6. Oxford: Oxford University Press for EETS, 2005–6.

Raby, F.J.E., ed. *The Oxford Book of Medieval Latin Verse.* Oxford: Clarendon Press, 1974.

Stewart, H.P. and E.K. Rand, eds. Anicius Manlius Torquatus Severinus Boethius, *De Consolatione Philosophiae.* Boston, MA: Harvard University Press, 1962.

3.6.2. Secondary sources

Aers, David. *Sanctifying Signs.* Notre Dame, IN: University of Notre Dame Press, 2004.

Bildhauer, Bettina. *Medieval Blood.* Cardiff: University of Wales Press, 2006.

Brewer, Derek and Jonathan Gibson, eds. *A Companion to the* Gawain-*Poet.* Cambridge: D.S. Brewer, 1997.

Burrow, J.A. *Langland's Fictions.* Oxford: Clarendon Press, 1993.

Burrow, John A. and Hoyt N. Duggan, eds. *Medieval Alliterative Poetry: Essays in Honour of Thorlac Turville-Petre.* Dublin: Four Courts Press, 2010.

Gallais, P. and Y.-J. Riou, eds. *Mélanges offerts à René Crozet.* 2 vols, Poitiers: Société d'Etudes Médiévales, 1966.

Kaske, R.E. 'The Speech of "Book" in *Piers Plowman*', *Anglia* 77 (1959):117–44.

Kean, P.M. 'Langland on the Incarnation', *Review of English Studies* 16 (1965): 349–63.

Kurath, H. *et al.*, eds. *Middle English Dictionary (MED).* Ann Arbor, MI: University of Michigan, 1954–2001.

Lawlor, Robert. *Sacred Geometry.* London: Thames and Hudson, 1982.

Schillebeeckx, Edward. *Christ the Sacrament of the Encounter with God.* London: Sheed and Ward, 1963.

Schmidt, A.V.C. 'Chaucer and the Golden Age', *Essays in Criticism* 26 (1976): 99–115.

——. *The Clerkly Maker.* Cambridge: D.S. Brewer, 1987.

——. 'Review of *A Companion to* Piers Plowman', *Journal of English and Germanic Philology* 89 (1990): 213–14.

——. '"Elementary" Images in the Samaritan Episode of *Piers Plowman*', *Essays in Criticism* 56 (2006): 303–23.

Simson, Otto Von. *The Gothic Cathedral.* London: Routledge and Kegan Paul, 1956.

Stock, Brian. *Myth and Science in the Twelfth Century.* Princeton, NJ: Princeton University Press, 1972.

Watson, Nicholas. 'Censorship and Cultural Change in Late-Medieval England: Vernacular Theology, the Oxford Translation Debate, and Arundel's Constitutions of 1409', *Speculum* 70 (1995): 822–64.

Wenzel, Siegfried. 'The Moor Maiden – A Contemporary View', *Speculum* 49 (1974): 69–74.

HELEN BARR

4 The Place of the Poor in 'the *Piers Plowman* Tradition'

4.0. Introduction

While none of the poems that comprise the core of 'the *Piers Plowman* Tradition' scale the imaginative and theological heights of *Piers Plowman*, they respond to important issues in *Piers*, and continue the discussion, often with a precise reprise of the diction of their predecessor.[1] In each of *Piers's* progeny there is space devoted to the plight of the less fortunate, those who are poor and vulnerable. The poems highlight the exploitation of the poor and the responsibilities of those who are better off to respect them, and to help them in their need. To what extent is their treatment of the poor precisely indebted to *Piers*?

4.1. *Piers Plowman*

Time and again, Langland returns to the question of the poor in all versions of his poem. As recent studies have shown, it was clearly an issue that vexed his social and poetic imagination, and answers to how society as a

---

1   All references to the *Piers* tradition poems are to *The Piers Plowman Tradition. A Critical Edition of Pierce the Ploughman's Crede, Richard the Redeles, Mum and the Sothsegger and The Crowned King*, ed. Helen Barr (London: Everyman, 1993). For discussion of the indebtedness to *Piers*, see Helen Barr, *Signes and Sothe: Language in the Piers Plowman Tradition* (Cambridge: D.S. Brewer, 1994).

whole must respond to the plight of the poor are not clear-cut.[2] The first version of the poem, the A text, ends with a bold and daring statement about the place of the poor: no one is saved sooner

> Þanne pore peple as plouȝmen, and pastours of bestis,
> Souteris and seweris – suche lewide iottis
> Percen wiþ a *Paternoster* þe paleis of heuene
> Wiþoute penaunce at here partyng, into þe heiȝe blisse.
>   (A XI 310–13)[3]

Salvation is seen to be most readily at hand for those who are poor: ploughmen; herdsmen; shoemakers, and seamstresses. They, with a simple Lord's Prayer, pierce the palisade of heaven with no penance at their deaths.[4] Whatever their hardship on earth, the kingdom of heaven is theirs for the asking; or so it seems. The extolling of the place of the poor, however worthy a championing position it is, begs more questions than it answers. What are the implications for the rest of society if such 'lewide iottis' are so readily saved? What does this say about the plight of those who are more fortunate? Does such a position suggest that it is actually better to be poor, and what does this mean for those who are in a position to help the needy? Would it be better for the poor to remain poor, for then, at least, the reward for the earthly misery would be eternal bliss?

2   See Anne M. Scott, *Piers Plowman and the Poor* (Dublin: Four Courts Press, 2004); David Aers, *Sanctifying Signs* (Notre Dame, IN: University of Notre Dame Press, 2004): 99–156; Margaret Kim, 'Hunger and need and the politics of poverty in *Piers Plowman*', *Yearbook of Langland Studies* 16 (2002): 131–68; Derek Pearsall, 'Poverty and poor people in *Piers Plowman*' in E. Kennedy, R. Waldron and J. Wittig (eds.), *Medieval English studies presented to George Kane* (Woodbridge, Suffolk: D.S. Brewer, 1988): 167–85; Geoffrey Shepherd, 'Poverty in *Piers Plowman*' in T.H. Aston, P.R. Coss, and C. Dyer (eds.), *Social Relations and Ideas* (Cambridge: Cambridge University Press, 1983): 169–89. Since the issue of poverty in *Piers* has received such ample treatment, my introductory comments address only those issues that are relevant to the depiction of poverty in the *Piers* tradition. My coverage of *Piers* is particularly indebted to David Aers's discussion.

3   All references are to *Piers Plowman: A Parallel-Text Edition of the A, B, C, and Z Versions*, ed. A.V.C. Schmidt, (London: Longman, 1995).

4   The chiming with Lollard polemic is discussed in Helen Barr, *Socioliterary Practice in Late Medieval England* (Oxford: Oxford University Press, 2001): 151.

Although these are resounding and courageous lines, they cannot hold the answer to questions about salvation, and to what society as a whole must do to address the situation of the poor. It is no accident, I think, that the A text stops with this most difficult problem, almost as if it brought the poet to an impasse. Versions of these lines are still present in the revisions to the poem represented by the B and C texts, but they are differently contextualized (B X 459–65; C XI 296–300). Discussion of the poor becomes increasingly bound up with meditation on the value of love, or charity, and how human beings should help and support each other. This is seen most noticeably in the speech that is given to Trajan in the B text, lines which have no counterpart in A:

> For Seint Johan seide it, and soþe arn hise wordes:
> *Qui non diligit manet in morte.*
> 'Whoso loueþ noʒt, leue me, he lyueþ in deeþ deyinge;
> And þat alle manere men, enemyes and frendes,
> Loue hir eyþer ooþer, and lene hem as hemselue.
> Whoso leneþ noʒt, he loueþ noʒt, Oure Lord woot þe soþe
> And comaundeþ ech creature to conformen hym to louye
> And [principally] pouere peple and hir enemyes after.
> For hem þat haten vs is oure merite to louye ...
> ... For our ioye and oure [iu]ele, Iesu Crist of heuene,
> In a pouere mannes apparaille pursueþ vs euere ...
> (B XI 176–85)

No less a person than Jesus Christ is figured as wearing poor man's clothes. Trajan forges a passionate plea to human beings to care for one another; there is a very important connection established between 'lening' and loving: '[w]hoso leneþ noʒt, he loueþ noʒt' (179). To 'lene' is to give; to provide, and hence to love. Christ is the paradigm, and commands humankind to follow his example. Trajan implores those wealthy enough to hold feasts not to invite the rich, but:

> ... calleþ þe carefulle þerto, þe croked and þe pouere;
> For youre frendes wol feden yow, and founde yow to quyte
> Youre festynge and youre faire ʒiftes – ech frend quyt so ooþer.
> Ac for the pouere I shal paie, and pure wel quyte hir trauaille
> That ʒyueþ hem mete or moneie and loueþ hem for my sake.
> (B XI 191–95)

The words of Luke 14:12–14 are here pressed into service to call for caring for the poor. Reward here is not for being poor in and of itself, but for loving the poor and helping them in their indigence. Trajan substantiates his remarks:

> Almiȝty God [myȝte haue maad riche alle] men, if he wolde,
> Ac for þe beste ben som riche and some beggeres and pouere.
> For alle are we Cristes creatures, and of his cofres riche,
> And breþeren as of oo blood, as wel beggeres as erles.
> For at Caluarie, of Cristes blood Cristendom gan sprynge,
> And blody breþeren we bicome þere, of o body ywonne,
> As *quasi modo geniti* gentil echone –
> No beggere ne boye amonges vs but if it synne made ....
> And we hise breþeren þoruȝ hym ybouȝt, boþe riche and pouere.
> Forþi loue we as leue children shal, and ech man lauȝe vp ooþer,
> And of þat ech man may forbere, amende þere it nedeþ,
> And euery man helpe ooþer – for hennes shul we alle.
>
> (B XI 196–210)

Christ's sacrifice on Calvary for love of his brethren is seen to be the ultimate template for how human beings should behave. Baptism into Christ's death makes all human beings one body, and therefore all, both rich and poor, should care for one another, united as they are through the blood of Christ into one body. It is better, argues Trajan, that some are rich and some are poor. God could have made all men rich, but chose not to do so. The inequality that exists between rich and poor offers an opportunity for love and mutual support. Just as Christ died on the cross to help his brethren, so too should all members of Christ's body, redeemed through his blood, help each other.

These ideas resurface in Passus XVIII. In his encounter with Lucifer, Christ explains both his legal right to the souls he has saved and also why it was imperative that he should save them:

> For blood may suffre blood boþe hungry and acale,
> Ac blood may noȝt se blood blede, but hym rewe ...
> For I were an vnkynde kyng but I my kyn holpe –
> And nameliche at swich a nede þer nedes help bihoueþ.
>
> (B XVIII 395–400)

Christ's redemption of all humankind is figured as helping the needy. In contrast to where the A text stops, the longer version of B expands on the meritorious position of the poor to consider the implications of the existence of poor people for all members of a social community. Poverty cannot be wished away, nor can the rich be faulted for being rich. What is most important, as Trajan's lines show, is that those who are poor and in need are supported. It is imperative for each member of Christ's body to help their 'bloody' brethren through 'lening'.

Of course, no single speech or passage in *Piers Plowman* holds all the answers to the solution of difficult issues. Langland's meditation on the plight of the poor becomes complicated by the presence in his society of those who are voluntarily poor, particularly the friars. In the B and C texts of the poem there are eulogies on the value of patient poverty. Patience and Recchelesnes are both given speeches that extol the values of voluntary poverty in terminology which is indebted to Franciscan spirituality.[5] But, it is very important that this praise for voluntary poverty in the poem comes from speakers who are not themselves friars. What we see of friars in the poem, in terms of what they do and how they live their lives, suggests that in the real world of economic necessity, the practice of voluntary poverty is much more vexed than those passionate speeches suggest. Whatever the Franciscan ideals of holding no property or money, the friars must do something to sustain their very existence. While friars were to live by alms, by benefactions from other members of the social community, what was intended as a way of supporting the friars in patient poverty becomes open to abuse and corruption. Friars resort to begging, a practice which, insistently in *Piers*, is openly criticized. Whether it is the fraudulent labourers of the Half Acre, or the narrator himself in C Passus V, begging for one's sustenance is seen as an act to be condemned.[6]

5   *Piers*, B XIV 103–319 (C XV 283–XVI 155); C XI 195–307. For discussion of the Franciscan influence see Lawrence Clopper, *Songes of Rechelesnesse: Langland and the Franciscans* (Ann Arbor, MI: University of Michigan Press, 1997), and cf. David Aers's repositioning of the debate, *Sanctifying Signs* (Notre Dame, IN: University of Notre Dame Press, 2004): 119–34.
6   See *Piers*, B VI 121–70 and C V 1–98.

This leaves Langland with a problem. How can he praise the virtues of poverty when the friars' practice turns indigence into vice? It is a dilemma that the poem does not solve. The poem closes with the collapse of the rebuilt Church, something for which friars are responsible. Not able to support themselves, the friars resort not only to begging but to the corrupt practice of selling penance for money. Friar Flatterer talks his way into the Barn of Unity and destroys the sacrament of penance by demanding privy payments for confession. So deadly are the attentions of the friar for the health of the human soul, that in a memorable line, Langland writes that 'Contricion hadde clene foryeten to crye and to wepe' (B XX 370). In contrast to Trajan's depiction of Christ as an exemplar of 'lening', the neediness of the friars results in deadly abuse of the souls of their fellow Christians. Instead of healing their fellow Christians, they poison them:

> The frere wiþ his phisyk þis folk haþ enchaunted,
> And plastred hem so esily [hij] drede no synne.
>
> (B XX 379–80)

Conscience, at the end of the poem, is left helpless and resolves to wander wide in the world in the search of *Piers Plowman*; the barn of Unity and the Christians within it left a helpless wreck in his wake, stranded by the 'phisyk' of the friars. As Conscience strides off, he wishes that

> ... freres hadde a fyndyng, þat for nede flateren.
>
> (B XX 384)

As David Aers has argued so well, the problem with the friars' claims to poverty in *Piers Plowman* is that it leaves them in a state of need which siphons off the alms and charity that ought to be given to the deserving poor: those who cannot work, and who refuse to beg, or whose sustenance is so meagre that they can barely survive. Conscience proposes that the friars had some kind of 'fyndyng' – an enigmatic word but one that suggests some kind of formal material help to prevent their flattering from need. The conclusion of the poem offers nothing more substantial than this inscrutably pious hope.[7]

---

7   David Aers, *Sanctifying Signs* (Notre Dame, IN: University of Notre Dame Press, 2004): 152–56.

This is not Langland's last word on the subject. The issue returns powerfully in the C-text of the poem. It is well known that one of the dramatic events deleted from the C-text is the scene of Piers's tearing of the Pardon in B. This omission has often been seen to make the poem less radical. But it seems to me that what is put in its place, especially given that it would have been written after Langland had finished the B-text, is differently, but importantly, an extremely daring discursive move. He replaces the overdetermined Pardon Scene with poetry that addresses the plight of the poor with direct, uncomplicated passion. Who is worthy to receive?

> Woet no man, as Y wene, who is worthy to haue;
> Ac þat most neden aren oure neyheboures, and we nyme gode hede,
> As prisones in puttes and pore folk in cotes,
> Charged with childrene and chief lordes rente;
> Þat they with spynnyng may spare, spenen hit on hous-huyre,
> Bothe in mylke and in mele, to make with papelotes
> To aglotye with here gurles that greden aftur fode.
> And hemsulue also soffre muche hunger,
> And wo in wynter-tymes, and wakynge on nyhtes
> To rise to þe reule to rokke þe cradel,
> Bothe to carde and to kembe, to cloute and to wasche,
> To rybbe and to rele, rusches to pylie,
> That reuthe is to rede or in ryme shewe
> The wo of this wommen þat wonyeth in cotes;
> And of monye oþer men þat moche wo soffren,
> Bothe afyngred and afurste, to turne þe fayre outward,
> And ben abasched for to begge and wollen nat be aknowe
> What hym nedede at here neyhebores at noon and at eue.
> This Y woet witterly, as þe world techeth,
> What other byhoueth þat hath many childrene
> And hath no catel but his craft to clothe hym and to fede,
> And fele to fonge þerto and fewe panes taketh.
> There is payne and peny ale as for a pytaunce ytake,
> And colde flesche and fische, as venisoun were bake.
> Fridays and fastyng days a ferthing-worth of moskeles
> Were a feste with suche folk, or so fele cockes.
> These were almusse, to helpe þat han such charges,
> And to conforte suche coterelles and crokede men and blynde.
>   (C IX 70–97)

And madden as the mone sit, more other lasse.
Careth they for no colde, ne counteth of non hete,
And aren meuynge aftur þe mone; moneyles þay walke ...
... Barfoot and bredles, beggeth they of no man.
And thauh a mete with the mayre ameddes þe strete,
A reuerenseth hym ryht nauht, no rather then another:
... Suche manere men, Matheu vs techeth,
We sholde haue hem to house and helpe hem when they come
(C IX 108–25).

Those most in need of help are not the friars. The needy are able-bodied, hard-working men and women; landless labourers whose wages and unpaid domestic work leave them and their children barely above subsistence level. Langland describes their lives in graphically minute detail. Even though they have employment, the jobs are so menial and part-time they can scarcely scrape together a living.[8] The deserving poor are also those who lack mental health. Unable to care for themselves or to operate in the social world, they go barefoot, without money, but they do not beg. These, says the narrator, are our neighbours; these are the people most worthy to receive alms. What is especially striking about these added passages is the subjectivity of the writing. There is no patronizing frame: no institutionalized book learning underwrites the address; there is no clever punning or abstraction. Langland takes off his clerkly cap and simply lets us *see* why a problem matters. Poverty is displayed in all its material starkness: an accumulated picture of lack, not a tangled mosaic of ideas.

For all the troubled treatment of the poor and of poverty in *Piers Plowman*, then, some clarity does emerge. Langland does not appear to champion poverty as a worthy state, although he does contrast the merits of such a position with the arrogant learning of greedy clerics when it comes to thinking of who is likely to be saved. There are serious reservations expressed about the social consequences of living in voluntary poverty, as evidenced by the treatment of the friars, however laudable the original ideals of St Francis. Where the place of the poor does matter so strongly

8   Derek Pearsall, 'Lunatyk lollares' in Piero Boitani and Anna Torti (eds.), *Religion in the Poetry and Drama of the Late Middle Ages* (Cambridge: Cambridge University Press, 1990): 163–78.

to the poet, however, is in terms of how the rest of society treats them. The passages in the C-text provide a contemporary call to alms for the people whom, in Trajan's terms, other members of society should 'lene' and 'love'. Just as Christ is figured as a blood brother who helps his brethren at their most acute time of need, so each and every one of us should help our poor neighbours, to relieve them of their involuntary suffering. The friars, and their ideals of poverty, obstruct the simple directive of charity, summed up in the commandment of the New Testament which Trajan quotes – 'love one another'.[9]

4.2. The *Piers Plowman* Tradition

How much of this finds its way into the four new poems of the *Piers Plowman* tradition? In none of the poems is there anything to compare with the powerful poetry of those C lines, or the complexities of the issues. In *Richard the Redeles* and *Mum and the Sothsegger*, the poet focuses chiefly on the abuse of the poor by more powerful members of society. In *Richard*, the retainers of Richard II are described as lawless and violent, and as agents of social anarchy; they 'bare adoun the pouere' (II. 39) and they cheat and rob them. There is nothing here that is distinctively Langlandian.[10] In *Mum*, the poor have a larger profile, and one that is arguably

---

9   John 13:34. This is also the advice of Kynde to Will in B XX 208, 'Lerne to loue'.
10   Similar comments are found in occasional political poetry: see *Historical Poems of the XIVth and XVth Centuries*, ed. R.H. Robbins (New York: Columbia University Press, 1959): 63/9–12; 144/14, and 152/41. The closest the *Richard* poet comes to sounding what may be a distinctively Langlandian note occurs in a single line. In Passus III of the poem, the narrator describes the ideal, fully functioning, political community: 'It is not vnknowen to kunnynge leodis,/That rewlers of rewmes around all the erthe/ Were not yffoundid at the frist tyme/To leue al at likynge and lust of the world,/But to laboure on the lawe as lewde men on plowes' (Passus III 263–7). This is not championing the poor as such, but in the valuing of the honest labour of the lowest members of society as a template for the responsibility with which rulers of the realm should

closer to *Piers*. As in *Richard*, there is concern that the poor are exploited at law. Lines 19–27 of the poem urge the importance of hearing the legal representations of the poor in court, and the nobility are warned against robbing the poor of their goods in line 1491. But in contrast to *Richard the Redeles* there is something of a religious inflection to discussion of the poor. When the narrator turns to the bag of books at the end of the poem, amongst its contents is a 'copie of couetise' (1683). A wealthy man has procured his riches through robbing the poor. In his will, however, he makes provision for them by leaving money for the building of hospitals. The narrator remarks:

> But while he had power of the penyes the poure had but lite.
> Hit is a high holynes and grete helth to the soule,
> A man to lyue in lustes alle his life-dayes
> And haue no pitie on the poure, ne parte with thaym nother,
> But holde it euer in his hande till the herte breke.
> But thenne he shapeth for the soule whenne the sunne is dovne,
> But while the day durid he delte but a lite;
> Now muche moste his merite be that mendeth so the poure,
> That gifeth his good for God-is sake whenne his goste is passed.
>   (*Mum*, 1688–96)

The poem goes on to comment that such post-death provision for the poor is useless as the executors of wills are so corrupt that instead of discharging the terms of the will, they keep all the money for themselves. 'Why shulde we dele for the dede? He dide not while he mighte' they are quoted as saying (1708). To give to the poor only after one is dead, and to refuse to help them when alive is wrong. The narrator comments, with bitter irony, that such behaviour is 'high holynes and grete helth to the soule' (1689). This is not alms, or charity, but spiritual opportunism. While the tenor of the remarks is not out of keeping with a Langlandian perspective, however, it would be hard to claim direct influence. Executors feature in Mede's entourage in *Piers*, C II 189, but criticisms of false executors, or

---

discharge their duties, there is a political edge not out of keeping with a Langlandian vision. The collapsing of the king into the ploughman is richly suggestive of the figure of Piers in Passus XVIII, whether or not there is a conscious recall.

making provision for the poor only in death, occur in other alliterative poetry. Wastour advises Wynnere not to hoard his wealth: 'thi sone and thi sektours ichone slees othere, ... A dale aftir thi daye dose the no mare / Þan a lighte lanterne late appone nyghte'.[11] The topos has penitential resonance; it appears in the Vernon lyrics: 'Tarry not till To-morrow', warns of the fraudulence of executors, ll. 37–48 with a refrain, '[t]rust nouȝt on hem after to-Morn'.[12]

Closer, perhaps to *Piers*, is the interaction in *Mum* between the narrator and the religious. The narrator is a poor man, who in his travels to all groups of society meets corruption and malpractice. The friars come under even heavier fire than in *Piers* (see lines 392–527).[13] Their lack of charity towards the poor is one of the milder criticisms:

> For though a frere be fatt and haue a ful coffre
> Of gold and of good, thou getys but a lite
> Forto bete thy bale, though thou begge euer.
> (451–3)

More dramatically, the *Mum*-poet shows us how monks treat the poor. The narrator goes to an Augustinian abbey:

> But for I was a meen man I might not entre;
> For though the place were y-pighte for poure men sake
> And eeke funded there-fore yit faillen thay ofte
> That thay doon not eche day do beste of alle.
> *Mutauerunt caritatem in cupiditatem. Sapiencia.*
> For the fundacion as the fundours ment
> Was groundid for God-is men, though hit grete serue.
> They koueiten no comers but yf thay cunne helpe
> Forto amende thaire mynstre and to maynteyne thaire rente,

11   *Wynnere and Wastoure*, ed. Stephanie Trigg (EETS OS 297 (1990)), ll. 305–6.
12   *The Minor Poems of the Vernon Manuscript Part II*, ed. F.J. Furnivall (EETS OS 117 (1901)), ll. 725–7.
13   For discussion of the antifraternal satire in *Mum*, see Helen Barr, *Signes and Sothe: Language in the Piers Plowman Tradition* (Cambridge: D.S. Brewer, 1994): 126–8, and *Socioliterary Practice in Late Medieval England* (Oxford: Oxford University Press, 2001): 166–9.

> Or in worke or in worde waite thaire profit,
> Or elles entreth he not til thay haue y-sopid.
> Thus thaire portier for my pouerete putt me thens,
> And grauntid me of his goodnesse to go where me luste
> And to wandry where I wolde without the gates.
>
> (*Mum*, 540–52)

The monks are shown to behave in a fashion exactly opposite to the passionate pleas to help the poor voiced by Trajan and the narrator in *Piers*. With a Langlandian echo, we are told that they do not do best because they turn charity into cupidity (543–54). The reprise of the Dowel motif from *Piers* underwrites the monks' refusal of hospitality unless their guests provide them with gifts and material goods for the benefit of their building. Dramatically, the porter of the monastery, rather than offering shelter and food to the poor narrator, actually ejects him for his poverty. There is real bite in the alliterative coupling of 'portier', 'pouerete' and 'putt' in line 550, and the ironic politeness in lines 551–2 of telling the narrator to go where he pleases without the gates. To place one's guest outside the gates is a violation of the code of hospitality. This passage is without the passionate poetry in *Piers* concerned with helping and 'lening' the poor, but the Langlandian echo is appropriate to the temper of the poet's remarks, even if the inhospitality topos is not distinctive to *Piers Plowman*.[14] In *Mum*, even if there is a trace of verbal echo, the concerns about the poor are more coincident with *Piers* than urgently informed by their great predecessor.

---

14   Closest to the treatment of inhospitality in *Piers* is the banquet scene with the doctor of divinity where the narrator and Patience are cold-shouldered and the friar eats all the pudding (B XIII 28–111). Jenni Nuttall has shown how the inhospitality topos was an important part of political narratives written during the reign of Henry IV: see 'Household Narratives and Lancastrian Poetics in Hoccleve's Envoys and Other Early Fifteenth Century Middle English Poems' in Cordelia Beattie, Anna Maslakovic and Sarah Rees Jones (eds.), *The Medieval Household in Christian Europe: Managing Power, Wealth and the Body* (Turnhout: Brepols, 2003): 91–106. It is an issue taken up also in the Digby-lyrics, where the poet uses the devotional topos of humankind refusing hospitality to God to comment simultaneously on human beings' lack of charity towards each other: Helen Barr (ed.), *The Digby Poems* (Exeter: University of Exeter Press, 2009).

4.3. *The Crowned King*

The remaining two poems are more distinctively Langlandian. *The Crowned King* is chiefly concerned with advice to King Henry V before setting sail to France in 1415.[15] But in its course there are lines devoted to urging the king to pay proper heed to the poor:

> The playnt of the pouere peple put thou not behynde,
> For they swope and swete and swynke for thy fode;
> Moche worship they wynne the in this worlde riche,
> Of thy gliteryng gold and of thy gay wedes,
> Thy proud pelure, and palle with preciouse stones,
> Grete castels and stronge, and styff walled townes.
> And yit the most preciouse plente that apparaill passeth,
> Thi pouere peple with here ploughe pike out of the erthe,
> And they yeve her goodes to gouerne hem euen.
> (Crowned King, 65–73)

The poor deserve to be properly governed because their work is essential to the prosperity of the realm. There is passion in this writing. The alliterative 'swope' 'swynke' and 'swete' for the king's food (66) forms a powerful contrast to the listing of the king's jewels, clothes and castles. A list of splendour having been built, however, there is a sudden twist in the argument. The most precious plant that surpasses apparel is that which the poor people dig out of the earth with their plough (72). The most precious commodity is therefore by inference the labour of the poor. In contrast to this precious plant, the poet has earlier figured the king's riches as 'mukke' (64). There is a distinctive Langlandian echo. This is how Holy Church describes the Incarnation:

---

15   Derek Pearsall provides astute commentary: see '*Crowned King*: War and Peace in 1415', in Jenny Stratford (ed.), *The Lancastrian Court* (Harlaxton Medieval Studies 13, 2001): 163–72.

And also þe plante of pees, moost precious of vertues:
For heuene myȝte nat holden it, so was it heuy of hymselue,
Til it hadde of þe erþe eten his fille.
And whan it hadde of þis fold flessh and blood taken,
Was neuere leef vpon lynde lighter þerafter,
And portatif and persaunt as þe point of a nedle,
That myȝte noon armure it lette ne none heiȝe walles.

                                                    (*Piers*, B I 152–8)

Here, the plant of peace is Love; the Incarnation; God becoming human flesh and blood in order to save human souls. If the echo of this passage in *Crowned King* is deliberate, then it invests the duty of the king to care for the position of the poor with resonances of Christ's redemptive action for all humankind. This is exactly how Christ describes his kingly duties in Passus XVIII of *Piers* (quoted above), and it is entirely consonant with the care for the poor championed by Trajan. Nor is this an isolated vision of kingship in *Crowned King*. While the primary focus of the poem is commentary on a political moment in an international arena, there is a transcendence to the writing granted by the poem's frame. The 'condicion of a kyng', writes the poet, should be that he 'comfort his peple' (133). To do this, the king is urged to follow the 'siker ensample that Crist hym-self sheweth' (137). The exemplar of kingship is 'Crist, crowned Kyng, that on Cros didest' (1). This, the first line of the poem, is repeated four lines before its close; it brings the poem full circle. Christ's love for humankind, and his redemptive sacrifice, is not only the template for the duty of the king to care for the poor in the lines which echo the 'plant of peace' passage, but informs the whole poem.

4.4. *Pierce the Ploughman's Crede*

So too, in *Pierce the Ploughman's Crede*, a Langlandian vision of the place of the poor is present in both verbal echo and in overall structure. The narrator's search for someone who can teach him the Apostles' Creed takes him to visit all the four orders of friars. None can help him. Desperate and disillusioned, he comes across a poor ploughman in a field:

I seigh a sely man me by opon the plow hongen,
His cote was of a cloute that cary was y-called,
His hod was full of holes and his heer oute,
With his knopped schon clouted full thykke;
His ton toteden out as he the londe treddede,
His hosen ouerhongen his hokschynes on eueriche a side,
Al beslombered in fen as he the plow folwede:
Twey myteynes, as mete, maad all of cloutes;
The fyngers weren for-werd and ful of fen honged.
This whit waslede in the fen almost to the ancle,
Foure rotheren hym by-forn that feble were worthen;
Men myghte reken ech a ryb so reufull they weren.
His wijf walked him with with a long gode,
In a cutted cote cutted full heyghe,
Wrapped in a wynwe schete to weren hire fro weders,
Barfote on the bare ijs that the blod folwede.
And at the londes ende laye a litell crom-bolle,
And thereon lay a litell childe lapped in cloutes,
And tweyne of tweie yeres olde opon a-nother syde,
And alle they songen o songe that sorwe was to heren;
They crieden alle o cry a carefull note.
The sely man sighede sore, and seide, 'Children, beth stille!'
This man loked opon me and leet the plow stonden,
And seyde, 'Sely man, why syghest thou so harde?
Yif the lakke lijflode lene the ich will
Swich good as God hath sent. Go we, leue brother'.

(*Pierce the Ploughman's Crede*, 420–46)

In contrast to the other poems, here we both see and hear the voice of the truly poor. Peres the Ploughman could have been one of the poor folk in the cottages of the C interpolations in *Piers Plowman*. He is able-bodied and works for his living, but in treacherously abject conditions. His clothing is tattered and scarcely protects him from his environment. Even more so is this the case with his wife, her feet cut with the ice on which she walks because she has no shoes. That the couple's children have to be left in the field in a little scrapbowl as they work dramatizes the extent of their need to work and their poverty. Of course, the portrait is sentimentalized but it is, nonetheless, a graphic realization of the living and working conditions of the hard-working involuntary poor who live barely above subsistence level.

What is markedly Langlandian is not only the detail of the description but the attitude of the ploughman towards his fellow man. Seeing the narrator and hearing him sigh, Peres's first words are to ask if he lacks sustenance, and if he does, he will 'lene' him, for he is his dear brother (444). Peres is a paradigm of Trajan and the C narrator's plea to offer our fellow human beings charity. This new poem responds both to the harsh realities of what it is like to live in poverty described so passionately in *Piers* and to the crucial injunction that, fully to follow Christ's example, one must have compassion on the needy. In *Crede*, one of the neediest members of the social community spontaneously offers charity to his fellow man.

The place of this episode in the structure of the poem can also be seen to have been influenced by *Piers Plowman*. Peres's concern for the narrator contrasts starkly to the actions of the friars that precede this episode. Throughout *Crede*, the friars' need for sustenance is described in terms that show how their greed despoils the poor. The decoration on the pillars of the sumptuous Dominican chapel costs the price of a plough-land of pennies (169). The lead decorations in the cloisters are so exquisite and elaborate that the agricultural yield of a huge shire would be insufficient to have provided for it all (191–7). The friary has enough dormitories to give lodging to the queen, and yet, the narrator observes sourly:

> ... thise bilderes wilne beggen a bagg-full of wheate
> Of a pure pore man that maie onethe paie
> Half his rente in a yer and half ben behynde.
>   (*Pierce the Ploughman's Crede*, 216–18)

The friars' need to beg results in superfluous, ostentatious living which is, quite literally, at the expense of the 'pure' poor who cannot meet the demands of their rent. These charges are echoed by Peres in his conversation with the narrator in the second half of the poem. In a pithy line, he says of the friars, 'with trauail of trewe men thei tymbren her houses' (723). The idealizing claims of the friars to a life of poverty are exposed as a hollow sham:

> Her pacience is al pased and put out to ferme,
> And pride is in her pouerte that litell is to preisen
>
> *(Pierce the Ploughman's Crede, 75–6)*

The ideal of fraternal involuntary poverty here has been transposed into pride. Repeatedly in the poem this issue is dramatized in the friars' treatment of the narrator. In contrast to Peres' immediate, unbidden request to 'lene' his brother, the friars consistently try to obtain money or goods from him and they offer him nothing in the way of material – or spiritual – nourishment. Peres tells the narrator that friars:

> ... chewen charitie as chewen schaf houndes.
> And thei pursueth the pouere ...
>
> *(Pierce the Ploughman's Crede, 663–4)*

This is as damning an indictment as any in the poem. The simile of the hounds chewing chaff is Langlandian.[16] Far from simply lacking charity, the friars show utter contempt for the concept, and instead persecute the poor. Peres explicitly contrasts the fraudulence of the friars with the misery of the poor who refuse to beg:

> All tho blissid beth that bodyliche hungreth;
> That ben the pore penyles that han ouer-passed
> The poynt of her pris lijf in penaunce of werkes,
> And mown nought swynken ne sweten but ben swythe feble,
> Other maymed at myschef or meseles syke,
> And here good is agon and greueth hem to beggen.
> Ther is no frer in feith that fareth in this wise ...
>
> *(Pierce the Ploughman's Crede, 619–25)*

Here again is graphic description of those who are poor because they have exhausted their working life through hard labour, or are injured, or sick with leprosy. And yet, in contrast to the pampered luxury of the friars,

---

16   Holy Church says of chaplains who are unkind to their kin that they '[c]hewen hire charite and chiden after moore', *Piers*, B I 193.

such poor penniless, like those who lack 'inwit' in the C-passages of *Piers*,
refuse to beg. While in *Piers Plowman*, Conscience's answer to the problem of the friars' voluntary poverty is that they should have some kind
of 'fyndyng', some kind of endowment, Peres's solution in *Crede* is much
more radical:

> Thei schulden deluen and diggen and dongen the erthe,
> And mene-mong corn bred to her mete fongen,
> And wortes flechles wroughte and water to drinken,
> And werchen and wolward gon as we wrecches vsen.
> (Pierce the Ploughman's Crede, 785–8)

Peres's solution to the problem of the friars is that their way of life should
disappear. Instead of their superfluous existence, which is a drain on the rest of
society, they should work, live, eat and dress as poor labourers. It is a position
that *Piers Plowman* never adopts, but it is clear from the discussion of the
poor in *Pierce the Ploughman's Crede* that there is unmistakeable influence
from Langland's poem. The poor are idealized and sentimentalized in a way
that exceeds their depiction in *Piers*, but this new poem reprises Langland's
relationship between the place of the poor in the economic world and the
place of the voluntarily poor friars. *Crede*'s discussion of poverty responds
both to individual passages and issues in *Piers* and also to its underlying structure and argument. Even while the *Crede*-poet adopts a position on the friars
which is far more radical than anything envisaged in *Piers*, his perception
that the problem of poverty in the economic world is linked to the problem
of the friars' involuntary poverty shows a reading of *Piers* which goes well
beyond reprising only its verbal texture or overt moral positioning.

4.5. Conclusion

Crede is usually seen to be a Lollard polemic against the friars – which it is.
But such polemic is inseparable from its brutally honest depiction of the
stark reality of involuntary poverty, and the importance of charity. In each
of the poems of the *Piers* progeny, there is a directness and clarity in their

treatment of the poor which strips out the tortured and tangled nature
of the discussion in *Piers*. But for all that, it is clear that the new poems
take much more than cursory inspiration from their poetic progenitor.
Especially in *Crowned King* and *Crede* we see the work of poets who were
sensitive readers not only of the declarative statements of *Piers* but also of
its verbal texture and its narrative strategies.

4.6. References

4.6.1. Primary sources

Barr, Helen, ed. *The Piers Plowman Tradition. A Critical Edition of Pierce the Plough-man's Crede, Richard the Redeles, Mum and the Sothsegger and The Crowned King*. London: Dent, 1993.
———. *The Digby Poems*. Exeter: University of Exeter Press, 2009.
Furnivall, F.J., ed. *The Minor Poems of the Vernon Manuscript Part II*. EETS OS 117. Oxford: Oxford University Press, 1901.
Langland, William. *Piers Plowman: A Parallel-Text Edition of the A, B, C, and Z Versions*, vol. I, ed., A.V.C. Schmidt. London: Longman, 1995.
Robbins, R.H., ed. *Historical Poems of the XIVth and XVth Centuries*. New York: Columbia University Press, 1959.
Trigg, Stephanie, ed. *Wynnere and Wastoure*. EETS OS 297. Oxford: Oxford University Press, 1990.

4.6.2. Secondary sources

Aers, David. *Sanctifying Signs*. Notre Dame, IN: University of Notre Dame Press, 2004.
Barr, Helen. *Signes and Sothe: Language in the Piers Plowman Tradition*. Cambridge: D.S. Brewer, 1994.
———. *Socioliterary Practice in Late Medieval England*. Oxford: Oxford University Press, 2001.
Clopper, Lawrence. *Songs of Rechelesnesse: Langland and the Franciscans*. Ann Arbor, MI: University of Michigan Press, 1997.

Kim, Margaret. 'Hunger and Need and the Politics of Poverty in *Piers Plowman*', *Yearbook of Langland Studies* 16 (2002): 131–68.

Nuttall, Jenni. 'Household Narratives and Lancastrian Poetics in Hoccleve's Envoys and Other Early Fifteenth Century Middle English Poems', in Cordelia Beattie, Anna Maslakovic and Sarah Rees Jones (eds.), *The Medieval Household in Christian Europe: Managing Power, Wealth and the Body*. Turnhout: Brepols, 2003: 91–106.

Pearsall, Derek. 'Poverty and Poor People in *Piers Plowman*', in E. Kennedy, R. Waldron and J. Wittig, eds., *Medieval English studies presented to George Kane*. Woodbridge, Suffolk: D.S. Brewer, 1988: 167–85.

——. 'Crowned King: War and Peace in 1415', in Jenny Stratford, ed. *The Lancastrian Court*. Harlaxton Medieval Studies 13 (2001): 163–72.

Scott, Anne M. *Piers Plowman and the Poor*. Dublin: Four Courts Press, 2004.

Shepherd, Geoffrey. 'Poverty in *Piers Plowman*' in T.H. Aston, P.R. Coss, and C. Dyer, eds. *Social Relations and Idea*, Cambridge: Cambridge University Press, 1983: 169–89.

5 'My Wyl is This' (*Canterbury Tales*. I [A] 1845):
Chaucer's Sense of Power in *The Knight's Tale*
and *The Clerk's Tale*

5.0. Introduction

As R.J. Meyer-Lee asserts in the recently published *Poets and Power from Chaucer to Wyatt*,[1] it could not be denied that the deposition of Richard II and the divorce of Henry VIII had surprisingly far-reaching effects on English literature; for the fall of Richard II enabled the rise of the Lancastrian dynasty, and the divorce of Henry VIII marked the beginning of the English Reformation. Recent studies have further demonstrated how Lancastrian ways of legitimation sometimes took very indirect cultural forms (including high-class vernacular verse).[2] Almost immediately after the enthronement of Henry IV, this verse begins to be concerned with power; that is to say, English poetry becomes more charged, albeit indirectly, with political import.

Generally speaking, no great contradiction can be seen between the utilitarian and the aesthetic in the Middle Ages, but it is also certain that the tendency not to have the means of a literary object be entirely transparent characterized the Ricardian period. Poets are therefore said to have

---

1 Cf. R.J. Meyer-Lee, *Poets and Power from Chaucer to Wyatt* (Cambridge: Cambridge University Press, 2007): 24–31.
2 Cf. Paul Strohm, *England's Empty Throne: Usurpation and the Language of Legitimation, 1399–1422* (New Haven, CT and London: Yale University Press, 1998): 173–95.

adopted strategies of indirection and displacement. The ambiguous description of Richard as God of Love in the prologue to *The Legend of Good Women* exemplifies these strategies, although this prologue is obviously not a political statement. On the other hand, beginning with John of Gaunt, the Lancastrians fully appreciated the political utility of literature. Indeed, it appears that after 1400 the Lancastrians demanded a poetry that could serve as a political weapon. With these backgrounds in mind, I would like to consider Chaucer's sense of power; discussion will concentrate chiefly on the ruler's speeches in *The Knight's Tale* and *The Clerk's Tale*.

5.1. The Sense of Power in *The Knight's Tale*

In *The Knight's Tale*, particularly in the speeches of Duke Theseus, Chaucer undoubtedly attaches exceptional importance to the speech of power because, in this poem, speech is the political vehicle by which a ruler expresses his own will and makes a broad response to his people in Athens. The following passage is a good example:

> *My wyl is this, ...*
> *Withouten any repplicacioun*
> (I [A]1845–6; italics mine)[3]

Theseus's speech, which is unhurried and assured, stands on traditional associations and ancient wisdom. His speech declares a coherent world in which logic and even style itself become weapons of power.[4] Generally speaking, authoritative speech seems to dwell on a given situation rather

---

3   L.D. Benson, (ed.), *The Riverside Chaucer*, 3rd edn, with a New Foreword by Christopher Cannon (Oxford: Oxford University Press, 2008).

4   When discussing the style of *The Knight's Tale* we cannot help remembering Charles Muscatine's apt criticism in *Chaucer and the French Tradition* (Berkeley, CA: University of California Press, 1957): 177–8.

than move it forward in any practical way. It goes without saying that the speech of power chiefly exists to make decisions; that is, it aims at resolving conflict, rather than opening an issue for discussion or seeking to generate response. Consequently, the speech of power does not require a listener, although the speech in general may assume a listener. The listener to the authoritative speech in *The Knight's Tale* is a silent presence. Even when a speech is delivered by a speaker other than Duke Theseus, since it issues from authority it has a majesty that demands silence, not response. When the herald makes his proclamation, opinion and dialogue are replaced by reverence and receptivity:

> An heraud on a scaffold made an 'Oo!'
> Til *al the noyse of peple was ydo*[5]
>
> (I [A] 2533–4)

The poem is full of characteristic speech like this. Though we know very well that the form of speech changes within a thousand year (cf. *Troilus and Criseyde*, II. 22–3), speech is so important, particularly in *The Knight's Tale*, that often the action of the tale seems to exist for the speech alone. Thus, the imprisonment of Arcite and Palamon and their falling in love with Emily provoke extensive philosophical speeches; their fighting in the woods causes Theseus's feeling of pity and his speech on the power of love; Arcite's illness draws lyrical lament (I [A] 2765–97); and finally, Theseus's subsequent sorrow is followed by Egeus's wisdom on the world's transmutation (I[A]2842–9). In all the scenes, listeners are present, but speeches are complete without listeners.

However, the description of Theseus before his final speech of the tale is the most conspicuous example of the speech of power because here his wisdom, his words, and his will are one:

---

5   In addition, it can be noted that 'stormy peple' (IV[E]995) are likened to the moon in *The Clerk's Tale*. Therefore it follows that self-sufficient speech is not related to interdependency.

His eyen sette he ...

... ...
> And after that right thus *he seyde his wille*:
>
> (I[A]2984–6)

Theseus's speech wholly expresses his rational view of events in the world; his speech is thus full of unquestioned authority. His final speech on 'the faire cheyne of love' (I [A] 2988) is the culmination of a tale in which the spoken word has greatness that could not be disputed or doubted. When we read *The Knight's Tale*, we momentarily experience a world in which speech can convey a cosmology and a reasoned conclusion.[6] As in *The Consolation of Philosophy*, Theseus's consolation helps to solve the problems that have been raised by Arcite and Palamon and the events of the poem.[7]

I would now like to consider the essence of the sense of power in *The Clerk's Tale*, and compare it with that of *The Knight's Tale*, which throws light on it, inasmuch as both tales posit a philosophical and social order and the presence of an absolute ruler, though admittedly there are differences between them. While the speech of authority in the case of Theseus is neither naked nor arbitrary, in that of Walter it is arbitrary and oppressive:

> Taak it agayn; *I graunte it of my grace.*
>
> (IV [E] 808)

---

6   As a consequence, Theseus's words at the end of the tale move Palamon and Emily to an action; cf. I[A] 3070–4.

7   Theseus's speech asserts a wisdom based on law and his cosmology would seem to unify human experience generally. To be sure, when viewed from the standpoint of the narrator [the Knight], speech seems to obey the rule of reason; however, for the next narrator [the Miller] it does not do so (cf. P.A. Olson, *The Canterbury Tales and the Good Society* (Princeton, NJ: Princeton University Press, 1986): 75–85; Alfred David, *The Strumpet Muse* (Bloomington, IN: Indiana University Press, 1976): 153; Paul Strohm, *Social Chaucer* (Cambridge, MA: Harvard University Press, 1987): 151. The Miller cannot accept the Knight's speech without accepting its values, because he says, 'I wol quite the Knyghtes tale' (I[A]3127; speech now establishes itself as the currency of conflict and that is why the majestic pace of Theseus's speech is replaced by the more rapid movement of everyday-life language. We can see here Chaucer's sense of reality. According to Paul Strohm's indication, we are to recognize that there are both 'ernest' and 'game' in *The Canterbury Tales*.

These are the words with which Walter addresses his wife, Griselda; and it is obvious that Walter seems to suppress pity and mercy in his speech. On the other hand, Theseus, by incorporating these qualities, exhibits a speech in which the private and the public blend into one another. Theseus is, as it were, moving from inner to outer, from the private to the public. He does not suppress mercy and pity in any sense. His speech aims to expose conflict and to subject initial emotions to thoughtful modification. *The Knight's Tale* emphasizes this quality by showing the process by which Theseus's speech translates an initial emotion into understanding and compassionate behaviour. This attention to the civilizing power of speech is quite admirable in *The Knight's Tale*.[8]

Theseus's speech in *The Knight's Tale* is supposed to be the tool by which the ruler tempers his judgement. Theseus's early question to the company of ladies (I [A] 905–6) is just one instance of several in which the Duke first questions aggressively and then responds judiciously and sympathetically. His words and behavior are similarly modified when he comes upon Arcite and Palamon. In short, speech tempers arbitrary judgements. Theseus's tribute to the god of love (I[A]1785–90) is the outcome of a lengthy inner deliberation in which anger is replaced by reason:

Yet in his resoun he hem bothe excused,

(I[A]1766)

And in *his gentil herte* he thoughte anon,

(I [A] 1772)

Being responsive to inner as well as outer impulses, Theseus's speech is the vehicle by which human emotions are to be understood. Assuredly, it testifies to Chaucer's instinctive openness in terms of speech that even Theseus, who is a most powerful speaker, still leaves room for dialogue.

---

8   Cf. Charles Muscatine's observation that Chaucer might be constantly aware of antagonistic elements (*ibid.*, 181). And William Frost shares the same opinion; cf. 'An Interpretation of Chaucer's *Knight's Tale*', *Review of English Studies* 25 (1949): 289–304.

5.2. The Sense of Power in *The Clerk's Tale*

In *The Clerk's Tale*, the sense of power is more arbitrary. Each question raised by the Griselda story about the psychological and spiritual appropriateness of the testing of Griselda is central to the medieval controversy about political order. According to A.P. d'Entrèves, the notion of absolute order is not compatible with the Christian notion of the absolute value of human personality.[9] That is to say, indiscriminate submission for the sake of unity of will, which lies at the very heart of absolutist political unity, may conflict with the value of the individual in a sense; this is a problem in which we might eternally be involved (IV [E] 800–1). When we see how speech is employed in *The Clerk's Tale*, we are conscious that at the centre of the tale lies a tension between the needs of the state and the value of the individual. Thus Griselda, in her absolute obedience to her husband Walter, is not unwilling to accept absolute authority and arbitrary speech as follows:

> For *I wol gladly yelden hire my place,*
> ...   .
> That *I shal goon, I wol goon whan yow leste.*
>   (IV [E] 843–7)

Evidently in *The Clerk's Tale*, the philosophical ground suggested by Theseus's speech disappears and, in turn, a diminished speech expressive of pure power appears.

The ruler's speech in both tales assumes a hierarchical order, but Walter's speech draws attention to the distance between himself and other people much more than does the speech of Theseus; for Walter's speech is nothing but a means of maintaining hierarchy. Consequently, Walter asserts sharp distinctions between himself and other people, and between himself and Griselda. The first meeting with Janicula [Griselda's father] and Griselda is a 'collacioun', i.e. a consultation (IV [E] 325):

9   Cf. A.P. d' Entrèves. *Dante as a Political Thinker* (Oxford: Clarendon Press, 1952): 49.

Have a collacioun, and wostow why?

(IV [E] 325)

The reader soon realizes that the regal terms, such as 'charge', 'assure', 'swere', 'grucche', 'requeste', and 'assente', denote the relationship among the speakers (cf. IV [E] 162–75); for the regal and political implications of the verb 'grucche' (IV [E] 170), A.L. Kellogg's essay is useful.[10]

In the first meeting with Griselda, Walter is also legalistic, referring to his questions as 'demandes' and asking whether Griselda will 'assente, or elles yow avyse?' (IV [E] 348–50). And the absolute obedience that Walter asks would deny the most important factor of being human (IV [E] 355–7). In *The Clerk's Tale*, the speaker and the listener are differentiated because of its legal framework for speech; therefore, Walter's speech is always curtailed or shortened, so that, for example, even in asking his people's agreement to the conditions for marriage, he phrases it as follows:

I prey yow, *speketh namoore of this matere.*

(IV [E] 175)

To Griselda's acceptance of the marriage contract (IV [E] 358–71), Walter simply responds:

'This is ynogh ... '

(IV [E] 365)

Walter is similarly economical in his comments to the people who gather outside: the brief directive to honour and love his wife Griselda is followed by 'ther is namoore to seye' (IV [E] 371). This phrase will be echoed by the sergeant when in his first encounter with Griselda he asks forgiveness and states the necessity of his mission. This sergeant is counted among 'swich folk' that 'wel kan / Doon execucioun in *thynges* badde' (IV [E] 521–2). He says to Griselda:

---

10   A.L. Kellogg. 'The Evolution of *The Clerk's Tale*: A Study in Connotation', in A.L. Kellogg. *Chaucer, Langland, Arthur: Essays in Middle English Literature* (New Brunswick, NJ: Rutgers University Press, 1972): 276–329.

Though I do *thyng* to which I am constreyned.
....
And so wol I; *ther is namoore to seye.*

$$\text{(IV [E] 527–32)}^{11}$$

5.3. Chaucer's Sense of Mutability

As I have explained, in *The Knight's Tale* the speech of power does its work openly: Theseus's speech reveals its reasonings and manifests the belief that gives it its authority. Conversely, the underlying rationale of Walter's speech in *The Clerk's Tale* remains hidden, and so its authority is quite arbitrary; obviously, Walter withholds explanations. To accomplish his end, he orders his sergeant to misinform Griselda, devises a false papal bull (IV [E] 736–49), sends secret letters, and uses 'open audience' (IV [E] 790) to lie to Griselda. Walter's speech, like that of Theseus, does not reveal its full intentions to anyone until the tale's end (IV [E] 1072–8); as a result, the secretive aspect of communication is emphasized.

Walter's speech, like Theseus's, does not seem to move between the private and the public; furthermore, it neglects the private for the public. In short, Walter's speech excludes his own emotions; while he notes Griselda's continued obedience, he hides his response:

Al *drery was his cheere* and *his lookyng,*

$$\text{(IV [E] 513)}$$

... *he caste adoun*
His eyen two ...

$$\text{(IV[E]668–9)}$$

---

11   The word 'thyng' is also applied by Griselda to herself in accepting her husband's order (IV [E] 504). And yet it is very effective here, suggesting the dryness or inhumanity of power itself demonstrated in Walter's selfishness, and clearly illustrating Chaucer's distinctive artistry. Cf. *The Shipman's Tale* (VII [B2] 217, 429).

The last reference to eyes is very interesting here, reminding us of the description of Theseus's eyes in *The Knight's Tale* (I [A] 1783, 2984). In general, it is said that human eyes are 'the window of the soul'; and so we should recognize the importance of the fact that Walter in *The Clerk's Tale* 'caste adoun / His eyen', and Theseus in *The Knight's Tale* 'gan looken up with eyen lighte'. But we must not lose sight of the difference between them; for in each case the 'eye' metaphor has a distinctive significance.[12] And Theseus's speech is the supreme manifestation of his understanding and his governance; on the other hand, Walter's speech characterizes a hiddenness that impairs its capacity to represent the human condition. As a result, Theseus's speech in *The Knight's Tale* provides a notable contrast to Walter's; in *The Clerk's Tale*, however, Walter's speech is implicitly contrasted with Griselda's speech.[13] Here, in *The Clerk's Tale*, Chaucer reminds his audience or readers that the kind of speech which Walter proposes is quite different from Theseus's speech in *The Knight's Tale*. We can thus see here the poet's artistic versatility.

Chaucer states the changeableness of the speech in *Troilus and Criseyde*, so it is better to take it up here:

> ... in forme of speche is chaunge
> Withinne a thousand yeer ...
>
> (*Troilus and Criseyde*, II. 24–5)

These are admirable, inscrutable, and universal words; because our speech is changeable, our behaviour is changeable, our body is changeable, our days are changeable, and power is changeable. In short, time will not abide with us; we cannot help but notice

12   David Wallace offers a helpful suggestion on 'eyes'. Perhaps Walter has seen, in Griselde's 'constance' a mystery that he cannot imagine. Cf. David Wallace. *Chaucerian Polity: Absolutist Lineages and Associational Forms in England and Italy* (Stanford, CA: Stanford University Press, 1997): 291–2.

13   The commons recognize that Griselde is concerned with the *commune profit*. But Walter informs Griselde that the commons have turned against her; cf. David Wallace. *Ibid.*, 290.

Ay fleeth the tyme; it nyl no man abyde. (IV[E] 119)

... ye se that *al this thyng hath ende*. (I [A] 3026)

These words might indeed be thought of as representing Chaucer's own philosophy.

5.4. Conclusion

When, therefore, Chaucer turns to the storytelling game he exposes different modes of speech to each other. His repeated return in *The Canterbury Tales* to issues of speech may suggest that he creates in the tale-telling game a fictive world in which to explore manifest conflicts. In particular, the contrast between the discursive world of *The Knight's Tale* and that of the fabliaux is only one example of the tendency of extremes to suggest each other, rather than to achieve resolution.

Chaucer's narratives, with their multiple characters and multiple points of view, have a tendency to aim at a distancing of the narrator's 'I' from the person of the poet. In respect of the relationship between first-person speaker and empirical poet, it is also important to remember that, with the advent of the Ricardian period, English narratives often presupposed a virtual conflation of speaker and poet. Presumably Chaucer has an artistic mind to distance voices that were conventionally conflated; particularly in *The Knight's Tale*, he plays with the distance between his empirical person and his textual *alter ego*.[14] In the end, Chaucer's sense of power was dramati-

---

14   In the fiction of the *Tales*, this is, of course, an exceedingly apt question, since the social identity of the tale-teller is so often important to the tale he or she supplies, and, indeed, the narrator is the only pilgrim whose social identity we do not know. If Chaucer were to answer the Host's question and supply this identity (e.g., 'I am Chaucer, clerk of the King's works') he would bring his empirical person fully into the poem. But Chaucer introduces this possibility only to sidestep it; cf. R.J. Meyer-Lee, *Ibid.*, 33.

cally timely, coming at a period in English history when severe and arbitrary restrictions were put on the spoken word in the city as well as in the court. Chaucer's development of frame narration in *The Canterbury Tales* thus suggests an immediate and virtually limitless possibility for study.[15]

5.5. References

5.5.1 Primary sources

Chaucer, Geoffrey. *The Riverside Chaucer*, ed. L.D. Benson. 3rd edn, with a New Foreword by Christopher Cannon. Oxford: Oxford University Press, 2008.

5.5.2. Secondary sources

Allen, J.B. and T.A. Moritz. *A Distinction of Stories: The Medieval Unity of Chaucer's Fair Chain of Narratives for Canterbury*. Athens, OH: Ohio State University Press, 1981.
Boitani, Piero and Jill Mann, eds. *The Cambridge Companion to Chaucer*. Cambridge: Cambridge University Press, 1987.
Brewer, D.S. *Chaucer: The Poet as Storyteller*. London: Macmillan, 1984.
Britnell, R.H. *The Commercialisation of English Society, 1000–1500*, 2nd edn. Cambridge: Cambridge University Press, 1996.
Carruthers, Leo, ed. *Heroes and Heroines in Medieval English Literature*. Cambridge: D.S. Brewer, 1976.
Cigman, Gloria. 'The Medieval Self As Anti-Hero', in Leo Carruthers, ed.: 164ff.
David, Alfred. *The Strumpet Muse*. Bloomington, IN: Indiana University Press, 1976.
d'Entrèves, A.P. *Dante as a Political Thinker*. Oxford: Clarendon Press, 1952.

---

15 According to Gloria Cigman, Chaucer has no great interest in heroics of any kind; the experiences undergone by Constance and Griselda are narrated as reportage rather than fiction. Cf. 'The Medieval Self As Anti-Hero', in Leo Carruthers, (ed.), *Heroes and Heroines in Medieval English Literature* (Cambridge: D.S. Brewer, 1994): 164.

Ellis, Steve, ed. *Chaucer: The Canterbury Tales*. London: Longman, 1998.

—— *Chaucer: An Oxford Guide*. Oxford: Oxford University Press, 2005.

Frost, William. 'An Interpretation of Chaucer's *Knight's Tale*', *Review of English Studies* 25 (1949): 289–304.

Ganim, John. 'Chaucer and the Noise of the People', *Exemplaria* 2 (1990): 71–88.

Hill, T.E. '*She, This in Blak*': *Vision, Truth, and Will in Geoffrey Chaucer's Troilus and Criseyde*. London: Routledge, 2006.

Jost, J.E., ed. *Chaucer's Humor*. New York: Garland, 1994.

Justman, Stewart. 'Medieval Monism and Abuse of Authority', *Chaucer Review* 11 (1976): 95–111.

Kellogg, A.L. 'The Evolution of *The Clerk's Tale*: A Study in Connotation', in *Chaucer, Langland, Arthur: Essays in Middle English Literature*. New Brunswick, NJ: Rutgers University Press, 1972: 276–329.

Kiser, Lisa J. *Truth and Textuality in Chaucer's Poetry*. Lebanon: University Press of New England, 1991.

Meyer-Lee, Robert. J. *Poets and Power from Chaucer to Wyatt*. Cambridge: Cambridge University Press, 2007.

Muscatine, Charles. *Chaucer and French Tradition*. Berkeley, CA: University of California Press, 1957.

Olson, Paul A. *The Canterbury Tales and the Good Society*. Princeton, NJ: Princeton University Press, 1986.

Rudd, Gillian. *The Complete Critical Guide to Geoffrey Chaucer*. London: Routledge, 2001.

Strohm, Paul. *Social Chaucer*. Cambridge, MA: Harvard University Press, 1989.

——, *England's Empty Throne: Usurpation and the Language of Legitimation, 1399–1422*. New Haven, CT: Yale University Press, 1998.

Wallace, David. *Chaucerian Polity: Absolutist Lineages and Associational Forms in England and Italy*. Stanford, CA: Stanford University Press, 1997.

YOSHIYUKI NAKAO

6 Textual Variations in *Troilus and Criseyde* and the Rise of Ambiguity

6.0. Introduction

The aim of this paper is to focus on some of the textual variations in *Troilus and Criseyde* and describe how they are likely to cause significant ambiguities. My discussion is threefold. First, I will propose a framework to describe ambiguities in Chaucer's language in general. Second, I will show the textual status of *Troilus and Criseyde* with regard to its language diversity in late fourteenth-century London, manuscript production, early and modern editions and varieties of readers. Third, I will deal with some of the textual variations in terms of ambiguity. My primary concern here is with those passages descriptive of Criseyde's shifting affections.

6.1. The Rise of Ambiguity: The Double Prism Structure

I will describe the double prism structure as a means of explaining how and why ambiguity is likely to occur. Empson's (1930) description of ambiguity is dependent on types of contexts, but this cannot easily be applied here because these contexts are not easily classified. My description is expression-orientated in that it operates according to the way in which these expressions can be observed and described, whether separately or in combination. Each variety of expression, whether it is a word or phrase, or the text as a whole, constitutes a layer of its own semantic production. In describing ambiguous expressions, I have given 'addresser' and 'addressee' more than 'accessory' importance (cf. Jakobson 1960: 353). This framework is diagrammed in Figure 6–1.

A represents a particular phenomenon which the writer, the first prism, observes; *B* represents his ways of cognizing *A*; *C* represents the expression which the first prism produces to represent *A*; *D* represents the second prism, the reader's way of reconstructing *B* through *C*; and finally *E* represents the reader's interpretation. If the second prism is controlled by *C* sufficiently to make clear the first prism's cognition and leads to only one reading, ambiguity is likely to be reduced. On the other hand, if the second prism is triggered by *C* to question the first prism's cognition, and to have, or fluctuate between, two or more readings, ambiguity is likely to be produced. The reason I use 'prism' here is that, whether phenomenon or expression, when it passes through the observers' eyes, it does not necessarily produce a straight line, but a refracted line or even a diffused reflection in accordance with their perceptions. I am using 'prism' as a metaphor for representing multiple 'refractions' in interpretations.

Note to Figure 6–1

1   The broken lines indicate that the second prism, the reader, cannot easily determine one stance or value. A phenomenon is susceptible to multivalence when allowing for different views of a single prism or between the two prisms. How the first prism, the writer, views the phenomenon is not always textually explicit but only suggestive, which calls for the reader's inference. An expression can semantically be easily determined but involved in complex pragmatic contexts; it may be open to varying interpretations. Furthermore, the real state of Chaucer's language, only existent through scribes, is open to discussion. On the other hand, I used solid lines for the reader's stance and his interpretation because the communicative value of the expression is finally realized by them and because the extent of their realization can be described, although his justification for them may depend on his assumption or inference.

2   Two broken lines in *B* and three solid lines in *D* indicate that they are not necessarily the same.

3   *E* assumes two cases: interpretation divided 'within one reader' and 'between readers.'

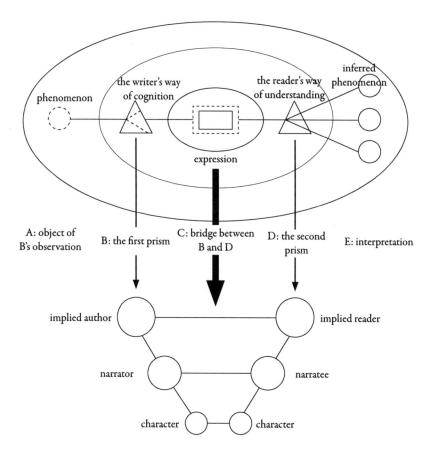

Figure 6–1 The double prism structure. From Yoshiyuki Nakao, *Chaucer no aimaisei no kozo* (*The Structure of Chaucer's Ambiguity*). Tokyo: Shohakusha, 2004. Reprinted with permission.

The factors *A* to *E* are equally important to the rise of Chaucer's ambiguity. Since we have no Ur-texts of Chaucer, there are uncertainties about what phenomenon he observed *(A)*, how he cognized it *(B)*, and how he expressed it *(C)*. Because of this, the reader's participation in the production of the text in question, i.e., his mode of cognition *(D)* and his interpretation *(E)* become all the more important.

A to *E* are thus fundamental factors involved in the rise of ambiguity. But the order of their application is not straightforward. Assuming the reader *D*'s response, the author may cognize the phenomenon *A* in such a way *B*. Through the expression *C*, the reader may assume the phenomenon *A* and the author's way of cognition of it *B*, and progress to his interpretation *E*. We cannot say to what extent Chaucer was conscious of the double prism structure. The first prism may be at one time strongly conscious of it, as shown in Chaucer's deliberate use of wordplay (*paronomasia*), and at others only weakly conscious of it, as when he is involved in the object of his observation so much so that he cannot censure it. The second prism is encouraged to assume the author's way of cognition in one way or another and progress to his interpretation. When the second prism's assumption of it varies, it is inevitable that ambiguities arise. Whichever type of ambiguity we may encounter, we can position it in the double prism structure and describe it with supporting evidence. The rise of ambiguity is thus explained by the double prism structure.

We have three more things to make clear regarding the diagram in Figure 6–1. First let us consider the contexts surrounding the constituent factors *A* to *E* of the double prism structure. For the tripartite division of these contexts my most immediate source is Su (1994: 67). His basis is the functionalist view of language, which covers pragmatic as well as linguistic meanings. The three circles from the inner through the intermediate to the outer are correspondent respectively to the metafunction (textual, interpersonal, ideational), the context of situation (field, participants, mode), and the context of culture (See Malinowski, in Ogden and Richards 1960: 296–336, and Halliday, 2004).

The inner circle *(C)* indicates, according to Su, the 'most immediate context, which includes the surrounding linguistic environment (from phrase and sentence to the entire poem as a linguistic construct), and the subject matter or topic of the text.' The intermediate circle indicates the 'immediate context of act of communication, which includes situational factors such as, among others, author–reader *(B/D)* relationship, and physical and social milieu.' In this paper the 'mode' of language is treated with the same degree of importance as 'field' and 'participants'. The 'mode' is concerned with how the textual transmission between the addresser and the addressee is made (spoken or written). The outer circle indicates the 'least immediate context', which includes circumstances of authorship, culture and tradition.' The phenomenon *(A)* in my framework can be traced from the words used to represent it, through the context of situation, further back to the context of culture. The courtly love and the heroine's betrayal of Troilus in *Troilus and Criseyde*, for instance, are adaptations from the traditional Trojan legend.

Second, in describing Chaucer's ambiguity I have taken into account not only the semantics but also the pragmatics of his language. Therefore my treatment of it is not based on the 'code model', but the 'inferential model' of communication, according to Sperber and Wilson (1999). In this perspective, what the first prism *(B)* intends to say is not delivered directly to the second prism *(D)*, but only indirectly.[1] This inferential model seems to suit Chaucerian discourse. His authorial voice is only perceivable through language, but the language is not necessarily his, but that of the scribes. The two prisms are often found in tension. The second prism (the reader) may challenge the first prism (the author) in that he is sensitive to what the first prism may not have been fully conscious about and even rewrites the expression *C*, as seen in the scribes' emendations.

[1]   Tadao Ito (1993) proposed the mechanism of literary ambiguity with regard to 'the processes of expression', focusing on the following processes: phenomenon to be observed→the speaker's view of it→the expression. And he holds, as regards the view of the phenomenon, that the sender and the receiver do not have the same basic perception. In other words, unlike the ideal speaker-hearer model, the interaction model assumes that the sender and the receiver have the same importance ('Varieties of Ambiguity in Medieval English Romances', the Ninth Congress of the Japan Society for Medieval English Studies, 1993 at Keio University). The double prism structure I propose here is based on this position of Ito's. This model is a basic framework to describe Chaucer's ambiguity in Nakao (2004). For further information, see Halliday's (2004) functional view of language (the interaction between ideational, interpersonal and textual components), Sperber and Wilson's (1999) explanation of the 'inferential model' and Su's (1994: 67) pragmatic as well as semantic description of poetic discourse (the basic 'Author(A)-Text(T)-Reader (R) form of written communication).

Third, the interaction between the two prisms B and D is only observable through the triply layered author–reader relationship in C, as shown in the latter half of the figure in Figure 6–1: character to character at the bottom, then narrator (in Chaucer's case the first-person narrator, whether reliable or unreliable) to narratee (the audience assumed to follow the narrator at one stage or another in the story through his inference) in the middle, and at the top the implied author (the author assumed to govern the whole text) and the implied reader (the reader assumed to ideally read the text). In reading the text, we are provided with an insight or at least a hint from a character or the narrator to see into the writer's perspective. There do occur uncertainties in the text as to who utters a speech, the narrator or a character, as in 'Free Indirect Speech' (see Leech and Short, 1981, and Fludernik, 1993). Those ambiguities are only perceivable and describable with our assumption of the different points of view. What is important here is to be sensitive to these different points of view and move between them, to progress to the interpretation E.

Theoretically, there is a difference in perspective between the 'writer' and the 'implied author', although they can be collapsed together. But here, in order to make the discussion simple, I use 'author' as a blanket term for both, except when I need to distinguish between them. The same principle is applied to the 'reader' and the 'implied reader'. The 'reader' includes such readers as the medieval audience, the scribes, modern editors and critics, the implied reader, and the view-shifting reader 'I', understood as an integrator of readings.[2] When describing ambiguities, I will specify these different kinds of readers.

---

2   I use 'the view-shifting reader "I"' to signify a reader who, standing at a vantage-point, can shift his views with ease (at one time identify himself with a character and at another with the narrator).

6.2. Textual Variations and the Rise of Ambiguity

6.2.1. *The double prism structure and metatext*

Chaucer's own manuscripts have never been discovered. We therefore have access to his writings only through the extant scribal manuscripts and modern editions. In this study I have used Benson (1987), currently the standard edition, in which the text of the *Troilus* is edited by Stephen Barney. Barney's *Troilus and Criseyde* is based on the Corpus Christi Cambridge manuscript (Cp), which is regarded as closest to Chaucer's original. However, since this is not that original itself, the reader needs to regard it with some scepticism, i.e. treat it as a metatext and actively participate in the reconstruction of the original.

We will pay particular attention to the reader in the double prism structure and investigate his inferences and choice of textual elements (words/ grammatical structures, including editors' punctuation/word order, etc.). Ambiguity is likely to arise when the reader cannot concentrate on one interpretation. Here among various readers involved in the evaluation of the text, we have highlighted those scribes engaged in its production, regarding them as the closest to Chaucer's editors, who are most concerned with textual problems when trying to identify the best text. Although readers of Chaucer's original or of the manuscript copies of his texts, they would perhaps have had the most challenging attitude to the text, even taking the role of the first prism (the poet) in that they could influence his texts by rewriting them. Before examining metatextual ambiguity, I shall discuss briefly the state of the language in Chaucer's times, the production of his manuscripts and the nature of his readers.

6.3. Linguistic Diversity in London and between the Scribes

The English of the fourteenth and fifteenth centuries in which the manuscripts of *Troilus and Criseyde* were copied was unstable and exposed to
a great deal of change on many levels. There was the blurring of the pronunciation of final *-e*, the variation of word forms, syntactic fluidity, the
enlargement of vocabulary, semantic diversification due to the coexistence
of synonymous words, dialectal mixture and other factors. Chaucer, as is
well known, was aware of this linguistic mutability:

> And for ther is so gret diversite
> In Englissh and in writyng of oure tonge,
> So prey I God that non myswrite the,
> Ne the mysmetre for defaute of tonge;
> And red wherso thow be, or elles songe,
> That thow be understonde, God I biseche![3]

At the end of *Troilus and Criseyde*, Chaucer expresses apprehension that
his language will not be copied properly. When copying it in this situation
of linguistic diversity, what problems did the scribes of the fourteenth and
fifteenth centuries face? How did they respond to the diversities of the English of this time? To what extent were the variations between them due to
arbitrary errors such as careless mistakes, dialectal variants and unnatural
syntax? Or from an 'integrated' point of view, are they no mere mistakes
but suggestive of ambiguities underlying the text? If there are two cases like
these, how can we distinguish between them? Taking into consideration
the apparently liberal, not to say slipshod attitude of scribes and editors
toward the text, I will attempt to make clear the process whereby ambiguity is likely to arise.

---

3   *Troilus and Criseyde* (hereafter *Tr*) 5.1793–8, ed. Stephen Barney, in Benson (1987).

6.3.1. Production of the manuscripts of Chaucer's texts[4]

In medieval times texts were produced by scribes copying the writer's original.[5] Chaucer's texts remain only as scribal manuscript copies.[6] There are no extant original texts by him. While scribes copied the original faithfully, they rewrote it according to their intention, or made a self-assertion (editing) through their dialectal or literary filtering (Brown 2000: 432). The great dismay experienced by Chaucer when checking manuscripts of his works is revealed in his short poem *Chaucers Wordes unto Adam, his Owene Scriveyn*:

> Adam scriveyn, if ever it thee bifalle
> Boece or Troylus for to wryten newe,
> Under thy long lokkes thou most have the scalle,
> But after my makyng thow wryte more trewe;
> So ofte adaye I mot thy werk renewe,
> It to correcte and eke to rubbe and scrape,
> And al is thorugh thy negligence and rape.

There was little editorial supervision of the manuscript production of Chaucer's secular works and little attention was paid to copyright or proofreading. The case is very different with religious works, where the *sententia*

---

4 Sections 6.3.1 to 6.3.4 are basically reproduced from Yoshiyuki Nakao, 'Towards a Parallel Text Edition of Chaucer's *Troilus and Criseyde*: A Study of Book 1.1– 28', *Universals and Variation in Language* 1 (Tokyo: The Center for Research on Language and Culture, Institute for Development of Social Intelligence, Senshu University, 2006): 89–92, to clarify the scribal and editorial backgrounds of *Troilus and Criseyde*.

5 '... because a MS. is a copy, and perhaps a copy of a copy ... of a copy, it has been taken to represent not the language of some one scribe or of some one place, but a conglomeration of the individual usages of all those scribes whose copies of the text stand between this present MS. and the original'. Michael Benskin and Margaret Laing, 'Translations and *Mischsprachen* in Middle English Manuscripts', in M. Benskin and M.L. Samuels (eds.), *So meny people Longages and Tonges: Philological Essays in Scots Medieval English Presented to Angus McIntosh* (MEDP: Edinburgh, 1981): 55.

6 There is an argument that *Equatorie of the Planets* is Chaucer's holograph, but this has not been substantiated.

of the text was checked by a supervisor. Although *Troilus and Criseyde* and Gower's *Confessio Amantis* are both secular works, the Gower text was, by contrast, copied under the strict control of a supervisor.[7] In Chaucer's case, it is absolutely necessary to be free from one edited text and observe it from a multi-textual point of view.

6.3.2. The sixteen manuscripts of Troilus and Criseyde (See Appendix)

There are two ways of understanding the manuscripts of *Troilus and Criseyde*. One is that variant manuscripts are due to Chaucer's revision. The other is that there is only one original and the variants are due to scribes. Root (1952) is closest to the former, and there he assumes Chaucer's revision in the order of what he calls the α, γ and β manuscripts, with β as the final one. His understanding of the stemma of *Troilus and Criseyde* is shown in Figure 6–2. Accordingly, Root assumes that the sixteen manuscripts were derived from the three exemplars set up ideally in Chaucer's revision stage. His edited text is based on the intermediate γ (Cp) and the final β (J).

On the other hand, Windeatt (1990) is closer to the third view and is critical of Root's linear and temporally distinct conception of Chaucer's revision, thinking that Chaucer wrote the text with every possible variation in mind. He assumes that Chaucer's revision, if any, was restricted to a short period and therefore cannot have been on a scale to warrant being called 'revision.'

---

7   Derek Pearsall, 'The Gower Tradition' in A.J. Minnis (ed.), *Gower's Confessio Amantis* (Cambridge: D.S. Brewer, 1983): 183. Copy after copy varies in only minute details – in contrast with the texts of Chaucer and Langland, often being copied by the same class of professional scribes. It may be that scribes were influenced by the presence of Latin, which tended to stabilize the English text with which it was associated, or it may be too that the shorter verse-lines, with their regularity of metre, were more readily held in mind as scribes copied line by line. There may have also been an effect on them because of the sense that they were dealing with a completely finished product. Gower's careful supervision of early production was important here: the poor quality of the majority of *Canterbury Tales* manuscripts shows by contrast the consequences of the absence of such supervision.

From the fact that there is found a mixture of the α, γ and β variants in one manuscript, Windeatt is sceptical of the assertion that Chaucer revised the text at distinctly different stages. He regards the γ (Cp) as the complete text and makes it the basic text in his edition, and the final β (J) as the scribes' revision. Instead of Root's sequential α/γ/β, he adopts Phetc/Cpetc/ Retc, respectively, on the basis of the unmixed types (Ph/Cp/R) of manuscripts. (For detailed information as to how these manuscript traditions emerge in the mixed-type manuscripts, see Windeatt 1990: 68–75). The textual transmission of the *Troilus* is so complex that Hanna (1996: 129) is moved to say that 'To cope with this particularly fluid context, I would suggest taking seriously the rhetorical ploys I have built into my argument – that approaches such as game theory may approximate the situation of much vernacular book production more fully than more sober notions.'

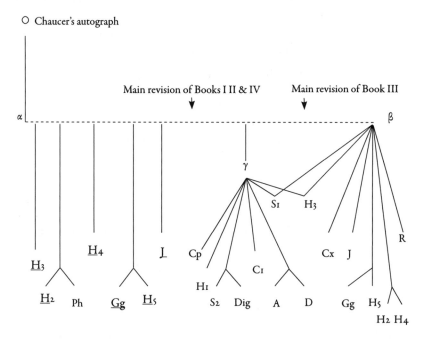

Figure 6–2 The stemma of *Troilus and Criseyde*. From R.K. Root, *The Textual Tradition of Chaucer's Troilus* (London: Kegan Paul, Trench, Trübner & Co., Ltd, 1916), p. 272.

Note to Figure 6–2

See R.K. Root, *The Textual Tradition of Chaucer's Troilus* (London: Kegan Paul, Trench, Trübner & Co., Ltd, 1916): 272. The broken line, α ... β, represents a single manuscript, Chaucer's own copy of the poem, progressively corrected and revised, until its text, originally α, becomes β. In the case of manuscripts of composite character, the α portion of the manuscript is represented by underscoring the designation.

6.3.3. Modern editions of Troilus and Criseyde

Other types of reader or modern editor show their way of reading the text in their editions. Scribes produced manuscripts based on the exemplars they had to hand without sufficient collation of variants. Editors, on the other hand, produce editions by collating variants and attempting to reconstruct the text to accord as closely as possible with Chaucer's original. They provide grammatical punctuation marks in their texts of a type that the scribes by and large did not use. Such punctuation as is used by the scribes is elocutionary in function, rather than grammatical. Modern editors give detailed annotations. Those of scribes, such as they are, are fragmentary marginalia. While the scribes assumed a particular type of reader, such as the projected owner of the manuscript, modern editors assume a wide readership. Moreover, it goes without saying that modern editors cannot be as sensitive to the connotations of idiomatic expressions as contemporary scribes.

There is not so much diversity in modern editions as in the manuscripts. For example, Windeatt (1990) uses the γ (Cp) tradition, except when he has serious textual problems, and Barney (1987), the received text we use here, consults Cp, Cl, and J, in that order of preference.[8]

---

8   The manuscripts modern editions are based on are as follows:
    Pollard (1898): based on J, and corrected throughout from readings of α and β types alone.

6.3.4. Kinds of readers

I have so far dealt with scribes and editors, but there were and are other kinds of readers. They are various, as shown below.

a. The writer: the writer as a reader (the writer sees himself objectively and self-critically)
b. The audience: the courtly audience who listened to Chaucer's narration directly from the author's mouth
c. The implied reader: the reader assumed to read the text ideally
d. Scribes: the bridge between the writer and the medieval readers
e. The owners of the manuscripts: the wealthy people inside and outside the court
f. Early editors: Caxton, Wynkyn de Worde, Thynne, etc.
g. Modern editors
h. The integrator of readings or the shifting apparatus of reading, 'I'

Skeat (1900): a close collation of Cl and Cp, taking Cl as the foundation, but correcting it by Cp, throughout.

Root (1926): In conjunction with Cp, it [J] has been used as a basic authority for the present edition.

Baugh (1963): basically that of MS Cp, with occasional readings of the Campsall and the St. John's College MSS.

Robinson (1957): Cp. β readings have been consistently rejected in this text, which is based throughout on the γ version.

Donaldson (1975): has adhered to Cp.

Warrington (1975): Not mentioned.

Howard (1976): Not mentioned.

Windeatt (1990): Cp (For the lacking parts of Cp, Cl is used) [*the J readings are also recognized (Nakao)*]

Barney, in Benson (1987): based on Cp. When Cp is rejected or deficient, this edition prints the readings of Cl or J, in that order.

Fisher (1989): Campsall with variants from Cp.

Shoaf (1989): based on Baugh.

In producing a text, the writer himself *(a)* may have seen his text with some distance and self-criticism, and modified it. Chaucer's modification is seen in his additions from Boethius' *De Consolatione Philosophiae* in *Troilus and Criseyde*, in the F/G versions of the Prologue to *The Legend of Good Women*, the order of *The Canterbury Tales*, etc. The primary (immediate) audience *(b)* who gave a direct response to Chaucer's narration included the king (Richard II), Queen Anne of Bohemia, the court officials, knights, courtly ladies, and writers (at the end of the *Troilus*, Chaucer dedicates it to the moralist Gower and the philosopher Strode). The secondary audience is much wider, including the middle class, and with the increasing production of manuscripts, perhaps some readers in a narrow sense who were able to read them, not an audience who just listened. This is evident from the following passage from *The House of Fame* (652–60):

> For when thy labour doon al ys,
> And hast mad alle thy rekenynges,
> In stede of reste and newe thynges
> Thou goost hom to thy hous anoon,
> And, also domb as any stoon,
> Thou sittest at another book
> Tyl fully daswed ys thy look;
> And lyvest thus as an heremyte,
> Although thyn abstynence ys lyte.[9]

Further, widening his conception of the readership, Chaucer may have taken into consideration those readers who could interpret the text as he himself did, including future readers *(c)*.

We have next scribes bridging the gap between the writer and the medieval readers who are confined to the fifteenth century *(d)*. They are the central readers here and they are the earliest critics of Chaucer's language and literature. Their rewritings include simple errors, paraphrases (changes that produce more limited and easier interpretations) and acts of

---

9   Cf. *Book of the Duchess* 49, *Parliament of Fowls* 15–25, *Tr* 5.1753, 5.1797, *Legend of Good Women* F 30.

creative self-assertion. Their editorial activity was also in accordance with the wishes of the owners of the manuscripts (*e*).[10]

Then we have early editors from the fifteenth century to the sixteenth century (*f*). The production of a large number of copies of the text different from that of manuscripts incurred a risk of inaccuracy brought about by economic considerations. The text was rewritten in accordance with the taste of the purchasers who wanted them. (They did not assume universal readers, although perhaps they took into account a few representative readers around them.) And insufficient collation of manuscripts was undertaken. We have then modern editors and critics (*g*). At this point we will deal with the modern editors' choice of words in conjunction with the variations in manuscripts. And finally, we have the integrator of readings, 'I' *(h)*.

6.3.5. Descriptions of textual ambiguities

As a phenomenon in the double prism structure described above, I have focused on the processes whereby Criseyde shifts her affections, or the extent to which that shift is positively or negatively described. How we should evaluate this phenomenon is not clear-cut, and the reader is called upon to participate in that interpretation. Criseyde is expected to accept her beloved gradually and with some prudence, because a courtly lady must exercise delay in accepting a lover and must not herself initiate the process. In medieval times, Christian morality and courtly idealism would

---

10   M.B. Parkes, Cp Ms. 'History', in M.B. Parkes and E. Salter, Introduction, *Troilus and Criseyde. Geoffrey Chaucer: A Facsimile of Corpus Christi College Cambridge MS 61* (Cambridge: D.S. Brewer, 1978): 11–12. 'The earliest identifiable person to have handled the manuscript is John Shirley (c. 1366–1456) of London, the literary entrepreneur, lender of books, and gossipy commentator on Chaucer's minor poems. ... Since the manuscript passed through the hands of John Shirley, the favorite candidate for the identification of the Anne Nevill referred to in the late-fifteenth-century note on fol. 101v is Anne, the daughter of Richard Beauchamp, Earl of Warwick, who was Shirley's chief patron.'

have forbidden explicit descriptions of physical love. In what follows, let us examine what words/phrases scribes or modern editors choose or reject, and how their interpretations differ.

6.3.6. Analysis of Troilus 2.636

> So lik a man of armes and a knyght
> He was to seen, fulfilled of heigh prowesse,
> For bothe he hadde a body and a myght
> To don that thing, as wel as hardynesse;
> And ek to seen hym in his gere hym dresse,
> So fressh, so yong, so weldy semed he,
> It was an heven upon hym for to see.
>
> (Tr 2.631–7)

In Book 1, Pandarus is told by Troilus about his love for Criseyde, and Pandarus promises to be a go-between for them. In Book 2, he visits Criseyde at her house, and tells her of Troilus's love for her. Immediately after this, Troilus makes a triumphal return to Troy and goes past her house. In the example below, the emphasis is on the shift in her affections and the effect the sight of him has on her. In seeing him in armour, she descries him as 'So fressh, so yong, so weldy ....' For *weldy* we have lexical variants as below.[11]

---

11   Materials I have used for the sources of variations between manuscripts: B.A. Windeatt (ed.), *Geoffrey Chaucer. Troilus & Criseyde: A new edition of 'The Book of Troilus'* (London: Longman, 1990), Wm. Michael Rossetti, *Chaucer's Troylus and Cryseyde* (from the Harl. MS. 3943) (London: Published for the Chaucer Society, 1873), F.J. Furnivall (ed.), *A Parallel Text Print of Chaucer's Troilus and Criseyde from the Campsall MS. of Mr. Bacon Frank, Copied for Henry V. When Prince of Wales, the Harleian MS. 2280 in the British Museum, and the Cambridge University Library MS. Gg.4.27* (London: The Chaucer Society, First Series, LXIII, LXIV, 1882), F.J. Furnivall and G.C. Macaulay (eds.), *Three More Parallel Texts of Chaucer's Troilus and Criseyde* (London: Published for the Chaucer Society. Kegan Paul, Trench, Trübner & Co. Limited, 1894–5), M.B. Parkes and E. Salter, Introduction, *Troilus and Criseyde Geoffrey Chaucer: A Facsimile of Corpus Christi College Cambridge MS*

Weldy]worþi Gg H3 H5 J R Cx W

While the α and γ manuscripts adopt *weldy*, the β manuscripts (Gg, H3, H5, J, R) read *worþy*. Further, the printed editions, Cx based on the β manuscripts and W based on Cx, adopt *worthy* (cf. Thynne: *weldy*). Eleven manuscripts have *weldy*, and five have *worþy*, a ratio of more than 2:1. We must assume that *weldy* was a strange word to scribes and likely to go through their filtering. We think this is why *weldy* is rewritten as *worþy*, signifying a typical attribute of a knight. Among modern editors, only Root adopts *worþy*, and this because he regards the β manuscripts as represent-ing Chaucer's final revisions.

It is clear that *weldy* is a relatively rare word.[12] This occurrence (*OED* s.v. *wieldy* 'capable of easily "wielding" one's body or limbs') and *unweldy* (*CT* IX (H) 55)[13] are the earliest citations in the *OED*. And while *weldy* appears once in Chaucer, *worþy* appears 184 times in his work (see Benson 1993). It should be noted that *unweldy* is used in the Hengwrt manuscript of *The Canterbury Tales*, the oldest and therefore probably closest to Chaucer's original (see Blake *et al.* 1994).

Further, there is an implication in *weldy* not mentioned by the *OED*. In the late fourteenth century the verb *weld* develops a sexual implication

---

61 (Cambridge: D.S. Brewer, 1978); M.B. Parkes and Richard Beadle, Introduction, *Poetical Works of Geoffrey Chaucer: a Facsimile of Cambridge University Library MS GG.4.27* (Cambridge: D.S. Brewer, 1980), Richard Beadle and J. Griffiths (eds.). *St. John's College, Cambridge, Manuscript L.1., A Variorum Edition of the Works of Geoffrey Chaucer* (Norman, OK: Pilgrim Books, 1983), microfilms from the libraries containing the *Troilus* manuscripts reproduced.

12 Examples from the *Canterbury Tales* of rare words being modified include: Thop VII 917 worly (Ch, El, Hg, Ph1)→worthy: Ad1, Bo1, Bo2, Cn, Dd, Ds, En1, En3, Ha3, Ha4, Ii, Ln2, Ma, N1, Ox, Ph2, Py, Se, To. MancP 55 unweldy (Hg, El)→vnwelde Ha4, La; vnweld Ld1; Ra2; vnweldly Ma; vn weldely G1; vnweli Ha3; vnwery Gg; wery En3 (Manly & Rickert 1940 (vol. 8): 147).

13 *OED* s.v. unwieldy: *1. Of persons, the body, etc.: Lacking strength; weak, impotent; feeble, infirm. 1386–1442. This word is quoted from MancP 55 as the earliest instance (it is found in the Hengwrt manuscript). It is natural to think that Chaucer knew the positive form *weldy*.

based on the original sense of 'wield one's limbs or weapons' (*OED* s.v. *wield*), with regard to which see Hanna's (1971) note on 'welde a womman' and Donaldson's comment (Donaldson 1979: 9). This sexual implication is present in the derived adjective *weldy*. Scribes rewriting the text and editors selecting from among their products give different images to the character of Troilus and that of Criseyde in her observation of him.

6.3.7. Analysis of Troilus 2.1274

> God woot if he sat on his hors aright,
> Or goodly was biseyn, that ilke day!
> God woot wher he was lik a manly knyght!
> What sholde I drecche, or telle of his aray?
> Criseyde, which that alle thise thynges say,
> To telle in short, hire liked al in-fere,
> His persoun, his aray, his look, his chere,
>
> His goodly manere, and his gentilesse,
> So wel that nevere, sith that she was born,
> Ne hadde she swych routh of his destresse;
> And how so she hath hard ben here-byforn,
> To God hope I, she hath now kaught a thorn,
> She shal nat pulle it out this nexte wyke.
> God sende mo swich thornes on to pike!
>   (*Tr* 2.1261–74)[14]

The context of the above is the following. In Book 2, Pandarus tries to persuade Criseyde to direct her love towards Troilus. On his second visit to her house, he consults Troilus and makes the following plan: Pandarus visits her house and will be in the process of persuading her to accept Troilus's love precisely when Troilus is passing her house on his triumphal return to

---

14   *OED*: s.v. *thorn* sb. 2. *fig.* (or in fig. context): Anything that causes pain, grief, or trouble; in various metaphors, similes and proverbial expressions, as a thorn in the flesh or side, a constant affliction c.1230. The example from *Tr* 3.1104 is quoted.

Troy, and she will naturally be captivated by his manly nature and appearance. The narrator observes this moment and comments upon it.

Mo is worthy of note here. What parts of speech belong with this word determine the reader's interpretation of its meaning: this is what determines the nature of the object of the verb *send*. While ten manuscripts have 'God sende mo swich thornes' as in the above, six manuscripts deviate as can be seen below.

> mo] *general people*: ȝow A Gg; mo folkes R
>   *specific person*: mo...on] hir m...o. D Sı Cx W; hir ... mo H5

Thus some authorities prefer a general interpretation, taking *mo* as 'yow' or 'mo folkes,' while others favour a specific interpretation, restricting the recipient to Criseyde with *mo* as 'more thorns.' The verb *send* is expected to take two objects (recipient and patient).

When faced with the potential ambiguities of linguistic expressions, scribes were likely to reduce them if they could do so with as little effort as possible. Applied to *mo*, this suggests that that word was in the original, and that they reduced its ambiguity with their minimum effort. R disregards the metrics of the line.

Mo is used as a noun and an adjective, both of which accord with Chaucer's usage. The *MED* quotes the above example as a noun, but there can only be one interpretation.

> *mo* n. 2. a) other persons: *CT* G 485, E 1039, D 663, *Tr* 1.613, *Tr* 2.1274.
> *mo* adj. 2. a) more in number, more numerous *Romaunt* 1834.

Editors also show embarrassment and confusion regarding *mo*, and determine its meaning each in their own way, as can be seen in the following.

> general people (*mo*=noun): Robinson, Windeatt, Howard, Benson (Barney) 'others'; Donaldson: me ('men')
> specific person (Criseyde) + 'more thorns' (*mo*= adjective): Benson (Barney), Skeat, Warrington, Shoaf; Donaldson: me ('me')

Barney is indecisive, taking *mo* as 'more' (adjective) primarily, and as 'people' (noun) secondarily. Robinson and Howard support the reading of 'people in general' but, differing from the scribes, are particular as to whom they refer. Robinson assumes that Pandarus is the speaker and in the pangs of love appeals to his beloved indirectly. Howard assumes that Chaucer plays the role of an enthusiastic supporter of love in general, putting forward the idea that it was right for courtly society of the late medieval period to accept love as part of *gentilesse*. At turning points in the story the narrator frequently draws the attention of the audience to this (1.22–9, 3.1222–5, 3.1324–37, 3.1373–93, 5.1835–41).[15]

In the case of a specific reading of *mo*, editors are obliged to paraphrase it. The normal reading is that Criseyde, who stands hesitantly on the threshold of a love affair, should be given more thorns of love. However, in a wider context where the audience has already been given information in Book 1 about Criseyde's coming betrayal of Troilus, the narrator might have suggested that more thorns should be sent to her.

Donaldson is bold enough to adopt the reading *me*, not found in any manuscript, unless it is a printing error in his edition. Moreover, since *e* and *o* are often difficult to distinguish in the scribal versions, it is possible that through a paleographical reconstruction of these two letters Donaldson has decided to understand *e*.[16] From the viewpoint of the collocation between *send* and its object pronoun, 'God send me ...' is repeated in Chaucer, but 'God send mo ...' is the only attested instance. *Me* is either a reduced form of *men* (not found in the Hengwrt manuscript of *The Canterbury Tales*) or the first-person pronoun. If we take *me* as the first-person pronoun, it is possible that the narrator, keeping some distance from love/lovers, is making a joke.[17]

---

15   Although we adopt the sense of 'people in general', the referent seems to be different according to the gender of the viewpoint adopted. From the male point of view, the wish is for women to experience more thorns of love. From the female point of view, we have a critical view of men's attitude to their love. This is because amongst the medieval nobility marriages based on pure love were scarce.

16   See the manuscript of St John's College, Cambridge for this.

17   The narrator parodies his poverty in the experience of love: 'For I, that God of Loves servantz serve, /Ne dar to Love, for myn *unliklynesse*, /Preyen for speed, al sholde I therfore sterve, /So fer am I from his help in derknesse' (*Tr* 1.15–18).

This is a unique example as regards the ambiguity of *mo*, and as far as the author, the first prism, is concerned, the ambiguity may be purely unintended. However, it induces the reader, the second prism, to adopt many points of view, and read into it several meanings.

6.3.8. *Analysis of Troilus 3.575–93*

> Nought list myn auctour fully to declare
> What that she thoughte whan he seyde so,
> That Troilus was out of towne yfare,
> As if he seyde therof soth or no;
> But that, withowten await, with hym to go,
> She graunted hym, sith he hire that bisoughte,
> And, as his nece, obeyed as hire oughte.
>
> But natheles, yet gan she hym biseche,
> Although with hym to gon it was no fere,
> For to ben war of goosissh poeples speche,
> That dremen thynges whiche as nevere were,
> And wel avyse hym whom he broughte there;
> And seyde hym, 'Em, syn I moste on yow triste,
> Loke al be wel, and do now as yow liste.'
>
> He swor hire yis, by stokkes and by stones,
> And by the goddes that in hevene dwelle,
> Or elles were hym levere, soule and bones,
> With Pluto kyng as depe ben in helle
> As Tantalus–what sholde I more telle?
>
> (*Tr* 3.575–93)

The context of the above is the following. In the epic time that elapses between the end of Book 2 and the beginning of Book 3, Troilus and Criseyde have their first meeting and he declares his love. In order to strengthen the relation between Troilus and Criseyde, Pandarus tries to make them meet at his house, then comes to her house and invites her to his house for supper. She hesitates to accept the invitation because she apprehends that if Troilus is there, it might bring about a scandal. However, she is strongly persuaded into accepting it.

First let us look at 3.579–80. The word order there is based on the Cp (γ) tradition, and is also that found in the α manuscripts. By contrast, the β manuscripts, H4, J, R, S1, as can be seen below, transpose 'withouten await' and 'she graunted.'

> But that she graunted with hym forto go
> Withoute awayt syn that he hir bisoughte

Along with the change of word order, *to* in line 3.579 is changed to *forto*, so as to accommodate the metre, and *that* now appears after *syn*. In this position it may either be interpreted as the pronoun object of *bisoughte* or as part of a compound causal conjunction *syn that*. Cx and W have the same word order as the β manuscripts.

Scribes tend to rewrite the original's poetic syntax into a prosaic and more predictable word order (Windeatt 1979: 136). They memorize and write one line after another line as they are read aloud. Lines of ten syllables are more subject to errors than those of eight, and *Troilus and Criseyde* is composed in ten-syllable rhyme royal stanzas. But here it should be noted that rewriting by the scribes extends over two lines, and this is deliberate on their part because the rhythm also has to be adjusted over two lines. Among modern editors, only Pollard and Root adopt this word order. Root uses the β manuscripts here as we saw in 3.6.

The position of the adverbial clause denoting manner 'withowten await' at the beginning of the line seems to make Criseyde's attitude towards Pandarus's invitation more vivid than the usual order.[18] This being the case, the narrator's claim that she acts only out of the sense of duty proper to a niece produces something of an anticlimax.[19] To accept the situation she is involved in by saying that her decision is inevitable is a pattern of behaviour repeated in the story. In accordance with the ideal of a courtly lady, she cannot enter into a potential scandal except under considerable pressure. If we were to remove this adverbial phrase from the beginning of the line

18   For details, see the relation between the word order and the information structure of for instance *Tr* 2.599 in Yoshiyuki Nakao, *Chaucer no aimaisei no kozo* (*The Structure of Chaucer's Ambiguity*) (Tokyo: Shohakusha, 2004).

19   For a similar example, see *Tr* 3.924.

and place it in its normal position, the subtleties of Criseyde's character might be reduced, but her honour would be preserved.

As regards the *await* in 'withowten await', this conversion of a verb to a noun is, according to the *OED*, the earliest in Chaucer. The scribes seem to have been baffled by this word and variation of the phrase is as below (see Windeatt 1990).

> that with-owten await] þerwith out H2 Ph; þat with owte more H5
> withowten] with H1; Without nayeng Cx.

The bolder rewriting is seen in H1, where the *out* in *withowten* is removed, thus producing the opposite meaning, so that Criseyde's prudence rather than her compliance is emphasized.

Next, let us look at the collocation between *most* and *trist on* (3.587). In Middle English, the first-person singular of the modal *most* has two basic forms: *must/e* and *most/e*. The Cp text has only the latter (incidentally the same is true of the Hengwrt manuscript of *CT*). Here it is formally impossible to distinguish between the superlative *most/e* and the auxiliary *most/e*. However, using the context we can distinguish them, perhaps with the sole exception of *Tr* 3.587, which is the odd man out.[20] As we have seen in the case of *mo*, the scribes attempted a minimal rewriting to obviate ambiguity. Windeatt (1990) notes the variants at 587 as follows:

> Most] moste CpD; mot GgH4 (mote); must H2H5Ph RCxTh

Here, six out of sixteen manuscripts clearly take *most/e* as a modal (as do the early printed books Cx and Th). These six are restricted to the α and β manuscripts, while the β (J) and the γ manuscripts (AClH1H3S1S2) are ambiguous.

---

20   Cf. 'Ye knowe ek how it is youre owen knyght,'
     And that *bi right ye moste upon hym triste*,
     And I al prest to fecche hym whan yow liste. *Tr* 3.915–17
     The scribal variants here are: *most* ADH1H3; *moste* ClCpS2; *muste* GgH4; *must*
     H2H5R; *missing* Dg. The word *moste* here can be reliably interpreted as a modal.

When we find *most/e* in the J and γ manuscripts, in which sense is it to be understood? When Criseyde leaves everything to Pandarus, does she do so because she 'trusts him most' or because 'she must trust him'? The editors cope with the difficulty as follows:

WINDEATT: perhaps 'must' rather than the adverb 'most', as some scribes thought.[21]
BENSON (BARNEY): 'must' is clearly preferable: Criseyde finds it useful to assert her dependency on her uncle.
ROBINSON: 'trust most'
BAUGH: adverb
ROOT: I take *triste* to be present indicative, and *most* the superlative; but it is possible that Chaucer wrote *moste* (pret. of *moot*) with infinitive *triste*. See variant readings.
DONALDSON: 'must'
SKEAT: *mot* (following Gg. 4. 27)
FISHER: 'must'
SHOAF: 'most'

The interpretations of the editors are divided into two groups.

modal: Windeatt, Benson (Barney), Donaldson, Skeat, Fisher
adverb: Robinson, Baugh, Root, Shoaf

Incidentally, modern translations are as follows:

COGHILL (1971): since I trust you best
STANLEY-WRENCH (1965): since I now trust most of all in you
TATLOCK & MACKAYE (1912): since I must trust you
WINDEATT (1998): since I must trust you
KARITA (1949): ichiban shinraishite imasu yueni [since I trust you most]
MIYATA (1979): itto goshinraishite rundesu mono [since I trust you most]

21   Windeatt (tr.), *Geoffrey Chaucer Troilus and Criseyde: A new translation by Barry Windeatt* (Oxford: Oxford University Press, 1998): 169. Windeatt translates *moste* in 'I moste on yow triste' (iii.587) as 'must' rather than the adverb 'moste', but notes that 'the construction in the original is – perhaps designedly – ambiguous.'

Tatlock and MacKaye and Windeatt support a modal and others the superlative of an adverb. Half the instances of *trist/trust* in *CT* [Hengwrt] and *Tr* (33 out of 66) collocate with adverbs (*wel*: 28/51; *most*: 5/15). Here in the overwhelming number of cases the word order verb-adverb prevails over adverb-verb. But with regard to the superlative *most/e* with various verbs such as *desireth, honouren, labouren, loue, entendeth, wynne, drede,* and *greueth,* the orders verb-adverb and adverb-verb compete with each other (see the note of Table 6–1 below). The collocation of *triste/trust* with adverbs or degree intensifiers is repeated, but the collocation of *triste/trust* with the modal *mot/most* is restricted to *Tr* 3.587 (an interpretation) and 3.916 among *The Canterbury Tales* and *Troilus and Criseyde* (it collocates with other modals (*wol/may/shal/wolde*) but very rarely). In terms of Chaucer's usage, the word to collocate with *triste/trust* is predictably an adverb.

[trust + adv]	trust–adv	adv–trust	*
CT: trust + wel	5	o	5/8
truste + wel	4	o	4/14
trusted + most	1	o	1/1
trusteth + wel	13	o	13/20
Tr:truste + wel	1	o	1/2
trusted + most	1	o	1/2
trustest + most	1	o	1/1
trusteth + wel	5	o	5/7
trist + most	1	1? (3.587)	2/11

Table 6–1 Order of verb-adverb/adverb-verb
*The number to the right of the oblique stroke '/' indicates the frequency of verbs and the number to the left indicates the frequency of the collocation between the adverb and the verb. For the word order of verb + *moost* (adv), we have consulted Blake, *et al.* (1994).
verb–*moost*: KnT 2767, WBT 895, WBT 932, WBT 959, SqT 444, ShT 172 *moost*–verb: KnT 2327, KnT 2409, KnT 2410, WBT 879, WBT 981, WBT 1088, FrT 1395, FranT 604. *Troilus and Criseyde* verb–*most*: 1.604, 1.720, 1.1019, 2.247, 2.1368, 2.1410, 4.561, 4.597, 4.1621, 5.592, 5.704, 5.1248 *most*–verb: 2.1150, 3.587, 3.1265, 5.1063, 5.1757.

In the courtly society of the fourteenth century, trust is an important virtue. When someone does someone good, the latter is often assumed to have an absolute trust in the former, as shown below.

> 'But for the love of God, I yow biseche,
> As ye ben he that I loue moost and triste,
> Lat be to me youre fremde manere speche,
> And sey to me, youre nece, what yow liste.'
> $(Tr\ 2.246-9)^{22}$

Taking into account the usual habit of courtly society, an adverbial reading is more natural. If her trust in Pandarus is imposed on her (the modal reading suggests this), the courtly relation between Criseyde and Pandarus will be weakened.

But with regard to the example of 3.587, the trustful relationship between Criseyde and Pandarus alone is not enough. A psychological reading rather than a social one is perhaps more appropriate for Criseyde in this situation. Judging from her question whether Troilus is at Pandarus's house (3.569), it seems to be her most earnest desire to see Troilus. However, because of the potential scandal, she cannot agree to Pandarus's invitation without some compelling reason to do so. Her obligation to trust Pandarus suggests her avoidance of taking responsibility. This is in accord with 'And, as his nece, obeyed as hire oughte' (3.581). Criseyde chooses to act thus and so leave responsibility to Pandarus. The modal use here is unnatural, but more appropriate for representing her psychology. (For a fuller discussion of this *most* from a philological point of view, see Nakao 2006b; and cf. Chaucer's repeated use of *and* for Criseyde's choices (Pearsall 1986)).

Next, let us look at the main clause 3.588 following the *syn* clause. The following is an expanded full list of variants from Windeatt (1990).

> Cp   Loke al be wel and do now as ȝow liste
>   A (well), Cl (lyste), D (alle, wele, you), H3 (whel, doo, you, lust),
>   H5 (all, well, ye), S1 (all, list), S2 (Luke, all, wele, <u>and</u> list)

---

22   Similar examples are: *Tr* 2.239–45, 2.411–13, 3.366 (Troilus→Pandarus), *Confessio Amantis* 8.1293, 'trawthe' in *Sir Gawain and the Green Knight* 2348.

Gg   Loke al be wel <u>and</u> do riȝt as ȝow lest [<u>and</u>: abbreviation expanded]
H1   Look al be wel do now as ȝow liste
H2   Loke al be wele y do now as ye lyste
H4   Looke as be weel for I do as you list
      R(wel, y, yow, liste), Cx (wel, yow, lyste), W (Loke, all, well, lyste),
      Th (Loke, nowe, lyst)
J   Loke al be wel for I do þt yow liste
Ph   Loke al be wele y do now as ȝow liste

In Middle English idiom, *do*, when collocating with the impersonal construction *as yow liste*, tends to be imperative. In the Hengwrt manuscript, five *do*s out of six collocate with an imperative.[23] The constructions in A, Cl, Cp, D, H3, H5, S1, S2, Gg and H1 are the most predictable. By contrast, *do*s in H2, J, R H4 and Cx are used as a finite verb. The *y* in the sense of 'I' in the H2 is perhaps due to the confusion of *y* with the virgule (/) or the abbreviation of *and* (&).

Loke and *do* in Cp are imperative, and there Criseyde leaves the responsibility for events to Pandarus. On the other hand, the latter half of the β line is 'for I do ...', which suggests responsibility for her action. This part of the quoted passage is uttered by Criseyde; and given what we know of Criseyde's moral and ethical make-up, the γ readings would seem to reflect Chaucer's intention most faithfully.

In answer to her request quoted above, Pandarus asserts that he will do it. Scribes rewrite his assertion (3.589), according to Windeatt (1990), in the following way:

ȝes] Cp; this GgH5JRTh; DH2H4Ph *om*; rest ȝis.

23   For the collocation between the imperative form of the verb and 'as yow liste,' we refer to Norman Blake *et al.* (eds.), *A New Concordance to 'The Canterbury Tales' Based on Blake's Text Edited from the Hengwrt Manuscript* (Okayama: University Education Press, 1994). Now *demeth as yow list*, ye that kan, KnT I (A) 1355. *Dooth as yow list*: I am here at youre wille. WBT III (D) 1016. Right *as yow list* gouerneth this matere. ClT V (E) 322. Ye ben oure lord: *dooth with your owene thyng Right as yow list*. Axeth no reed of me. ClT V (E) 652–3. *Dooth as yow list*; haue youre biheste in mynde FranT V (F) 627.

However, even though we have determined the words from the manuscripts, to what he said 'yes' or 'this' still remains uncertain.[24] Here neither scribes nor editors can manifest their readings; and what 'yes' or 'this' refers to depends on the second prism, the reader.

6.3.9. Analysis of Troilus 5.1240–1

> So on a day he leyde hym doun to slepe,
> And so byfel that yn his slep hym thoughte
> That in a forest faste he welk to wepe
> For love of here that hym these peynes wroughte;
> And up and doun as he the forest soughte,
> He mette he saugh a bor with tuskes grete,
> That slepte ayeyn the bryghte sonnes hete.
>
> And by this bor, faste in his armes folde,
> Lay, kyssyng ay, his lady bryght, Criseyde.
> For sorwe of which, whan he it gan byholde,
> And for despit, out of his slep he breyde,
> And loude he cride on Pandarus, and seyde:
> 'O Pandarus, now know I crop and roote.
> I n'am but ded; ther nys noon other bote'.
>
>   (*Tr* 5.1233–46)

The above depicts the famous scene where Troilus sees what he judges to be evidence of Criseyde's infidelity in a dream. Here (5.1240–1) we find an instance of the strong activation of the double prism structure. The subject of the double prism structure 'embracing' itself is social and collaborative, and psychologically even dynamic (shifting from negative attitude to positive or vice versa), bringing about ambiguities on the part of the reader as to who is the trigger of the action and who is the triggered. The fact that the above quotation is the narrator's reconstruction of Troilus's dream makes this problem further confusing. We are asked to infer how

---

24   See the note by B.A. Windeatt (ed.), *Geoffrey Chaucer Troilus & Criseyde: A new edition of 'The Book of Troilus'* (London: Longman, 1984; rev. paperback edn 1990): 281, citing A.C. Spearing.

the narrator grasps Troilus's dream, and then how Troilus himself feels in that dream. The first prism, the writer himself, seems to be involved in such a complexity that his linguistic control of it is likely to be loosened. If this is right, it would be no wonder that the reader is strongly encouraged to challenge the first prism based on his or her assumptions. Therefore the boundary between the two prisms is made imprecise.

Scribal and editorial variations are pointed out by Chickering (1990). Through the double prism structure, I have reinterpreted them with a focus on their psychological background. Scribes and modern editors are divided in the choice of words, as shown below.

> Manuscript variations of 5.1240
> *his*: AClH4; *hir*: D, Gg (*hyre*) H1R (*hyr*) S1S2Th (*her*); omission H2H3PhCx (CpDgH5 lack this line)
>
> Modern editorial variations of 5.1240
> *his*: Robinson, Barney (Benson), Skeat, Baugh, Warrington, Howard (note. The image is of Criseyde held by and kissing the boar); *hir/her*: Root, Donaldson, Fisher, Pollard

Pronouns may go beyond a sentence boundary to a discourse structure as regards the determination of their reference. They were often a cause of errors for scribes, who copied one line after another line of the original text. It often happens that those pronouns are modified after rereading (later scribes were also involved in their modification). However, the lines above are written by scribes without showing any traces of modification. They chose pronouns with confidence and were still divided in their choice. *His* refers to the boar, *her* to Criseyde, and the ellipsis of *his/her* suggests no concern with who is more active in the process of 'folding', or perhaps it is intended to suggest reciprocity of their action. Modern editors choose either *his* or *her*. No editors adopt ellipsis of pronouns.[25] They fulfill the

---

25   About the pronominal ellipsis of a similar construction, see 'hente/streyne/take/folde, etc .... in (zero pronoun) armes.' Regarding the scribal variation of the construction, we have consulted B.A. Windeatt (ed.), *Geoffrey Chaucer. Troilus & Criseyde: A new edition of 'The Book of Troilus'* (London: Longman, 1984; paperback edn 1990). And hym *in armes* took, and gan hym kisse. *Tr* 3.182

metrical demands of the line and then consider the problem of who is more active in the 'folding', the boar or Criseyde.

The act of 'folding' is characterized by reciprocity, and who initiates it cannot easily be determined. Therefore, which is original and which is scribes' revision is hard to determine. This applies to kissing. Scribes did not add grammatical punctuation to the lines. Editors restrict their readings by punctuation as regard to who kisses whom. The punctuation of 5.1241 is seen below.

> a.   Windeatt [his]; Donaldson/Fisher (her)
>   Lay kissing ay his lady bright, Criseyde
> b.   Baugh (his)
>   Lay, kissing ay his lady bright, Criseyde
> c.   Robinson/Benson (his); Root/Pollard (her)
>   Lay, kissing ay, his lady bright, Criseyde

From a structural point of view, we have a locative inversion here (By this bor ... lay ... Criseyde). Regarding a, there is no pause between *Lay* and *kissing*, and if we regard *his lady bright* as an inverted subject, the one initiating a kiss is construed as Criseyde. The comma after *his lady bright* indicates the appositive relation to Criseyde. This reading is syntactically supported. Since *the bor* is governed by the preposition *by*, it cannot conceivably be the subject of the 'kiss' verb. Incidentally, we find a caesura before *his lady bright* in the manuscripts H3 and H4, and the editions Cx and W. This suggests the impossibility of *his lady bright* as an object.

------

        armes] hire a. A
    He hire *in armes* faste to hym hente. *Tr* 3.1187
        armes faste to hym] hise a.t.h.f. H2 Ph
    This Troilus *in armes* gan hire streyne, *Tr* 3.1205
        Gg: þus Troylus in his armys streyne hire gan
    Therwith he gan hire faste *in armes* take, *Tr* 3.1359
        in]in his Ph
    Took hire *in armes* two, and kiste hire ofte, *Tr* 4.1219
        armes] his a. H2 Ph

Regarding b, we have a comma between *Lay* and *ay kissing his lady bright*, and there seems to be some distance between the collocation of *Lay* and the inverted subject *Criseyde*. There may be no difference between a and b about the agent of 'kissing.' Here, however, *kissyng his lady bright* is highlighted as a unity.

Regarding c, since there are commas both before and after *kissing ay*, the separation due to the participial construction is reinforced. The reciprocal action of the boar and Criseyde seems to be brought into relief (see Chickering 1990: 103).[26]

Whether Criseyde is active in 'folding'/'kissing' is classified as below.

    a. active in both folding and kissing
    b. active in folding, but passive in kissing
    c. passive in folding, but active in kissing
    d. passive in both folding and kissing

The reading making Criseyde the most active is adopted by Pollard/Donaldson (a), and c, the intermediate reading making her passive in 'folding' but active in 'kissing', is adopted by Robinson/Barney/Skeat/Howard. But b, the reading making her active in 'folding' but passive in 'kissing', is not adopted by any editors. Nor is d, the reading making her the most passive.

Let us now examine the psychology of the scribes and editors vis-à-vis a and c. In the case of a, Criseyde is active in the action of physical love, which suggests her conscious infidelity. This is a big departure from the ideal of a courtly lady and to that extent a radical reading. On the other hand, c, the intermediate reading, seems to correspond to Chaucer's original, *Il Filostrato*, as seen in the following.

---

26   A similar example is the degree of relatedness between the participial construction 'Retornyng ...' (*Tr* 5.1023) and its expected main clause.

E poi appresso gli parve vedere
Sotto a' suoi piè Criseida, alla quale
Col grifo il cor traeva, ed al parere
Di lui, Criseida di così gran male
Non si curava, ma quasi piacere
Prendea di ciò che facea l' animale,
Il che a lui sì forte era in dispetto,
Che questo ruppe il sonno deboletto.

(*Il Filostrato* 7.24.1–8)

(And then afterwards it seemed to him that he saw beneath its feet Cressida, whose heart it tore forth with its snout. And as it seemed, little cared Cressida for so great a hurt, but almost did she take pleasure in what the beast was doing. This gave him such a fit of rage that it broke off his uneasy slumber. [Translation from Griffin and Myrick, modified. (1978)])

If Chaucer has taken his lead from the original, this interpretation is natural.[27] And if Chaucer sees the boar's arm as reflecting that of Diomede (the dream is interpreted in this way by Cassandre later), it is natural for the bold and aggressive boar to be the one doing the 'folding.' Further, it is best to reveal Criseyde's 'slydynge' (*Tr* 5.825) character. In that way, the image of her being controlled by the boar/Diomede, and of her normal instincts being aroused, follows naturally, so that she herself gradually becomes active and kisses him back.

Incidentally, a reading whereby the boar is active both in 'folding' and 'kissing' (d) is one which is most sympathetic to Criseyde in that it is best calculated to preserve her honour as a courtly lady. This would have met with the approval of the sympathetic reader. However, because it is too idealistic, it ignores what she really is. In linguistic terms, the relation between

27 *MED* s.v. *bor* n.: 1. a) An uncastrated male swine (either wild or domestic) d) *breme as–*, fierce as a wild boar; *brust as a–*, bristly as a boar, bristling (or showing anger) like a boar; *wod as wild–*, raging like a wild boar. 3. A representation of a boar; *her.* a boar in a coat-of-arms. 4. a) Man likened to a wild boar; esp., King Arthur, Edward III.

the boar (subject) and 'kissyng ay his lady bright' is very weak.[28] Thus the readers' view of Criseyde determines their choice of pronouns/syntax, and their choice of pronouns/syntax informs their view of Criseyde.[29] Finally,

28 Modern translations of the quotation in question

Tatlock, J.S.P. and P. MacKaye, *The Modern Reader's Chaucer. The Complete Works of Geoffrey Chaucer Now First Put into Modern English* (London: The Macmillan Company, 1912):
As he roamed up and down through the forest, he dreamed he saw a boar with great tusks lying asleep in the heat of the bright sun, and by this boar, folding it fast in her arms and continually kissing it, lay his bright Criseyde.

Margaret Stanley-Wrench (tr.), *Troilus and Criseyde by Geoffrey Chaucer* (London: Centaur Press Ltd., 1965):
And by this boar's side, folded in its arm
Lay kissing it, Criseyde, his lady bright,

Coghill, Nevill (tr.), *Geoffrey Chaucer Troilus and Criseyde* (London: Penguin, 1971):
And close beside it, with her arms enfolding,
And ever kissing it, he saw Criseyde;

Windeatt, B.A. (tr.), *Geoffrey Chaucer Troilus and Criseyde: A new translation by Barry Windeatt* (Oxford: Oxford University Press, 1998):
And beside this boar, tightly clasped in his arms and continually kissing, lay his fair lady, Criseyde.

Karita, Motoshi (tr.). *Koi no toriko (Caught in Love)* (Tokyo: Shingetsusha, 1949):
shikamo inoshishino katawarani, sonoudenishikato dakare, kuchizukeshitsutsu jibunno kagayakashii joseino kuriseidega yokotawatteita. (By the boar, folded in its arms, lay kissing his bright lady Criseyde)

Miyata, Takeshi (tr.), *Turoirasu to Kuriseide (Troilus and Criseyde)* (Nishinomiya: Otemae Women's University Anglo-Norman Institute, 1979):
sobaniha sonoinoshishino udeni shikkaridakarenagara, utsukushii aijin kuriseidega yokotawatteite, shikirini seppun shiteirunodesu. (By the boar, folded in its arms, lay his beautiful lover Criseyde, ever kissing)

29 The double syntax regarding *folde* (pp) and *kissing* may be an instance of what Renaissance rhetoric calls amphibology. Amphibology in medieval times is generally regarded as a misuse of language, not an artifice of rhetoric. If we can say that the double syntax is positively used, Chaucer may have used it quite unconventionally in his times. Cf. G.D. Willcock and A. Walker, *The Arte of English Poesie by George Puttenham: 'Amphibologia or the Ambiguous'* (Cambridge: Cambridge University Press Library Edition, 1936): 260.

the scribes and modern editors of the second prism are differentiated in their interpretations, and thus ambiguity becomes inevitable.

6.4. Conclusion

Through the double prism structure, we have focused on a particular phenomenon – Criseyde's fluctuating affections, investigated how the first prism (the author) observed and expressed it, and considered how the scribes and modern editors representing the second prism responded to the expression of the first prism, and described how their rewriting or choice of expressive items led to differences in interpretation or ambiguity.

While scribes tried to copy Chaucer's original (or a copy of it) as faithfully as possible, they sometimes made simple mistakes that were hard to admit contextually. However, those parts I have dealt with are more or less generally agreed to be correct and cannot be said to be incorrect with certainty. The variants found there may be said to be due to differences

---

Then haue ye one other vicious ſpeach with which we will finiſh this Chapter, and is when we ſpeake or write doubtfully and that the ſence may be taken two wayes, ſuch ambiguous termes they call *Amphibologia*, we call it the *ambiguous*, or figure of ſence incertaine, as if one ſhould ſay *Thomas Taler* ſaw *William Tyler* dronke, it is indifferent to thinke either th'one or th'other dronke. Thus ſaid a gentlman in our vulgar pretily notwithſtanding becauſe he did it not ignorantly, but for the nonce.

I ſat by may Lady ſoundly ſleeping,
My miſtreſe lay by me bitterly weeping.

No man can tell by this, whether the miſtreſe or the man, ſlept or wept: ...

The word amphibology of *Troilus and Criseyde* 4.1406 is quoted as an earliest instance in *OED* 1 'ambiguous discourse.' I am indebted to the late professor David Burnley, who kindly commented on this construction which 'was criticised in medieval times by lawyers striving after unambiguous wording.'

of opinion on the part of the characters, the narrator, and the author in relation to Criseyde's fluctuating affections.

How far she was actively responsible is a disputed matter, and this led to scribal variations. Faced with rare words, word order influenced by the poetic medium and the psychological nature of the content, they revised them through a process of filtering. They tended to convert these potentially ambiguous expressions to semantically more general or more limited ones to suit their own viewpoints or those of the manuscripts' owners. However, in getting together the scribal variants, we have found that they are sensitive to the possibility of the ambiguous nature of the original text. Significantly enough, they are involved in the production of the *Troilus* text not only as a reader but as a (re)writer of Chaucer's original.

The scribal variation in manuscripts requires another second prism (the editors) to choose one variant or another in the process of textual reconstruction. They chose one and rejected another and also showed their way of reading through their punctuation. However, in the totality of reading the text, it was found that scribes and editors were limited in interpretation, where the view-shifting reader, 'I', was required to participate in it. When the text allows for multiple choices, every variant is and is not Chaucer's. Every variant is and is not a fact. Chaucer can be situated midway between a multiplicity of texts.

6.5. References

6.5.1 Primary sources

Baugh, A.C., ed. *Chaucer's Major Poetry.* Englewood, NJ: Prentice-Hall, 1963.
Benson, Larry D., ed. *The Riverside Chaucer:* 3rd edn, based on *The Works of Geoffrey Chaucer,* ed. F.N. Robinson. Boston, MA: Houghton Mifflin Company, 1987.
Beadle, Richard, and J. Griffiths, eds. *St. John's College, Cambridge, Manuscript L.1., A Variorum Edition of the Works of Geoffrey Chaucer.* Norman, OK: Pilgrim Books, 1983.

Blake, N.F., ed. *The Canterbury Tales Edited from the Hengwrt Manuscript*. London: Arnold, 1980.

Brewer, D. S,. and L.E. Brewer, eds. *Troilus and Criseyde (abridged) by Geoffrey Chaucer*. London: Routledge & Kegan Paul, 1969.

Davis, Norman, ed. *Sir Gawain and the Green Knight*. 2nd edn. Oxford: Clarendon Press, 1967.

Donaldson, E.T., ed. *Chaucer's Poetry: An Anthology for the Modern Reader*. New York: The Ronald Press Company, 1975.

Fisher, J.H., ed. *The Complete Poetry and Prose of Geoffrey Chaucer*. 2nd edn. New York: Holt, Rinehart and Winston, 1989.

Furnivall, F.J., ed. *A Parallel Text Print of Chaucer's Troilus and Criseyde from the Campsall MS. of Mr. Bacon Frank, Copied for Henry V. When Prince of Wales, the Harleian MS. 2280 in the British Museum, and the Cambridge University Library MS.Gg.4.27*. London: The Chaucer Society, First Series, LXIII, LXIV, 1882.

Furnivall, F.J., and G.C. Macaulay, eds. *Three More Parallel Texts of Chaucer's Troilus and Criseyde*. London: Published for the Chaucer Society. Kegan Paul, Trench, Trübner & Co. Limited, 1894–5.

Griffin, N.E., and A.B. Myrick, eds. and trs. *The Filostrato of Giovanni Boccaccio*. New York: Octagon Books, 1978.

Hanna, Ralph III, ed. *The Auntyrs off Arthure at the Terne Wathelyn*. Manchester: Manchester University Press, 1971.

Howard, D.R., ed. *Geoffrey Chaucer. Troilus and Criseyde and Selected Short Poems*. New York: New American Library, 1976.

Macaulay, G.C., ed. *The English Works of John Gower*. 2 vols, EETS ES. 81 and 82, 1900–1.

Manly, J.M. and E. Rickert, eds. *The Text of the Canterbury Tales: Studied on the Basis of All Known Manuscripts*. 8 vols. Chicago & London: The University of Chicago Press, 1940.

Parkes, M.B., and Richard Beadle. Introduction. *Poetical Works of Geoffrey Chaucer: a Facsimile of Cambridge University Library MS Gg.4.27*. Cambridge: D.S. Brewer, 1980.

Parkes, M.B., and E. Salter. Introduction. *Troilus and Criseyde Geoffrey Chaucer: A Facsimile of Corpus Christi College Cambridge MS 61*. Cambridge: D.S. Brewer, 1978.

Pollard, A.W., et al., eds. *The Works of Geoffrey Chaucer* (The Globe Edition). London: Macmillan, 1898.

Robinson, F.N., ed. *The Works of Geoffrey Chaucer*. London: Oxford University Press, 1957.

Root, R.K. *The Textual Tradition of Chaucer's Troilus*. Published for the Chaucer Society. London: Kegan Paul, Trench, Trübner & Co., 1916.

——.ed. *The Book of Troilus and Criseyde by Geoffrey Chaucer*. Princeton, NJ: Princeton University Press, 1952.

Rossetti, Wm. Michael, ed. *Chaucer's Troylus and Cryseyde* (from the Harl. MS. 3943). London: Published for the Chaucer Society, 1873.

Shoaf, R.A., ed. *Geoffrey Chaucer. Troilus and Criseyde*. East Lansing, MI: Colleagues Press, 1989.

Skeat, W.W., ed. *The Complete Works of Geoffrey Chaucer*. Vol II. *Boethius and Troilus*. 2nd edn. Oxford: Clarendon Press, 1900.

Warrington, J., ed. *Geoffrey Chaucer. Troilus and Criseyde*. London: J.M. Dent & Sons, 1975.

Windeatt, B.A., ed. *Geoffrey Chaucer. Troilus & Criseyde: A new edition of 'The Book of Troilus.'* London: Longman, 1984 (paperback edn 1990).

6.5.2. Secondary sources

Benskin, Michael, and Margaret Laing, 'Translations and *Mischsprachen* in Middle English Manuscripts,' in M. Benskin and M.L. Samuels, eds. *So meny people Longages and Tonges: Philological Essays in Scots Mediaeval English Presented to Angus McIntosh*. Edinburgh: Middle English Dialect Project, 1981: 55–106.

Benson, Larry D., ed. *A Glossarial Concordance to The Riverside Chaucer*. New York and London: Garland Publishing, 1993.

Blake, Norman, David Burnley, Masatsugu Matsuo and Yoshiyuki Nakao, eds. *A New Concordance to 'The Canterbury Tales' Based on Blake's Text Edited from the Hengwrt Manuscript*. Okayama: University Education Press, 1994.

Brown, Peter, ed. *A Companion to Chaucer*. Oxford: Blackwell, 2000.

Chickering, H. 'Unpunctuating Chaucer,' *The Chaucer Review*, 25.2 (1990): 97–109.

Coghill, Nevill, trans. *Geoffrey Chaucer. Troilus and Criseyde*. London: Penguin, 1971.

Davis, N., *et al.*, eds. *A Chaucer Glossary*. Oxford: Clarendon Press, 1979.

Donaldson, E.T. *Speaking of Chaucer*. London: Athlone Press, 1970.

Empson, W. *Seven Types of Ambiguity*. Harmondsworth: Penguin Books, 1930. 2nd edn 1947.

Fludernik, L.D. *The Fictions of Language and the Languages of Fiction: The Linguistic Representation of Speech and Consciousness*. London and New York: Routledge, 1993.

Godefroy, Frédéric, ed. *Lexique de L'Ancien Français*. Paris: Librairie Honoré Champion, 1965.

Halliday, M.A.K. *An Introduction to Functional Grammar*. London: Arnold, 2004.

Halliday, M.A.K. and R. Hasan, *Cohesion in English*. London: Longman, 1976.

Ito, Tadao. 'Varieties of Ambiguity in Medieval English Romances', the Ninth Congress of the Japan Society for Medieval English Studies, at Keio University, unpublished, 1993.

Jakobson, Roman. 'Closing Statement: Linguistics and Poetics', in T.A. Sebeok ed., *Style in Language*, 350–7. Cambridge, MA: The MIT Press, 1960.

Jimura, Akiyuki, Yoshiyuki Nakao and Masatsugu Matsuo, eds. *A Comprehensive List of Textual Comparison between Blake's and Robinson's Editions of* The Canterbury Tales. Okayama: University Education Press, 1995.

——. eds. *A Comprehensive Textual Comparison of* Troilus and Criseyde: *Benson's, Robinson's, Root's, and Windeatt's Editions*. Okayama: University Education Press, 1999.

——. eds. *A Comprehensive Collation of the Hengwrt and Ellesmere Manuscripts of The Canterbury Tales: General Prologue*. *The Hiroshima University Studies, Graduate School of Letters*, vol. 82, Special Issue, No. 3, 2002.

Karita, Motoshi, trans. *Koi no toriko (Caught in Love)*. Tokyo: Shingetsusha, 1949.

Kurath, H., S.M. Kuhn and R.E. Lewis, eds. *Middle English Dictionary*. Ann Arbor, MI: The University of Michigan Press, 1954–2001.

Leech, G. and M. Short. *Style in Fiction*. London: Longman, 1981.

Matsuo, Masatsugu, Yoshiyuki Nakao, Shigeki Suzuki and Takao Kuya, eds. *A PC-KWIC Concordance to the Works of Geoffrey Chaucer Based on Robinson (1957)*. Unpublished. 1986.

Miyata, Takeshi, trans. *Turoirasu to Kuriseide (Troilus and Criseyde*. Nishinomiya: Otemae Women's University Anglo-Norman Institute, 1979.

Nakao, Yoshiyuki. 'Chaucer no aimaisei no kozo: *Troilus and Criseyde* 3.12–15 "God loveth ..." wo chushin ni' (The Structure of Chaucer's Ambiguity: A Focus on *Troilus and Criseyde* 3.12–15 'God loveth ...'), Masahiko Kanno, ed. 'FUL OF HY SENTENCE' eigogoironshu (*FUL OF HY SENTENCE: Essays in English Lexical Studies*). Tokyo: Eihosha, 2003: 21–33.

——. *Chaucer no aimaisei no kozo (The Structure of Chaucer's Ambiguity)*. Tokyo: Shohakusha, 2004.

——. 'Towards a Parallel Text Edition of Chaucer's *Troilus and Criseyde*: A Study of Book 1.1–28', *Universals and Variation in Language*, vol. 1. Tokyo: Center for Research on Language and Culture, Institute for Development of Social Intelligence, Senshu University, 2006: 89–114.

——. 'The Interpretation of *Troilus and Criseyde* 3.587: "syn I moste on yow triste"', in Michiko Ogura, ed., *Textual and Contextual Studies in Medieval English: Towards the Reunion of Linguistics and Philology*. Frankfurt am Main: Peter Lang, 2006: 51–71.

Ogden, C.K., and I.A. Richards. *The Meaning of Meaning: A Study of the Influence of Language upon Thought and of the Science of Symbolism.* 10th edn. London: Routledge & Kegan Paul, 1960.

Oizumi, Akio, ed. *A Complete Concordance to the Works of Geoffrey Chaucer, Programmed by K. Miki.* Hildesheim: Olms-Weidmann, 1991.

Pearsall, Derek. 'The Gower Tradition,' in A.J. Minnis ed., *Gower's Confessio Amantis.* Cambridge: D.S. Brewer, 1983: 179–97.

——.'Criseyde's Choices,' *Studies in the Age of Chaucer: Proceedings*, No. 2 (1986): 17–29.

Root, R.K. *The Textual Tradition of Chaucer's Troilus.* London: Kegan Paul, Trench, Trübner & Co., Ltd., 1916.

Simpson, J.A., and E.S.C. Weiner, eds. *The Oxford English Dictionary.* 2nd edn. Oxford: Clarendon Press, 1989.

Sperber, D. and D. Wilson. *Relevance: Communication and Cognition.* Oxford: Basil Blackwell, 1986.

Stanley-Wrench, Margaret, trans. *Troilus and Criseyde by Geoffrey Chaucer.* London: Centaur Press Ltd., 1965.

Su, Soon Peng. *Lexical Ambiguity in Poetry.* London and New York: Longman, 1994.

Tatlock, John S.P. and Arthur G. Kennedy, eds. *A Concordance to the Complete Works of Geoffrey Chaucer.* Washington: The Carnegie Institution of Washington, 1927.

Tatlock, J.S.P., and P. MacKaye. *The Modern Reader's Chaucer. The Complete Works of Geoffrey Chaucer Now First Put into Modern English.* London: Macmillan, 1912.

Wetherbee, W. *Chaucer and the Poets: An Essay on Troilus and Criseyde.* Ithaca, NY and London: Cornell University Press, 1984.

Willcock, G.D., and A. Walker, eds. *The Arte of English Poesie by George Puttenham.* Cambridge: Cambridge University Press Library Edition, 1936.

Windeatt, B.A. 'The Scribes as Chaucer's Early Critics,' *Studies in the Age of Chaucer.* 1 (1979): 119–41.

——. trans. *Geoffrey Chaucer. Troilus and Criseyde: A new translation.* Oxford: Oxford University Press, 1998.

Appendix 6–1: The 16 manuscripts of *Troilus and Criseyde*

A   London, British Library, MS Additional 12044
Cl   The Campsall MS, now New York, Pierpont Morgan Library, MS M 817
Cp   Cambridge, Corpus Christi College, MS 61
D   University of Durham Library, MS Cosin V. II. 13
Dg   Oxford, Bodleian Library, MS Digby 181
Gg   Cambridge University Library, MS Gg.4.27
H1   London, British Library, MS Harley 2280
H2   London, British Library, MS Harley 3943
H3   London, British Library, MS Harley 1239
H4   London, British Library, MS Harley 2392
H5   London, British Library, MS Harley 4912
J   Cambridge, St John's College, MS L.1
Ph   Formerly Phillipps 8252, now San Marino, Huntington Library, MS HM 114
R   Oxford, Bodleian Library, MS Rawlinson Poet.163
S1   Oxford, Bodleian Library, MS Arch. Selden B.24
S2   Oxford, Bodleian Library, MS Arch. Selden, Supra 56

7 A Comprehensive Textual Comparison of *Troilus and Criseyde*: Corpus Christi College, Cambridge, MS 61 and B.A. Windeatt's Edition of *Troilus and Criseyde* (1990)

7.0. Introduction

We have sixteen extant manuscripts of *Troilus and Criseyde* apart from the fragments.[1] Among those used as a copy text is Corpus Christi College, Cambridge MS 61 (henceforth Cp).[2] Windeatt (1990: 69), for instance, uses Cp as a copy text. However, he edits the manuscript in various ways, on the one hand, by attempting to reconstruct Chaucer's original as closely as possible, on the other hand, by modernizing it to some degree for the convenience of modern readers.

Cp is available to us in a transcription by Furnivall and Macaulay (1894–5) and in a facsimile reproduced by Parkes and Salter (1978). Through these texts *per se*, however, it is far from easy to obtain the linguistic profiles of Cp in a systematic as well as quantitative way. For this linguistic investigation, it is a desideratum to digitalize the manuscript. Ideally, it is

1 For an explanation of the various manuscripts, see R.K. Root, *The Textual Tradition of Chaucer's Troilus*. Published for the Chaucer Society (London: Kegan Paul, Trench, Trübner & Co., 1916), and Yoshiyuki Nakao's chapter in this volume.

2 We would like to express our thanks to the three Cambridge libraries for permission to examine the following manuscripts: Corpus Christi College, Cambridge, MS 61 (Corpus Christi Parker Library), Cambridge University Library MS Gg.4.27 (University Library), St John's College, Cambridge, MS L.1 (St. John's College Library).

expected that digitalization of the sixteen manuscripts will be carried out, and that a parallel text of them will be available on a CD-ROM or in a book format with its KWIC index and various word-lists. (Part of the sixteen manuscripts of the *Troilus* I.1–28 is transcribed and machine readable as a case study in Nakao, 2006). Those manuscripts produced in the fifteenth century are expected to offer first-class linguistic information as a database for the historical survey of English and also for literary researches, as is seen in the case of the manuscripts of the *Canterbury Tales*.[3]

Jimura, Nakao and Matsuo published in 1999 a comparative collation of the four editions: Robinson (1957), Benson (1987), R.K. Root (ed.), *The Book of Troilus and Criseyde* by Geoffrey Chaucer (Princeton, NJ: Princeton University Press, 1952) and B.A. Windeatt (ed.), *Geoffrey Chaucer. Troilus & Criseyde: A new edition of 'The Book of Troilus'* (London: Longman, 2nd edn., 1990). This collation had a further task, to make clear the links between the edited texts and the manuscripts they are based on. In view of this, the present project is an attempt to make a comprehensive textual collation between Cp and Windeatt's edition (Windeatt hereafter) as a case study and to describe the similarities and dissimilarities between them systematically as well as quantitatively and, as a result, to contribute to the textual criticism of Chaucer. In this chapter, we will give outlines of this project and suggest its significance with illustrative examples.

3   For the concordances to the manuscripts (Hengwrt and Ellesmere) of *The Canterbury Tales* and a collation between those manuscripts and the edited texts (N.F. Blake (ed.), *The Canterbury Tales edited from the Hengwrt Manuscript* (London: Arnold, 1980), F.N. Robinson (ed.), *The Works of Geoffrey Chaucer* (London: Oxford University Press, 1957), Larry D. Benson (ed.), *The Riverside Chaucer.* Third edn. based on *The Works of Geoffrey Chaucer* edited by F.N. Robinson (Boston, MA: Houghton Mifflin, 1987), see N.F. Blake, D. Burnley, M. Masatsugu and Y. Nakao (eds.), *A New Concordance to 'The Canterbury Tales' Based on Blake's Text Edited from the Hengwrt Manuscript* (Okayama: University Education Press, 1994), A. Jimura, Y. Nakao and M. Matsuo (eds.), *A Comprehensive List of Textual Comparison between Blake's and Robinson's Editions of The Canterbury Tales* (Okayama: University Education Press, 1995) and Y. Nakao, A. Jimura and M. Matsuo, 'A Project for a Comprehensive Collation of the Hengwrt and Ellesmere Manuscripts of *The Canterbury Tales*: The General Prologue', in J. Nakamura, N. Inoue and T. Tabata (eds.), *English Corpora under Japanese Eyes* (Amsterdam and New York: Rodopi, 2004): 139–50.

7.1. The Cp Manuscript

According to M.B. Parkes and E. Salter (1978: 2), Windeatt and Jane Roberts (2005), Cp has the following features.[4] This manuscript was completed between 1385 when Chaucer finished writing the *Troilus* and 1456 when its owner John Shirley died. Roberts (2005: 194) restricted the year of Cp's production to the first quarter of the fifteenth century (c.1415–25). Cp was written on vellum in folio (318 × 220 mm), having 151 + 2 leaves (the verso of the first leaf is the *Troilus* Frontispiece). For the writing of letters, lines were laid out of 213–15 × 122–4 mm with a narrow margin of 25 mm and a wide margin of 65 mm. The manuscript contains only the *Troilus*. Two scribes were involved in it. The first scribe wrote most of it, actually every leaf except for 17r–32v, which were by the second scribe. The style of handwriting is *littera quadrata*, a variant of *textura*.

Parkes and Salter (1978) make no specific reference to the dialect of the scribes, while Roberts (2005: 194) confines the location of their dialects to 'London to St. Albans'. This is evidenced, for instance, in the third-person plural forms *hire*, *hem*, the third-person singular verb form *–eth*, and the present participle form *–ing/e*. Cp is noted for the *Troilus* Frontispiece, one interpretation of which is that it depicts Chaucer addressing King Richard II, Queen Anne and their courtiers (Parkes and Salter: 23). The king's face was apparently erased. What significance this bears seems to be determined by our reconstruction of the political context the manuscript was produced in. This remains enigmatic.

---

4   M.B. Parkes and E. Salter, Introduction, *Troilus and Criseyde, Geoffrey Chaucer: A Facsimile of Corpus Christi College Cambridge MS 61* (Cambridge: D.S. Brewer, 1978); B.A. Windeatt (ed.), *Geoffrey Chaucer Troilus & Criseyde: A new edition of 'The Book of Troilus'* (London: Longman, 1990); and Jane A. Roberts, *Guide to Scripts Used in English Writings up to 1500* (London: The British Library, 2005).

7.2. Digitalization of Cp: Toward a Comprehensive Collation between Cp and Windeatt (1990)

The digitalization of Windeatt has already been completed. In this project, we have digitalized Cp as closely as possible. Generally, the more closely we transcribe the manuscript, the more distant we become from its modern edition. Windeatt gives a great deal of his edition to Cp, as is seen in his 'Readings'. For instance, morphologically, dealing with monosyllabic adjectives ending in consonants, he determines the existence and the non-existence of a final –*e* according to its grammatical system. He expands the abbreviations of letters, and edits the capitals and word divisions according to modern conventions. Although no punctuation marks such as the virgula are found in Cp, he distinguishes chunks of the text by commas, periods, question marks, etc. to facilitate the modern readers' comprehension of it.

In the next section, we will show the methodology for digitalizing Cp, the basic text of Windeatt. For the method of collation we have adopted, see Jimura, Nakao and Matsuo (1995); Jimura, Nakao and Matsuo (1999); Jimura, Nakao and Matsuo (2002); and Nakao, Jimura and Matsuo (2004).

7.3. Processing of the Letters in Cp

7.3.1 Missing lines

For referencing of the lines in Cp, we follow Windeatt. The missing lines are as follows: I 859, I 890–6, IV 491–532, IV 708–14, IV 1388 (second half) – IV 1409 (first half) inclusive, V 1223–74. Those lines are marked by '<Missing>', as in: Cp: I 890 <Missing>.

7.3.2. Processing of the letters within the text

7.3.2.1. Special letters and ornaments

We have created several external fonts and employed them for the special letters and ornaments in Cp. They mainly follow the conventions and fonts adopted in *the Digital Hengwrt* and are usually placed after the letter even if they are placed above it in Cp. The list of the external fonts is given at the end of this paper as Appendix 7–1.

7.3.2.2. Inserted words and letters

For these, the following conventions are used.

< > indicates a string of (redundant) spaces of unclear/obscure letters, the number of spaces between < > roughly corresponding with that of Cp:

> Cp:II 425 Right for this fy < > o lady myn pallas
> Cp: III 50 < >ay al this mene while Troilus

{nX} indicates the expansion of a capital letter, the figure *n* representing the size of the capital.

> Cp: II 1 {8O}wt of; Cp: IV 29 {7L}iggyng

[ ] stands for letters inserted above the line.

> Cp:14r I 485 And made his mete his [foo] and ek his ſorwe

7.3.3. Letters outside the text

Marginalia and catchwords are shown by a pair of asterisks as in

> * Canticus Troili *(130v)
> * whan they vnto the *(127v)

Latin and other foreign words and phrases are not marked but left as they are.

> le v~re T 142v (v~re=votre)

7.4. Some Linguistic Features of Cp

There are various linguistic features ascribed to Cp, which depart consider-
ably from Windeatt, whose copy-text is Cp. Those features are manifested
in metrics/phonology, morphology, orthography (kinds of letters such
as short s and long s, abbreviations, etc.), lexis, syntax and punctuation.
Here we will limit ourselves to and illustrate with examples the final –e of
monosyllabic adjectives ending in consonants, spacing problems in word-
divisions, the fusion of words and capitals. In this chapter, giving a sample
of a comprehensive collation between Cp and Windeatt, we will show how
such features are represented in the two texts.

7.4.1. Monosyllabic adjectives ending in consonants[5]

7.4.1.1. The existence of a grammatically unnecessary final –e

Cp:I 515 That is the man of ſo grete ſapience   (emphasis ours)
Cp:I 523 But alſo colde in loue towardes the
Cp:I 528 A lord to me it were a grete comforte

---

5   See J.D. Burnley, 'Inflections in Chaucer's Adjectives', *Neuphilologische Mitteilungen*
     83 (1982): 170 on those adjectives that may be pronounced as monosyllables. They
     can be divided into two major classes: those that are invariably written with a final
     -e, such as *wilde, shene, deere, leene, trewe, kene, clene, grene, meke, poure, large, riche*
     (Class I); and those that end in a consonant in their uninflected form (Class II).
     The first class is derived largely from Old English *ja-* and *jo-*stem adjectives, with
     analogical additions from other sources. The second class consists of OE *a-* and
     *o-*stem adjectives, also with analogical additions. It is this second class that exhibits
     inflexional change in the language of the Hengwrt MS, and it is with them that we
     shall be concerned. The adjectives that have been examined are: *long, short, round,
     wyd, deep, hard, hoot, derk, blynd, bold, brood, next, neigh, sad, syk, heigh, glad, bright,
     smal, soor, swift, sharp, reed, whit, grey, blak, cold, old, strong, yong, wys, fair, greet,
     good, proud, blew, fals, fressh, fyn, cler, wayk, sleigh*. For the suffixes of the ME strong
     and weak adjective paradigms, see Robert A. Peters, 'Chaucer's Language', *Journal
     of English Linguistics. Occasional Monographs I* (Washington: Western Washington
     University Press, 1980): 80–1.

Cp:II 21 A <u>blynde</u> man kan nat Iuggen wel in hewis
Cp:II 636 So <u>freſſhe</u> ſo ʒong ſo weldy ſemed he
Cp:II 811 Now hoot now <u>colde</u> but thus bitwixen tweye
Cp:II 818 And other of hire wōmen a <u>grete</u> route
Cp:II 987 In <u>grete</u> diſeſe abideth for the peyne
Cp:II 1271 And how that ſhe hathe <u>harde</u> ben here byforn
Cp:II 1299 What ſholde I make of this a <u>longe</u> ſermoun
Cp:II 1510 Now thynk nat ſo for thow doſt <u>grete</u> folie
Cp:II 1569 <u>Grete</u> hono͡ did hem Deiphebus certeyn

7.4.1.2. The omission of a grammatically necessary final –e

Cp:I 951 And next the <u>derk</u> nyght the glade morwe
Cp:II 54 Whan Phebus doth his <u>bryght</u> bemes ſprede
Cp:II 317 The <u>good</u> wise worthi freſſhe and free
Cp:II 383 But alwey <u>good</u> Nece to ſtynte his woo
Cp:II 1203 Now <u>good</u> Nece be it neuere ſo lite
Cp:II 1572 My <u>good</u> brother Troilus the ſyke

7.4.2. Spacing problems in word division

7.4.2.1. Inflectional morpheme, *y/i* + past participle

(1) [ynome]

Cp:I 242 Than they that han be moſte with loue <u>ynome</u>
Cp:I 382 ffrom euery wight <u>yborn</u> al outrely
Cp:I 741 With which the maker is hym ſelf <u>ybeten</u>
Cp:II 586 Ther were neuere two ſo wel <u>ymet</u>

(2) [Icloſed]

Cp:II 968 <u>Icloſed</u> ſtoupen on hire ſtalk lowe

(3) [I iaped]

Cp:I 318 Repentynge hym that he hadde euere <u>I iaped</u>
Cp:II 570 Ne neu'e was to wight ſo depe <u>I ſworne</u>
Cp:II 1749 Las tyme <u>I loſte</u> I dar nought with ʒow dele

(4) [y born]

Cp:II 298 As creature in al this world <u>y born</u>–
Cp:II 535 That to myn hertes botme it is <u>y ſounded</u>
Cp:II 583 That han ſwich oon <u>y kaught</u> with outen net
Cp:II 789 But harm <u>y doon</u> is doon who ſo it rewe
Cp:II 792 How ofte tyme hath it <u>y knowen</u> be
Cp:II 973 Thi myght thi grace <u>y heried</u> be it here
Cp:II 1236 That ȝe to hym of harde now ben <u>y wonne</u>
Cp:II 1245 ffor truſteth wel to long <u>y doon</u> hardyneſſe

7.4.2.2. Space in a word/compound

(1) function words

Cp:I 243 And ſtrengest folk bien <u>ther with</u> ouerecome
Cp:I 988 <u>Wher fore</u> I am and wol ben ay redy
Cp:II 82 <u>With Inne</u> a paued perlour and they thre
Cp:II 714 <u>With outen</u> nede ther I may ſtonde in grace
Cp:I 415 Compleyne <u>I wis</u> thus poſſed to and fro
Cp:I 433 <u>In to</u> hire honde and with ful humble chere
Cp:II 1375 To haue a manere routhe <u>vp on</u> my woo
Cp:I 457 That to <u>hym ſelf</u> a thouſand tyme he ſeyde
Cp:I 169 <u>A mong</u> thiſe othere folk was Criſeyda
Cp:III 903 But this thyng ſtant al in <u>a nother</u> kynde

(2) content words

Cp:V 1796 Ne the this myſmetre for <u>de faute</u> of tonge
Cp:I 409 If harme <u>a gree</u> me wherto pleyne I thenne
Cp:III 1409 ffor it <u>a cordeth</u> nought to my matere
Cp:V 1460 To purpos how that fortune <u>ouer throwe</u>
Cp:I 186 <u>By holding</u> ay the laddies of the town
Cp:II 408 And ſhe be gan to breſte <u>a wepe</u> a noon
Cp:IV 613 God help me ſo ſhe nyl nat take <u>a grief</u>
Cp:I 572 Go hennes <u>a wey</u> for certes my deyinge
Cp:I 569 Hath gided the to ſen me <u>lange wiſſhinge</u>
Cp:II 152 As frendes doon whan thei ben mette <u>y fere</u>

7.4.3. Fusion of words

Cp:I 5 My purpos is er that I parte <u>froye</u>
Cp:I 368 It was to hym <u>aright</u> good auenture
Cp:I 662 ʒet to hymſelf his konnyng was <u>fulbare</u>
Cp:II 372 What who wol demen though he ſe <u>aman</u>
Cp:I 884 Of hire eſtat <u>nagladder</u> ne of ſpeche
Cp:I 690 ḟfor to truſten ſ<u>omwhight</u> is a preue
Cp:II 1617 So heynous <u>thatmen</u> myghte on it ſpete
Cp:I 681 And telle me plat what is <u>thencheſoun</u>
Cp:II 276 And ſeyde lord ſo faſt ʒe <u>mauiſe</u>
Cp:II 1566 Right to <u>theffect</u> with outen tales mo

7.4.4. Capitals ('nece' and 'em' referring to the social relation between Criseyde and Pandarus are capitalized)

Cp:II 249 And ſey to me ʒoure <u>Nece</u> what ʒow liſte
Cp:II 251 And ſeyde gladly leue <u>Nece</u> dere
Cp:II 472 In honoˆ than myn <u>Emes</u> lyf to leſe
Cp:II 499 Tyl at the laſte O good <u>Em</u> qdˀ ſhe tho

We have observed in Cp morphological features, spacing problems in word divisions (space in a single word and no space between words) and capitals. In section 7.5, we will have a look at how these features are transformed or remain the same in Windeatt.

7.5. Collation Concordance between Cp and Windeatt (1990): A Sample

We will give a sample (II 1566–83) of a comprehensive collation between Cp and Windeatt as Appendix 7–2. The first line is from Cp and the second from Windeatt. If the corresponding lines of the two texts are identical,

only the Cp line is given. The symbol # indicates that one text lacks the
equivalent form/s of the other. When encountering ambiguous text in Cp,
we have consulted Furnivall and Macaulay (1894–5)[6] and Windeatt.

7.6. Conclusion

Through the collation above we can detect easily how Cp and Windeatt
differ from each other. There is an instance of 7.4.1.1 in 'Grete hono͡'
(II 1569), where MS *Grete* is transformed into *Gret* in Windeatt according to the strong declension of that adjective. On the other hand, 'my
good brother' (II 1572) of 7.4.1.2 is transformed into 'my goode brother'
in Windeatt according to the weak declension of that adjective. We have
an instance of 7.4.2.1. (3) in 'I loſte' (II 1749), the two forms of which are
hyphenated as one word in Windeatt.

We have shown examples of words divided by spaces: in 7.4.2.2. (1)
function words – 'With outen' (II 714), 'Up on' (II 1375), and 'i wis' (I 415)
are all hyphenated in Windeatt while 'him ſelf' (I 457) remains the same
in Windeatt and 'A mong' (I 169) are connected to each other without
any space in Windeatt; (2) content words – 'a gree' (409) is hyphenated in
Windeatt while 'By holding' (I 186) are connected to each other without
any space in Windeatt. We have instances of 7.4.3, the fusion of words:
'theffect' (II 1566) (< the effect) which remains the same in Windeatt and
'thatmen' (II 1617) (< that men), which is divided into two words according
to modern convention in Windeatt. We have instances of 7.4.4, capitalized
'Nece' (II 249), which remains the same in Windeatt.

We find that Windeatt is sensitive to the grammatical use of final –*e*
as regards monosyllabic adjectives ending in consonants and thus to the
metrical structure of the line (iambic pentameter). This is not true of the

---

6   F.J. Furnivall and G.C. Macaulay (eds.), *Three More Parallel Texts of Chaucer's Troilus
     and Criseyde*. Published for the Chaucer Society. (London: Kegan Paul, Trench,
     Trübner & Co., 1894–5).

Cp scribes. Cp deviates a great deal from modern conventions in the treatment of word division and the fusion of words. What sort of morphological system is at work in the practice of the Cp scribes? The space after the bound morpheme *i/y* in the past participle form in Cp seems to highlight the metrical structure of the line. The fact that *nece* and *em* are capitalized in Cp is worthy of note. Windeatt seems to support this practice and retains it in his edition. We have published a collation concordance to Cp and Windeatt (see Nakao, Matsuo, and Jimura (2009)), which is expected to offer data of first-class importance, such as statistical data on linguistic features of both Cp and Windeatt. It is our sincere hope to contribute in this way to the textual criticism of the *Troilus* and Chaucer as a whole.

7.7. References

7.7.1. Primary sources

Benson, Larry D., ed. *The Riverside Chaucer*. 3rd edn, based on *The Works of Geoffrey Chaucer*, ed. F.N. Robinson. Boston, MA: Houghton Mifflin, 1987.

Blake, N.F., ed. *The Canterbury Tales edited from the Hengwrt Manuscript*. London: Arnold, 1980.

Furnivall, F.J. and G.C. Macaulay, eds. *Three More Parallel Texts of Chaucer's Troilus and Criseyde*. Published for the Chaucer Society. London: Kegan Paul, Trench, Trübner & Co., 1894–5.

Jimura, Akiyuki, Yoshiyuki Nakao and Masatsugu Matsuo, eds. *A Comprehensive List of Textual Comparison between Blake's and Robinson's Editions of The Canterbury Tales*. Okayama: University Education Press, 1995.

——— eds. *A Comprehensive Textual Comparison of Troilus and Criseyde: Benson's, Robinson's, Root's, and Windeatt's Editions*. Okayama: University Education Press, 1999.

——— eds. *A Comprehensive Collation of the Hengwrt and Ellesmere Manuscripts of The Canterbury Tales: General Prologue*. *The Hiroshima University Studies*, Graduate School of Letters, vol. 82, Special Issue, No. 3, 2002.

Nakao, Yoshiyuki, Masatsugu Matsuo and Akiyuki Jimura, eds. A *Comprehensive Textual Collation of Troilus and Criseyde: Corpus Christi College, Cambridge, MS 61 and Windeatt (1990)*. Tokyo: Senshu University Press, 2009.

Parkes, M.B. and E. Salter. Introduction. *Troilus and Criseyde. Geoffrey Chaucer: A Facsimile of Corpus Christi College Cambridge MS 61.* Cambridge: D.S. Brewer, 1978.

Robinson, F.N., ed. *The Works of Geoffrey Chaucer.* London: Oxford University Press, 1957.

Root, R.K., ed. *The Book of Troilus and Criseyde by Geoffrey Chaucer.* Princeton, NJ: Princeton University Press, 1952.

Stubbs, Estelle, ed. *The Hengwrt Chaucer Digital Facsimile.* Leicester, UK: Scholarly Digital Editions, 2000.

Windeatt, B.A., ed. *Geoffrey Chaucer Troilus & Criseyde: A new edition of 'The Book of Troilus'.* London: Longman, 1984, repr. 1990.

7.7.2. Secondary sources

Blake, Norman, David Burnley, Masatsugu Matsuo and Yoshiyuki Nakao, eds. *A New Concordance to 'The Canterbury Tales' Based on Blake's Text Edited from the Hengwrt Manuscript.* Okayama: University Education Press, 1994.

Burnley, J.D. 'Inflections in Chaucer's Adjectives', *Neuphilologische Mitteilungen* 83 (1982): 169–77.

Hanna, Ralph III. *Pursuing History: Middle English Manuscripts and Their Texts.* Stanford, CA: Stanford University Press, 1996.

Nakao, Yoshiyuki. 'Towards a Parallel Text Edition of Chaucer's *Troilus and Criseyde*: A Study of Book 1.1–28', *Universals and Variation in Language*, vol. 1. The Center for Research on Language and Culture, Institute for Development of Social Intelligence, Senshu University, 2006: 89–114.

Nakao, Yoshiyuki, Akiyuki Jimura and Masatsugu Matsuo. 'A Project for a Comprehensive Collation of the Hengwrt and Ellesmere Manuscripts of *The Canterbury Tales*: The General Prologue', in Nakamura, Junsaku, Nagayuki Inoue and Tomoji Tabata, eds., *English Corpora under Japanese Eyes.* Amsterdam and New York: Rodopi, 2004. 139–50.

Peters, Robert A. 'Chaucer's Language', *Journal of English Linguistics. Occasional Monographs I.* Washington: Western Washington University Press, 1980.

Roberts, Jane. *Guide to Scripts Used in English Writings up to 1500.* London: The British Library, 2005.

Root, R.K. *The Textual Tradition of Chaucer's Troilus.* Published for the Chaucer Society. London: Kegan Paul, Trench, Trübner & Co., 1916.

Appendix 7–1:
List of external fonts adopted (thorns and yoghs are excluded)

name	symbol	MS image	example
macron	–		wō man
p bar 2	ꝑ		ꝑuerbe
lower p flower	ꝑ		ꝑaunter
one upper dot	·		ny˙ ght
two upper dot	··		gn¨te
ff left longer	ff		ffor
ff right longer	ff		ffor
inverted comma	ᵔ		neuᵔe
long s	ſ		ſhape
macron2	˄		harp˄

We would like to thank the Corpus Christi Parker Library, Cambridge, for permission to use the special fonts in MS 61.

Appendix 7–2: Sample of collation (Wn = Windeatt)

Cp:II 1566 Right to theffect with outen tales mo
Wn:II 1566   withouten
Cp:II 1567 Whi al this folk aſſembled in this place
Wn:II 1567   assembled
Cp:II 1568 And lat vs of hire ſaluynges pace
Wn:II 1568   saluynges
Cp:II 1569 Grete hono͡ did hem Deiphebus certeyn
Wn:II 1569 Gret honour
Cp:II 1572 My good brother Troilus the ſyke
Wn:II 1572   goode   syke
Cp:II 1573 Lith ʒet and therwith # gan to ſike
Wn:II 1573   therwithal he   sike
Cp:II 1576 Compleyned ek Eleyne of his ſikneſſe
Wn:II 1576   siknesse
Cp:II 1578 And euery wight gan waxen for acceſſe
Wn:II 1578   accesse
Cp:II 1579 A leche anon and ſeyde in this manere
Wn:II 1579   seyde
Cp:II 1581 But ther ſatte on al liſt hire nought to teche
Wn:II 1581   sat   oon   list
Cp:II 1582 That thoughte beſt koude I ʒet ben his leche
Wn:II 1582   best
Cp:II 1583 After compleynte hym gonnen they to preyſe
Wn:II 1583   preyse
Cp:II 1584 As folk don that whan ſom wight hath bygonne
Wn:II 1584   ʒet   som
Cp:II 1585 To preiſe a man and # with pris hym reiſe
Wn:II 1585   preise   vp   reise
Cp:II 1586 A thouſand fold ʒet heigher than the ſonne
Wn:II 1586   thousand   sonne
Cp:II 1589 He naughte forgate hire preiſynge to conferme
Wn:II 1589   naught forgat   preisynge
Cp:II 1590 Herde al this thyng Criſeyde wel I nough
Wn:II 1590   Criseyde   i-nough
Cp:II 1592 ffor which with ſobre cheere hire herte lough
Wn:II 1592 ffor   sobre
Cp:II 1593 ffor who is that ne wolde hire glorifie
Wn:II 1593 ffor

8 The Old English Equivalents for *Factum Esse* and the Salisbury Psalter

8.0. Introduction

Geworden, the past participle of the Old English verb *(ge)weorðan* 'become', 'happen', 'be made', 'be done', etc.,[1] is often found with *beon/wesan/weorðan* and is used very frequently in translating Latin *factum esse*[2] literally. In the two papers I wrote in 1979 (*'Wæs Geworden'* and *'Factum esse and Wesan Geworden'*), where I investigated a limited number of Old English works, I observed that the influence of Latin *factum esse* on Old English *wesan geworden* appears (a) in the periphrasing of the simple forms of *(ge)weorðan* meaning 'become, happen' and (b) in the extension of the meaning into 'be made'. Later, with the help of the Microfiche Concordance to Old English[3] (which covers almost all the Old English works), I learned how the examples of *wesan geworden* were distributed among Old English works. The expression has a large number of examples in translations from Latin

---

1   The definition in *A Concise Anglo-Saxon Dictionary* by Clark Hall is: '±weorðan[3] (u, y) *to become, get, be* (passive auxiliary), *be done, be made, CP: happen, come to pass, arise, take place, settle*: (+) impers. *get on with, please, agree, AO, Chr: think of, occur to*'. The impersonal use above will be left out of consideration since the past participle of the impersonally employed *(ge)weorðan* combines not with *wesan* but with *habban*.

2   'Fîô, fierî, factus sum, *be made, be done, become*, was used by the Romans as the passive of the simple verb faciô. ... the perfect system is quite regular as the normal passive of faciô; factus, -a, -um est, factus erat, factus sit, factus esset, factus esse, etc'. (Wheelock, *Latin* 173). 'faciô, -ere, fêcî, factum, make, do, accomplish, ...; passive: fîô, fierî, factus sum' (419).

3   *A Microfiche Concordance to Old English*, compiled by Antonette diPaolo Healey and Richard L. Venezky (Toronto: University of Toronto Press, 1980). See References.

and Bible-related works and, among these, the interlinear Psalter glosses have the greatest number.

Most of the results seem to be harmonious with my previous studies but one does not. The Salisbury Psalter Gloss [PsGlK] has extremely few occurrences of *wesan geworden* among the Psalter glosses. There are many examples of *factum esse* in K, but glossed mostly with *wesan gedon* rather than with *wesan geworden*. What brought this exceptional phenomenon to PsGlK instead of the regular glossing of *factum esse* with *wesan geworden*? This is what I shall pursue in this chapter.

8.1. *Wesan Geworden*: Its Distribution and the Examples in PsGlK

8.1.1. *The distribution of wesan geworden in Old English works*

The examples of *wesan geworden*, with more than 30 variant spellings of *geworden*,[4] total 1,461. Table 8–1 illustrates the number of variants in each genre:[5]

---

4   The variant spellings of *geworden* are: *geuorden, geuordeno, geweordon, gewoerden, gewordan, geworde, geworden, gewordena, gewordene, gewordenne, gewordeno, gewordenu, gewordne, gewordon, gewordyn, gewordyne, gewordyny, gewordys, geworþan, geworþen, geworþene, gewurden, gewurdene, gewurþen, giworden, giwordne, giwordon, iworden, iwordene, iworþen, iwurþen, worden, wordene.*

5   *A Microfiche Concordance to Old English*, compiled by Healey and Venezky (1980) is the source for the frequency word counts of Section 1. D (Glossaries), E (Runes), and F (Inscriptions) contain no example of *wesan geworden*. Examples of *habban geworden* are only five in all: 2 in A (*Beo* 2024, *Jud* 257), 3 in B (*Or* 4 12.208.22, *ChronC* (Rositzke) 918.5, *ChronD* (Classen-Harm) 918.1.6). No instance occurs in C.

Genre	Poetry		Prose		Glossed Texts		Total	
wesan geworden	39	2.7%	555	38.0%	744	50.9%	1338	91.6%
beon geworden	3	0.2%	59	4.0%	23	1.6%	85	5.8%
weorðan geworden	1	0.1%	37	2.5%	0	0.0%	38	2.6%
Total	43	2.9%	651	44.6%	767	52.5%	1461	100.0%

Table 8–1 All Old English texts

8.1.2. Poetry

Forty-three examples of *wesan geworden* appear in poetry. The fifteen examples (35%) from the *Paris Psalter* (PPs) and the seven examples (16%) from *Christ* A, B and C make up more than half of all the examples in poetry (see Table 8–2).

Short title[1]	Cameron number	*wesan geworden*		*beon geworden*		*weorðan geworden*		Total	
GenA,B	A1.1	4	9.3%	0		0		4	9.3%
Dan	A1.3	1	2.3%	0		1	2.3%	2	4.7%
Sat	A1.4	2	4.7%	0		0		2	4.7%
Dream	A2.5	1	2.3%	0		0		1	2.3%
El	A2.6	2	4.7%	0		0		2	4.7%
ChristA,B,C	A3.1	6	14.0%	1	2.3%	0		7	16.3%
GuthA, B	A3.2	1	2.3%	0		0		1	2.3%
Beo	A4.1	2	4.7%	0		0		2	4.7%
PPs	A5	15	34.9%	0		0		15	34.9%

Met	A6	1	2.3%	0		0		1	2.3%
CEdg	A10.3	2	4.7%	0		0		2	4.7%
Msol	A13	0		1	2.3%	0		1	2.3%
LPr	A20	0		1	2.3%	0		1	2.3%
PsFr	A24	1	2.3%	0		0		1	2.3%
MPs	A51	1	2.3%	0		0		1	2.3%
Total		39	90.7%	3	7.0%	1	2.3%	43	100.0%

Table 8–2 A: Poetry
[1] *A Microfiche Concordance to Old English* (1980) is the source for short titles.

8.1.3. Prose

Two hundred and six (32%) prose examples appear in the section of Alfredian and Other Translations, 189 (29%) in Anonymous Homilies, 161 (25%) in Biblical Translations, with these three sections comprising 86% of all prose examples (see Table 8–3).

Cameron number	Section	*wesan geworden*	*weorðan geworden*	*beon geworden*	Total
B1	Works of Ælfric	26 (4%)	6	3	35 (5%)
B2	Works of Wulfstan	12	3	1	16 (2%)
B3	Anonymous Homilies	145 (22%)	11 (2%)	33 (5%)	189 (29%)
B4	Prose Romance, Vision Literature	1	1	0	2
B5	Prose Dialogues	2	0	0	2
B6	Letters	1	0	0	1
B7	Proverbs	0	0	0	0
B8	Biblical Translations	143 (22%)	9	9	161 (25%)
B9	Alfredian and Other Translations	198 (30%)	0	8	206 (32%)

B10	Rules for Monks and Canons	4	o	o	4
B11	Confessional and Penitential Texts	2	o	o	2
B12	Liturgical Texts, Creeds, Prayers	o	2	o	2
B13	Ecclesiastical Laws and Institutes	3	3	o	6
B14	Laws of England	o	1	o	2
B15	Charters in English	1	o	o	1
B16	Records	o	o	o	o
B17	Chronicles and Historical Texts	3	1	o	4
B18	Lists of Kings, Saints, and Bishops	o	o	o	o
B19	Martyrology	9	o	o	9
B20	Computus	2	o	1	3
B21	Medical Texts	o	o	4	4
B22	Other Scientific Texts	o	o	o	o
B23	Folklore	o	o	o	o
B24	Notes and Commonplaces	1	o	o	1
B25	Runic Texts	o	o	o	o
B26	Cryptograms	2	o	o	2
B27	Directions to Readers, Scribbles	o	o	o	o
B28	Colophons, Inscriptions, Names	o	o	o	o
	Total	555 (85%)	37 (6%)	59 (9%)	651 (100%)

Table 8–3 B: Prose

Tables 8–4 to 8–23 illustrate the occurrences in each section.

Text	Cameron number	*wesan geworden*	*weorðan geworden*	*beon geworden*	Total
ÆCHom I	B1.1	12 (34%)	0	2	14 (40%)
ÆCHom II	B1.2	3	2	0	5
ÆLS	B1.3	2	1	0	3
ÆHom	B1.4	5 (14%)	1	0	6 (17%)
ÆHomM	B1.5	0	1	0	1
Æ (Tracts)	B1.6	0	0	0	0
ÆLet	B1.8	1	0	0	1
ÆGram	B1.9.1	2	0	1	3
ÆTemp	B1.9.4	1	1	0	2
Total		26 (74%)	6 (17%)	3 (9%)	35 (100%)

Table 8–4   B1: Works of Ælfric

Text	Cameron number	*wesan geworden*	*weorðan geworden*	*beon geworden*	Total
WHom (Eschatological Homilies)	B2.1	1	1	0	2
WHom 6 (The Christian Faith)	B2.2.1	1	1	0	2
WHom (Archiepiscopal Functions)	B2.3	2	1	1	4
WHom (Evil Days)	B2.4	8 (50%)	0	0	8 (50%)
Total		12 (75%)	3 (19%)	1 (6%)	16 (100%)

Table 8–5   B2: Works of Wulfstan

Text	Cameron number	*wesan geworden*	*weorðan geworden*	*beon geworden*	Total
HomS	B3.2	49 (26%)	1	15 (8%)	65 (34%)
LS	B3.3	73 (39%)	8 (4%)	4	85 (45%)
HomU	B3.4	15 (8%)	2	13 (7%)	30 (16%)
HomM	B3.5	8 (4%)	0	1	9 (5%)
Total		145 (77%)	11 (6%)	33 (17%)	189 (100%)

Table 8–6 B3: Anonymous homilies

Text	Cameron number	*wesan geworden*	*weorðan geworden*	*beon geworden*	Total
ApT	B4.1	1	1	0	2
Total		1	1	0	2

Table 8–7 B4: Prose romance, vision literature

Text	Cameron number	*wesan geworden*	*weorðan geworden*	*beon geworden*	Total
Sol	B5.1, B5.3	2	0	0	2
Total		2	0	0	2

Table 8–8 B5: Prose dialogues

Text	Cameron number	*wesan geworden*	*weorðan geworden*	*beon geworden*	Total
Let 1 (Sisam)	B6.1	1	0	0	1
Total		1	0	0	1

Table 8–9 B6: Letters

Text	Cameron number	*wesan geworden*	*weorðan geworden*	*beon geworden*	Total
Heptateuch	B8.1	16 (10%)	1	2	19 (12%)
Psalms 1–50	B8.2	10 (6%)	0	1	11 (7%)
Gospels	B8.4	95 (59%)	5	4	104 (65%)
Apocrypha	B8.5	22 (14%)	3	2	27 (17%)
Total		143 (89%)	9 (6%)	9 (6%)	161 (100%)

Table 8–10 B8: Biblical translations

Text	Cameron number	*wesan geworden*	*weorðan geworden*	*beon geworden*	Total
CP	B9.1	6	0	1	7
Or	B9.2	3	0	0	3
Bo	B9.3	2	0	0	2
Solil	B9.4	1	0	0	1
GD[1]	B9.5	87 (42%)	0	2	89 (43%)
Bede	B9.6	98 (48%)	0	4	102 (50%)
Alc (Warn 35)	B9.7	1	0	1	2
Total		198 (96%)	0	8 (4%)	206 (100%)

Table 8–11 B9: Alfredian and other translation
[1] The examples of both C and H are included.

Text	Cameron number	*wesan geworden*	*weorðan geworden*	*beon geworden*	Total
BenR	B10.3	4	0	0	4
Total		4	0	0	4

Table 8–12 B10: Rules for monks and canons

Text	Cameron number	*wesan geworden*	*weorðan geworden*	*beon geworden*	Total
Conf	B11.1.1–11	2	0	0	2
Total		2	0	0	2

Table 8–13 B11: Confessional and penitential texts

Text	Cameron number	*wesan geworden*	*weorðan geworden*	*beon geworden*	Total
Lit 3.2 (Thorpe)	B12.3.2	0	1	0	1
LitBen 7.5 (Ure)	B12.7.5	0	1	0	1
Total		0	2	0	2

Table 8–14 B12: Liturgical texts, creeds, prayers

Text	Cameron number	*wesan geworden*	*weorðan geworden*	*beon geworden*	Total
WPol	B13.2–6	3	3	0	6
Total		3	3	0	6

Table 8–15 B13: Ecclesiastical laws and institutes

Text	Cameron number	*wesan geworden*	*weorðan geworden*	*beon geworden*	Total
LawGrið	B14.51	0	1	0	1
Total		0	1	0	1

Table 8–16 B14: Laws of England

Text	Cameron number	*wesan geworden*	*weorðan geworden*	*beon geworden*	Total
Ch 1202(HarmD 8)	B15.2.7	1	0	0	1
Total		1	0	0	1

Table 8–17 B15: Charters in English

Text	Cameron number	*wesan geworden*	*weorðan geworden*	*beon geworden*	Total
ChronD (Classen-Harm)	B17.8	1	1	0	2
ChronE (Plummer)	B17.9	2	0	0	2
Total		3	1	0	4

Table 8–18 B17: Chronicles and historical texts

Text	Cameron number	*wesan geworden*	*weorðan geworden*	*beon geworden*	Total
Mart	B19.1–6	9	0	0	9
Total		9	0	0	9

Table 8–19 B19: Martyrology

Text	Cameron number	*wesan geworden*	*weorðan geworden*	*beon geworden*	Total
ByrM 1 (Crawford)	B20.20.1	2	0	1	3
Total		2	0	1	3

Table 8–20 B20: Computus

Text	Cameron number	*wesan geworden*	*weorðan geworden*	*beon geworden*	Total
Lch I (Herb)	B21.1.1.2	0	0	1	1
Lch III (Foetus)	B21.4	0	0	3	3
Total		0	0	4	4

Table 8–21 B21: Medical texts

Text	Cameron number	*wesan geworden*	*weorðan geworden*	*beon geworden*	Total
Notes 10.2 (Nap)	B24.10.2	1	0	0	1
Total		1	0	0	1

Table 8–22 B24: Notes and commonplaces

Text	Cameron number	*wesan geworden*	*weorðan geworden*	*beon geworden*	Total
Crypt 1.1 (Först)	B26.1.7	2	0	0	2
Total		2	0	0	2

Table 8–23 B26: Cryptograms

8.1.4. Interlinear glosses

573 examples (76%) occur in the Psalter glosses and thirty-five examples (5%) in the Canticles of the Psalter. The interlinear glosses to the Gospels contain 109 examples (14%). *Factum esse* is often glossed with the periphrastic forms *aweorðan* in the Lindisfarne Gospels but the occurrences of those examples are excluded here (see Table 8–24).[6]

Text	Cameron number	*wesan geworden*	*weorðan geworden*	*beon geworden*	Total
BenRGl	C4	5	o	o	5
LibScEcc	C6	1	o	o	1
PsGlC(Cambridge)	C7.1	57 (7%)	o	1	58 (8%)
PsGlE(Harsley)	C7.3	54 (7%)	o	5	59 (8%)
PsGlL(Bosworth)	C7.4	14 (2%)	o	o	14 (2%)
PsGlJ(Arundel)	C7.5	61 (8%)	o	1	62 (8%)
PsGlH(Tiberius)	C7.6	35 (5%)	o	1	36 (5%)
PsGlA(Vespasian)	C7.7	62 (8%)	o	1	63 (8%)
PsGlG (Vitellius)	C7.8	53 (7%)	o	1	54 (7%)
PsGlD(Roeder)	C7.9	39 (5%)	o	2	41 (5%)
PsGlF(Stowe/Spelman)	C7.10	61 (8%)	o	1	62 (8%)
PsGlI (Lambeth)	C7.11	67 (9%)	o	1	68 (9%)
PsGlB (Junius)	C7.12	57 (7%)	o	2	59 (8%)
PsGlK (Salisbury)	C7.13	6 (1%)	o	o	6 (1%)
Psalter Glosses Subtotal		566 (75%)	o	16 (2%)	582 (76%)

6   The occurrences of '*factum esse* = *wesan/beon aworden*' are: MtGl(Li) 1, MkGl(Li) 11, LkGl(Li) 77, JnGl(Li) 18, LkHeadGl(Li) 1. No example is found in MtArgGl(Li), MtHeadGl(Li), MkArgGl(Li), LkArgGl(Li), JnArgGl(Li), JnHeadGl(Li).

Bible, Gospels	C8	109 (14%)	o	o	109 (14%)
PsCa	C11	35 (5%)	o	o	35 (5%)
MonCa	C12	10	o	o	10
LibSc	C15	6	o	5	11
ProgGl	C16	o	o	1	1
HyGl	C18	8	o	o	8
IsGl	C19	1	o	o	1
LibScSen	C20	1	o	o	1
DurRitGl	C21	2	o	o	2
OccGl 49(Zupitza)	C49	o	o	1	1
Total		744 (97%)	o (0%)	23 (3%)	767 (100%)

Table 8–24   C: Interlinear glosses

8.1.5.

The preceding tables show an uneven distribution of *wesan geworden* in Old English texts, where translations from Latin and works related to the Bible tend to abound with examples.[7] The Psalter Glosses have the most examples, and we shall return to Table 8–24 to look into the distribution more closely.

7   F.M. Wheelock writes in his *Latin Literature* (New York: Barnes and Noble, 1969): 223. '**Factum est**, *it happened, it came to pass:* common in the Vulgate'.

8.2. The Distribution of *Wesan Geworden* in the Psalter Glosses

Among the Psalter glosses, only K has an extremely small number of examples of *wesan geworden*, for the length of L is only about one-fifth that of the other manuscripts. The 'number of citations' illustrates the length of each manuscript in the Old English machine-readable corpus.[8]

Psalter gloss	*wesan/weorðan/ beon geworden*		Number of citations	
PsGlC (Cambridge)	58	10.1%	2452	9.2%
PsGlE (Harsley)	59	10.3%	2397	9.0%
PsGlL (Bosworth)	5	0.9%	446	1.7%
PsGlJ (Arundel)	62	10.8%	2457	9.3%
PsGlH (Tiberius)	36	6.3%	1889	7.1%
PsGlA (Vespasian)	63	11.0%	2407	9.1%
PsGlG (Vitellius)	54	9.4%	2407	9.1%
PsGlD (Roeder)	41	7.2%	2455	9.3%
PsGlF (Stowe/Spelman)	62	10.8%	2427	9.1%
PsGlI (Lambeth)	68	11.9%	2447	9.2%
PsGlB (Junius)	59	10.3%	2357	8.9%
PsGlK (Salisbury)	6	1.0%	2388	9.0%
Psalter glosses total	573	100.0%	26529	100.0%

Table 8–25 The length of each Psalter gloss

8   This and part of the following data are based on the Dictionary of Old English Project, University of Toronto, *The Complete Corpus of Old English in Machine Readable Form*, First Version (Oxford: Oxford Text Archive, 1990). I am grateful to Mr. Masatoshi Kawada of Kanto Gakuin University Computer Center for dividing the data on the magnetic tape into floppy diskettes.

As was mentioned in 8.1., the use of *wesan geworden* closely depends on Latin *factum esse*, and *factum esse* in the Psalter Glosses is mostly glossed with (*wesan*) *geworden*. In the five manuscripts C, L, A, F and B, *factum esse* is exclusively glossed with (*wesan*) *geworden*. In the manuscripts other than K, the examples of *factum esse* glossed with an Old English verb other than *wesan geworden* are very few: E 1 (1.72%),[9] J 1 (1.64%),[10] H 2 (4.26%),[11] G 3 (4.92%),[12] D (Roeder) 3 (4.92%),[13] I 1 (1.64%).[14] In K, on the other hand, the examples of *factum esse* with an Old English gloss other than *wesan geworden* amount to 50 (87.7%),[15] and all of them are glossed with (*wesan*) (*ge*)*don*.

In the Rushworth Gospels, an interlinear gloss where Latin is rather freely rendered into Old English, less than 10% of the examples of *factum esse* are glossed with *wesan gedon* and there are far more examples of *wesan geworden* (see Table 8–26).

9   PsGlE 138.22: Þurhfulfremede fioung ic fioung hie fiend *geworhte sindon* me [Perfecto odio oderam illos inimici *facti sunt* michi].

10   PsGlJ 117.23: Fram drihtne *gedon is* þæt & is wundorlic on eagum hurum [A domino *factum est* istud et est mirabile in oculis nostris].

11   PsGlH 68.11: [Et operui in ieiunio animam meam et *factum est* in opprobrium mihi] &/ ic oferwreah on fæstenne sawle mine & *gedon is* on hops me. 105.36: [et seruierunt sculptilibus eorum; et *factum est* illis in scandalum] & hy þeowodon deofolgildon heora & *gedon is* him on æswinc.

12   PsGlG 37.7: Yrmþum *geswenced ic eom* & gedrefed eom oð ende on ende ælce dæge geunrotsod ic ineod/ [Miser *factus sum* et curuatus sum usque in finem tota die contristatus ingrediebar]. 68.11: & ic oferwreah on fæstene/ sawle mine & *gedon is* on hospe me [Et operui in ieiunio animam meam et *factum est* in obprobrium mihi]. 105.36: & hy þeowodon deofolgildum heora/ & *gedon is* him on æswinc [et seruierunt sculptilibus eorum et *factum est* illis in scandalum].

13   PsGlD (Roeder) 68.11: & ic oferwreah on fæstene sawle & *gedon* [no equivalent for *est*] on hosp [Et operui in ieiunio animam meam et *factum est* mihi in obprobrium]. 105.36: & hy ðeowodon deofolgildum heora & *gedon is* him on æswic [et seruierunt sculptilibus eorum et *factum est* illis in scandalum]. 117.23: Fram drihtne *gedon is* & is wundurlic on eagum urum [a domino *factum est* et est mirabile in oculis nostris].

14   PsGlI 32.9: Forðan þe he sylf cwæð & *geworhta vel gewurdone* synt he bebead gesceapene hig synt [Quoniam ipse dixit et *facta sunt* ipse mandauit et creata sunt].

15   K has, in all, 57 examples of *factum esse* with an Old English gloss.

factum esse	occurrence	%
wesan geworden	13	38.2%
(ge)wearð, wurdon	9	26.5%
wesan (ge)worht	5	14.7%
wesan gedon	3	8.8%
gelamp	3	8.8%
geworden	1	3.0%
Ru¹ Total	34	100.0%

Table 8–26 The Rushworth Gospels 1
Mitsu Ide, '*Factum esse* と [and] *wesan geworden*', *Metropolitan* 23 (1979): 25.

There are some examples of *factum esse* rendered into *wesan gedon* in prose translations of the Bible:

Matt 11.20[16]

Latin:

[Tunc coepit exprobrare ciuitatibus in quibus *factae sunt* plurimæ uirtutes eius]

KJ:

[Then began he to upbraid the cities wherein most of his mighty works were done ...]

Li:

ða ongann of-sceomage vel forcuoeða ðæm burgum in ðæm *geworden weron* swiðe monige mæhto his ...

Ru¹:

þa in-gonn æt-witan cæstrum in ðæm ðe *geworhte wærun* þa mængistu mægen his

---

16   Ide, '*Factum esse* と [and] *wesan geworden*': 31.

WSCp:

Ða ongan he hyspan þa burga on þam *wærun gedone* manega hys mægena ...

WSH:[17]

Þa on-gan he hysfan þa burga on þam *wæren gedon* [*wæron gedone*][18] manega his mænega

It follows from the above that what is peculiar to the Psalter interlinear gloss K is not the presence itself of the examples of *wesan gedon* (instead of *wesan geworden*) corresponding to *factum esse*, but the extremely high frequency of its occurrence.

8.3. Seven Examples of *Wesan Geworden* in PsGlK

In PsGlK, where fifty (87.7%) out of fifty-seven examples of *factum esse* with an Old English gloss are rendered into (*wesan*) (*ge*)*don*, there are still seven examples of *factum esse* = *wesan geworden*, which we will investigate to see whether their usage differs from the examples of *wesan gedon*. The seven examples are the following:

---

17   Hatton = Ker 325. Bodleian. Hatton 38(4090) s. xii/xiii.
18   Royal = Ker 245. British Museum, Royal I A. xiv s. xii². 'The Old English translation of the Gospels, the so-called West Saxon Gospels, composed in the tenth century, was still being copied, transmitted and studied at Christ Church, Canterbury, in the late twelfth century, as evidenced by London, BL, MS Royal I A XIV, a copy made at the time from an eleventh-century exemplar (Oxford, Bod. Lib., MS Bodley 441), the former, in turn, becoming the exemplar for Bod. Lib., MS Hatton 38, a copy made *c*. 1200, also at Canterbury'. Margaret Gibson, T.A. Heslop, and Richard W. Pfaff (eds.). *The Eadwine Psalter: Text, Image, and Monastic Culture in Twelfth-Century Canterbury* (London and University Park, PA: The Modern Humanities Research Association in conjunction with the Pennsylvania State University Press, 1992): 136.

K 37.15:

geworden eom swa man na gehyrende & na hæbende on muþe his steorspæce [Et *factus
sum* sicut homo non audiens et non habens in ore suo redargutiones]

K 68.4:

ic swanc clypiende hase *gewordene synd* goman mine geteorudan egan mine þonne
ic hihte on god mine [Laboraui clamans *rauce factæ sunt* fauces meæ defecerunt oculi
mei dum spero in deum meum]

K 72.23:

swa nyten *geworden ic eom* beforan þe & ic æfre mid þe [Vt iumentum *factus sum*
apud te et ego semper tecum]

K 118.150:

geneahlæhte ehtende me unrihtwisnes of æ soþlice þinre feor *gewordene synd* [Adpro-
pinquauerunt persequentes me iniquitati a lege autem tua longe *facti sunt*]

K 125.1:

on gecyrringe hæftned *geworde we synd swa frefrede* [In conuertendo dominus captiuitatem Sion *facti sumus sicut consolati*]

K 125.3:

gemyclud don us *geworde we synd* blissiend [Magnificauit dominus facere nobiscum
facti sumus lætantes]

K148.5:

forþam he cwæð & *gewordene* [no Old English word corresponds to *sunt*] he bebead
& gesceappene synd [Quia ipse dixit et *facta sunt* ipse mandauit et creata sunt][19]

---

19 Cf. (B1.5.13) ÆHex 123: [Ipse dixit et *facta sunt*, ipse mandauit et creata sunt]: He sylf
hit gecwæð and *hi wurdon geworhte*, he sylf hit bebead and hi wurdon gesceapene.

As far as the subjects of *wesan geworden* are concerned, four out of the above seven have first-person subjects. Among the rest is an example with the subject *goman mine* [*fauces meæ*], but examples of *wesan gedon* with first-person subject also occur in 21.15, 29.8, 30.12, 30.13, 37.7, 68.9, 68.12, 70.7, 78.4, 78.8, 87.5, 101.7 (2 examples), 101.8, 118.83 in K, for a total of fifteen times in all. Whether the subject is the first person or not does not seem to decide the use of *wesan geworden* in PsGlK.

Nor does the meaning seem to be relevant in choosing *wesan geworden* instead of *wesan gedon*. The verb (ge)*weorðan* means both 'become, happen' and 'be done, be made'. Although it is often difficult to decide to which meaning an example belongs, most of the above seven examples are used in the sense 'become'. But the fifty instances of *wesan gedon* include examples of *beon gedon* 'to become, be'. *Dictionary of Old English* cites three examples from PsGlK:[20]

PsGlK 70.7:

swaswa foretacn **gedon** ic eom manegum & þu fylstend strang *tamquam prodigium factus sum multis et tu adiutor fortis* (ABCDEFGHIJ forms of *geworden*).

PsGlK 82.11:

hi forwurdon n **gedone** synd swa cwæd eorðan *disperierunt in Endor facti sunt ut stercus terræ* (ABCDEFGHIJ forms of *geworden*).

PsGlK 101.7:

gelice **gedon** ic eom stangeallan on westne gedon ic eom swa nihthrem on solere *similis factus sum pellicano solitudinis factus sum sicut nicticorax in domicilio* (ABCDEFGHIJ forms of *geworden*).

We cannot say, therefore, that *wesan geworden* in PsGlK is used to mean 'become, happen' or *wesan gedon* 'be done, be made'.

---

20   **gedon**, Past part. of (ge)**don**, 1.c.

There is another piece of evidence for the irrelevance of meaning in employing *wesan geworden* instead of *wesan gedon*. In 32.9 *wesan gedon* expresses the same thing described in 148.5:

K 32.9:

he cwæð & *gedone synd* he bebead & gesceapene synd [Quoniam ipse dixit et *facta sunt* ipse mandauit et creata sunt]

8.4. Examination of Some Possible Factors Related to the Frequent Use of *Wesan Gedon* in K

8.4.1. The examples of 'factum esse ≠ wesan geworden' in the Psalter manuscripts other than K

It is not only in PsGlK that we can find examples of *wesan gedon*, etc., that is, examples of *factum esse* that are not rendered by *wesan geworden*. There are eleven examples of this kind in the Psalter glosses.

I 32.9:

forðan þe he sylf cwæð & *geworhta vel gewurdone synt* he bebead gesceapene hig synt [Quoniam ipse dixit et *facta sunt* ipse mandauit et creata sunt]

G 37.7:

yrmþum geswenced ic eom & gedrefed eom oð ende on ende ælce dæge geunrot-sod ic ineod [*Miser factus sum* et curuatus sum usque in finem tota die contristatus ingrediebar]

In the following three places, D has *(wesan) gedon*.

105.36

D(R): & hy ðeowodon deofolgildum heora & *gedon is* him on æswic [et seruierunt sculptilibus eorum et *factum est* illis in scandalum]

H: *gedon is*

G: *gedon is*

68.11

D(R): & ic oferwreah on fæstene sawle & *gedon* on hosp [Et operui in ieiunio animam meam et *factum est* mihi in obprobrium]

H: *gedon is*

G: *gedon is*

117.23

D(R): fram drihtne *gedon is* & is wundurlic on eagum urum [a domino *factum est* et est mirabile in oculis nostris]

J: *gedon is*

138.22

E: þurhfulfremede fioung ic fioung hie fiend *geworhte sindon* me [Perfecto odio oderam illos inimici *facti sunt* michi]

Among the above eleven examples, both the instances of 'become, happen' and 'be made, be done' are included. All the corresponding parts in K have *wesan gedon*. These eleven examples, like the seven examples of *wesan geworden* in K, do not suggest that *wesan geworden* and *wesan gedon* are used differently from each other in K.

8.4.2. Examination of some other aspects of PsGlK and the Psalter glosses

We have been unable to ascribe the frequent use of *wesan gedon* in K to a certain difference of meaning or use between *wesan gedon* and *wesan geworden*. We shall now turn to some other aspects.

There is no instance of the Latin expression *factum est (ut)* ... (It happened that ...) in the Psalter. The frequent use of *wesan gedon* in K does not correspond to any particular Latin expression.

Concerning the dialects of the Psalter Glosses, A is Early Mercian and K is, with all the others, Late West-Saxon.[21]

K was written later than most of the other Psalter Glosses. 'It was written in the later tenth century in South-Western England, probably at the fashionable nunnery of Shaftesbury, and continued in use there for more than three hundred years. Long after the Norman Conquest, about the beginning of the twelfth century, it was thought worth while to copy into it an interlinear Old English translation which again goes back to the tenth century, a great formative period in English history' (Sisam & Sisam, p. v). But since E, which was written later in *c.* 1150 (Sisam & Sisam, p. ix), has no instance of *wesan gedon* and as many as 59 examples of *wesan geworden*, we cannot simply ascribe the frequent use of *wesan gedon* in K to the situation where the verb *weorðan* was becoming less and less used.

'At folios 41b and 75b another hand has filled in a few lines of gloss' (Sisam & Sisam, p. 14) but no example of *wesan gedon* or *wesan geworden* occurs there. Judging from the microfilm of the manuscript K,[22] the rare use of *wesan geworden* in K is not in a different hand or caused by interpolation.

The interrelationships of the Psalter glosses are also irrelevant here. The glosses that are more or less dependent on type D are E (corrections), F, G, H, J, L and K (Sisam & Sisam, §112).

---

21   According to the 'Genre, Date, and Dialect description (DD)' of the *Dictionary of Old English Corpus*, A is GEA (Glossary Early Anglian) and all the others are GLS (Glossary Late Saxon).

22   I am grateful to Prof. Kazuyoshi Yamanouchi of Tokyo Metropolitan University for letting me use the microfilm he ordered from Southampton University.

There is one thing that attracts our attention. In the five manuscripts C, L, A, F and B, where all the examples of *factum esse* are glossed with *wesan geworden*, there are very few instances of the simple forms of *(ge) weorðan*. A has no simple finite form of *(ge)weorðan* and all the examples in A are of the past participle *geworden*. C, L, F and B have respectively three, three, six and two examples of the simple finite form, while in K there are fifteen examples, the highest figure in the Psalter Glosses. Tables 8–27 and 8–28 illustrate these.

	Latin	C	E	L	J	H	A
019.004	pinguefiat	gefættige gewyrðe					
019.004	fiat						
030.019	fiant				geweorþe		
030.019	efficiantur	syn gefremyde	sien geworðen				
031.009	fieri						
032.022	Fiat	Geweorðe					
034.005	Fiant						
034.006	Fiat						
036.018	erit						
040.014	fiat						
040.014	fiat						
060.003	anxiaretur				angud wearþ	angud wearð	
068.023	Fiat						
068.026	Fiat			Geweorðe			
077.008	Ne fiant		Þæt hy ne werðen				

	Latin	C	E	L	J	H	A
077.065	excitatus				aweht wearþ		
077.065	est					wearð	
079.018	Fiat						
105.017	est						
108.007	fiat						
108.019	Fiat						
113.016	fiant						
118.076	Fiat						
118.080	Fiat						
118.173	Fiat						
121.007	Fiat			Geweorþe			
129.002	Fiant			geweorðe			

Table 8–27 The simple finite forms of *(ge)weorðan* (the first half)

	Latin	G	D (Roeder)	F	I	B	K
019.004	pinguefiat						
019.004	fiat			sy vel geweorðe			
030.019	fiant	synd vel gewurðe		geweorðe	gewurðun		gewyrþan
030.019	efficiantur		gewerþen				
031.009	fieri						gewyrþan
032.022	Fiat			Geweorðe	Gewurðe		
034.005	Fiant			Geweorðe	Beon hig vel gewurðun hig		Gewyrðan
034.006	Fiat				Gewurðe		Gewyrðe
036.018	erit						weorð
040.014	fiat				Gewurðe		
040.014	fiat				gewurðe vel sy þæt		
060.003	anxiaretur		angud wearð				
068.023	Fiat			Geweorðe			Gewyrþe
068.026	Fiat				Geweorðe		Gewyrðe
077.008	Ne fiant						
077.065	excitatus	awreht wearð		aweht wearð			
077.065	est		wearð				
079.018	Fiat						gewyrþe

	Latin	G	D (Roeder)	F	I	B	K
105.017	est				wearð		
108.007	fiat					geweorðe	gewyrþe
108.019	Fiat						Gewyrþe
113.008	fiant					geweorðen	gewyrþað
118.076	Fiat						Gewyrþe
118.080	Fiat						Gewyrþe
118.173	Fiat						Gewyrþe
121.007	Fiat						Gewyrþe
129.002	Fiant						

Table 8–28 The simple finite forms of *(ge)weorðan* (the second half)

This makes clear that the correspondence between the Latin verb *facere* (including the active forms) and Old English *(ge)weorðan* and *(ge)don* is irrelevant to our problem. What is relevant to us is the correspondence between Latin *factum esse* and its Old English equivalents. What is still more relevant is whether the Latin past participle *factum*, with or without *esse*, is glossed with *geworden* or with *gedon* or with some other verb. Our scope of investigation, therefore, will now be the Old English rendering of the Latin past participle *factum* in the interlinear glosses, including *facto* (and other forms) used as the ablative absolute.

8.5. The Equivalents of *Factum* in the Old English Glosses

The past participle *factum* can take a variety of forms. As the past participle of the intransitive verb *fio*, it can be used in the forms *factus, facta, factum* (singular), or *facti, factae, facta* (plural). The ablative absolute requires the forms *facto, facta* (singular) or *factis* (plural). Although Old English *(ge)weorðan* is an intransitive verb, the use of *(ge)worden* as a gloss goes beyond the above Latin forms. There are examples of accusative forms *(factam, factos*, etc.) glossed with *geworden*.

> JnGl (Ru)2.9:
> [ut autem gustauit architriclinus aquam uinum *factam* et ...] ðæt wutudlice inberigde ðe aldormon ðæt wæter to wine *giworden* & ...

Table 8–29, therefore, includes as *factum* all the Latin past participle forms that have *(ge)worden* as one of their Old English equivalents. In such cases, *geworden* is in rivalry with *gedon*. Those forms are 11 in all: *factæ, factę, facta, factae, factam, facte, facti, facto, factos, factum, factus*. There were no examples of *geworden* glossed to *factorum, factarum*, etc.

Factum, facti, factis, facto, facta glossed with the Old English noun *dæd(a)* have been excluded. I have excluded examples with no Old English equivalent.

I have also counted double glosses with different Old English verbs separately, but examples like '*geworden is vel uæs*' have been counted as one.

Ker	MS	Texts
203	Vespasian A. i	PsGlA
203	Vespasian A. i	PsCaA 1
203	Vespasian A. i	PsCaA 2
287	Pierpont Morgan Library 776	OccGl 50.1.2
335	Junius 27	PsGlB
292	Auct. D. 2. 19	MtGl(Ru)
292	Auct. D. 2. 19	MtGl(Ru)
292	Auct. D. 2. 19	LkGl(Ru)
292	Auct. D. 2. 19	JnGl(Ru)
249 art. a	Royal 2 B. v	PsGlD (Roeder)
249 art. a	Royal 2 B. v	PsCaD (Roeder)
165	Nero D. iv	MtGl(Li)
165	Nero D. iv	MtArgGl(Li)
165	Nero D. iv	MtHeadGl(Li)
165	Nero D. iv	MkGl(Li)
165	Nero D. iv	MkArgGl(Li)
165	Nero D. iv	LkGl(Li)
165	Nero D. iv	LkArgGl(Li)
165	Nero D. iv	LkHeadGl(Li)
165	Nero D. iv	JnGl(Li)
165	Nero D. iv	JnArgGl(Li)

Century	*worden**	*don***	*worht****	others	Verbs (= Others)
s. ix	64				
s. ix	4				
s. ix	3				
s. ix-x²	2				
s. x¹	62				
s. x	25	3	5	7	*wæs(3), gelamp(3), cwom(1)*
s. x	26		2		
s. x	63				
s. x	29				
s. x med	59	3			
s. x med	6				
s. x²	43		1	1	*was*
s. x²	3				
s. x²	2				
s. x²	27		2		
s. x²	1				
s. x²	88				
s. x²	1				
s. x²	3				
s. x²	31				
s. x²	2				

Ker	MS	Texts
165	Nero D. iv	JnHeadGl(Li)
106 art. c	Durham A. iv. 19	DurRitGl 1
106 art. d	Durham A. iv. 19	DurRitGl 2
106 art. d	Durham A. iv. 19	DurRitGlAbbrev
106 art. d	Durham A. iv. 19	DurRitGlCom
40	CCCC 173	SedGl 2.1 (Meritt)
129	B.M., Add. 37517	PsGlL
129	B.M., Add. 37517	PsCaL
8	Brussels 1650	Ald V 1
100 art. a	GL. KGL. SAM. 2034	CuthGl 1 (Metitt)
107A art. 1	Durham B. III. 32	HyGl 2 (Stevenson)
107A art. 2	Durham B. III. 32	MonCa 1 (Korhammer)
280 art. 1	Lambeth 427	PsGlI
280 art. 1	Lambeth 427	PsCaI
308	Bodl. Bodley 319 (2226)	IsGl
13	Ff. 1. 23	PsGlC
13	Ff. 1. 23	PsCaC
79	Pembroke	PsGlPem 1
271	Stowe 2	PsGlF
271	Stowe 2	PsCaF
320	Digby 146	AldV 13.1
160 arts. a, b	Julius A. vi	HyGl 3 (Gneuss)

Century	*worden**	*don***	*worht****	others	Verbs (= Others)
s. x²	3		I		
s. x²	II				
s. x²	I				
s. x²	2	I			
s. x²	6		I		
s. x–xi(?)		I			
s. xi in.	14				
s. xi in.	3				
s. xi¹	2				
s. xi¹	I				
s. xi¹	6				
s. xi¹	5				
s. xi¹	63		I	I	*gehælde*
s. xi¹	2		3		
s. xi¹	I				
s. xi med.	62				
s. xi med.	4		3		
s. xi med.	I				
s. xi med.	64				
s. xi med.	2				
s. xi med.	I				
s. xi med.	7				

Ker	MS	Texts
186 art. 1	Tiberius A. iii	BenRGl
186 art. 6	Tiberius A. iii	RegCGl
186 art. 7a	Tiberius A. iii	ProgGl 1
186 art. 7g	Tiberius A. iii	ProgGl 7
199 art. a	Tiberius C. vi	PsGlH
208 art. c	Vespasian D. xii	MonCa 3 (Korhammer)
224 art. a	Vitellius E. xviii	PsGlG
224 art. a	Vitellius E. xviii	PsCaG
256 art. 1	Royal 7 C. iv	LibSc
256 art. 2	Royal 7 C. iv	LibScEcc
232	B.M., Harley 863	PsCaHar
256 art. a	Bodleian, Auct.F. 3.6	PrudGl 8
134 art. 1	B.M., Arundel 60	PsGlJ
134 art. 1	B.M., Arundel 60	PsCaJ
379	Salisbury 150	PsGlK
379	Salisbury 150	PsCaK
91	Trinity R. 17.1	PsGlE
91	Trinity R. 17.1	PsCaE

Century	*worden**	*don***	*worht****	others	Verbs (= Others)
s. xi med.	8	I		I	*eom*
s. xi med.	3	16		I	*gemacedum*
s. xi med.	3				
s. xi med.		I			
s. xi med.	45	2			
s. xi med.	4			I	*is*
s. xi med.	60	2		I	*geswenched*
s. xi med.	4				
s. xi med.	6	I			
s. xi med.	I				
s.xi (3rd quarter)	3				
s.xi (3rd quarter)				I	*gestrenged*
s. xi²	63	I			
s. xi²	5				
s. xi/xii	7	52			
s. xi/xii	3	2			
s. xii med.	59		I		
s. xii med.	7				
Total	**1,086**	**86**	**20**	**14**	
Percentage	**90.0%**	**7.1%**	**1.7%**	**1.2%**	

Table 8–29 The equivalents of *factum* in interlinear glosses (in the chronological order of manuscripts)
* Under *worden* are grouped *geworden, aworden, giwoden, gewordenre, (a)warð, gewearð, wurdon, wyrdon*, etc. ** In the *don* group are *gedon, gedonum, ungedon*, etc.
*** *Worht* represents *geworht, aworht, giwyrcan*, etc.

Ninety per cent of *factum* is glossed with *geworden*. *Geworden* appears quite frequently in PsGlE, written later than K. The practice of glossing *factum* with *geworden* continues from s. ix (PsGlA) through s. xii med. (PsGlE).

Gedon occurs eighty-six times in all; specifically, fifty-two examples in PsGlK, two (*factus est mihi in salutem*) in PsCaK, thirty-two in other works. ÆGram, which is outside the interlinear glosses, also has one occurrence. The examples can be found sporadically from the rather freely glossed Ru¹ of s. x through the late Old English period, and comparatively frequently in s. xi med.

As to the place of the manuscripts containing *factum* = *gedon*, BenRGl, RegCGl, ProgGl 7 are in the MS British Museum, Cotton Tiberius A. iii, ff. 2–173 (s. xi med.), which is 'almost certainly a manuscript described in the medieval catalogue of Christ Church, Canterbury' (Ker p. 248). LibSc is also 'identifiable in the medieval Christ Church, Canterbury, catalogue' (Ker p. 324) and the 'gloss is mainly in a hand of s. xi med.' (ibid.).²³ PsGlD, too, 'was at Christ Church, Canterbury, in s. xi and later' (Ker p. 320). However, PsCaE in MS Cambridge, Trinity College R. 17.1(987) (s. xii med.), which was 'written at Christ Church, Canterbury' (Ker 136), does not have *factum* = *gedon*, though it has *facere* = *don*. On the other hand, PsGlG,²⁴ PsGlH and PsGlJ 'form a close group: all three are assigned to the period 1050–75, and all were produced at Winchester' (Sisam & Sisam §116). The interrelationship among these and the oldest Ru¹ or our K is unknown. K was probably still in the Benedictine nunnery at Shaftesbury in the thirteenth century.²⁵ Unlike the case of *factum* = *geworden*, it is difficult to find the tradition of glossing *factum* = *gedon*.

Examples of *factum* = *geworht* account for only 1.7% and are sporadic in time.

---

23   PsGlK and RegCGl are both in Hofstetter's Group II (= 'Those [texts] which favour vocabulary which does not conform to the Winchester usage' (Hofstetter, *ASE* 151)), and both favour *(ge)gearwian* for 'prepare', *mægen* for 'power', *ege* for 'terror, fear', *hreowsung* for 'repentance' and *ofermod-* for 'pride' (Hofstetter (1987) Nr. 214 & Nr. 229). RegCGl has 'a surprisingly large number of lexical affinities with the *Liber*'. (Getty xxx).

24   s. xi med. 'Written probably at Winchester' (Ker p. 301).

25   Celia Sisam and Kenneth Sisam (eds.), *The Salisbury Psalter*. EETS OS 242 (Oxford: Oxford University Press, 1959): §§10 & 24.

8.6. The Uniqueness of PsGlK

Unlike the case of *factum = geworden, factum = gedon* does not seem to have constituted a tradition in the Old English period. The frequent use in K, therefore, might be considered to be a unique phenomenon uninfluenced by other manuscripts or people. PsCaK, a work in the same manuscript (Salisbury 150), shares this distinctiveness. There are some other features that they alone share.

8.6.1. *The equivalents of 'factus est mihi in salutem' and 'salui facti sunt' in Old English Interlinear Glosses*

There are forty-four examples of *factus es(t) mihi in salutem* and fifteen examples of *salui facti sunt (sumus)* and *salua facta est*, reaching a total of fifty-nine examples. LibSc has one example (34.3), MtGl(Li) one (9.22), and MtGl(Ru) two (9.22, 14.36), all of which are the type *salui facti sunt (sumus)*, *salua facta est*. PsCa (Canticles of the Psalter) has seventeen instances.[26] All except five of these are examples of *geworden*. The only exceptions are the five instances of *gedon*, which occur in PsGlK (three examples) and in PsCaK (2). The five consist of four examples of *factus es(t) mihi in salutem* and one example of *salui facti sunt*.

> PsGlK 21.6
>> salui facti sunt [hale gedone synd]
> PsGlK 117.21
>> factus es mihi in salutem [gedon is me on hæle]
> PsGlK 117.28
>> factus es mihi in salutem [gedon þu eart me on hæle]
> PsCaK 2.2
>> factus est mihi in salutem [gedon eart me on hæle]
> PsCaK 5.2
>> factus est mihi in salutem [gedon is me on hæle]

---

26   PsCaC 2.2, PsCaC 5.2, PsCaE 2.2, PsCaE 5.2, PsCaJ 2.2, PsCaJ 5.2, PsCaA1 2.3, PsCaA1 5.1, PsCaG 2.2, PsCaD 2.2, PsCaD 5.2, PsCaF 2.2, PsCaF 5.2, PsCaI 2.2, PsCaI 5.2, PsCaK 2.2, PsCaK 5.2.

As can be seen in Table 8–29, MtGl(Ru) and LibSc have examples of *gedon* in other cases but do not have the ones used in this expression.

8.6.2. *The equivalents of 'amen (amen)' in Old English Interlinear Glosses*

Latin *amen* is translated in Interlinear Glosses by various Old English expressions: *soðlic(e)* (*vel soð is*) (58), *soð* (52), *si hit swa* (25), *soð is* (*vel soðlice*) (5), *sy swa* (5), *swa hit gewurðe* (4), *þæt si* (3), *swa beo hit* (2), *gealage vel sy swa* (2), *fiað* (2), *swa hit æfre/ gelim* (1) and no gloss (52). *Amen amen* is translated into *soð is soðlice* (19), *soð is soð is* (13), *soðlice soð is* (9), *soðlice soðlice (vel)* (3), *soð soðlice* (2), *soðlice soð* (2), *soð soð* (1). Among these, *þæt si* can be found only in PsCaK 16.18, 17.6 and AsPrGl 3 1.1, that is, in MS Salisbury 150, the manuscript containing PsGlK.

8.7. *Geworden* versus *Gedon* in Other Works

In this section, we shall look more closely into the examples of *geworden*, *gedon*, etc., in some other works in order to understand the uniqueness of PsGlK.

8.7.1. *RegCGl*

Regularis concordia (RegCGl) in Table 8–29 gives us interesting examples. It has one example of *factum est = gedon wæs* (8.20). Examples of ablative absolute are nineteen. Of the nineteen, fifteen have *gedon*; that is, *facto signo* ('when the bell is rung'), ten;[27] *cena facta* ('when supper is over'), one (9.38); *capitulo facto*, three (2.179, 4.29, 5.147); *factaque oratione*, one (3.37). Of the

27   2.51, 2.103, 2.129, 2.205, 2.277, 3.47, 5.134, 5.144, 7.12, 7.20.

remaining four, three have *geworden*, one has *gemakedum* (just preceded by *quo peracto* = *þam gedonum*) as their Old English gloss.[28] And the three examples of *geworden* all correspond to *mane facto* ('at daybreak').

RegCGl 5.129:

[*Mane facto* in caena domini conueniant ad primam qua sonore dicta et canonico more scilicet deus in nomine tuo] *mergene gewordenum* on gereorde cuman ætgædere to prime þam be sone gecweden & preostlicum gewunan gewislice.

RegCGl 7.20:

[Si uero necdum dies fuerit sique priori uisum fuerit *facto signo* qui uoluerint lectulis suis pausent usque dum *mane facto* agant ut supradictum est] gif soþlice na þænne gyt dæg byþ & gif þam ealdre geþuht byþ *gedonum tacne* þa þe wyllan on beddum hyra slapan oð þæt mergene *mergene gewordene* don swa herbufan gecweden ys.

RegCGl 13.34:

[siminus ordinentur fratres qui sine intermissione psalmodie uacent residentes circa corpus die noctuque sequenti donec *mane facto* corpus terre commendetur] gif þæt na byþ beon gescyfte gebroþrum þa buton forlætincge to sealmsange geæmtian sittende abutan þæt lic on dæge & nihte fyligendre oþ þæt *mergene gewordenum* þæt lic eorþan beo betæht.

They are used in the sense 'become, get, be' instead of the sense 'be done, be made'. On the other hand *facto signo* corresponds to *gedonum tacne*, e.g.,

RegCGl 2.205:

[et *facto* signo agant orationem deinde sextam post sextam eant ad mensam] & *gedonum tacne* hi don gebed syþþan middæg æfter middæge gan to mysan.

28   RegCGl 2.265: [Inde pulsata tabula eant ad mandatum secundum regule edictum quo *peracto facto* signo in ecclesia initietur collatio rursumque dato tintinnabuli signo refectorium introeant caritatis gratia] syþþan gecnucedre tabulan gan to æfter regules bebode þam *gedonum gemacedum* tacne on cyrcean si ongunnen æfenræding & eft gesealdum þære bellan tacne beodærn inngan mid soþre lufe gife.

In this connection all the three examples of *facto (primo) signo* (when the (first) signal has been given) in the Benedictine Rule have *geworden*.[29]

8.7.2. Possible alternatives to wesan geworden

Latin *factum esse* was the perfect form of the verb *fieri* and the passive of the verb *facere*.[30] The Old English verb *(ge)weorðan* was used in the senses *to become, be done, be made, happen, come to pass, arise, take place*, etc.[31] A verb used generally as an alternative of *wesan geworden* must have these meanings. The verb *gelimpan*, which occurs three times as a gloss to *factum esse* in Ru¹,[32] cannot be a general equivalent.

Visser gives three alternatives to *wesan geworden* in translating *factum esse: wesan gedon, was made* and *wesan geworht*.[33] These seem to have been likelier to be used than simple verb forms, especially in glossing, in that both *factum* and *esse* have their Old English counterparts.[34] Visser only enumerates examples of them found in Old, Middle and Modern English works. But these three were not used indiscriminately in the Old English period. Bede has a large number of examples of *factum esse*. They, together with

---

29 BenRGl 53.12 [facto signo] gewordenre tacne; 54.17 [facto signo] gewordenem tacne; 82.11: [Facto autem primo signo] gewordenum forecnyll.

30 'Fiô, fierî, factus sum, *be made, be done, become*, was used by the Romans as the passive of the simple verb faciô.... the perfect system is quite regular as the normal passive of faciô; factus, -a, -um est, factus erat, factus sit, factus esset, factus esse, etc'. (Wheelock *Latin* 173). 'faciô, -ere, fêcî, factum, make, do, accomplish, ...; *passive:* fiô, fierî, factus sum' (419).

31 The definition in Clark Hall (ed.), *A Concise Anglo-Saxon Dictionary* (Cambridge: Cambridge University Press, 1960) is: '±weorðan³ (u, y) *to become, get, be* (passive auxiliary), *be done, be made*, CP: *happen, come to pass, arise, take place, settle*: (+) impers. *get on with, please, agree*, AO, Chr: *think of, occur to*'. The impersonal use above will be left out of consideration since the past participle of the impersonally employed *(ge)weorðan* combines not with *wesan* but with *habban*.

32 Ru¹, 11.1, 13.53 & 19.1.

33 Visser, F. Th. *An Historical Syntax of the English Language*, vol. 3, second half (Leiden: E.J. Brill, 1973): §1900.

34 For this principle, see Knud Sørensen, 'Latin Influence on English Syntax: A Survey with a Bibliography', *Travaux du Cercle Linguistique de Copenhague* 11 (1957): 143.

the examples in Ælfric and *Oxford English Dictionary* (*OED*), give some
clues to the adoption of *wesan gedon* as the alternative to *wesan geworden*
in K.

8.7.2.1. *Wesan gemacod(e)*

'The word is not very frequent in OE' (*OED*, s.v. 'make', Etymology). K
has indeed only one active example of this verb[35] and no passive ones. In
Bede, which has 102 examples of *factum esse*, no example of *macian* occurs.
The only passive example in 'Alfredian and Other Translations' (B9) is in
CP 18.135.7.

In the works of Ælfric, the passive forms occur four times: in ÆHom
20: 43, 21 324, 22 202, and in Ælet1 (Wulfsige Xa) 114. Their subjects are
respectively *eunuchi*, *næddre*, *sylfren god* and *eower reaf*, none of which
represents an action or event.

In the *OED*, no Old English examples are among the passive quotations of 'make' rendering Latin *fieri* 'to begin to exist', 'to take place', 'to
be', 'to become', etc. ('make' 9e, 48f & 49e & d). The scarcity of *macian* in
Old English is mentioned in 'I. Senses in which the object of the verb is
a product or result. * To bring into existence by construction or elabora-
tion': Not common until late in OE.; the L. *facere* is usually rendered by
gewyrcan. In 'V. To do, perform, accomplish. 57' we find: 'From the 12th
c. *make* (corresponding to L. *facere*, F. *faire*) has been extensively used with
a noun of action as object, where the older language would have used the
verb ȝewyrcan (WORK) or *dón* (DO)'.

Wesan gemacod(e), so little used, does not seem to have been in a position to be a general equivalent of *factum esse* in K.

8.7.2.2. *Wesan geworht(e)*

The verb *gewyrcan* was more widely used. In the section 'The word frequency
counts listed alphabetically' in the *Old English Concordance* (microfiche),
the numbers of occurrences in Old English are the following: *gemacod*,

---

35   PsGlK 7.16.

9; *gemaced*, 4; *geworht*, 243; *geworhte*, 498.[36] The Ru¹ has five instances of
wesan (ge)worht corresponding to *factum esse*, along with three examples
of *wesan gedon*.[37]

In Bede, there are thirteen examples of *wesan geworht(e)*. The subjects
of the verb are the following: 'church' (3.104.32, 7.40.24, 15.62.2, 17.90.13),
Romaburh (9.42.28), *ceastre & torras & stræta & brycge* (9.44.5), *fæsten*
(9.46.8), *þa* (followed by *ðe monna hondum geworhte wæron of eorðlicum
timbre, oðþe of treom, oðþe of stanum*) (16.224.12), *treowgeweorc* (3.272.4),
þyrel (3.272.6), *hus* (26.354.18) and *þurh* (5.396.19). Whether large or small,
they are what result from having been built, constructed or made. The other
one is in 6.176.6: *ðæt weorc þære cirican huhugu healf wæs geworht*. This may
be grouped together or the subject may represent the act of constructing
or building.

The examples in ÆCHomI (17) & II (12)[38] show the same tendency,
though here only two[39] have as subject what is built. The other subjects are
what come to be or are made: *heofen, ealle þing* (four times), *þa gesceafta, se
sunu, ... menn* (three times), *we, deorwyrðe, sealfe, reaf*, etc. The two examples *wurdon geworhte* with the subject *fela wundra* or *wundra forwel fela*
are accompanied by *ðurh ðone halgan cuðberht* (ÆCHom II, 10 84.95) or
ðurh geearnungum his eadigan lifes (ÆCHom II, 10 90.331), respectively.
Four examples of *wesan geworht(e)* have a complementary adjective or a
noun phrase like the following: *swiþost gif hi* [= *treowa*] *beoð unsæpige
geworhte*[40] or *Þeah gif wifman bið werlice geworht*.[41]

---

36   Cf. *gedone* 58, *gedoan* 3, '*gedon* 822' includes infinitive examples. Jn(WSCp) has only
one example. Jn (WSCp) 13.2: & þa Drihtnes þenung <u>wæs gemacud</u> ... [Et cena
<u>facta</u> ...]

37   Ru¹, 11.20, 11.21(twice), 11.23(twice). *Sindun worht* in 14.2 corresponds to *inoperan-
tur*. The examples of *wesan gedon* are in 18.31, 23.15 & 28.11. See also Visser, F. Th.
An Historical Syntax of the English Language. vol. 3, second half (1973): §1900,
p. 2051.

38   ÆCHomI: 1 12.19, 1 16.1, 2 40.12, 4 70.16, 6 102.22, 8 122.13, 9 142.12, 12 188.28, 12
188.32, 15 220.8, 18 256.30, 19 264.18, 20 278.19, 20 280.13, 25 360.2, 29 424.1, & 29
424.6. ÆCHomII: 3 19.19, 3 25.202, 10 84.95, 10 90.331, 12.1 117.268, 23 203.123 (twice),
25 209.92, 34 256.47, 38 287.264, 43 320.54, & 45 339.121.

39   ÆCHomII, 23 203.123 (þa gebytlu) & 38 287.264 (seo cyrce).

40   ÆCHomI, 6 102.22.

41   ÆCHomI, 12 188.32. The other ones are in ÆCHomI, 1 12.19 & 12 188.28.

8.7.2.3. *Wesan gedon (e)*

At '†14' of 'I. Transitive senses' of the verb *do* in *OED* is the definition: 'In pass., rendering L. *fieri, factum esse*: To be brought about, come to pass, happen. Obs.' Although the first citation dates from Wycliffe, *wesan gedon* was already used in rendering Latin *factum esse* in the Old English period, as the examples in K and others show.

In Bede, there are sixteen examples of *wesan gedon*. Two of them with the subject *Eadwinis heafod* and *his lichama* are used in the sense 'place'.[42] One with *he* as its subject corresponds to Latin *fuerat ... sociatus*.[43] There are examples with *wund* or *bryce ne daro* as their subjects.[44] What is quite different from *wesan geworht* or *wesan gemacond* is that all the other ten examples have a subject representing an event, occurrence or action and are used in the senses 'to happen, take place, be done'.[45] When examples about miracles are compared, unlike the two of *wesan geworht* in ÆCHomII, the one of *wesan gedon* (Bede 3 11.188.30) has no *ðurh*-phrase: *he hine gelomlice herde secgan in þære mægðe bi þæm* wundrum, *þe æt þæm banum þæs arwyrðan cyninges* gedon wæron.

ÆCHomI & II have seven and fourteen instances respectively of *wesan gedon*. Except one,[46] all are about an event, occurrence or action and they mean 'to happen, take place, be done'.[47] Fourteen of them have *hit* (referring to an event, action, and the like) as its subject and three have *þis*. A *þæt*-clause is the subject of I, 34 518.30. No example with a building as its subject occurs in these works.

---

42 Bede 2 16.148.28.
43 Bede 5 17.452.15.
44 *wund*: Bede 2 8.124.8 and 4 18.308.14. *bryce ne daro*: Bede 3 1.158.1.
45 BedeHead 1.10.10, 3 10.186.33, 3 11.188.30, 322.252.1, 4 32.380.17, 4 33.380.30, 5 1.386.24, 5 3.392.11, 5 4.396.5, 5 17.450.18.
46 ÆCHomI, 22 324.16: and þurh tocyme þæs halgan gastes mennisce men wurdon gedone to godum;
47 ÆCHomI, 37 564.1, 10 162.13, 16 230.30, 26 374.15, 34 502.29, 34 518.30; II, 3 22.117, 4 29.17, 8 68.30, 11 103.374, 13 135.241, 13 135.253, 15 154.157 (twice), 16 161.10, 26 213.16, 26 216.95, 28 222.50, 35 262.82, 38 282.70.

In K, only active examples of *macian*[48] and *wyrcan*[49] occur and no passive forms of these verbs are used. *Wesan gedon* is found along with *wesan
geworden*. What is common to the latter two is that they are used in the
sense 'to happen, to take place' in addition to 'be made' with or without a
complementary adjective, preposition *to*, etc.[50] It is suspected that the possibility of this sense of *wesan gedon* has led the glossator of the Salisbury
Psalter to adopt it when glossing the frequently used *factum esse*.[51] Sisam
writes: 'where D has a variety of renderings for a Latin word, the scribe of K
usually restricts himself to one'. Though most of the examples in the Psalter
have a complementary adjective or noun and are not used in this manner,
an Old English expression without the sense 'to happen' was probably not
an appropriate one for the glossator of K to use frequently in glossing the
examples of *factum esse* in the Bible.

8.7.3. *The growth of wesan gedon*

Each of the following two examples is taken from a gloss and has *tonitruum*
'thunder' as its subject:

JnGl (Ru) 12.29:

[turba ergo quae stabat et audiebat dicebat *tonitruum factum est* alii dicebant angelus
ei locutus est] ðe here forðon ðeðe stod & giherde cwedun *ðunor ðætte aworden wæs*
oðre cwedun engel him sprecende wæs.

ProgGl 7 (Först) 14:

[Si media nocte *tonitruum factum fuerit* famem magnam significat] Gif on midre
nihte *þunorrad gedon bið* ungor micelne getacnað.

---

48   PsGlK 7.16.
49   PsGlK 9.5, 9.16, 35.13, 43.2, 67.29, 73.17 (twice), 76.4, 79.10, 85.9, 94.5, 94.6, 95.5,
     117.24, 118.73, 120.2, 138.5.
50   See Joseph Bosworth and T. Northcote Toller, *An Anglo-Saxon Dictionary*, Supplement
     (Oxford: Oxford University Press, 1955), 'don' III. *to make*; 'gedon' V, VI, etc.
51   See note 6.

The former, JnGl(Ru), dates from the tenth century,[52] and the verb is *aworden wæs*. The corresponding part of the Lindisfarne Gospels (s. x²)[53] is *aworden uoere*. The latter, Prognostics (ProgGl 7 14(CaCC)), dates from the middle of the eleventh century[54] and has *gedon bið*. The difference may be ascribed to the development of *(ge)don*.

If we go from the interlinear glosses to the prose GD, we find *gedon* and *geworden* used in the same way (see Table 8–30):

GD	C	H	Yerkes	
22. 7	*gedon*	*geworden*	(No. 233)	'it happened that'
172. 4	*gedone*	*gewordene*	(No. 2761)	'had taken place'
172.12	*gedon*	*geworden*	(No. 2767)	'it happened that'

Table 8–30 *Gedon* and *geworden* in GD

GD 1 (C) 2.22.6:

& swa hit *wæs gedon*, þæt se fæder wearð to swa mycelre monþwærnysse/ gelæded, & þa gewearð seo eadmodnys þæs geongran to lareowe þam abbude.

GD 1 (H) 2.22.6:

& swa *wæs geworden*, þæt se abbod wearð getogen to mycelre geþwærnysse, & wearð þæs gingran eadmodnys þam abbode to lareowe.

GD 2 (C) 35.171.34:

Þam deacone wafiendum for þus mycclum wundre se Godes wer Benedictus him sæde æfter endebyrdnysse ealle þa wisan, þe þær *gedone wæron*. || GD 2 (C) 35.172.4: & þa sona in Cassinum þære stowe he onbead þam æwfæstan were Theoprobo þæt, þæt he onsænde þære ylcan niht man to Capuanan þære byrig, & þæt he sylf ongeate

52   Ker 292.
53   Ker 165.
54   Ker 186 art. 7g.

& eft þider gebude, hwæt geworden wære be Germane þam biscope. | GD 2 (C)
35.172.11: Þa *wæs* þæt swa *gedon*, þæt þone arwyrþestan wer Germanum þone biscop
se ærendraca, þe þider onsænded wæs, gemette þa forðferedne.

GD 2 (H) 35.171.30:

Ðam diacone þa wafiendum for þus mycelum wundre se Godes wer be endebyrd-
nesse gerehte þa þing, þe þær *gewordene wæron*, & on Casino þam stocwic þam eaw-
fæstan were Theoprobo þær rihte bebead, þæt he on þære ylcan nihte asende sumne
mann to Capuanan þære byri & gewiste & him eft gecyðde, hwæt wære geworden
be Germane þam bisceope. | GD 2 (H) 35.172.10: Ða *wæs geworden*, þæt se þe þyder
asended wæs gemette eallunga forðferedne þone arwurðan wer Germanum bisceop,
& he þa smeaþancollice axiende oncneow, þæt his forðsið wæs on þam ylcan timan,
þe se drihtnes wer oncneow his upstige to heofonum.

MS H is perhaps older than C,[55] and in C *gedon* is used in the three places
above.

The next one is from an eleventh-century entry of Chronicle E:

ChronE (Plummer) 1066.15:

& man cydde Harolde cyng hu hit *wæs* þær *gedon & geworden*. & he com mid myc-
clum here Engliscra manna. & gemette hine æt Stængfordes brycge. & hine ofsloh.
& þone eorl Tostig. & eallne þone here ahtlice ofercom.

Denison writes: 'the individual probabilities seem to be that *gedon* is a
passive participle 'done' and *geworden* an intransitive perfect participle
'happened' – yet they are coordinated complements of a single occurrence
of BE. Such examples actually call the distinction into question' (§12.4.3).
This example also seems to indicate that *wesan gedon* and *wesan geworden*
were coming to be used in a similar fashion.

---

55   C: Ker 60; Cambridge, Corpus Christi College 322; s.xi²; Wærferth's original transla-
      tion (Yerkes xvi). H: Ker 328A; Bodleian, Hatton 76 (4125); s.xi¹.; revision (Yerkes
      xvi). Yerkes considers 'C and H, both written in the eleventh century, quite possibly
      at Worcester' (xvi).

The *Middle English Dictionary* further attests the development of *wesan gedon* in this direction. It says that *ben don* was used in the sense of 'happen' and gives a prose example, 'a faithful rendering of the Latin' Vulgate, from a 'South-western text' 'of the early fourteenth century'.[56]

> 4.(a) To cause (sth.); make (sth. happen), cause (sb. to do or experience sth.), have (sth. done); *ben don, happen*; **be it don**, so be it; **as it was don**, as it was; *it is (was)* ~, *it came to pass*; ....

> (a) a1325(c1280) SLeg.Pass.(Pep)1541: Þo by-gonne *tenebres, þat* in-to al þe eorþe *were ydon*, In þe sixte tyd of þe day.

Two of the three corresponding parts in the West-Saxon Gospels have *wesan geworden*.[57]

I have been examining the examples of *wesan gedon*, but except those in the Salisbury Psalter, I have not encountered an example of *wesan gedon*

---

56   SLeg.Pass.(Pep) = *The Southern Passion Edited from Pepysian MS 2344*, ed. B.D. Brown, EETS OS 169(1927 for 1925): 1–92. [BR 483]]. | xvi: In MS. Pepys 2344 (from which no pieces have heretofore been printed) we have a useful South-western text, ... | xviii: *P.* Pepys MS 2344, 183–237. A manuscript of 528 pages, forty-seven lines to a page; numerous initials in colours; a fine regular hand of the early fourteenth century | xl: *P* This manuscript is south-western, with Midland shading notably in forms replacing O.E. *u*. It appears to have been copied from a text less influenced by Midland dialect (cf. no. 7). *P* has in common with H the dialectal form *wordle* 137, 212, 398, 1064, &c. (but *world* 373, 1029, 1030). | lv: For those portions of the *Southern Passion* which are immediately concerned with the life of Jesus, the Vulgate has supplied the entire substance, and, to a large extent, the phrasing .... The language of this portion of the poem has apparently been transferred directly from the open page of the Vulgate, since it corresponds as a rule, even in minute details, with the Latin text .... the language of the poem, in so far as it is concerned with the material of the Vulgate, is, as has been said, a faithful rendering of the Latin of the source. | lix: [*S.P.*] 1541–1545 [Vulgate] Matt. xxvii. 45; Marc. xv. 33; Luc. xxiii. 44.

57   Mt (WSCp) 27.45: Witodlice fram þære sixtan tide *wæron gewurden* þystru ofer ealle eorðan oþ þa nigoþan tid. Mk (WSCp) 15.33: And þære syxtan tide *wurdo* þystru *gewordene* geond ealle eorðan oð nontide. Lk (WSCp) 23.44: Þa wæs nean seo syxte tid, & þystro *wæron* ofer ealle eorþan oð þa nigoþan tide, & sunne wæs aþystrod & þæs temples wahryft wearð toslyten on middan.

used in the sense of 'become'. The *Middle English Dictionary* does not have 'be or become' among the definitions of *ben don*.[58]

The *Dictionary of Old English* puts 'in glosses' in parentheses after the definition '*beon gedon* "to become, be"' and three out of four illustrations are from the Salisbury Psalter.

All these things seem to indicate that the examples of *wesan gedon* in the sense of 'be' or 'become' do not represent a widespread use in the days of the Salisbury Psalter.

8.8. Conclusion

Of the 1,461 examples of *wesan geworden* in Old English, as many as 767 (52%) are in Glossed Texts, and 76% of these (582 examples) occur in the Psalter glosses. This expression was an almost regular equivalent to Latin *factum (esse)* in the interlinear gloss, where the language 'gehorcht zweifellos in vielerlei Hinsicht eigenen Gesetzen' (Kornexl, ccxxv). *Wesan geworden* is used in glossing all the instances of *factum esse* in the ninth-century PsGlA. Its almost exclusive use in rendering *factum esse* continued even in the mid-twelfth-century PsGlE.

The situation outside the interlinear glosses, however, seems to have been different, and the glossator of the Salisbury Psalter was not a slavish copyist of D, the Royal Psalter. The words he rejected and chose 'about the beginning of the twelfth century' were 'the adjustments he made to the speech of his own day' (Sisam & Sisam, p. v).[59] *Wesan geworden*, which had traditionally been employed especially in glosses for *factum esse* and was eventually to be obsolete, was rejected probably because it was rather archaic and was not a familiar, everyday word to the scribe of the Salisbury Psalter.

---

58   Kurath, Hans, *et al.* (eds.), *Middle English Dictionary* (Ann Arbor, MI: University of Michigan Press, 1954–2001) has 'be or become' as the definition of 'ben made'.

59   'Certain words in D are rejected with fair consistency: ... perhaps becoming obsolete, e.g. *afeorrian* (K *afeorsian*), *atynan* (K *openian*), *cneoris* (K *cneornes*, with analogical suffix), *fæmne* (K *mægden*), *gehat* (K *behæs*), *ofergytan* (K *forgytan*), *symle* (K *æfre*)' (Sisam and Sisam, eds., *The Salisbury Psalter*. EETS OS 242 (1959): §77).

Wesan gedon was employed because it was a newer, more common expression, it seems, outside interlinear glosses in the senses 'to happen,' etc. But the expression seems to have been confined to glosses in the sense 'to become.' Sisam writes: 'where D has a variety of renderings for a Latin word, the scribe of K usually restricts himself to one — the commonest in his day' (§76). So, the frequent use of *wesan gedon*, instead of *wesan geworden*, in the Salisbury Psalter is not entirely a mistake[60] but seems to have been partly an adjustment by the scribe to the speech of his own day and partly a mechanically extended application of *wesan gedon* to *factum esse* in the sense 'to become.'[61]

8.9. References

8.9.1. Primary sources

Brown, Beatrice Daw, ed. *The Southern Passion*. EETS OS 169. 1927. New York: Kraus Reprint, 1971.

Clemoes, Peter, ed. *Ælfric's Catholic Homilies: The First Series Text*. EETS SS 17. London: Oxford University Press, 1997.

60   For the ignorance and mistakes of the glossator of K, see the Sisams' introduction (V. Method of Glossing & VI. Spelling of the Gloss). See also Derolez, R. (ed.), *Anglo-Saxon Glossography* (Brussels: Paleis der Academiën, 1992): 24.

61   This chapter has developed out of four presentations. 1 'Old English *(ge)weorðan* and *(ge)þyncan*'. Symposium '英語における迂言化の契機 [Verbal Periphrases in Old and Middle English]'. The Modern English Association (Keio University; 17 May 1991). 2 '*Factum esse = Wesan Gedon* in the Salisbury Psalter'. The 12th National Conference of the English Linguistic Society of Japan (University of Tokyo, Hongo Campus, 13 Nov. 1994). 3 'Factum Esse の古英語訳 と The Salisbury Psalter [The Old English Equivalents for *Factum Esse* and the Salisbury Psalter]'. The 13th Meeting of the Eastern Branch of the Japan Society for Medieval English Studies (Kawamura Woman's University; 28 June 1997). 4 'The Old English Equivalents for *Factum Esse* and the Salisbury Psalter'. International Medieval Congress (University of Leeds; 14 July 1997). I am grateful to all those who commented on my presentations, especially to Prof. Shigeru Ono, Kazuyoshi Yamanouchi and Michiko Ogura, although of course I alone am responsible for any errors.

Getty, Sarah Sovereign. *An Edition, with Commentary, of the Latin/Anglo-Saxon 'Liber-Scintillarum'.* Dissertation. University of Pennsylvania, 1969. Ann Arbor, MI: UMI, 1970.

Gibson, Margaret, T.A. Heslop and Richard W. Pfaff, eds. *The Eadwine Psalter: Text, Image, and Monastic Culture in Twelfth-Century Canterbury.* London and University Park, PA: The Modern Humanities Research Association in conjunction with the Pennsylvania State University Press, 1992.

Godden, M.R., ed. *Ælfric's Catholic Homilies: The Second Series Text.* EETS SS 5. London: Oxford University Press, 1979.

Kornexl, Lucia, ed. *Die 'Regularis Concordia' und ihre altenglische Interlinearversion.* München: Wilhelm Fink Verlag, 1993.

Logeman, H., ed. *The Rule of S. Benet: Latin and Anglo-Saxon Interlinear Version.* EETS OS 90. 1888. Millwood, NY: Krauss Reprint, 1981.

Sisam, Celia and Kenneth Sisam, eds. *The Salisbury Psalter.* EETS OS 242. Oxford: Oxford University Press, 1959.

8.9.2. Secondary sources

Bosworth, Joseph and T. Northcote Toller, eds. *An Anglo-Saxon Dictionary*, Supplement. Oxford: Oxford University Press, 1955.

Cameron, Angus, *et al.*, eds. *Dictionary of Old English, D.* Toronto: Pontifical Institute of Mediaeval Studies, 1986.

Denison, David. *English Historical Syntax: Verbal Constructions.* London and New York: Longman, 1993.

Derolez, R., ed. *Anglo-Saxon Glossography.* Brussels: Paleis der Academiën, 1992.

The Dictionary of Old English Corpus. Toronto: Dictionary of Old English, 1993 Release.[62]

Dictionary of Old English Project, University of Toronto. *The Complete Corpus of Old English in Machine Readable Form.* 1st version. Oxford: Oxford Text Archive, 1990.

Hall, J.R. Clark, ed. *A Concise Anglo-Saxon Dictionary.* 4th edn. Cambridge: Cambridge University Press, 1960.

Healey, Antonette diPaolo and Richard L. Venezky, comp. *A Microfiche Concordance to Old English: The List of Texts and Index of Editions.* Toronto: University of

---

62   I am grateful to Professor Peter Clemoes for permission to use his text of Ælfric's Catholic Homilies, First Series, for my research purposes.

Toronto Press, 1980. (The editions of the Old English texts cited with abbreviations in this chapter are those listed in this book).

Hoffsteter, Walter. *Winchester und der spätaltenglische Sprachgebrauch: Untersuchungen zur geographischen und zeitlichen Verbreitung altenglischer Synonyme.* München: Wilhelm Fink, 1987.

——. 'Winchester and the Standardization of Old English Vocabulary', in Peter Clemoes, ed. *Anglo-Saxon England* 17, Cambridge: Cambridge University Press, 1988: 139–61.

Ide, Mitsu. '*Factum esse* と [and] *wesan geworden*', *Metropolitan* 23 (1979): 17–45.

——. '*Wæs Geworden*'. *Metropolitan Linguistics* 3 (1979): 1–25.

Ker, N.R. *Catalogue of Manuscripts Containing Anglo-Saxon.* Oxford: Clarendon Press, 1957.

Kurath, Hans, *et al.* eds. *Middle English Dictionary.* Ann Arbor, MI: University of Michigan Press, 1954–2001.

Simpson, J.A. and E.S.C. Weiner, eds. *The Oxford English Dictionary.* 2nd edn. Oxford: Clarendon Press, 1989.

Sørensen, Knud. 'Latin Influence on English Syntax: A Survey with a Bibliography', *Travaux du Cercle Linguistique de Copenhague* 11 (1957): 131–55.

Visser, F. Th. *An Historical Syntax of the English Language.* vol. 3, second half. Leiden: E.J. Brill, 1973.

Wheelock, Frederic M. *Latin: An Introductory Course Based on Ancient Authors.* 3rd edn. New York: Barnes and Noble, 1963.

——. *Latin Literature.* New York: Barnes and Noble, 1969.

Yerkes, David. *The Two Versions of Wærferth's Translation of Gregory's Dialogues.* Toronto: University of Toronto Press, 1979.

AKIYUKI JIMURA

9 On the Decline of the Prefix *y-* of Past Participles

9.0. Introduction

Present-day English often shows a marked discrepancy between word forms and their pronunciations. The words 'know', 'walk' and 'climb' as spelled do not correspond to their pronunciations, because they respectively lose one or more sounds, such as the initial sound /k/ (aphaeresis), the medial sound /l/ (syncope) and the final sound /b/ (apocope). By contrast, in Middle English word forms more often coincide with their pronunciations.

We may easily find the coexisting variant word forms in Middle English, when reading the extant manuscripts carefully. Examples include the word forms of past participles with both *y*-prefix and ø-prefix. At the earliest stages, the prefix *ge-* was also attached to the stems of parts of speech other than verbs. It has disappeared in present-day English (via the weakened *y-/i-* forms), though the equivalent form remains in German. This paper discusses a historical perspective or process affecting the prefix *y-*, which came to be used only in a few archaic words such as 'yclept' or 'yclad'.

In Early Middle English, I will investigate variant word forms in the four manuscripts of *Ancrene Wisse* written mainly in the thirteenth century. *A* is Cambridge, Corpus Christi College, MS 402 (Corpus); *C* is London, British Library, MS Cotton Cleopatra C. vi (Cleopatra); *N* is London, British Library, MS Cotton Nero A. xiv (Nero); and *V* is Oxford, Bodleian Library, MS Eng. Poet. A. 1 (Vernon). For detailed information on the manuscripts, I have consulted T. Kubouchi and K. Ikegami (eds.), *The Ancrene Wisse: A Four-Manuscript Parallel Text. Preface and Parts 1–4* (Frankfurt am Main: Peter Lang, 2003) and *Parts 5–8 with Wordlists*

(Frankfurt am Main: Peter Lang, 2005). It is said that A, C and N were written in the first half of the thirteenth century: A c.1230, C between c.1225 and c.1230, and N between c.1225 and 1240, while V was written in the last quarter of the fourteenth century between the 1380s and 1390s. MS A shows dialectal features of the West Midlands, whereas C, N and V show features of the Southwest Midlands. Additionally, A and V show formal stylistic features, while C and N have informal and private features of language.[1]

I will use the language of Geoffrey Chaucer (1340?–1400) and William Langland (1330?–87) as my examples of late fourteenth-century English. There are three representative versions of *Piers Plowman*. The A version was written between 1368 and 1374, the B version around 1377, and the C version between 1379/1381 and c.1385.[2] We can see some features of language change in the second half of the fourteenth century, when comparing the language of A, B and C. It is said that A shows the dialect of the Southwest of England, B that of the Midlands, and C that of the West Midlands. Thus, we understand that A reflects the language features of Southern English.

The language of Chaucer was maintained by several scribes after Chaucer's death. As is well known, the Hengwrt manuscript and the Ellesmere manuscript are the representatives that show marked language features of the first half of the fifteenth century. William Thynne (?–1546) edited Chaucer's *The Romaunt of the Rose* in 1532. Interestingly, Thynne added the prefix *y-* to past participles mainly in the first 2,000 lines of *The Romaunt of the Rose*.[3] It is an important fact that the sixteenth-century editor Thynne took the trouble to add the prefix *y-* to the past participles, ignoring the

1   T. Kubouchi, 'Modernity and Archaism in the *Ancrene Wisse* Revisited' (in Japanese), *SIMELL* 21 (2006): 67, 72.
2   See George Kane, 'The Text', in J.A. Alford (ed.), *A Companion to* Piers Plowman (Berkeley, CA: University of California Press, 1988): 175–221. For more recent discussion of the dating, see A.V.C. Schmidt, *Piers Plowman: A Parallel-Text Edition, Vol. II.* (Kalamazoo, MI: Medieval Institute Publications, 2008): 273–81.
3   L.D. Benson (ed.), *The Riverside Chaucer*, 3rd edn. (Boston, MA: Houghton Mifflin, 1987): 1198.

original word form of the manuscript. It is not too much to say that the prefix *y-* is an archaic word form, descended from Old English, which characterizes the language of the poet Chaucer. This feature, in due course, reflects the language of the sixteenth century, where an archaic use of the prefix *y-* is followed in the language of Edmund Spenser (1552?–99) and John Milton (1608–74).

9.1. Middle English

9.1.1. Ancrene Wisse

I will look at the word form *icleopet* in the four aforementioned manuscripts of *Ancrene Wisse* (the italics in the cited passage are mine.)

A 3r04, V372ra48
A   & for his muchele halinesse *icleopet* godes broðer.
C   & for his / muchel halinesse *icleoped* godes broðer.
N   & for his muchele halinesse ᴣ *icleo-/ped* godes broþur.
V   and for his muchel halynesse. *I.cle-/ped* godus broþur.

The other instances are as follows: A 35r22, V377vb60; A 35r03, V377rb80; A 48v04, V380rb15; A 48v06, V380rb17; A 8ov10, V385vb52; A 86v06, V386vb57. The exception is A 51v12, V380vb50, where 'icleopet' is used in A and C, while 'i_cleoped' and 'i_clepet' are found in N and V respectively. Most examples show that there exists a marked difference between the three manuscripts A, C and N and the Vernon manuscript, which uses the capital letter *I* as the prefix. A small letter *i* is attached as a prefix, without using any space between *i* and *cleopet* in A, C, and N. The prefix *i-* is marked, as is shown in the capital *I-*, which may indicate that the scribe tried to preserve older language features or needed to identify his or her situation in society.

9.1.2. Piers Plowman

When we investigate 'clepe' in *Piers Plowman*, here cited from the Athlone Editions of the A, B and C versions, only one example of prefix *y-* is
used in the A text; we cannot find a past participle with prefix *y-* in the
other texts. Since the A text is thought to have been originally written in a
South-western dialect, it may be that the retention of the prefix *y-* in that
text is to be explained on the grounds of regional dialect.

> A.11.21   Þat suche craftis conne [to counseil ben <u>yclepid</u>],
> B.10.21   [That] swiche craftes k[onne] to counseil [are] <u>cleped</u>
> C.11.18   That coueite can and caste thus ar <u>cleped</u> into consayle.[4]

9.1.3. Chaucer

Tables 9–1 and 9–2 show examples of prefix *i-* or *y-* in Benson's text. The
data of the tables are based on A. Jimura, 'A Historical Approach to English:
Notes on Word Forms in Chaucer's English,' *Studies in Modern English:
The Twentieth Anniversary Publication of the Modern English Association*
(Tokyo: Eichosha, 2003): 31–44.

The abbreviation of the names of tales follows L.Y. Baird-Lange and
H. Schnuttgen (eds.), *A Bibliography of Chaucer 1974–1985* (Cambridge:
D.S. Brewer, 1988).

9.1.3.1. Word forms in Benson's edition of Chaucer's works

First, I examine some general characteristics of word forms in Chaucer's
English, on the basis of Benson's edition (henceforth BN) of Chaucer's
works.

---

4   J.S. Wittig (ed.) *Piers Plowman: Concordance* (London: The Athlone Press, 2001).

	CT	BD	HF	Anel	PF	Bo	TC	LGW	ShT	ASTR	Rom
finde	0	0	0	0	0	0	0	0	1	8	0
fond	12	5	6	1	3	0	17	8	3	17	11
fonden	0	0	0	0	0	0	1	0	0	0	0
foond	31	0	0	0	0	0	0	0	0	0	0
found	0	2	2	1	0	0	1	0	1	0	1
founde	15	5	1	0	1	4	9	8	3	4	15
founden	9	0	0	0	0	0	7	2	0	1	6
fownde	0	0	0	0	0	0	1	1	0	0	0
fownden	0	0	0	0	0	0	4	0	0	0	0
fynd	1	0	0	0	0	0	0	0	0	1	0
fynde	76	4	8	2	8	7	44	21	6	3	27
fynden	9	0	0	0	0	3	7	1	0	2	2
ifounde	0	0	0	0	0	2	1	0	0	0	0
yfounde	6	1	0	0	0	0	1	1	0	0	0
yfynde	2	0	0	0	0	0	0	2	0	0	0

Table 9–1 Frequency of 'finde' and its related words
Note. The form 'yfynde' is the infinitive and the forms 'ifounde' and 'yfounde' are the past participle. The form 'founde' excludes both the verb meaning 'try' or 'seek' and the verb meaning 'build' or 'erect', and the form 'founden' excludes the past participle of the verb meaning 'try' or 'seek'.

Examples include:

fynde	For, quyk or deed, right there ye shal me fynde (FranT 1336)
yfynde	And herbes shal I right ynowe yfynde (SqT 470)
founde	He looketh up and doun til he hath founde (RvT 4059)
yfounde	And whan that she hir fader hath yfounde (MLT 1152)

	CT	BD	HF	Anel	PF	Bo	TC	LGW	ShT	ASTR	Rom
iknowe	0	0	1	0	0	8	0	0	0	0	0
know	0	0	0	0	1	0	3	0	1	7	0
knowe	83	5	8	2	4	34	31	10	5	58	21
knowen	40	1	6	0	0	49	12	4	2	2	12
yknowe	5	1	1	1	0	0	2	0	0	0	0
yknowen	2	0	0	0	0	0	2	0	0	0	0

Table 9–2 Frequency of 'know' and its related words

Examples are:

iknowe   every wyght hath iknowe, thei wenen that tho (*Bo* 5 pr 4.133)
knowen   hymself yif so be that he hath knowen me or now (*Bo* 1 pr 2.24).

Generally speaking, the prefix *y-* or *i-* tends to be dropped in Chaucer's English. The form 'ifounde' occurs twice and 'iknowe' eight times in *Boece*.

9.1.3.2. Some notes on word forms in several editions of
          Chaucer's *The Canterbury Tales*

This section aims to investigate the actual states of word forms in several editions of Chaucer, based upon A. Jimura, 'A Historical Approach to English: Notes on Word Forms in Chaucer's English,' *Studies in Modern English: The Twentieth Anniversary Publication of the Modern English Association* (Tokyo: Eichosha, 2003). First, I will consider the word forms among three editions of *The Canterbury Tales*: Blake's edition (henceforth BL), BN and Robinson's edition (henceforth RB).[5] The number in round brackets after the instances shows the frequency.

---

5   N.F. Blake's edition of *The Canterbury Taless: Edited from the Hengwrt Manuscript* (London: Edward Arnold, 1980) is based upon the Hengwrt Manuscript; while

I have checked the frequency of the different forms: the first shows the word found in BL, the second in BN, and the third in RB. BL uses the form without the prefix *y-* twenty-five times where BN and RB use the form with the prefix *y-*. On the other hand, BL uses the form with the prefix *y-* sixteen times where BN and RB use the form without the prefix *y-*. The instances consist of two groups. The first group shows where BL has the initial letter loss, while BN and RB do not. The second shows where BN and RB have the initial letter loss, while BL does not.

Benson's *The Riverside Chaucer*, 3rd edn (1987) and F.N. Robinson's *The Works of Geoffrey Chaucer*, 2nd edn (Boston, MA: Houghton Mifflin, 1957) are edited from the Ellesmere Manuscript. Simon Horobin, *The Language of the Chaucer Tradition* (Cambridge: D.S. Brewer, 2003): 3 states that 'studies of Chaucer's language must be firmly based upon an understanding of the manuscripts themselves, and on the relationships between these manuscripts'. Our study of the relationships between the manuscripts and the editions of *The Canterbury Tales* is reported in Y. Nalao, A. Jimura and M. Matsuo, 'A Project for a Comprehensive Collation of the Hengwrt and the Ellesmere Manuscripts of *The Canterbury Tales*: General Prologue', *English Corpora under Japanese Eyes: JAECS Anthology Commemorating Its 10th Anniversary* (Amsterdam: Rodopi, 2004): 139–50. We have also published our joint projects: A. Jimura, Y. Nakao., M. Matsuo, N.F. Blake and E. Stubbs (eds.), 'A Comprehensive Collation of the Hengwrt and the Ellesmere Manuscripts of *The Canterbury Tales*: General Prologue', *Hiroshima University Studies*, Graduate School of Letters, 62, Special Issue 3, 2002 and A. Jimura, Y. Nakao, and M. Matsuo (eds.). '"The General Prologue" to *The Canterbury Tales*: A Comprehensive Collation of the Two Manuscripts (Hengwrt and the Ellesmere) and the Two Editions (Blake [1980] and Benson [1987])', *Hiroshima University Studies*, Graduate School of Letters, Vol. 68, Special Issue, 2008. D. Burnley, *The Sheffield Chaucer Textbase* (Sheffield: University of Sheffield, 1990). A. Jimura, Y. Nakao and M. Matsuo (eds.) *A Comprehensive List of Textual Comparison between Blake's and Robinson's Editions of The Canterbury Tales* (Okayama, Japan: University Education Press, 1995).

blessed: yblessed: yblessed (1)	born: yborn: yborn (1)
broght: ybroght: ybroght (1)	clepid: ycleped: ycleped (1)
comen: ycome: ycome (1)	comen: ycomen: ycomen (1)
dight: ydight: ydight (1)	drawe: ydrawe: ydrawe (1)
fynde: yfynde: yfynde (1)	graunted: ygraunted: ygraunted (1)
holden: yholden: yholden (1)	knowe: yknowe: yknowe (1)
knowen: yknowen: yknowen (1)	maad: ymaad: ymaad (1)
proeued: ypreved: ypreved (1)	shadowed: yshadwed: yshadwed (1)
shapen: yshapen: yshapen (1)	shaue: yshave: yshave (1)
slawe: yslawe: yslawe (1)	stynt: ystynt: ystynt (1)
taken: ytaken: ytaken (1)	thonked: ythanked: ythanked (1)
wedded: ywedded: ywedded (1)	wroght: ywroght: ywroght (2)

Table 9–3 Group one: BL with initial letter loss, BN/RB without

yblessed: blessed: blessed (1)	yborn: born: born (1)
yclothed: clothed: clothed (1)	ydeled: deled: deled (1)
ygeten: geten: geten (1)	ygraunted: graunted: graunted (1)
yholde: holde: holde (1)	ylost: lost: lost (1)
ypayd: apayed: apayed (1)	ysayd: sayd: ysayd (2)
yshaue: shave: shave (1)	ytake: take: take (1)
ytold: toold: toold (1)	ywedded: wedded: wedded (1)
ywriten: writen; writen (1)	cf. ypayd: apayed: apayd (1)

Table 9–4 Group one: BN/RB with initial letter loss, BL without

In *The Canterbury Tales*, BL seems to prefer the word forms without the prefix *y-*. It is thought that the Hengwrt MS, on which BL is based, had been commenced while Chaucer was alive. As is well known, this manuscript gives a different impression from the Ellesmere MS, which has beautifully coloured ornate initials, and is carefully written and decorated. The Heng-wrt MS scribe seemingly wrote Chaucer's works in a great hurry. Both RB and BN are edited as standard texts of Chaucer's works, according to the Ellesmere MS, which is thought to have been written about ten years later by the same scribe as the Hengwrt MS. The fact that the earliest Chaucer manuscript, Hengwrt, has left word forms closer to Modern English may indicate that the word form without prefix *y-* was prevalent in Chaucer's lifetime. By contrast, the Ellesmere MS, gorgeously decorated, may be supposed to prominently display a conservative language feature such as the form with prefix *y-*, as though this were an identified characteristic of Chaucer's language.

Furthermore, the fact that some foreign words adopted from Old French or Old Norse came to possess prefix *y-*, as in *ygraunted* or *ytaken*, allows us to think that English has considerable flexibility to Anglicize foreign elements appropriately. Then a professional scribe or editor appar-ently checked and inspected English spellings in order to accommodate foreign words at that time; and this textual tradition of Chaucer's works leads to the editorial technique found in Thynne's edition in the Early Modern English period.

9.2. Early Modern English

I will now investigate the existence of prefix *y-* in Thomas Malory (1405?–71) as an example of English of the second half of the fifteenth century, in Edmund Spenser for sixteenth-century English, and in John Milton for seventeenth-century English.

9.2.1. Malory's English

With regard to Malory's English, Yuji Nakao indicates that the Winchester MS uses prefix *i-* or *y-* more often than the 1485 edition of William Caxton (1422?–92).[6] He says that there are fourteen examples with that prefix in the Winchester MS, and only two examples in Caxton's edition. It would not be strange that a conservative language feature of Old English remained in the Winchester MS written in the southern area of England.

9.2.2. Spenser's English

According to C.G. Osgood, some of the examples with prefix *y-*, excluding *ycleped*, are quoted from *The Faerie Queene* as follows:

> Boue all the sonnes that were of earthly wombes ybore (III. iv. 21. 9)
> ... I leaue you, my liefe, yborn of heauenly berth. (I. iii. 28. 8–9)
> And cole blacke steedes yborne of hellish brood, (I. v. 20. 8)
> A Satyres sonne, yborne in forrest wyld, (I. vi. 21. 1)
> Of th' high descent, whereof he was yborne, (I. vii. 10.2)
> A Faerie was, yborne of high degree, (III. vi. 4. 3)
>
> it for his lemans sake / Ybuilded all of glasse, by Magic powre (III. ii. 20. 6–7)
> It was a vaut ybuilt for great dispence, (II. ix. 29. 1)[7]

---

6   Yuji Nakao, 'Interchangeability of Prefixed and Non-Prefixed Words in the Winchester Malory and Caxton's Malory', *Journal of the College of Humanities* 11 (2004): 47–79.

7   C.G. Osgood (comp. and ed.), *A Concordance to the Poems of Edmund Spenser* (Gloucester, MA: Peter Smith, 1963).

ybent	yblent	ybore	ykindled	yplaste	yssewd
yborn	yborne	ybownd	ylincked	yplight	ywandred
ybredd	ybrent	ybrought	ymett	yrent	ywounded
ybuilded	ybuilt	ycarud	ymixt	yrockt	ywritt
yclad	ycladd	ycled	ymolt	yshrowded	ywrought
yclothed	ycouered	ydrad	ymounted	yslaine	
ydred	yfed	yfostered	ypaid	yslaked	
yfraught	yfretted	yglaunst	ypaynted	yspent	

Table 9–5 Spenser's use of *y*-prefix words

The prefix *y-* in three kinds of past participle of *bear* such as *ybore, yborn,* and *yborne* has a weak or light stress. Two word forms *ybore* and *yborne* are used as rhyme words. The forms such as *ybuilded* and *ybuilt* are closely connected with the metrical necessity, because the former has three syllables and the latter two syllables.

9.2.3. Seventeenth-century English

According to G.L. Brook (1958: 133), the prefix *ge-* of the past participle in Old English became *y-* in Early Middle English and had been one of the language features of southern dialects for a long time.[8] However, this prefix disappeared in Later Middle English. On the other hand, Miltonic *yclept,* as Brook says, remains as an archaic word form even in seventeenth-century English. An example is: 'In heaven *yclept* Euphrosyne,' ('L'Allegro', 12),[9] where past participle with prefix *y-* reminds us of Spenserian use in *The Faerie Queene* (III v 8). The other example is *ychained* ('On the Morning of Christ's Nativity', xvi), according to the *OED.*

8   G.L. Brook, *A History of the English Language* (London: André Deutsch, 1958).
9   J. Carey and A. Fowler (eds.) *The Poems of John Milton* (London: Longman, 1968, 1980).

9.3. Conclusion

In this chapter, we have seen a historical change of prefix *y*-, investigating some notable examples in *Ancrene Wisse*, Langland, Chaucer, Malory, Spenser, and Milton. We are able to recognize some marked characteristics of every period in the history of English. It is now further necessary to look at every period more minutely in order to discern a connection between periods, but we might have almost established a certain predictable line between them. However, I would now like to bring forward evidence to explain sufficiently why archaic word forms such as *yclept* and *yclad* have remained in Modern English. According to the *Oxford English Diction-ary* (*OED*), *yclept* was frequently used as an archaic literary form in the 1500s and 1600s. Is it a coincidence that the language feature of adding the prefix *y*- to past participles, though minor, is seen in an age of developing strength for Britain? The establishment of the Anglican Church apparently corresponded to a wider tendency to return to the Anglo-Saxon period, as Thynne insisted on using the prefix *y*- when he edited Chaucer's texts in the Early Modern English period. A passage in *Shirley* (1849) by Charlotte Brontë (1816–55), quoted by the *OED*, reveals an archaic use of *yclept*, as in 'the old and tenantless dwelling *yclept* Fieldhead,' where *yclept* is used with conscious archaism in reference to a deserted and old-fashioned house that has been empty for the past ten years. When we look at the column of City Notes in the *Westminster Gazette*, dated 23 February 1900, we find an interesting passage: 'The Associated South Soudan Extended Gold Mines Corporation, Limited, *yclept* in the market Suds, should not be a thing of the very distant future',[10] where the *OED* changed the name of an African country *Soudan* into *London*. Even though it were an intentional mistake or an accidental occurrence, we should notice that Sudan was in a ruinous condition in the year of 1900, the year after Sudan was governed by the union of Britain and Egypt in 1899. In such a serious historical period, it might be significant that a newspaper journalist used *yclept* in order to

10   This quotation is from the microfilm in British Library.

make the reader perceive it as something dignified, humorously evoking an imaginary and still unestablished company. In this way, an archaic word *yclept* has survived until today, imparting an old-fashioned or out-of-the-way atmosphere. Is this *yclept* English humour?

9.4. References

9.4.1. Primary sources

Benson, L.D., ed. *The Riverside Chaucer*, 3rd edn. Boston, MA: Houghton Mifflin, 1987.

Blake, N.F., ed. *The Canterbury Tales: Edited from the Hengwrt Manuscript*. London: Edward Arnold, 1980.

Brontë, C. *Shirley*. London: John Murray, 1920.

Burnley, D. *The Sheffield Chaucer Textbase*. Sheffield: University of Sheffield, 1990.

Carey, J., and A. Fowler, eds. *The Poems of John Milton*. London: Longman, 1968, 1980.

Jimura, A., Y. Nakao and M. Matsuo, eds. *A Comprehensive List of Textual Comparison between Blake's and Robinson's Editions of The Canterbury Tales*. Okayama, Japan: University Education Press, 1995.

——, eds. "'The General Prologue" to *The Canterbury Tales*: A Comprehensive Collation of the Two Manuscripts (Hengwrt and the Ellesmere) and the Two Editions (Blake [1980] and Benson [1987])', *Hiroshima University Studies*, Graduate School of Letters, vol.68, Special Issue, 2008.

Kubouchi, T. and K. Ikegami, eds. *The Ancrene Wisse: A Four-Manuscript Parallel Text. Preface and Parts 1–4* (2003); *Parts 5–8 with Wordlists* (2005). Frankfurt am Main: Peter Lang, 2003 and 2005.

Robinson, F.N., ed. *The Works of Geoffrey Chaucer*, 2nd edn. Boston, MA: Houghton Mifflin, 1957.

Schmidt, A.V.C., ed. *Piers Plowman: A Parallel-Text Edition of the A, B, C and Z Versions. Vol,. II. Introduction, Textual Notes, Commentary, Bibliography and Indexical Glossary*. Kalamazoo, MI: Medieval Institute Publications, 2008.

9.4.2. Secondary sources

Baird-Lang, L.Y. and H. Schnuttgen. *A Bibliography of Chaucer 1974–1985.* Cambridge: D.S. Brewer, 1988.

Brook, G.L. *A History of the English Language.* London: André Deutsch, 1958.

Horobin, S.C.P. *The Language of the Chaucer Tradition.* Cambridge: D.S. Brewer, 2003.

Jimura, A. 'A Historical Approach to English: Notes on Word Forms in Chaucer's English,' *Studies in Modern English: The Twentieth Anniversary Publication of the Modern English Association.* Tokyo: Eichosha, 2003. 31–44.

Kane, G. 'The Text', in J.A. Alford ed., *A Companion to Piers Plowman.* Berkeley, CA: University of California Press, 1988. 175–221.

Kubouchi, T. 'Modernity and Archaism in the *Ancrene Wisse* Revisited', (in Japanese) *SIMELL* 21 (2006): 65–82.

Nakao, Y. 'Interchangeability of Prefixed and Non-Prefixed Words in the Winchester Malory and Caxton's Malory', *Journal of the College of Humanities* 11 (2004): 47–79.

Nakao Y., A. Jimura and M. Matsuo. 'A Project for a Comprehensive Collation of the Hengwrt and the Ellesmere Manuscripts of *The Canterbury Tales*: General Prologue', *English Corpora under Japanese Eyes: JAECS Anthology Commemorating Its 10th Anniversary.* Amsterdam: Rodopi, 2004. 139–50.

OED = Oxford English Dictionary, the. (1989) 2nd edn. Oxford: Oxford University Press.

Osgood, C.G., comp. and ed. *A Concordance to the Poems of Edmund Spenser.* Gloucester, MA: Peter Smith, 1963.

Wittig, J.S., ed. *Piers Plowman: Concordance.* London: The Athlone Press, 2001.

HIROSHI YONEKURA

10   Compound Nouns in Late Middle English: Their Morphological, Syntactic and Semantic Description[1]

10.0. Introduction

In Old English, compounding words was one of the most effective means of increasing vocabulary. This process of word formation played an especially important role in poetic diction. The Norman Conquest, however, transformed this linguistic situation;[2] the more frequent use of compounds was not observed in Middle English. In the words of Bradley (1904), 'this tendency was fostered by the circumstance that the two fashionable languages, French and Latin, make very little use of composition.' Consequently, for example, the Old English compound noun *lǽcecrǽft* (originally meaning 'leechcraft') gave place to the simple word *medicine* (OF *medicine* and L *medicina* 'healing or medical art') in Middle English.[3]

---

1   I would like to express my gratitude to A.V.C. Schmidt for his helpful comments. I am also grateful to Professor Larry Walker of Kyoto Prefectural University for his suggestions concerning stylistic improvements in this article. All remaining errors, of course, are my own.

2   See David Burnley, 'Lexis and Semantics', in Norman Blake (ed.), *The Cambridge History of the English Language*. vol. II: 1066–1476 (Cambridge: Cambridge University Press, 1991): 441, Hans Sauer, *Nominalkomposita im Frühmittelenglischen* (Tübingen: Max Niemeyer Verlag, 1992): 7–10, 719–21 and Hiroshi Yonekura, 'A Descriptive Study of Word Formation in Chaucer', PhD dissertation (Tsukuba University, 2004): 596.

3   However, the coumpound *lechecraft* is still used in Middle English: for example, Chaucer, KnT 2745, Tr 4.436; Malory *Wks* 1218/29.

The question of how compound words were coined with the purpose of enriching English vocabulary is very important in order to throw some light on the development of the English language. However, this subject of word formation has not until recently received very much attention from scholars and students working in the field of linguistics. As Kastovsky (1985) remarks, 'A comprehensive history of English word-formation has still to be written'.[4]

Therefore, the goal of the present paper is to provide a descriptive investigation of this processing of word formation, particularly of compound nouns in Late Middle English from a morphological, syntactic and semantic point of view. Although the decline of compounding has been noticeable from the Middle English period onward, the productivity of compound nouns remains very high throughout all the periods. This is the reason why special emphasis is placed upon compound nouns in the present paper.

10.1. Theoretical Ground

Here, as a theoretical ground, I take mainly Marchand (1969) and Sauer (1992). The compound word is defined as a *syntagma*, consisting of a *determinant* and a *determinatum* on the basis of Marchand's (1969) principle.[5]

---

4   See Dieter Kastovsky, 'Deverbal Nouns in Old and Middle English: From Stem-Formation to Word-Formation', in Jacek Fisiak (ed.), *Historical Semantics: Historical Word Formation* (Berlin, New York and Amsterdam: Mouton, 1985): 221. However, Dalton-Puffer (1996), Trips (2009) and Mühleisen (2010) deal with Middle English morphology influenced by Old French, the development of *-hood*, *-dom* and *-ship* in the history of English, and word-formation patterns in the period from Middle English to Present-day English, respectively. What is more worthy of notice is the fact that Bauer (2001), Plag (2003), Plag (2004), Lieber (2004), Lieber (2005), and Brinton and Traugott (2005) have made a close examination of morphological productivity and constraints on productivity as well as word-formation processes and productive lexical innovations.

5   See Hans Marchand, *The Categories and Types of Present-Day English Word-Formation: Synchronic-Diachronic Approach.* 2nd edn. (München: C.H. Beck'sche Verlagsbuchhandlung, 1969): 3. Both Dieter Kastovsky, 'Word-formation, or: at the

This syntagma contains both a simple form (e.g. *bonde-men* 'serf' ParsT 752)[6] and a complex form (e.g. *counting-bord* 'counting table' ShipT 83).

The morphological type refers to a morphological structure that is constituted of two or more word-classes. For example, the word *bonde-man* has a morphological structure consisting of a noun *bonde* and a noun *man*. The compounds are also analyzed on the basis of the syntactic deep structure, which indicates the 'underlying sentence'. Therefore, the underlying structure of the compound noun *bonde-man* is 'The man is a peasant (=*bonde*)'.

Here one more important thing concerning the syntactic deep structure is the concept 'type of reference'. The type of reference denotes which part of the underlying sentence becomes the determinatum of the morphological structure.[7] The underlying sentence of the compound *bonde-man* is 'The man is a peasant' so that the second element *man* is the determinatum of the compound in question. This type of reference is called Subject-type because the second element *man* occurs in a subject position of the underlying sentence.

There are three more types of reference. One is Object-type, as in *bene-straw* (MerT 1422), where the underlying sentence is 'The plant (=*bene*) yields straw', and the second element *straw* appears as an object of the sentence. Another is Adverbial-type, as in *dong-carte* (NPT 3036), where the underlying sentence is 'They carry dung in the cart', and the second element *carte* occurs in an adverbial phrase. A third is Predication-type, as in *toth-ake* (*Rom*A 1098), where the underlying sentence is 'The tooth aches', and the second element *ake* functions as a predicate. Moreover, the semantic information is obviously to be observed within the underlying sentence.

---

crossroads of morphology, syntax, and the lexicon', *Folia Linguistica* 10 (1977) and Sauer, *Nominalkomposita im Frühmittelenglischen* also adopt Marchand's definition. For an example, in *harpe-stryng* (Chaucer, *House of Fame* 777), the compound noun is a syntagma that unites a determinant *harpe* with a determinatum *stryng*.

6   All the quotations of Chaucer's works are taken from Larry D. Benson (ed.), *The Riverside Chaucer*. 3rd edn. (Boston, MA: Houghton Mifflin; London: Oxford University Press, 1987). The abbreviations are also based upon Benson (1987: 779). In relation to *The Romaunt of the Rose*, the present essay deals only with Fragment A.

7   In more detail see Marchand, *The Categories and Types of Present-Day English Word-Formation*: 32–4. A noteworthy fact is that the type of reference is rather appropriate to compound nouns (Sauer, *Nominalkomposita*: 713).

10.2. Noun/Noun

First of all, the Noun/Noun compounds are classified into two basic kinds of compounds: *copula compounds* and *rectional compounds*.

10.2.1. Copula compound

The copula compound is a compound that has an underlying syntactic structure of 'B is (like) A' on semantic grounds, as in *oak tree* ('The tree (=B) is an oak (=A)'). Moreover, this compound is subdivided into four types: (a) an attributive compound, (b) a subsumptive compound, (c) a tautological compound, and (d) a compound containing a comparison.

10.2.1.1. Attributive compound

This compound has an underlying sentence 'B is A', as in *somer sesoun* [OE+OF] 'spring' (Bo 2.pr.5.67), where the underlying sentence is 'The season is summer.' Other examples are *bondeman* [OE+OE] 'a serf or servant' (Gower, *Confessio Amantis* 8.1358), *cowkynde* [OE+OE] 'cattle or cow-kind' (*Piers Plowman B* 11.340), *morow tyde* [OE+OE] 'daybreak' (Malory, *Wks* 27/10), *morne-while* [OE+OE] 'morning time' (*Alliterative Morte Arthure* 2001), *myst-hakel* [OE+OE] 'cloak of mist' (*Sir Gawain and the Green Knight* 2081).[8]

---

8   The texts examined here are G.C. Macaulay (ed.), *The English Works of John Gower*, 2 vols. (EETS ES 81, 82) (London: Oxford University Press, 1968), A.V.C. Schmidt (ed.), *William Langland: The Vision of Piers Plowman: The B Text*. (2nd edn) (London: Dent. Reprinted, with revisions and corrections, 1997), E.V. Gordon (ed.), *Pearl* (Oxford: Clarendon Press, 1980), Richard Morris (ed.), *Early English Alliterative Poems in the West Midland Dialect of the Fourteenth Century* (EETS OS 1) (London: Oxford University Press, 1965), W.R. Barron (ed.), *Sir Gawain and the Green Knight* (New York: Manchester University Press, 1974), R.W. Chambers and Marjorie Daunt (eds.), *A Book of London English 1384–1425* (Oxford: Clarendon

10.2.1.2. Subsumptive compound

The subsumptive compound indicates that the first element (=determinant) is included in the second element (=determinatum), as in *mankynde* [OE+OE] 'mankind' (*Cleanness* 278, Gower *CA* 2.3108, MilT 3521), where the underlying sentence is 'The kind is man'. However, it may be very difficult to distinguish this kind of compound and an attributive compound, from a semantic point of view. In *cowkynde* [OE+OE] (*PPl.B* 11.340) mentioned above, for example, *cow* is regarded as a logical subclass of *kynde* (=species).⁹ Compounds of this sort are scarcely observed in the corpus examined.

10.2.1.3. Tautological compound

In this compound, the first element is similar in meaning to the second element, as in *pecok* [OE+OE] 'peacock' (*Tr* 1.210, *PPl.B* 12.228, Gower *CA* 5.6498). The underlying sentence of the compound *pecok* may be 'The cock (=*cok*) is a peacock (=*pe*)'. In other words, the compound in question is characteristic of its tautological or repeated use of both elements. Similarly the following examples are found: *wod-schawe3* [OE+OE] 'grove' [*wod* n.=grove + *schawe3* n.=forest] (*Pearl* 284), *margery perle* [OF+OF] 'pearl' [*margerye* n.=pearl + *perle* n.=pearl] (*Cleanness* 556), *tile*

Press, 1931), Eugène Vinaver (ed.), *The Works of Sir Thomas Malory*. 3 vols. (Oxford: Clarendon Press, 1969, 3rd edn by P.J.C. Field, 1990), and Edmund Brock (ed.), *Morte Arthure, or The Death of Arthur*. (EETS OS 8) (London: Oxford University Press, 1967). The abbreviations used henceforth are Malory *Wks* (=*The Works of Sir Thomas Malory*), Gower *CA* (=*The English Works of John Gower*), *Gawain* (=*Sir Gawain and the Green Knight*), *LondonE* (=*A Book of London English 1384–1425*), *Morte Arth* (=*Morte Arthure, or The Death of Arthur*), *PPl.B* (= *The Vision of Piers Plowman: The B-Text*).

9   Sauer (1992: 722) distinguishes as attributive compound from a subsumptive compound. He gives *henne-fugeles* ('hen-birds') or *marbel-stone* as an example of a subsumptive compound. In Marchand (1969: 40–1), *oak tree* is given as a subsumptive compound, because *oak* represents the species and *tree* the genus. On the other hand, *girl friend* is regarded as an attributive compound.

stones [OE+OE] 'brick' [*tile* n.=brick + *ston* n.=stone] (*LondonE* 158.559), *caremane* [ON+OE] 'male, man' [*care* n.=a man + *mane* n.=man] (*Morte Arth* 957).

10.2.1.4. Compound containing a comparison

There are some compounds where the second element is compared to something, as in *goshauk* [OE+OE] 'goshawk' (*Morte Arth* 4001). Here the underlying sentence is considered to be 'The hawk is like a goose'. Other examples are *houndfyssh* [OE+OE] 'small shark' (MerT 1825), *pescoddes* [OE+OE] 'pea-pods' (*PPl.B* 6.291), *waxlok* [OE+OE] 'wax-like curls' (*Cleanness* 1037), *ketille-hatte* [OE+OE] 'helmet' (*Morte Arth* 3516), *sperhauk* [OE+OE] 'sparrow hauk' (*Tr* 3.1192, Malory *Wks* 828/3).

10.2.2. Rectional compound

The rectional compound comprises the syntagma that is not 'analysable on an attributive basis'.[10] In short, the underlying sentence of this compound is not rewritten by the use of the verb *be*.[11] The rectional compound is divided into three types on the basis of the types of reference: Subject-type, Object-type, and Adverbial-type.

10.2.2.1. Subject-type

This type belongs to the class of compounds where the determinatum functions as a subject in the underlying sentence. Therefore, these combinations are formulable as 'B lives in, at, on A', 'B rules A', 'B contains A', etc. For example, *ale-stake* [OE+OE] 'tavern sign' (GP 667) is the compound in which the second element (=determinatum) *stake* works as a subject, as in

---

10   See Marchand, *The Categories and Types of Present-Day English Word-Formation*: 40.

11   In *carte-hors* (*HF* 944), for example, the underlying sentence of this compound is not 'The horse is a cart' but 'The horse draws the cart'.

the underlying sentence 'The stake indicates ale'. The compounds of this type comprise such instances as *plowman* [OE+OE] 'plowman, farmer' (*PPl.B* 5.537), *lade-sterne* [OE+OE] 'loadstar' (*Morte Arth* 751), *heuen-ryche* [OE+OE] 'kingdom of heaven' (*Patience* 14), *wynt-hole* [OE+OE] 'wind-pipe' (*Gawain* 1336), *horse knave* [OE+OE] 'stableboy' (Gower *CA* 4.1399), *hede-shete* [OE+OE] 'sheet at head of bed' (Malory *Wks* 394/26).

10.2.2.2. Object-type

In compounds of this type, the determinatum occurs as an object in the underlying sentence 'The bed (=A) has straw (=B)' of *bedstraw* [OE+OE] 'straw for bedding' (MerT 1783). Similarly we find such examples as *rug-gebon* [OE+OE] 'back-bone' (*PPl.B* 5.343), *sonnebeame* [OE+OE] 'ray of sunlight' (Malory *Wks* 865/19), *Scomerfare* [OF+OE] 'piracy' (Gower *CA* 8.1391), *eye-liddis* [OE+OE] 'eyelid' (*Morte Arth* 3952), *bed-syde* [OE+OE] 'bedside' (*Gawain* 1193), *helle-hole* [OE+OE] 'pit of hell' (*Cleanness* 223), *rak-hokes* [?OE+OE] 'rake-hooks' (*LondonE* 169.907).

10.2.2.3. Adverbial-type

In the compound of this type, the determinatum appears as an adverbial phrase in the underlying sentence. Therefore, these combinations are formulable as 'A lives in, at B' or 'They find A in B' as in the underlying sentence 'They find hazel (=A) in the wood (=B)' of *haselwode* [OE+OE] 'hazel thicket' (*Tr* 5.505). The following instances belong to the compounds of this type: *hede-rapys* [OE+OE] 'head-ropes' (*Morte Arth* 3668), *waterpot* [OE+OE] 'water-pot' (Gower *CA* 3.673), *punfolde* [OE+OE] 'pinfold' (*PPl.B* 5.624), *mete-whyle* [OE+OE] 'mealtime' (Malory *Wks* 205/20), *bordnaill* [OE+OE] 'spike-nail' (*LondonE* 158.547).

10.3. Noun's/Noun (Genitive Compounds)

The question of whether the compound of this type is a real compound or not is a highly controversial issue, because some scholars regard this compound as a syntactic combination. Marchand (1969: 65) remarks that 'It will be impossible to tell when exactly /s, z/ came to be regarded as a derivative element and when combinations of this group acquired compound status'.[12] In our texts examined, there are some examples in which it is often difficult to distinguish genitive compounds from syntactic genitive groups. Take *asses cheke* [OE+OE] (MkT 2038) for example. *MED* (s.v. *asse* n.) also gives *asse cheke*, where the noun *asse* is used in a common case, with the note that this combination was originally a genitive phrase and later a compound. It would be interesting to follow up this point further, but this is not our present concern, so only a few instances are given here.

The genitive compounds are classified into two kinds: (a) a copula compound and (b) a rectional compound.

10.3.1. Copula compound

The compound of this kind is sporadically used in our corpus. The underlying sentence of this composite is 'B is A' as in such examples as *mannes creature* [OE+OE] 'human creature' (*Tr* 2.417) [underlying sentence: 'The creature is man']; *heddys-mene* [OE+OE] 'headman, chief man' (*Morte Arth* 281) [underlying sentence: 'The man is a chief']; *shames deth* [OE+OE] 'a shameful death' (*LGW* 2072) [underlying sentence: 'The death is shameful']; *nyhtes tide* [OE+OE] 'night time' (Gower *CA* 1.860) [underlying sentence: 'The time is night'].

---

12   Also see Sauer, *Nominalkomposita*: 17.

10.3.2. Rectional compound

The rectional compounds are further divided into three subtypes: Subject-type, Object-type and Adverbial-type.

10.3.2.1. Subject-type

This type belongs to the compounds where the determinatum works as subject in the underlying sentence. Examples are *sterisman* [OE+OE] 'steersman' (*HF* 436) [underlying sentence: 'The man guides the course of a ship (=*stere*)']; *kynnesmen* [OE+OE] 'kinsmen' (*PPl.B* 15.247) [underlying sentence: 'The men belong to the same kin']; *kyngesbenche* [OE+OE] 'the highest court of law, King's Bench' (*LondonE* 105.21) [underlying sentence: 'The bench is placed for the king']; *sonde3mon* [OE+OE] 'messenger' (*Cleanness* 469) [underlying sentence: 'The man has a message'].

10.3.2.2. Object-type

This type is a compound which has an underlying syntactic structure 'A has B' on semantic grounds, as in *domesman* [OE+OE] 'judge' (MkT 2490) [underlying sentence: 'Judgment (=*domes*) has its man']; *kingesriche* [OE+OE] 'community governed by a king' (Gower *CA* 5.4202); *kingeshalve* [OE+OE] 'king's behalf' (Gower *CA* 2.1042), *swynes-heed* 'pig's head, a fool' (RvT 4262); *piggesnye* [OE+OE] 'pig's eye' (MilT 3268); *loves rage* [OE+OE] 'fervor of love' (Gower *CA* 1.2620).

10.3.2.3. Adverbial-type

This compound has an underlying syntactic construction 'A begins on B' as in *Newerys day* [OE+OE] 'New Year's Day' (Malory *Wks* 192/12) [underlying sentence: 'A new year begins on that day'].

10.4. Adjective/Noun

As with the genitival compounds, opinions are divided on the morphological interpretation of adjective/noun compounds. Owing to the loss of the
inflectional endings of the adjectives, Adjective/Noun compounds became
morphologically identical with the syntactic combination 'adjective +
noun' in Middle English.[13] For example, in *trewe-love* [OE+OE] 'faithful
love' (MilT 3692), according to *MED* (s.v. *true-love* n.), this compound
is always distinguishable from a simple syntactic combination. Since this
controversial subject is not part of our investigation here, however, only a
few instances are given for illustration. Generally speaking, the compound
of this sort has an underlying syntactic structure 'B is A', just as in that of
trewe-love (MilT 3692): 'Love is faithful (=*trewe*)'. Other examples are:
grene-wode [OE+OE] 'greenwood' (FrT 1386), *bale-deeth* [OE+OE] 'bale-
ful death' (*PPl.B* 18.35), *sauffgarde* [OF+OF] 'custody, security' (Malory
Wks 773/34), *fre-man* 'a free man' (*LondonE* 134.114), *quikselver* [OE+OE]
'metallic mercury, quicksilver' (Gower *CA* 4.2475), *mydnyȝt* [OE+OE]
'midnight' (*Gawain* 2187).

10.5. Numeral/Noun

The compound of this type raises the same problem as the *categories* Adjec-
tive/Noun or Noun's/Noun do. In other words, there are cases where we
cannot distinguish the compound from a syntactic noun phrase from a
semantic point of view. This compound also has the underlying structure 'B
is A'. Only a few examples are observed in our corpus: *twelmonth* [OE+OE]
'a year' (*Gawain* 298), *syxtyfolde* 'sixty thicknesses' (Malory *Wks* 225/8),
seven nyght [OE+OE] 'a week' (NPT 2873), *fourtenyght* [OE+OE] 'two
weeks' (Gower *CA* 4.1418).

---

13   See Sauer, *Nominalkomposita*: 723.

10.6. Pronoun/Noun

Sauer (1992: 724) points out that although the compound of this type is sporadically found in Old English and Early Middle English, it slightly productive in Late Middle English. In our corpus, however, only Chaucer employs the Pronoun/Noun compound. The underlying sentence is 'B is A', as in *she-ape* [OE+OE] 'female ape' (ParsT 424) [underlying sentence: 'The ape is female'], *she-wolf* [OE+OE] 'female wolf' (MancT 183 [underlying sentence: 'The wolf is female'].

10.7. Verb/Noun (Verb Stem/Noun)

In this compound the determinant (or the first element) appears as a verb stem or a verb that is derived by addition of a zero morpheme. The compound of this type is considered to originate 'from compounds with a deverbal noun as determinant, where in some cases the deverbal noun could then be immediately identified with the verb.'[14]

In Middle English the distinction in form between the verb and the noun, which were distinct in Old English, was almost impossible owing to the weakening and the loss of endings (for example, OE *lufu* (n.) and *lufian* (v.) > ME *luue* > ModE *love*). In consequence of this historical development, the compound Verb/Noun is sometimes difficult to distinguish morphologically from the compound Noun/Noun, as in *brymstoon* [ME+OE] 'brimstone' (ParsT 548), where *brym* may be understood as either a deverbal noun with zero morpheme or a verb stem.[15] The compound of this type is divided into subtypes on the basis of underlying syntactic structure: Subject-type, Object-type, and Adverbial-type.

14   See Sauer, *Nominalkomposita*: 725.
15   Sauer (1992: 601) interprets *brymston* as the compound Verb (verb stem) / Noun. Moreover, in Smith's (1971: 130) view, the first element *brym* had become obscured by Chaucer's time.

10.7.1. Subject-type

In the compound Verb / Noun, the determinatum (or the second element) functions as a subject in the underlying sentence, as in *tredefowel* [OE+OE] 'a sexually vigorous bird' (MkT 1945)[16] [underlying sentence: 'The bird (=fowl) treads']. Other examples are *workmen* [OE+OE] 'workmen' (*Pearl* 507), *drawe-brigge* [OE+OE] 'drawbridge' (*Morte Arth* 2474).

10.7.2. Object-type

In this type, the determinatum (or the second element) appears as an object in the underlying sentence, as in *pykeharneys* [ON+OF] 'plunderer of armour' (*PPl.B* 20.263) [underlying sentence: 'They plunder armour' (=*harneys*)']. Other examples are cachepol 'minor officer of the law' (*PPl.B* 18.46), *brewecheste* [OE+OE] 'trouble-maker' (*PPl.B* 16.43) [underlying sentence: 'Someone stirs up strife (=*cheste*)'], *pykepurs* [ME+OE] 'pick-purse, pickpocket' (KnT 1998).

10.7.3. Adverbial-type

The compound of this type is a combination where the determinatum occurs as an adverbial phrase in the underlying structure. Only one example is found in Chaucer: *wheston* [OE+OE] 'whetstone' (*Tr* 1.631) [underlying sentence: 'They whet something on the stone'].

---

16 *MED* (s.v. *treden* v.) understands *trede* as a verb, while *OED* reads this word as a noun. Moreover, Smith (1971: 84) points out that the word *trede* is a nominalized verb.

10.8. Noun/V+*ere*

In Sauer's view, the compound Noun/V+*ere* (i.e. noun/deverbal agent noun in –*ere*) was first created in Old English.[17] This compound forms agent nouns so that only subject-type combinations are found in our corpus. Examples are: *market-betere* [OE+OE] 'one who hangs around markets' (RvT 3936) [underlying sentence: 'The beater beats in the market'], *nyghtcomeris* [OE+OE] 'comers by night, nocturnal thief' (*PPl.B* 19.144), *tale-tellers* [OE+OE] 'tale-bearers, tattlers' (*PPl.B* 20.300), *footballpleyer* [OE+OE] 'football player' (*LondonE* 148.236) [underlying sentence: 'The player plays football'], *Sothseiere* [OE+OE] 'one who foretells' (Gower *CA* 7.2348), *torchebereres* [OF+OE] 'torch-carriers' (*LondonE* 145.135).

10.9. Noun/Verb+Ø (Noun/Zero Derived Deverbal Noun)

The compound of this type probably goes back to Old English[18] where we find such combinations as *nihtwaco* 'night-wake' (*Seafarer* 7),[19] *ellorsið* 'journey elsewhere, = death' (*Beowulf* 2451).[20] From a syntactic-semantic viewpoint, the majority of these compounds belong to a predication-type, but several indicate a subject-type.

---

17 See Sauer, *Nominalkomposita*: 726–7.
18 See Marchand, *The Categories and Types of Present-Day English Word-Formation*: 76 and Sauer, *Nominalkomposita*: 726.
19 The quotation is taken from Ida Gordon (ed.), *The Seafarer* (Old and Middle English Texts) (London: Manchester University Press, 1979).
20 The example is quoted from R.D. Fulk, Robert E. Bjork, and John D. Niles (eds.), *Klaeber's Beowulf* (Toronto & Others: University of Toronto Press, 2009).

10.9.1. Subject-type

In this type, the second element functions as a subject in the underlying structure, as in *love-drynke* [OE+OE] 'a love potion' (WBT 754, Gower *CA* 6.111) [underlying sentence: 'The drink induces love'].

10.9.2. Predication-type

The second element of the compound occurs as a predicate in the underlying sentence, as is clear from the following examples: *love-daunces* [OE+OE] 'lovers' dances' (*HF* 1235) [underlying sentence: 'They dance because of love'], *toothaches* [OE+OE] 'toothache' (*PPl.B* 20.82) [underlying sentence: 'The tooth aches'], *Sonne set* [OE+OE] 'sunset' (Gower *CA* 7.4913), *þunder þrast* [OE+OE] 'thunderbolt' (*Cleanness* 952), *timberwork* [OE+OE] 'woodwork' (Gower *CA* 5.2179), *almes-dede* [OE+OE] 'charitable act' (Malory *Wks* 973/10) [underlying sentence: 'They do mercy (=almes)'].

10.10. Noun/V+*ing* (Noun/Deverbal Action Noun in –*ing*)

The compound of this type is also traced back to Old English and is productive from Early Middle English onward, though most of these have been formed in the Modern English period.[21] Syntactically, this compound forms action nouns, so that the determinatum or second element works as a predicate in the underlying sentence, as in *fyr-makynge* [OE+OE] 'fire-making' (KnT 2914) [underlying sentence: 'They make a fire'], *luf-laȝyng* [OE+OE] 'loving laugh' (*Gawain* 1777) [underlying sentence: 'They laugh in a friendly way'], *luf-talkyng* [OE+ON] 'lovers' conversation' (*Gawain* 927) [underlying sentence: 'The lovers talk in court'], *sonne-risyng* [OE+OE] 'sunrise'

---

21   See Marchand, *The Categories and Types of Present-Day English Word-Formation*: 75.

(*PPl.B* 18.67) [underlying sentence: 'The sun rises'], *luf-longyng* [OE+OE] 'longing of love' (*Pearl* 1152) [underlying sentence: 'They long for love'].

In the compound *bakbityng* [OE+OE] 'back-biting, slandering someone behind his back' (ParsT 493) [underlying sentence: 'They bite someone's back / from behind'], *MED* (s.v. *bak-biting* ger.) regards the first element *bak* as a noun, while *OED* (s.v. *back-biting* n.) considers *back* to be an adverb. The same thing is said of *hom-comynge* [OE+OE] 'homecoming' (*Tr* 5.503) [underlying sentence: 'They come home']. In Smith's (1971: 84) view, the word *hom* is regarded as a noun but *OED* (s.v. *home-coming* n.) understands that *home* is an adverb. *MED* (s.v. *hom-coming(e* ger.), however, avoids making any definite comment on the matter. In this connection, the following examples are worthy of note: *here-beyng*[22] [OE+OE] 'existence here, present life' (*PPl.B* 14.141), *welwillinge*[23] [OE+OE] 'happiness, pleasure' (Gower *CA* 3.599), *welcoming* [OE+OE] 'an act of welcoming someone home' (Gower *CA* 2.671). In these examples each of the first elements *here* and *wel* works as an adverb.

10.11. Verb+*ing*/Noun
(Deverbal Action Noun in –*ing*/Noun)

In this compound the first element Verb+*ing* is analyzed as a verbal noun in –*ing*, not as a present participle. These combinations have already been observed in Old English (e.g., *leorning-cniht* 'pupil', *ræding-boc* 'reading-book'),[24] but 'none of the words used today are older than Middle English.'[25]

---

22 In *MED* (s.v. *her* adv.), *her being(e* 'life on earth' is given under the item 'cpds. & comb.'.

23 *MED* (s.v. *wel-willing(e* ger.) understands that this compound is derived from the combination of *wel* (adv.) and *willing(e* (ger.).

24 See Herbert Koziol, *Handbuch der englischen Wortbildungslehre*. Zweite, neubearbeitete Auflage. (Heidelberg: Carl Winter, Universitätsverlag): 60.

25 See Marchand, *The Categories and Types of Present-Day English Word-Formation*: 69.

From a syntactic-semantic point of view, the compounds of this type are divided into two subtypes: Object-type and Adverbial-type.

10.11.1. Object-type

The combination of this type has an underlying structure where the second element works as an object. In our corpus, only one example is found: *spendyng silver* [OE+OE] 'spending money' (CYT 1018) [underlying sentence: 'They spend money (=silver)'].

10.11.2. Adverbial-type

The adverbial-type is illustrated by *chasynge spere* [OE+OE] 'hunting-spear' (*Morte Arth* 1823) [underlying sentence: 'They hunt with a spear'], where the second element *spere* appears as an adverbial phrase. Other examples are *countyng-bord* [OF+OE] 'counting table' (ShipT 83) [underlying sentence: 'They count on the board'], *wipynge-cloth* [OE+OE] 'dishcloth' (*LondonE* 180.1250) [underlying sentence: 'They wash dishes with a cloth'], *with-drawynge Chamber* [OE+OF] 'small room for private conversations' (*LondonE* 175: 1078) [underlying sentence: 'They withdraw into their chamber'], *rennynge houndis* [OE+OE] 'hunting dogs' (Malory *Wks* 102/30) [underlying sentence: 'They hunt with hounds'].

10.12. The Distribution of Compound Nouns

Throughout the course of this essay, we have seen that there are quite a few variations of the compound nouns in Late Middle English. The distribution of the different kinds of compound nouns is shown in Table 10–1.

Noun/Noun (copula compound)

	OE+OE	OF+OF	OF+OE	OE+OF	Total
verse:	79	5	2	3	89
prose:	7	1	2	0	10

Noun/Noun (rectional compound)

	OE+OE	OF+OF	OF+OE	OE+OF	Total
verse:	251	14	18	5	288
prose:	49	2	9	1	61

Noun's/Noun (copula compound)

	OE+OE	OF+OF	OF+OE	OE+OF	Total
verse:	2	0	0	0	2
prose:	0	0	0	0	0

Noun's/Noun (rectional compound)

	OE+OE	OF+OF	OF+OE	OE+OF	Total
verse:	40	0	0	0	40
prose:	8	0	0	4	12

Adjective/Noun

	OE+OE	OF+OF	OF+OE	OE+OF	Total
verse:	81	13	7	3	104
prose:	17	9	4	2	32

Numeral/Noun

	OE+OE	OF+OF	OF+OE	OE+OF	Total
verse:	4	0	0	0	4
prose:	2	0	0	0	2

Pronoun/Noun

	OE+OE	OF+OF	OF+OE	OE+OF	Total
verse:	1	0	0	0	1
prose:	1	0	0	0	1

Verb (stem)/Noun					
	OE+OE	OF+OF	OF+OE	OE+OF	Total
verse:	14	1	0	1	16
prose:	4	0	1	0	5

Noun/Verb+*ere*					
	OE+OE	OF+OF	OF+OE	OE+OF	Total
verse:	4	0	1	0	5
prose:	7	0	3	0	10

Noun/Verb+Ø					
	OE+OE	OF+OF	OF+OE	OE+OF	Total
verse:	30	1	0	1	32
prose:	4	0	0	0	4

Noun/Verb+*ing*					
	OE+OE	OF+OF	OF+OE	OE+OF	Total
verse:	14	0	1	1	16
prose:	3	0	1	0	4

Verb+*ing*/Noun					
	OE+OE	OF+OF	OF+OE	OE+OF	Total
verse:	2	0	2	1	5
prose:	2	0	0	1	3

Table 10-1 Distribution of kinds of compound nouns

The distribution in Table 10-1 shows that the combination Noun/Noun is most prominent in its type-frequency in both verse[26] and prose, followed

26 Here 'verse' covers alliterative, rhymed, and alliterative-rhymed writing. The verse works examined in this essay are, in rhymed verse: Chaucer's *The Canterbury Tales* (excluding *The Tale of Melibee* and *The Parson's Tale*, *The Book of the Duchess*, *The House of Fame*, *The Legend of Good Women*, *The Parliament of Fowls*, *The Romaunt of the Rose* Fragment A, *Troilus and Criseyde*, *The Complaint to his Lady*, *The Complaint*

by the compounds Adjective/Noun, Noun's/Noun, and Noun/Verb+Ø, in order of frequency. On the other hand, both the compound Numeral/ Noun and the compound Pronoun/Noun are seldom employed in Late Middle English. What is more important is that the pattern [OE+OE][27] is the most common etymological feature that creates the compound noun in Late Middle English. This linguistic characteristic is worthy of note when we take into consideration that Old French had a great influence upon Late Middle English following the Norman Conquest. The other point to observe is that all kinds of compound nouns sporadically occur in the prose works.

Moreover, our notice will be directed only to the distribution that represents syntactic and semantic characteristics of the compound Noun/ Noun (copula compound and rectional compound), which is used with highest frequency.

Noun/Noun (copula compound) attributive:	OE+OE	OF+OF	OF+OE	OE+OF	Total
Verse	50	4	2	2	58
Prose	7	1	2	0	10
tautological:	OE+OE	OF+OF	OF+OE	OE+OF	Total
Verse	11	1	0	1	13

---

of Mars, *The Former Age, Fortune, An ABC, The Complaint unto Pity, The Complaint of Chaucer to his Purse, The Complaint of Venus, Womanly Noblesse, Against Women Unconstant, Lenvoy de Chaucer a Scogan* and *The English Works of John Gower*; in unrhymed alliterative verse: *The Vision of Piers Plowman, Morte Arthure, Cleanness and Patience*; in alliterative and rhymed verse: *Sir Gawain and the Green Knight, Pearl*. The prose works treated in the present paper are: Chaucer's *The Tale of Melibee, The Parson's Tale, Boece, A Treatise on the Astrolabe; The Works of Sir Thomas Malory; A Book of London English 1384–1425.*

27   The combinations such as OE+OE, OF+OF, OF+OE, OE+OF denote etymological features of each compound noun, respectively. Here the feature OE includes Old Norse and Middle English and the feature OF also refers to Anglo-French as well as Latin.

Prose	o	o	o	o	o
subsumptive:	OE+OE	OF+OF	OF+OE	OE+OF	Total
Verse	7	o	o	o	7
Prose	o	o	o	o	o
comparison:	OE+OE	OF+OF	OF+OE	OE+OF	Total
Verse	11	o	o	o	11
Prose	o	o	o	o	o

Table 10–2 Distribution of Noun/Noun copula compounds

Table 10–2 shows the type-frequency of the copula compound nouns on the basis of semantic factors. As is obvious from this table, the proportion of attributive use is significantly largest in both verse and prose, followed by tautological use and use containing a comparison, which are extremely infrequent. In this case, also, the etymological composite of the copula compound nouns in attributive use is [OE+OE] in both verse and prose.

Table 10–3 indicates the type-frequency of the rectional compound nouns on a syntactic and semantic basis in the underlying structure of the compound in question.

Noun/Noun (rectional compound)

subject-type:	OE+OE	OF+OF	OF+OE	OE+OF	Total
Verse	126	1	6	1	134
Prose	28	2	6	1	37
object-type:	OE+OE	OF+OF	OF+OE	OE+OF	Total
Verse	94	12	9	3	118
Prose	20	o	3	o	23
adverbial-type:	OE+OE	OF+OF	OF+OE	OE+OF	Total
Verse	31	1	3	1	36
Prose	1	o	o	o	1

Table 10–3 Type-frequency of rectional compound nouns

From the rest of this investigation, we realize that the use of compounds of this kind is most remarkable in a subject-type in both verse and prose. And the object-type compounds have the largest distribution following the subject-type compound nouns. What is also worthy of notice is that the etymological feature [OE+OE] is most prominent in each type in both verse and prose.

Here I shall treat the distribution of the copula compound nouns under the headings of alliteration and rhyme.

Noun/Noun (copula compound)

attributive:	OE+OE	OF+OF	OF+OE	OE+OF	Total
alliteration[1]	15	2	1	1	19
Rhyme	35	2	1	2	40
tautological:	OE+OE	OF+OF	OF+OE	OE+OF	Total
Alliteration	5	0	0	0	5
Rhyme	6	1	0	1	8
subsumptive:	OE+OE	OF+OF	OF+OE	OE+OF	Total
Alliteration	6	0	0	0	6
Rhyme	1	0	0	0	1
comparison:	OE+OE	OF+OF	OF+OE	OE+OF	Total
Alliteration	7	0	0	0	7
Rhyme	4	0	0	0	4

Table 10–4 Distribution of alliteration and rhyme
[1] Here 'alliteration' covers both rhymed and unrhymed alliterative verse.

First of all, Table 10–4 reveals that the proportion of compound nouns in the rhymed works is larger in both attributive and tautological uses than that in subsumptive use and comparison. Next, the point to notice is that the etymological feature [OE+OE] is most prominent in compounds of this kind in both alliteration and rhyme.

Finally, I focus upon type-frequency of the rectional compound nouns in both alliteration and rhyme.

Noun/Noun (rectional compound)

subject-type:	OE+OE	OF+OF	OF+OE	OE+OF	Total
Alliteration	56	1	4	1	62
Rhyme	70	0	2	0	72
object-type:	OE+OE	OF+OF	OF+OE	OE+OF	Total
Alliteration	22	3	3	3	31
Rhyme	72	9	6	0	87
adverbial-type:	OE+OE	OF+OF	OF+OE	OE+OF	Total
Alliteration	9	1	1	1	12
Rhyme	22	0	2	0	24

Table 10–5 Distribution of alliteration and rhyme

As is evident from Table 10–5, under all three types the occurrence of compounds of this kind is most marked in the rhymed works. In addition, Table 10–5 shows that compounds composed of the etymological feature [OE+OE] appear with highest frequency in the rhymed works.

10.13. On the Underlying Sentence

As has been mentioned above, in this chapter the syntactic and semantic description of the compound nouns is made on the basis of their underlying sentences. However, there are some cases where a given compound noun can often be paraphrased by two different sentences.

For example, the compound *bedstraw* 'straw for bedding' (MerT 1783) may have the underlying sentence 'They fill the bed with straw', in which case the compound can be classified as an adverbial-type. But it is also r possible that its underlying sentence may be 'The bed has straw', of which the compound is discussed as an object-type.[28] In *parissh clerk* 'parish clerk' (MilT 3312), we may paraphrase this compound either by the sentence 'The parish has a clerk' (so that the compound is classified as an object-type), or a sentence such as 'The clerk is in charge of the parish' may be assumed (so that it is classified as a subject-type).

In the underlying sentence of the compound *boxtre pipere* 'pipe-maker' (*PF* 178), either 'They make a pipe out of boxwood' or 'The pipe-maker (=*pipere*) uses boxwood (=*boxtree*)' may be assumed. When the former is taken, the compound boxtree pipere may be understood as an object-type. When the latter is adopted, however, the compound may be dealt with as a subject-type. In a second example, *pykeharneys* 'plunderer of armour' (*PPl.B* 20.263) the compound may be rewritten as either 'They plunder armour (=*harneys*)' (here an object-type), or 'The man despoils those slain in battle of their armour' (here an adverbial-type).

In Sauer's (1992) view, 'the possibility of two (or more) paraphrases for the same cpd [=compound] reflects one of the functions of cpds, namely to condense information.'[29]

10.14. Compound Nouns or Noun Phrases

The analysis of compound nouns raises a very difficult question about the criterion for a compound. Some scholars have asserted that we recognize a compound by finding out whether the determinant or first element can be separable from a determinatum or the second element. In Adams' (1973: 57) opinion, for example, the sequence *small talk* cannot be premodified

---

28 Charles Campbell Smith, 'Noun + Noun Compounds in the Works of Geoffrey Chaucer', PhD dissertation (New York University, 1970): 114 points out that 'it is a little difficult to decide to what extent human action is felt to be involved'. Therefore, as the underlying sentence of this compound, 'The bed has straw' is better.

29 See Sauer, *Nominalkomposita*: 719.

by an adverb *very*. To put it in other words, the first element *small* cannot be separated from the second element *talk*. Therefore, the composite *small talk* is a compound noun. On the other hand, in the sequence *wet day* we can say *very wet day*, so that this sequence is understood only as a noun phrase, which consists of an adjective and a noun.

According to Jespersen (1949: 185), a compound may be identified as such by other features that may distinguish it from a simple noun phrase. In short, Jespersen states that the singular form is used even if the idea of the first element of the sequence is plural, as in *tear gas*, which means 'gas which causes tears'.

Some scholars, such as Koziol (1937: 46–7), insist that the criterion of a compound is based upon the psychological unity of a combination. He says there is a difference of stress between a compound and a syntactic sequence. In other words, he seems to advocate stress as a criterion of a compound, as in *gréen hòuse*, which means 'a glass building in which plants that need protection from cold weather are grown' and *grèen hóuse*, which refers to 'a house painted green'.[30]

As is evident from what has been discussed so far, it is almost impossible for us to make a clear-cut distinction between a compound and a noun phrase, even in Present-day English. In Early English, there is no more decisive way to establish whether a noun phrase is a compound or not. The difficulty of answering the question of what is a compound is reflected in the explanations given in *MED* as well as in *OED*. Although the compound nouns are registered as entry words in these dictionaries, many sequences are given under the items such as 'compounds and combinations', 'combinations and phrases'. Here some examples are shown for illustration.

---

30   R.B. Lees, *The Grammar of English Nominalizations* (The Hague: Mouton, 1960) and Marchand, *The Categories and Types of Present-Day English Word-Formation* (1969) have also adopted the criterion of accentuation on the first element to define the compound.

1) *clowe-gelofre* 'clove-gillyflower' (*Rom* A 1368)

This compound is recorded under the entry word *clo(ve* in *MED*, while *OED* registers this combination as a compound. However, the combination in question is written either as a compound or a noun phrase in *Mandeville's Travels*.[31] As a noun phrase we have:

> And summe destyllen *clowes of gylofre* and of spikenard of Spayne (36/24–25)

And as a compound noun:

> And in that contree and in other contrees thereabouten growen many trees that beren *clowe gylofres* and ... of many other spices. (191/22–192/3)

2) *whete-seed* 'grain of wheat' (WBT 143)

Neither *MED* nor *OED* registers this sequence as a compound, but *MED* (s.v. *whete* n.) records the combination under the item 'in cpds. and phrases' and *OED* (s.v. *wheat* n.) understands the sequence as 'Comb.'.

The same thing is true of other examples such as *herde-gromes* 'herdsmen' (*HF* 1225), *bonde-folk* 'serfs' (ParsT 754), *mayster-toun* 'main city' (*LGW* 1591), *loue-drury* 'courtly love' (Thop 895), *plom-rule* 'plumb-rule' (*Astr* 2.38.9) (this last recorded as a compound noun in *OED*).

3) *castel wal* 'castle wall' (WBT 263)

This example is registered as a compound only under the item '1b' in *MED* (s.v. *castel* n.) and under the item 'Comb.' in *OED* (s.v. *castle* n.). However, this sequence is sometimes separable in Chaucer's English. As a noun phrase we find:

> Which was from us but a lyte –
> A long *castel with walles* white, (*BD* 1317–18)

---

31   The quotations are taken from M.C. Seymour (ed.), *Mandeville's Travels* (Oxford: Clarendon Press, 1969).

As a compound noun:

> Thou seyst men may nat kepe a *castel wal,*
> It may so long assailed been overall. (WBT 263–64)

These different combinations may be formed due to metrical demand or rhyme. The same thing is true of the following examples.
As a noun phrase:

> Wher that a *pot with water* nome
> Sche hath, and broghte it into house, (Gower *CA* 3.656–57)

As a compound:

> And she set doun hir *water pot* anon, (ClT 290)

> The *waterpot* sche hente alofte (Gower *CA* 3.673)

However, the following difference is not related to metre or rhyme.
As a noun phrase:

> And at the *chamber-dore* they abyde. (*LGW* 1718)

4) *fern-asshen* 'ashes of fern' (SqT 254)

Neither *MED* nor *OED* gives us a clear-cut answer as to whether this sequence is a compound or not. *MED* (s.v. *fern* n.) records it as *fern ashes, ashes of fern,* while *OED* (s.v. *fern* n.) registers this example under the item 'Comb. *fern-ashes*'. In this connection, the citation below is worthy of consideration.

> But nathelees somme seiden that it was
> Wonder to maken of *fern-asshen* glas,
> And yet nys glas nat lyk ashen of fern;
> (SqT 253–55)
> [But some said that it was extraordinary that glass is made of ashes of fern, though glass is not like ashes of fern.]

The phrase *asshen of fern* in the third line is rhymed with the word fern in
the next line 256 (But, for they han yknowen it so *fern*). We can say with
fair certainty that the word's appearance in rhyming position is what caused
the separation of the elements of the sequence. Much the same is true of
the following example:

> Ye have ynough, pardee, of *Goddes sonde*:
> Com doun to-day, and lat youre bagges stonde. (ShipT 219–20)

5) *eyen syght* 'the sense of sight' (MerT 2260)

This combination is recorded as a compound noun in both *MED* (s.v.
eie-sight n.) and *OED* (s.v. *eyesight* n.). However, when a pronoun or an
article is placed before the word *eyen*, the separation is observed, as in the
following examples.

> it maketh hym coveite, ... by *sighte of his eyen* as to erthely thynges,
>   (ParsT 336)
> Tho fastnede sche a litel the *syghte of hir eyen*,
>   (Bo 3.pr.2.1–2)
> the same rowndnesse of a body, otherweys the *sighte of the eighe* knoweth it,
>   (Bo 5.pr.4.143–44)

The same may apply to the following instances. As a noun phrase we
find:

> *Joye of this world*, for tyme wol nat abyde; (MLT 1133)

> Tho[u] enclyned to that party for bobbaunce and *pryde of the worlde*,
>   (Malory *Wks* 933/31–32)

> Heeld yet the *chamber of his paleys* riche (KnT 2525)

> with alle the *beemes of the sonne* hir brothir, hideth the sterres that ben lasse;
>   (Bo 1.m.5.7–8)

And as a compound noun:

> Hise *worldes joyes* ben so grete,
> Him thenkth of hevene no beyete; (Gower *CA* 1.2683–84)

> Of werre it helpeth forto ryde,
> For coveitise and *worldes pride*. (Gower *CA* 3.2469–70)

> Yit was no *paleis-chaumbres* ne non halles; (*Former Age* 41)

> That serchen every lond and every streem,
> As thikke as motes in the *sonne-beem*, (WBT 867–68)

6) *shames deeth* 'a shameful death' (MLT 819)

In both *MED* (s.v. *shame* n.) and *OED* (s.v. *shame* n.), this sequence is given as *shame(e* deth and as *shames death*, but this combination is not registered as a compound noun. In this sense, the following example may be worthy of notice.

> To maken hire on *shameful deeth* to deye. (MLT 592)

10.15. Conclusion

In this chapter I have limited the discussion to the compound nouns in Late Middle English. As is obvious from what has been said so far, the decline of compounding is more prominent in the Middle English period in comparison with the Old English period. In the corpus examined here, however, various kinds of compound nouns are observed. In particular, the copula compound nouns and the rectional compound nouns are employed with highest productivity.

Although the remarkable influence of French upon Middle English has been long noted, the most frequent pattern of etymological features that constitute these compound nouns is [OE+OE].[32] Contrary to general belief, in the history of English there are few cases where the compound nouns contain a French etymological feature. As our investigation has focused on only a few verse and prose works in the Late Middle English period, it would be necessary to examine a much larger body of linguistic data in order to make clearer the characteristics of the compound nouns.

As stated in sections 14 and 15, the problem we have to consider in more detail is how to decide the underlying sentences that are essential for a syntactic and semantic description of the compounds. And the question of what would be the best way to determine the compound nouns remains unsolved. In other words, it is a more or less arbitrary matter how we identify an item as a compound or a noun phrase. At the same time, several examples given in section 15 show that the distinction between compound nouns and noun phrases remains unstable in Late Middle English.

10.16. References

10.16.1. Primary sources

Barron, W.R., ed. *Sir Gawain and the Green Knight*, New York: Manchester University Press, 1974.

Benson, Larry D., ed. *The Riverside Chaucer*. 3rd edn. Boston, MA: Houghton Mifflin; London: Oxford University Press, 1987.

Brock, Edmund, ed. *Morte Arthure or The Death of Arthur* (EETS OS 8). London: Oxford University Press, 1967.

32   As noted in Yonekura, 'A Descriptive Study of Word Formation in Chaucer' (2004): 621, and *Studies in English Word Formation: Some Synchronic-Diachronic Problems* (Tokyo: Eichosha, 2005): 144, the etymological feature [OE+OE] is overwhelmingly marked in constituting compound nouns in Chaucer.

Chambers, R.W. and Marjorie Daunt, eds. *A Book of London English 1384–1425*. Oxford: Clarendon Press, 1931.

Fulk, R.D., Robert E. Bjork and John D. Niles, eds. *Klaeber's Beowulf*, Toronto & Others: University of Toronto Press, 2009.

Gordon, E.V., ed. *Pearl*. Oxford: Clarendon Press, 1980.

Gordon, Ida, ed. *The Seafarer* (Old and Middle English Texts). London: Manchester University Press, 1979.

Macaulay, G.C., ed. *The English Works of John Gower*. 2 vols. (EETS ES 81, 82). London: Oxford University Press, 1968.

Morris, Richard, ed. *Early English Alliterative Poems in the West Midland Dialect of the Fourteenth Century* (EETS OS 1). London: Oxford University Press, 1965.

Schmidt, A.V.C., ed. *William Langland: The Vision of Piers Plowman: The B Text*. 2nd edn. London: Dent. Reprinted, with revisions and corrections, 1997.

Seymour, M.C., ed. *Mandeville's Travels*. Oxford: Clarendon Press, 1969.

Vinaver, Eugène, ed. *The Works of Sir Thomas Malory*. 3 vols. 3rd edn. Oxford: Clarendon Press, 1990.

10.16.2. Secondary sources

Adams, Valerie. *An Introduction to Modern English Word-Formation*, English Language Series 7, London: Longman, 1973.

Bauer, Laurie. *Morphological Productivity*, Cambridge Studies in Linguistics 95, Cambridge: Cambridge University Press, 2001.

Bradley, Henry. *The Making of English*. Rev. by Simeon Potter. London: Macmillan, [1904] 1968.

Brinton, Laurel J., and Elizabeth Closs Traugott. *Lexicalization and Language Change*, Research Survey in Linguistics, Cambridge: Cambridge University Press, 2005.

Burnley, David. 'Lexis and Semantics', in Norman Blake ed., *The Cambridge History of the English Language*. vol. II: 1066–1476, Cambridge: Cambridge University Press, 1991: 409–99.

Dalton-Puffer, Christiane. *The French Influence on Middle English Morphology*, Topics in English Linguistics 20, Berlin and New York: Mouton de Gruyter, 1996.

Jespersen, Otto. *A Modern English Grammar on Historical Principles*. Part II. London: George Allen & Unwin, 1949.

Kastovsky, Dieter. 'Word-formation, or: at the Crossroads of Morphology, Syntax, and the Lexicon', *Folia Linguistica* 10 (1977): 1–33.

———. 'Deverbal Nouns in Old and Middle English: From Stem-Formation to Word-Formation', in Jacek Fisiak, ed., *Historical Semantics: Historical Word Formation*, Berlin, New York and Amsterdam: Mouton, 1985: 221–61.

Koziol, Herbert. *Handbuch der englischen Wortbildungslehre*. Erste Ableitung. Heidelberg: Carl Winter, Universitätsverlag, 1937.

———. *Handbuch der englischen Wortbildungslehre*. Zweite, neubearbeitete Auflage. Heidelberg: Carl Winter, Universitätsverlag, 1972.

Kurath, Hans, Sherman M. Kuhn, and Robert E. Lewis, eds. *Middle English Dictionary*. Ann Arbor, MI: University of Michigan Press, 1954–2001. [*MED*]

Lees, R.B. *The Grammar of English Nominalizations*. The Hague: Mouton, 1960.

Lieber, Rochelle. *Morphology and Lexical Semantics*, Cambridge Studies in Linguistics 104, Cambridge: Cambridge University Press, 2004.

———. 'English Word-formation Processes: Observations, Issues, and Thoughts on Future Research', in Pasvol Stekauer and Rochelle Lieber, eds., *Handbook of Word-Formation*. Dordrecht: Springer, 2005: 375–427.

Marchand, Hans. *The Categories and Types of Present-Day English Word-Formation: Synchronic-Diachronic Approach*. 2nd edn. München: C.H. Beck'sche Verlagsbuchhandlung, 1969.

Mühleisen, Susanne. *Heterogeneity in Word-Formation Patterns: A Corpus-Based Analysis of Suffixation with -ee and its Productivity*, Studies in Language Companion Series 118, Amsterdam: John Benjamins, 2010.

Plag, Ingo. *Word-Formation in English*, Cambridge Textbooks in Linguistics, Cambridge: Cambridge University Press, 2003.

———. 'Syntactic Category Information and the Semantics of Derivational Morphological rules', *Folia Linguistica* 38 (2004): 193–225.

Sauer, Hans. *Nominalkomposita im Frühmittelenglischen*. Tübingen: Max Niemeyer Verlag, 1992.

Simpson, John A. and Edmund S.C. Weiner, eds. *The Oxford English Dictionary*. 2nd edn. Oxford: Clarendon Press, 1988. [*OED*]

Smith, Charles Campbell. 'Noun + Noun Compounds in the Works of Geoffrey Chaucer.' PhD dissertation, New York University, 1970.

Trips, Carola. *Lexical Semantics and Diachronic Morphology*, Linguistische Arbeiten 527, Tübingen: Max Niemeyer Verlag, 2009.

Yonekura, Hiroshi. 'A Descriptive Study of Word Formation in Chaucer', PhD dissertation, Tsukuba University, 2004.

———. *Studies in English Word Formation: Some Synchronic-Diachronic Problems*. Tokyo: Eichosha, 2005. [In Japanese]

11 Robert Henryson's Rhymes between 'Etymological –ē and –ī' and the Special Development of Unstressed /i/

11.0. Introduction

Denton Fox's excellent edition of Robert Henryson's complete poems, *The Poems of Robert Henryson* (Oxford: Clarendon Press, 1981), provides an Appendix, where Fox discusses some of the interesting rhymes of Henryson (492–4). In Section Two, he deals with rhymes between etymological –ē (i.e. ME long close /e:/) and –ī (i.e. ME long /i:/). He says that these 'mixed rhymes' are difficult to explain away and, citing the line-numbers in which such rhymes occur, asks us to see the notes to each of these lines. In the notes, he briefly comments to the effect that Henryson would ordinarily avoid such rhyming, and continues:

> It seems likely, as A. J. Aitken has suggested to me, that these sounds had fallen together by Henryson's time, but that he generally followed the traditional practice of earlier poets. (493)

Altogether he finds fifteen rhymes of this kind in all, including three in *The Bludy Serk*, Henryson's authorship of which, he says, remains doubtful (439) and one in *The Fables*, which occurs in lines where he finds textual uncertainty (250–1).

The rhymes that Fox alleges to be of etymological -ē with -ī, however, need to be re-examined: one rhyme must be struck out, since this is not a 'mixed rhyme' but a pure rhyme on ME /e:/ in all the words involved; and there are in fact three more rhymes to be added as 'mixed' in Henryson's poems.

The first purpose of the present paper is to give the complete list of Henryson's rhymes between 'etymological -ē and -ī'. The second is to present my view of how these two sounds came to have fallen together. As Middle English philology has firmly established that ME long close /eː/ and long /iː/ never merged in the course of their developments, the identification of these two can only be explained from a special development of unstressed /i/ to /iː/ under the influence of secondary stress, which E.J. Dobson fully discusses in his *English Pronunciation 1500–1700* (Oxford: Clarendon Press, 1968): §§275, 350.

If this interpretation is approved, Henryson's rhymes of this kind, with some exceptions, can be taken as direct evidence for the development of ME /eː/ to early Modern English /iː/, as well as the diphthongization of ME /iː/. In sections 11.6 to 11.11, I shall discuss which rhymes are conclusive pieces of evidence for the changes, and which are not. And in the last two sections, 11.12 and 11.13, I shall point out that the use of this kind of rhyme is by no means confined to Henryson, but is found elsewhere in Scottish and non-Scottish poets among his contemporaries as well as those before and long after him.

11.1. Henryson and His Language

Robert Henryson is perhaps best-known to modern readers for his *Fables*, animal fables based on *Aesop* and the tale of *Reynard the Fox*, or *The Testament of Cresseid*, which was composed as a sequel to Chaucer's *Troilus and Criseyde*. Among his shorter poems, *Robene and Makyne*, a lovers' debate in a countryside, may be most famous.

Little is known of his life. Though dates around c.1430–c. 1505 are sometimes assigned to Henryson, the biographical details proposed by some scholars remain speculative. The only thing considered certain is that he lived in the second half of the fifteenth century. There is no piece of evidence to show his date of birth. His date of death, however, is inferred with some certainty, thanks to William Dunbar's *Lament for the Makars*, where Dunbar names Henryson among dead poets. This indicates that Henryson died before Dunbar composed this poem, which is considered c.1505. In the same poem, Dunbar associates him with Dunfermline, in Fife, East Scotland; the connection of Henryson with Dunfermline has not been questioned (Fox xiii–xxv).[1]

The type of language Henryson used is, therefore, Early Middle Scots. Though there are some changes peculiar to Scots, this language agrees in the main with a northern variety of Middle English in the second half of the fifteenth century.[2]

11.2. Complete List of Rhymes between 'Etymological –ē and –ĭ'

The rhymes Fox gives as etymological –ē with –ĭ are the following, cited in order of appearance in Fox's edition. I give a number in parentheses to each, and this number is used throughout when referring to these rhymes:

The Fables (Fables)
1) 1126/28/29 de (inf.) "die": fle (inf.) "flee": mortifie (inf.) "bring into subjection"
2) 2082/83 spedilie (adv.) "quickly": (vpon) hie (adj.) "loudly"
3) 2112/14 (on) hie (adj.) "loudly": trewlie (adv.) "truly"
4) 2264/65 me (pron.): trewlie (adv.) "truly"
5) 2301/03 hastelie (adv.) "hastily": me (pron.)

---

1   Dunbar's *Lament for the Makars*, lines 81–2 runs as follows:
    In Dunfermelyne he (= Death) has done roune
    With Maister Robert Henrisoun. (Douglas Gray (ed.), *The Oxford Book of Late Medieval Verse and Prose*, Oxford: Clarendon Press, 1985: 318).
2   On the phonological developments of Older Scots, see especially A.J. Aitken, *The Older Scots Vowels: A History of the Stressed Vowels of Older Scots from the Beginnings to the Eighteenth Century* (ed.), Caroline Macafee (Glasgow: The Scottish Text Society, 2002).

6)   2406/08 subtellie (adv.) "treacherously": me (pron.)
7)   2411/12 haistelie (adv.) "hastily": supple (n.) "help"
8)   2449/51/52 ee (n.) "eye": fantasie (n.) "fancy": buttrie (n.) "storeroom"

The Testament of Cresseid (Testament)
9)   296/98/99 3e (pron.): degre (n.) "degree": modifie (inf.) "assess"

Orpheus and Eurydice (Orpheus)
10)   65/67/68 liberalite (n.) "liberality": ermonye (n.) "music": kne (n.) "knee"
11)   419/20 be (3 pr. sg. subj.): poesie (n.) "poetry"

The Bludy Serk (BS)
12)   58/60/62/64 deir (adj.) "dear": de (inf.) "die": bludy (adj.) "bloody": sy (inf.) "see"
13)   73/75/77/79 de (inf.) "die": bludy (adj.) "bloody": me (pron.): fre (adj.) "free"
14)   97/99/101/03 Trinitie (n.) "Trinity": lady (n.): tre (n.) "tree": fell (pt. sg. of "fall")

Robene and Makyne (RM)
15)   18/20/22/24 A B C (n.) "primer": fre (adj.) "free": dre (2 pr. sg. subj.) "endure": previe (adj.) "secret"

Fox's list is defective, in that it contains one rhyme that is not 'mixed' and lacks three 'mixed rhymes' that should be included. The rhyme that must be excluded from the list is 15. The last word *previe* in this rhyme may have been taken as having 'etymological -$\bar{\imath}$', rhyming with the other three words with 'etymological –$\bar{e}$'. But this is not true. *Previe* < OF *privé* is a word having 'etymological –$\bar{e}$'. Middle English poets often rhymed the second syllable of this word properly with ME /e:/ as in Chaucer's *Miller's Tale* in *The Canterbury Tales* I(A) 3201/02 *privee* (adj.): *see* (inf.) (*The Riverside Chaucer*, ed. Benson: 68).

The three rhymes that should be added in the list are the following:

Testament
16)   62/63 destenie (n.) "destiny": wretchitlie (adv.) "with great misery"
17)   121/23/24 desteny (n.) "destiny": (in) hy (n.) "in haste": angerly (adv.) "angrily"
18)   470/72 destenye (n.) "destiny": cry (n.)

The seventeen rhymes given above in 1 to 18 (except for 15) are the only rhymes between 'etymological –ē and –ī' that Henryson has. All of these rhymes involve ME /e:/ or /i:(ə)/ in the final syllable of disyllabic or polysyllabic words.

11.3. ME /e:/ and /i:(ə)/ in Rhymes Other than 'Mixed Rhymes'

Henryson often uses such ME /e:/ and /i:(ə)/ in word-final position as rhymes, but he elsewhere keeps them apart. As well as the above 'mixed rhymes', there are eighty-one rhymes in which ME /e:/ in the final syllable of disyllables or polysyllables is used, and fifty-nine rhymes in which ME /i:(ə)/ in the final syllable of disyllables or polysyllables is used. These are all self-rhymes, i.e. ME /e:/ rhymes only on ME /e:/ itself and ME /i:(ə)/ on ME /i:(ə)/ itself.

Examples of ME /e:/-rhymes are: *Fables* 390/92/93/95 *the* (pron.): *se* (inf.): *honestie* (n.): *degre* (n.) and 824/26 *pietie* (n.) "pity": *he* (pron.), where all the words used have ME /e:/. The examples of ME /i:(ə)/-rhymes are: *Testament* 359/61/62 *reddy* (adj.) "ready": *(in) hy* (n.) "in haste": *ly* (pr. pl.) "lie down" and 387/89/90 *priuely* (adv.): *espy* (inf.): thairby (adv.) "from there", where all the words used have ME /i:(ə)/.

In addition to these, there are forty-seven monosyllables with ME /e:/ rhyming on itself, e.g. *Testament* 351/53 *sche* (pron.): *me* (pron.) and eight monosyllables with ME /i:(ə)/ rhyming on itself, e.g. *Fables* 2868/70 *cry* (inf.): *I* (pron.). This is also the case with ME /e:/ and ME /i:/ followed by consonant(s). Henryson does not rhyme ME /e:/ and ME /i: / together. A sole exception would be a case of *tyre* (inf.) and *tyrit* (pp.) "become weak" <OE *tīorian*, *tēorian*, which normally have /e:r/ in ME, rhyming with ME /i:r/ (*Fables* 560, 2536; *Testament* 516; *Against Hasty Credence* 42). Although the current pronunciation of *tire* with /aiə/ is derived from ME /i:r/, this /i:/-form is not fully explained and OE **tīran* is assumed to be an etymon (*OED* s.v. *tire* v¹).

As shown above, the bulk of Henryson's rhymes depending on ME /e:/ and ME /i:(ə)/ are self-rhymes, in which, as Fox says, the poet 'followed the traditional practice of earlier poets' (493). Such normal self-rhymes are of no interest linguistically, whereas the exceptional 'mixed rhymes' are interesting in that they indicate the actual pronunciation Henryson knew.

11.4. Influence of Secondary Stress Advanced by E.J. Dobson

E.J. Dobson observes that the presence of some form of secondary stress, in late ME or early Modern English, caused the lengthening of vowels in post-tonic syllables (§§264–83). The lengthening particularly relevant to the interpretation of rhymes between etymological –*ē* and –*ī* is that of unstressed /i/ to /i:/ under secondary stress, which Dobson discusses in sections 275 and 350.

He reports that such lengthening occurred in: (a) words with ME *ĭ* < OE, ON *ĭg* (OE – *īc*) in the suffixes –*y* (*bloody, body*, etc.) and –*ly* (*heavenly, boldly*, etc.), (b) words with French or Latin *i*, (e.g. *determine, crocodile, Florentine, mercy, cherries, caitive*), (c) words with OF –*é(e)* (e.g. *destiny, dishonesty, majesty, university, pity, army, country*), being assimilated to the native *ĭ* < *ĭg*, and (d) words with OF –*ie* (e.g. *history, injury, glory, copy*). He shows that the secondary stress could occur not only in syllables not immediately following the main stress, but also in syllables immediately following the main stress. This explains why the lengthening was brought about in the final syllable of disyllables as well as that of polysyllables. When the secondary stress was not given, short unstressed /i/ remained short and coexisted with the lengthened /i:/.

The linguistic situation where these two forms existed side by side is shown by the spellings used in *Welsh Hymn* (dated about, or rather somewhat before, 1500 (Dobson 1: 3)), or by the statements of sixteenth- and seventeenth-century grammarians or orthoepists. It should be remembered that the long stressed /i:/ in word-final position was not altogether an artificial pronunciation invented by poets when necessitated by rhyme, but was a real one supported by various writings on contemporary pronunciation.

11.5. Henryson's Use of Lengthened /iː/

I propose that this type of new /iː/ that developed from unstressed /i/ under the influence of secondary stress can justify Henryson's rhymes between 'etymological –ē and –ī'. The words I take as having such new /iː/ in each of the rhymes in the list above are the following: *mortifie* (inf.) < F. *mortifier* in the rhyme 1; suffix –*ly* < ON –*liga* in rhymes 2, 3, 4, 5, 6, 7; *fantasie* (n.) < OF *fantasie, buttrie* (n.) < AN *boterie,* *buterie in 8; *modifie* (inf.) < F. *modifier* in 9; *ermonye* (n.) < OF *harmonie* in 10; *poesie* (n.) < OF *poesie* in 11; *bludy* (adj.) < OE *blōdig* in 12, 13; *lady* (n.) < OE *hlǣfdige* in 14; *destenie/desteny/destenye* (n.) < OF *destinée* in 16, 17, 18.

The process of lengthening of the final syllable of these words, if we follow Dobson §275, may be explained as follows: At the outset, ME word-final /iː(ə)/ derived from OF –*ie* (1, 8, 9, 10, 11) and from OE or ON *-ĭg* (2, 3, 4, 5, 6, 7, 12, 13, 14) were reduced to unstressed /i/. ME word-final /eː/ from OF –*ée* (16, 17, 18) had been assimilated to the OE or ON suffix with /iː/ < -*ĭg* and was also reduced to unstressed /i/. Then, if the secondary stress was re-imposed on this kind of unstressed /i/, it was lengthened and new /iː/ arose.

Henryson rhymes this new /iː/ with ME /eː/ (from 1 to 14, though there are some ambiguous cases), as well as with pre-existing ME /iː/ (from 16 to 18, though one of these is ambiguous). In what follows, I shall call the former type of rhymes, i.e. rhymes between the new /iː/ and ME /eː/, A-type, and the latter, i.e. rhymes between the new /iː/ and older ME /iː/, B-type. I shall examine three different kinds of /iː/ in the argument that follows. So, for clarity's sake, I shall designate, when necessary, /iː/ derived from unstressed /i/ as 'new /iː/' and /iː/ derived from ME /eː/ as 'e.m.E (early Modern English) /iː/', to differentiate these from ME /iː/ derived from OE *ī* or OF *i* etc.

The A-type of rhymes presupposes that ME /eː/ has already shifted to e.m.E (Early Modern English) /iː/ and that pre-existing ME /iː/ has already started, if not completed, diphthongization. Otherwise the newly lengthened /iː/ would have been diphthongized as well, making it impossible to rhyme with e.m.E /iː/ derived from ME /eː/. The pronunciation intended in the A-type of rhymes would have been [iː]. The B-type of rhymes suggests that new /i:/ arose before the date of diphthongization of ME /i:/ and shared its subsequent diphthongization. Although the B-type does not in itself prove the diphthongization of ME /i:/, it is reasonable to consider that the pronunciation implied in the B-type of rhymes would have been a diphthongized one, something like [əi], since the A-type of rhymes presupposes that the diphthongization has already occurred.

Such rhyming practice in Henryson indicates that the imposition of secondary stress and the consequent lengthening of unstressed /i/ to new /i:/ occurred separately in two different periods, one before and the other after the date of diphthongization of ME /i:/.

Apart from these A and B types of 'mixed rhymes', there are many self-rhymes involving ME /e:/ or ME /i:(ə)/, which I have mentioned in 11.3 above. In those self-rhymes, which by far predominate, it is not adequate to postulate the use of long new /i:/ from unstressed short /i/, though it is possible, because word-final ME /e:/ or /i:(ə)/ would have escaped shortening, if stress is retained in it. For example, in the rhyme 15, which Fox takes for 'mixed' (see 11.2 above), the final syllable of *previe* with OF -*é* is rhymed with ME /e:/. It is possible to interpret this rhyme as new /i:/ from /i/ < ME /e:/ in *previe* rhyming with e.m.E /i:/ from ME /e:/. But this is far from conclusive, since *previe* could retain ME /e:/ in its final syllable. The existence of new long /i:/ from unstressed /i/ can only be proved in 'mixed rhymes', which admit of no other explanations than to postulate this /i:/. It follows that it is in 'mixed rhymes' that the shift of ME /e:/ to e.m.E /i:/ and the diphthongization of ME /i:/ can be known to have occurred.

The change of ME /e:/ to e.m.E /i:/ and the diphthongization of ME /i:/ are the earlier developments among the series of changes in pronunciation which affected long vowels known as the Great Vowel Shift. These two shifts are considered to have occurred perhaps before the mid-fifteenth century.[3]

---

3   Aitken postulates in section 20.1 that Early Scots /e:/ (= ME /e:/) seems to have been raised to near [i:] by the mid-fifteenth century. He continues that ME /i:/ began diphthongizing apparently not till after *c*1400, and before the mid-fifteenth

11.6.   Conclusive Evidence for the Shift of ME /e:/ to e.m.E /i:/

In the preceding section, I mentioned that A-type 'mixed rhymes' indicate the shift of ME /e:/ to e.m.E /i:/. But not all A-type rhymes can be considered as evidence for the shift. It is the following nine rhymes that can be taken as conclusive evidence for this:

Fables
4)   2264/65 me (pron.): trewlie (adv.) "truly"
5)   2301/03 hastelie (adv.) "hastily": me (pron.)
6)   2406/08 subtellie (adv.) "treacherously": me (pron.)

Testament
9)   296/98/99 3e (pron.): degre (n.) "degree": modifie (inf.) "assess"

Orpheus
10)   65/67/68 liberalite (n.) "liberality": ermonye (n.) "music": kne (n.) "knee"
11)   419/20 be (3 pr. sg. subj.): poesie (n.) "poetry"

BS
12)   58/60/62/64 deir (adj.) "dear": de (inf.) "die": bludy (adj.) "bloody": sy (inf.) "see"
13)   73/75/77/79 de (inf.) "die": bludy (adj.) "bloody": me (pron.): fre (adj.) "free"
14)   97/99/101/03 Trinitie (n.) "Trinity": lady (n.): tre (n.) "tree": fell (pt. sg. of "fall")

The reason I consider these as conclusive evidence for the change of ME /e:/ to e.m.E /i:/ is that new /i:/ derived from unstressed /i/ in the suffix *–ly* (in the rhymes 4, 5, 6) and in words ending in OF *–ie* (in 9, 10, 11) or in OE *-ĭg* (in 12, 13, 14) is rhymed, at least once in each set, with unambiguous

---

* century, since it is *a priori* likely that the diphthongization was first triggered by the encroachment of ME /e:/ upon [i:]. On the Great Vowel Shift of ME /e:/ and ME /i:/ in Older Scots, see Aitken §20, especially 108–17.

ME /e:/. Its sources are OE *ē* (in *me* < OE *mē* in 4, 5, 6, 13 and *ȝe* < OE *gē* 9) and OE *ēo* (in *kne* < OE *knēo* 10, *be* < OE *bēo* 11, *sy* < OE *sēon* 12, *fre* < OE *frēo* 13 and *tre* < OE *trēo* 14). These rhymes prove that ME /e:/ in these monosyllabic words has already developed into /i:/, otherwise these ME /e:/-words could not have rhymed with new /i:/ from unstressed /i/.

The rhymes 9, 10 and 14 involve respectively words with OF *–é*, *degre*, *liberalite* and *Trinitie*. This implies that OF *–é* in the final syllable of these words was pronounced [i:], which can be explained as coming either from ME /e:/ < OF *–é* with retention of stress, or from unstressed /i/ < ME /e:/ < OF *–é* with reduction of stress. In the case of *degre*, however, the [i:] in *-gre* is more likely to have come directly from stressed ME /e:/, since *de-* perhaps continued to be treated as a prefix with no stress. Similarly, *de* (inf.) in 12 and 13 is proved to have had e.m.E /i:/ < ME /e:/ < late OE *ēg-* (cf. 11.7 below).

The rhymes 12 and 14 are consonantally imperfect, *deir* 12 and *fell* 14 being thrown in among other words without -/r/ or -/l/. Such practice is very uncharacteristic of Henryson. Fox suggests that such loose rhymes may have been a part of Henryson's sophisticated imitation of Scots ballads, though there remains a question about his authorship (438–9)

11.7. New /i:/ Rhymes with Late OE *ēg-*

The following three rhymes are not satisfactory evidence for the shift of ME /e:/ to e.m.E /i:/, since in these rhymes new /i:/ derived from unstressed /i/ in the suffix *–ly* (in 2, 3) and OF words ending in *–ie* (in 8) is rhymed solely with words with late OE *ēg-*: *hie* "high" < Late OE *hēg-*, inflected form of *hēh* (in 2 and 3) and *ee* (n.) "eye" < OE (Anglian) *ēge* (in 8). As the reflex of late OE *ēg-* (i.e. late OE /e:/ + /j/ + vowel) varied in ME between /e:/ and /i:(ə)/ or /ai/, it is not certain that these rhymes were intended between new /i:/ from unstressed /i/ and ME /e:/.

Fables

2)   2082/83 spedilie (adv.) "quickly": (vpon) hie (adj.) "loudly"
3)   2112/14 (on) hie (adj.) "loudly": trewlie (adv.) "truly"
8)   2449/51/52 ee (n.) "eye": fantasie (n.) "fancy": buttrie (n.) "storeroom"

ME /e:/ for late OE *ēg-* was characteristic of Northern ME and of Scots (Aitken §6. 3. 2). In fact, Henryson's rhyming practice shows that ME /e:/ was his own usual form: except for the three rhymes given here, he elsewhere regularly rhymes late OE *ēg-* with ME /e:/ of various origin.[4]

However, in view of the fact that the Scottish Poet Gavin Douglas (? 1475–1522) in *The Eneados* rhymes *hie* (adj.) with *sky* (n.) < ON *skȳ* (5/6)

---

4   Elsewhere, Henryson uses words with OE *ēg-* in sixty-seven rhymes. All the words used are proved to have had ME /e:/, rhyming with OE *ē*, OE *ēo*, etc. in monosyllabic words. It may be noted that *hie* "high" is always spelled so, though ME /e:/ is attested. It is known that the spelling <hie> was common in sixteenth-century writings (*DOST* s.v. *Hie* (adj.)), in which all important witnesses for Henryson were surveyed. The following are the words with ME /e: / for OE *ēg-* proved by rhymes:

de(e)/die/dy (v.) 'die' < early ME *dēge* (< OE **dēgan*): *Fables* 1815, 1876, 1968, 2002, 2208, 2462, 2514, 2732, 2886, 2919; *Orpheus* 316; *BS* 60, 73; *The Ressoning betuix Deth and Man (RD)* 3, 26; *RM* 8; *The Thre Deid Pollis (TD)* 14.
dre (v.) 'endure' < OE *drēogan*: *Fables* 2916; *RM* 22.
e(e) (n.) 'eye' < OE (Anglian) *ēge*: *Fables* 384, 995, 1161, 1637, 1756, 2041, 2127; *Orpheus* 410, 453, 621; *The Abbey Walk* 5.
ene/eyne (n. pl.) 'eyes': *Fables* 1345, 1991; *Testament* 176, 191, 498; *Orpheus* 119, 150; *TD* 22.
fle (n.) 'fly (insect)' < OE *flēoge*: *Fables* 2045, 2402.
fle (v.) 'fly' < OE *flēogan*: *Fables* 1639, 1666.
hie (adj., adv.) 'high' < late OE *hēg-*, inflected form of *hēh*: *Fables* 264, 307, 371, 467, 871, 2599, 2761; *Testament* 550; *RM* 70.
le (n.) 'tract of green grass land' < late OE *lēg-*, inflected form of *lēh*: *Fables* 1793, 2512.
le/lie (v.) 'speak falsely' < OE *lēogan*: *Fables* 1993; *Testament* 252; *Against Hasty Credence* 4; *The ressoning Betuix Aige and Youth* 31; *RD* 12.
leid (pt. of *le*) 'spoke falsely': *Sum Practysis of Medecyne* 17.
sle (adj.) 'clever' < late OE *slēg-* < ON *slœg-r*: *Fables* 2913.

with ME /i:/ on the one hand, and on the other with *be* (v.) (91/92), *sey* (n.) "sea" < OE ǣ² (95/96) and *se* (v.) (133/34) with ME /e:/ (Gray 324–27), it must be considered possible that Henryson could treat words with late OE *ēg-* variously, sometimes as having ME /e:/, and sometimes as ME /i:(ə)/.[5]

11.8. New /i:/ Rhymes with 'Supple' (n.)

Similarly, the following rhyme is not good evidence for the change of ME /e:/ to e.m.E /i:/:

Fables
7)   2411/12 haistelie (adv.) "hastily": supple (n.) "help"

In this rhyme, the final syllable of the noun *supple* is rhymed with the suffix *-ly*. It is confirmed that Henryson's *supple* (< OF *so(u)pleer* (v.)) had ME /e:/ by another rhyme in which *supple* (*Fables* 2043) is rhymed with ME /e:/ of unambiguous quality in *be* (n.) 'bee' < OE *bēo* as well as with OE *ēg-* in *fle* (n.) 'fly (insect)' < OE *flēoge*. It seems possible, however, that the noun *supple*, which was used mainly in Scottish, had ME /i:(ə)/ beside ME /e:/, as is suggested by the fifteenth-century form *supplye* which *OED* gives under *supply* (n.). Therefore, it is not clear whether the poet intended to rhyme new /i:/ from unstressed /i/ in *-ly* with ME /e:/ or ME /i:(ə)/. For this reason, it is better to exclude this rhyme from conclusive evidence for the shift of ME /e:/ to /i:/.

5   Wright in *The English Dialect Grammar* records *ī* in *sky* n. Nhb. (= North Northumberland) (§178). This *ī* must have come from ME /e:/ for ON *ý*. But ME /i:/ for ON *ý* in *sky* is confirmed by Douglas's rhyme *skyis* (pl.): *rys* (inf.) 'rise' < OE *rīsan* (*The Eneados* 129/30 in Gray 327), in which ON *ý* in *skyis* is rhymed with OE *ī* in *rys*. Henryson's rhymes also attest ME /i:/ in *sky*, e.g. *Fables* 1683/84 *plesandly* (adv.): *sky* (n.); *Orpheus* 495/96 *sky* (n.): *ly* (inf.) 'lie down'.

11.9. New /iː/ with Textual Ambiguity

There is one more rhyme that is unsuitable as evidence to prove the change of ME /eː/ to e.m.E /iː/. In the following rhyme, the authenticity of the rhyme word *mortifie* is doubted:

Fables
1) 1126/28/29 de (inf.) "die": fle (inf.) "flee": mortifie (inf.) "bring into subjection"

Fox indicates the textual difficulty in the rhyme word *mortifie* with ME /iː(ə)/. This word is found in the three earliest of the complete witnesses, but another witness has different wording in line 1129 and gives as the rhyme word *see* (inf.) with ME /eː/ instead. Fox says that none of the witnesses preserves the authorial text (note to ll. 1129–31).

11.10. New /iː/ Identified with ME /iː/

Now I turn to the B-type of Henryson's 'mixed rhymes' in which new /iː/ developed from unstressed /i/ in word-final ME /eː/ <OF –*ee* is rhymed with pre-existing older ME /iː/. The word with new /iː/ used here is *desteny/ destenye/destenie* < OF *destinée*. This word appears in three rhymes, and the following two are certain to prove that new /iː/ was identified with pre-existing ME /iː/, which subsequently became diphthongized:

Testament
17) 121/23/24 desteny (n.) "destiny": (in) hy (n.) "in haste": angerly (adv.) "angrily"
18) 470/72 destenye (n.) "destiny": cry (n.)

In these rhymes, the final syllable of *desteny/destenye* is rhymed with unambiguous ME /i:/ in *hy* (n.) < ME *hīen* (v.) < OE *hīgian* (in 17) and *cri* (n.) < OF *cri* (in 18).

The rhyme 17 also involves *angerly* with the suffix *–ly*, which indicates that this suffix must have had ME /i:/. ME long /i:/ in the suffix *–ly* can be explained in two different ways, either retention or reduction of secondary stress, just as in the cases of OF words ending in *–é* discussed in 11.6 above. If the secondary stress was retained in *-ly*, ME long /i:/ could have been kept intact in that suffix. If the secondary stress was lost, ME long /i:/ would have been reduced to unstressed /i/; then, with the subsequent re-imposition of secondary stress, this /i/ would have been lengthened to be identified with ME /i:/.

It may be noted that the suffix *–ly* is elsewhere rhymed with ME /e:/ (in rhymes 4, 5, 6). It follows that the pronunciation of the vowel of suffix *–ly* varied between [əi] and [i:], and that Henryson could choose either of these as he liked.

11.11. New /i:/ Rhymes with the Suffix *–ly*

The remaining B-type of 'mixed rhyme' is the following:

Testament
16)   62/63 destenie (n.) "destiny": wretchitlie (adv.) "with great misery"

In this rhyme, new /i:/ in the final syllable of *destenie* and the suffix *–ly* are rhymed together. As it is possible that ME /i:/ in *–ly* can be assumed to come either from ME long /i:/ or from unstressed /i/ (as mentioned in Section 11.10 above), this rhyme does not prove the identification of the new /i:/ in *destenie* with pre-existing ME long /i:/.

Moreover, the rhyme allows two other different explanations. One is to consider this as A-type, assuming that the new /i:/ from unstressed /i/ in the suffix *–ly* rhymes with e.m.E /i:/ from ME /e:/ in *destenie*. The other is to take this as a self-rhyme, assuming that new /i:/ from unstressed /i/ in both words rhymes with each other.

A rhyme having such ambiguity cannot be used for any kind of evidence, though one thing is clear: that the pronunciations of the final syllable of *destenie* and *wretchitlie* were identical, either [əi] or [i:].

11.12. 'Mixed Rhymes' in ME Poets Other than Henryson

The use of 'mixed rhymes' is not confined to Henryson. From the Scottish poems contained in Bawcutt and Riddy's edition of *Longer Scottish Poems, Vol. 1* and Gray's edition of *Late Medieval Verse and Prose*, I have found the following:

From *Longer Scottish Poems, Vol.1:*
Richard Holland (died c. 1482), *The Buke of the Howlat* (written between 1445 and 1452)
1) 638/40/42/44 hie (adv.): be (inf.): "Pewewe" (onomatopoeia): pultre (n.) "poultry" < OF pouletrie
2) 738/39/40 the (pron.): ladye (n.) < OE hlǣfdǐge: fre (adj.)
3) 795/ 97/ 99/ 801 "Banachadee" (Gaelic *beannachadh De* "the blessing of God"): the (pron.): the (pron.): Irischerye (n.) "Irish people" (Irisch + -ery < OF –erie)

The Taill of Rauf Coilyear (late fifteenth century)
4) 337/39/41/43 kne (n.): thre (num.): chevalrie (n.) < OF chevalerie: se (pr. pl.)
5) 713/15/17/19 semelie (adj.) < ON sœmiligr : e (n.) "eye": gle (n.) "enjoyment" < OE glēo: me (pron.)
6) 774/75/76 fee (n.) "feudal right" < AN fee, fie, OF fé, fié: be (inf.): cumpany (n.) < AN compainie, OF compa(i)gnie
7) 904/05/06 Tartarie (n.) "Tartar empire" < F. Tartarie: be (inf.): the (pron.)

Sir David Lindsay (c.1486–1555), *The Historie of Squyer Meldrum*
8) 921/22 pietie (n.) "pity" < OF pité: mercie (n.) < OF merci
9) 1242/43 crueltie (n.) < OF crualté: mercie (n.)
10) 1497/98 crueltie (n.): mercie (n.)

Alexander Hume (c. 1556–1608), *Of the Day Estivall*
11)   42/44 see (inf.): busilie (adv.) "busily" < OE bysig + suffix –ly < ON –liga

From *Late Medieval Verse and Prose:*
William Dunbar (born ? c. 1460), *Lament for the Makars* (printed in 1508)
12)   59/60 tragidie (n.) [*text* trigide] < OF tragedie: me (Latin pron. acc.) "me"

The preceding rhymes 1–12 (except for Lindsay's 8, 9 and 10) are A-type of 'mixed rhymes' in which new /iː/ derived from unstressed /i/ rhymes with ME /eː/. These can be taken as conclusive evidence for the shift of ME /eː/ to e.m.E /iː/, since just as in Henryson's rhymes discussed in Section 11.6 above, new /iː/ from OF –*ie* (*pultre* in the rhyme 1, *Irisherye* 3, *chevalrie* 4, *cumpany* 6, *Tartarie* 7, *tragidie* 12), OE –*dĭg* (*lady* 2) and ON –*ig* in the suffix –*ly* (*semelie* 5, *busilie* 11) rhymes, at least once in each set, with unambiguous ME /eː/ in monosyllables such as *be* (inf.), *fre* (adj.) or *fee* (n.). These rhymes are conclusive evidence for the change of ME /eː/ to e.m.E /iː/.

In Lindsay's rhymes 8, 9 and 10, however, word-final ME /eː/ < OF –*é* in *pitie* 8 and *crueltie* 9, 10 rhymes with word-final ME /iː/ < OF –*i* in *mercie* 8, 9, 10. As ME /eː/ or ME /iː/ in the final syllables of disyllables or polysyllables were variable, the pronunciations implied in these rhymes are ambiguous. These are the same type of rhymes as Henryson's rhyme 16 discussed in Section 11.11 above, which allow several different interpretations to be made.

The rhymes listed above constitute 'mixed rhymes' in the works of poets who were Henryson's near contemporaries or who were later than him. I cannot find any of these among works of Scottish poets earlier than Henryson, such as the portion of *The Kingis Quair*, possibly by James I (1396–437), or that of *The Bruce* written in 1375 by John Barbour (c. 1320–95), which are extracted in these two anthologies and in Sisam's *Fourteenth Century Verse and Prose*.

This does not necessarily mean that the raising of ME /eː/ to e.m.E /iː/ and the diphthongization of ME /iː/, both of which are prerequisites for rhymes between 'etymological –*ē* and –*ī*', were unknown before Henryson's times. The absence of such 'mixed rhymes' may simply be due to the fact that the scope of my examination of earlier Scottish poems was not wide enough. But it seems likely that their absence is merely fortuitous, considering the usage of 'mixed rhymes' in non-Scottish poets.

I have elsewhere demonstrated that even though e.m.E /iː/ for ME /eː/ became prevalent in this period, there were some ME poets who never used this new pronunciation in rhymes. As far as I have ascertained, the earliest of 'mixed rhymes' clearly showing the shift of ME /eː/ to e.m.E /iː/ appeared in an Exeter text dated c. 1380. With the turn of the century, the use of this type of rhyme suddenly became common and after 1450 it became more and more extensive.

This gradual increase of 'mixed rhymes' certainly reflects the spread of new pronunciations. Some poets did not hesitate to use new pronunciations creating new types of rhymes, but others were reluctant to do so. The poets of the first half of the fifteenth century, Hoccleve and Lydgate, were the examples of the latter; in them I have so far found none. But their French contemporary Charles of Orleans, who wrote English poems for an English public after twenty-five years' imprisonment in England, was an example of the former. He uses many. From the first sequence of Ballades (with eighty-two ballades, totalling 3070 lines) I have found forty-one rhymes of this type.

In the second half of the century in which Henryson lived, there was the author, or the translator of the Dutch original, of the morality play *Everyman*, who used these new pronunciations in twenty-four rhymes among the total of 921 lines. For him, this type of new rhyme seems to have been a favourite.[6]

---

6   The earliest of 'mixed rhymes' appears in the metrical romance *Sir Ferumbras*, preserved in the autograph manuscript, Ashmole 33 of Bodleian Library, Oxford. A and B types of 'mixed rhymes' co-exist in this text, as in the case of Henryson: e.g. A-type: *me* (pron.) 4518: *companee* (sb.) 'company'; B-type: *pyty* (sb.) 'pity' 4729: *cry* (sb.). (The line-numbers cited here are from Herrtage's EETS edition (1879, rpt. 1966).) The first appearance of 'mixed rhymes' in *Sir Ferumbras* and their continuous use after *Sir Ferumbras* are shown and discussed in my article in *NOWELE* (1997).

11.13. Conclusion

Fox points out (493) that practically all the rhymes between 'etymological *ē* and *ī*' he finds in *Fables*, i.e. the rhymes numbered 2 to 8 (leaving aside 1 on grounds of textual problems), given in Section 11.2, occur within a segment of less than 400 lines, the rhymes 2 and 3 being in *The Fox, the Wolf, and the Cadger* and the rest (4 to 8) in *The Fox, the Wolf, and the Husbandman*.

Fox suggests the possible reasons for the fact that the occurrences of such rhymes are confined to these two fables among the Prologue and thirteen fables that make up the whole *Fables*:

1) These two fables are written in a fairly low style and Henryson may have thought it appropriate to use such rhymes here.
2) These two fables and perhaps also *The Wolf and the Wether*, which are omitted from one of the important manuscripts for Henryson, may have been written at a later date than the other ten fables.
3) Either or both of these fables were written by someone else.

None of these suggestions, however, seems to me tenable. Firstly, it must be remembered that Henryson used rhymes between 'etymological -*ē* and -*ī*' elsewhere in his poems, including *Testament* and *Orpheus* (see Section 11.2), which are certainly not written in a low style and which arouse no doubts about Henryson's authorship. Secondly, Henryson as a poet of the latter half of the fifteenth century was late enough to know the early Modern English /i:/ for ME /e:/ and was probably familiar with the rhyming practice in which this /i:/ is combined with /i:/ in the final syllable of disyllabic or polysyllabic words.

Though it seems true to say that an accomplished Middle English poet tended to avoid such rhyming, probably because he was skilful enough to find satisfactory traditional rhymes easily, I do not think that the use of 'mixed rhymes' immediately implies a lower style or a later date of composition, or the work of some other poet. Again, the fact that 'mixed rhymes' occur only in these two fables and not in the others can better be explained as simply a matter of chance. Henryson does not seem to have felt rhymes between 'etymological -ē and -ī' to be something special, and so he must have been free to use such type of rhymes when necessary.

I have discussed in the preceding sections how Henryson's rhymes between 'etymological -ē and -ī' can be interpreted as rhymes in which the reflex of ME /e:/ and that of ME /i:/ are rhymed with /i:/ which arose from unstressed /i/ due to re-imposition of secondary stress in the final syllable of dissyllabic or polysyllabic words. In Section 11.12, I demonstrated that the use of such rhyming was not an idiosyncrasy of Henryson, but a rhyming practice that became more and more common from the fifteenth-century onwards.

This rhyming was handed further down to later poets without any modification. William Wordsworth's rhymes like *me* (pron.): *continually* (adv.): *silently* (adv.) and *glee* (n.): *company* (n.) (Gardner 502, 506) perhaps do not arouse special interest in present-day readers. They can simply take these rhymes as normal /i:/-rhymes, though they may feel the accentuation on the suffix –*ly* or on the final syllable of *company* strange. They may also wonder how to pronounce the final syllable of Wordsworth's *majesty* and *obscurity* in the rhymes *by* (adv.): *majesty* (n.): *lie* (pr. pl.): *sky* (n.) and *dry* (adj.): *obscurity* (n.) (Gardner 503, 507). They may dismiss these rhymes as inexact, /i/ (or artificially lengthened /i:/) in the suffixes being combined with /ai/ in the monosyllables. Indeed, the former type of rhyme in Wordsworth is a direct descendant of Henryson's A-type of 'mixed rhymes', in which /i:/ from unstressed /i/ is rhymed with ME /e:/. And the latter two are legitimate successors of Henryson's B-type of 'mixed rhymes', in which /i:/ from unstressed /i/ is rhymed with ME /i:/.

From the viewpoint of historical phonology, these are the important rhymes between 'etymological -ē and -ī', which imply the great changes of pronunciation that began to occur at the end of the Middle English period.

11.14. References

11.14.1. Primary sources

Benson, Larry D., gen. ed. *The Riverside Chaucer*. 3rd edn. Boston, MA: Houghton Mifflin, 1987.

Bawcutt, Priscilla and Felicity Riddy, eds. *Longer Scottish Poems, vol. 1, 1375–1650*. Edinburgh: Scottish Academic Press, 1987.

Fox, Denton, ed. *The Poems of Robert Henryson*. Oxford: Clarendon Press, 1981.

Gardner, Helen, ed. *The New Oxford Book of English Verse 1250–1950*. Oxford: Clarendon Press, 1972.

Gray, Douglas, ed. *The Oxford Book of Late Medieval Verse and Prose*. Oxford: Clarendon Press, 1985.

Herrtage, Sidney J., ed. *The English Charlemagne Romances, Part I, Sir Ferumbras: Edited from the Unique Manuscript Bodleian MS Ashmole 33*, EETS ES 34. Oxford: Oxford University Press, 1879 rpt. 1903, 1966.

Sisam, Kenneth, ed. *Fourteenth Century Verse & Prose*. Oxford: Clarendon Press, 1921, rpt. 1962.

11.14.2. Secondary sources

Aitken, A.J. ed. Caroline Macafee. *The Older Scots Vowels: A History of the Stressed Vowels of Older Scots from the Beginnings to the Eighteenth Century*. Glasgow: The Scottish Text Society, 2002.

A Dictionary of the Older Scottish Tongue (DOST), 1931–2002, in *The Dictionary of the Scots Language*, <http://www.dsl.ac.uk>, accessed 4 March 2011.

Dobson, E.J. *English Pronunciation 1500–1700*. 2nd edn. 2 vols. Oxford: Clarendon Press, 1968.

Ikegami, Masa. 'Rhyme Evidence of the Great Vowel Shift in the *Ashmole Sir Ferumbras* (c. 1380)', *NOWELE (North-Western European Language Evolution)*, 30. Odense: Odense University Press, 1997: 3–19.

The Oxford English Dictionary (OED). 2nd edn. Oxford: Clarendon Press, 1989.

Wright, Joseph. *The English Dialect Grammar*. Oxford: Henry Frowde, 1905.

AKINOBU TANI

12 Word Pairs or Doublets in Caxton's *History of Reynard the Fox*: Rampant and Tedious?[1]

12.0. Introduction

This study aims at examining the use of word pairs (WPs) or doublets in Caxton's *History of Reynard the Fox* (*Reynard*), with special reference to their frequency and etymological make-up, to shed more light on what is called 'rampant use' of WPs by Caxton.

WPs are defined by Malkiel (1959:113) as 'the sequence of two words pertaining to the same form-class, placed on an identical level of syntactic hierarchy, and ordinarily connected by some kind of lexical link'. WPs have some semantic relations between the members like synonymy, complementarity or antonymy. Examples are found in the opening of *Reynard*:

> In this historye ben wreton the parables / goode lerynge / and dyuerse poyntes to be merkyd / by whiche poyntes men maye lerne to come to the subtyl knoweleche of suche thynges as dayly <u>ben vsed and had</u> in the counseyllys of <u>lordes and prelates gostly and worldly</u> / and / also emonge marchantes and other comone peple (*Reynard* 6/2–6) (underlining mine)

1   This is a revised version of the paper presented at 14 ICEHL in Bergamo, Italy. My sincerest thanks go to Professor Graham Caie and Professor Jeremy Smith, both of University of Glasgow for their generous help, and to Professor Manfred Markus of University of Innsbruck for helpful comments at the conference. All the quotations of *Reynard* are made from N.F. Blake's edition (William Caxton, *The History of Reynard the Fox*, EETS OS 263, ed. N.F. Blake (London: Oxford University Press, 1970), referenced by page and line.

This type of phraseology was one of the most important rhetorical ornaments frequently employed by medieval writers, and has long been recognized by critics of medieval English literature.

Jespersen (1972:90) considers Caxton's use of WPs as 'quite a mannerism'. In a similar vein, Bennett (1970:210) claims that 'in Caxton it [the practice of using pairs of synonymous words] has become a stylistic trick'. Yet Blake (1969:141) points out 'some controversy among Caxton scholars as to whether he used too many of them', and the same author (1991:256), discussing the WPs in *Reynard*, finds them 'by no means excessive' just from the comparison with the original. So what can we say about the actual use of WPs in Caxton's works? To examine this problem, this study addresses the frequency of WPs in *Reynard*; but in considering it, other relevant problems of this type of phraseology will be addressed as well.

12.1. Frequency of WPs in *Reynard*

To explore the problem posed by Blake (1969:141), we need an objective count of the frequency of WPs in comparison with the total number of words in *Reynard*. For this purpose, the e-text based on Blake's edition was compiled,[2] according to which the total number of words in the text of *Reynard* runs to 48,861 words. The results are summarized in Table 12–1.[3] This table shows the frequency according to conjunctions used in WPs.

---

2   I would like to thank Mr. Tadamasa Nishimura, formerly Professor of Kansai Gaidai
     College, for allowing me to use the e-text of Blake's edition which he compiled for
     his personal use.
3   The WPs treated in this study are only those consisting of one-word members and
     exclude those consisting of phrase members because of the etymological analysis.

Conj	# of WPs	# of WPs/1,000 wds
and	701	14.3
or	62	1.3
ne	69	1.4
nor	1	
Total	833	17

Table 12–1   Frequency of WPs per 1,000 words

The results demonstrate (a) that the total number of WPs in *Reynard* is 833, and (b) that the overall frequency of WPs per 1,000 words in *Reynard* is seventeen. To examine the nature of WPs in *Reynard*, data from other works is necessary. According to Tani (forthcoming) which examines the frequency of WPs in the same manner as this study, the average frequency of WPs per 1,000 words is 16.2 in Chaucer's entire prose works.[4] (Among Chaucer's prose works, *the Tale of Melibee* uses WPs most frequently, amounting to twenty-four per 1,000 words.)[5] The frequency of WPs in *Reynard* and Chaucer's prose is thus very similar. When compared with Chaucer's use of WP in his prose works, therefore, Caxton's use can be called moderate.

4   Inna Koskenniemi, *Repetitive Word Pairs in Old and Early Middle English Prose* (Turku: Turun Yliopisto, 1968), points out that the work with highest frequency in early ME is *Seinte Marherete* from the frequency per page. This is, however, inaccurate because the number of words on a page differs depending on editions. Using the e-text of ICAMET Corpus, Akinobu Tani, '*Thesaurus of Old English* for Early Middle English: An analysis in light of word pairs in the "Katherine Group" lives' in Christian Mair, Reinhard Heuberger in Collaboration with Josef Wallmannsberger, (eds.), *Corpora and the History of English. Paper Dedicated to Manfred Markus on the Occasion of His Sixty-Fifth Birthday* (Heidelberg: Carl Winter, Universitätsverlag, 2006): 293–303 shows that the frequency of WPs per 1000 words in the saint lives of the 'Katherine Group' runs to 21.1, and that in *Sainte Marherete* to 24.2 which is similar to the frequency in the *Melibee* where Chaucer deliberately augmented WPs to the OF original (cf. also A. Tani, 'Word Pairs or Doublets in Chaucer's Prose Works' (forthcoming).

5   On Chaucer's addition of WPs in the *Melibee* to his original, see Ralph W.V. Elliott, *Chaucer's English* (London: André Deutsch, 1974), Diane Bornstein, 'Chaucer's *Tale of Melibee* as an Example of the "Style Clergial"', *Chaucer Review* 12 (1978): 236–54 and Tani, 'Word Pairs or Doublets' (forthcoming).

What matters more than the problem of raw frequency is our different *perceptions* of the frequency of WPs when reading Chaucer's works and Caxton's *Reynard*. We do not feel that Chaucer is overdoing the use of WPs, yet in *Reynard* or Caxton's other works, the use of WPs strikes modern readers as rampant and results in such comments as 'mannerism' (Jespersen) and 'a stylistic trick' (Bennett). But why do we *feel* the use of WPs in Caxton to be rampant? According to my examination, the answer lies firstly, in his repetition of WPs, secondly, in his use of banal WP members, and thirdly, in the etymological makeup of the members of Caxton's WPs.

12.2. Repetition of WPs in *Reynard*

12.2.1. WPs consisting of the same members in the same member order

First, such WPs were selected as having the same members including some variations like singular or plural, having the same member order, and occurring more than once. The results demonstrate that there are sixty-seven types or 206 tokens of WPs with the same members and the same member order. These examples account for 24.7 per cent of the total of 833 WPs. The sixty-seven types of WPs show variety in frequency, ranging from those occurring twice to those occurring twelve times, as Table 12–2 shows.

Frequency of repetition	Types of WPs
2 times	40
3 times	12
4 times	4
5 times	4
6 times	2
7 times	3

9 times	1
12 times	1
Total	67

Table 12–2 Repetition of WPs

Out of WPs with the same members and the same member order, those WPs occurring more than three times are listed in Table 12–3.

12 times	kinge + queen
9 times	frendes + lignage
7 times	honour + worshipe
	lyf + good
	night + daye
6 times	right + lawe
	mysdo + trespace
5 times	drede + fere
	speke + saye
	traytour + morderar
	wyf + children
4 times	answerd + said
	hunter + hounde
	lord + lady
	oth + promise

Table 12–3 WPs used more than three times with same members and member order

The most frequent type of WPs is that consisting of *kinge* and *quene*, followed by *frendes* and *linages*, and then by *honour* and *worship*. Concerning these WPs, except for *night and day*, *speke and saye* and *answerd and said*, all of them are actually closely related to the subject matter of *Reynard*. For the tale consists of small episodes narrating how Reynard the fox *misdid and trespassed* other animals to their *dread and fear*, how these animals complained to the king and his court for the *right and law*, calling the fox *traitour and murderer*, and how *honour and worship* was regained ironically not by the animals but by Reynard. So these WPs in *Reynard* happened to relate closely to the subject matter.[6] Yet I do not consider this stylistic feature to be deliberately aimed at by Caxton, because the distribution of such phrases in the whole text is random and their occurrences very few in terms of the entire body of WPs.

Among fourteen types of these most frequent WPs having the same members and member order, nine are made up of members both of which are of Old English (OE) origin:

> how the foxe shal flatre the kynge and quene (*Reynard* 34/22–23)
> REynard answerd and said ... (*Reynard* 90/4)
> he said god thanke yow my lord and my lady that ... (*Reynard* 88/12–13)

All of them except for *hunter ne hound* and *lyf and good* are very traditional and formulaic, and four types alliterate. Yet they contribute little to the plot of the tale, rather they give a colloquial touch to the work.

12.2.2. WPs containing the same first members

Yet more interesting, many types of WPs have the same first members with variation in the second members. And the reason for focusing solely on such WPs is that it is the first members that draw readers' attention, considering the linear nature of our experience of language. The count of such WPs containing the same first members and occurring more than once goes up to 542 examples, accounting for 65.1 per cent or approximately two-thirds of all the WPs in *Reynard*. Out of such WPs, those occurring more than four times are listed in Table 12–4.

---

6   In this connection, see Will Héraucourt, 'Das Hendiadyoin als Mittel zur Hervorhebung des Werhaften bei Chaucer', *Englische Studien* 73 (1939): 190–201 for discussion of the relation of the WPs to the moral concepts in Chaucer's prose texts, specifically the *Parson's Tale*.

1st mem.	Freq	1st mem.	Freq	1st mem.	Freq
frendes	16	nyghte	7	doon	6
kynges	15	mysdoo	7	traytours	5
grete	12	honour	7	sorowe	5
good	11	harme	7	scatte	5
hurte (n)	7	flatre	7	pardone	5
lyf	9	cryed	7	myght	5
loue	9	spoken	6	made	5
worshipe	8	redynge	6	fowl	5
right	8	mysdedes	6	false	5
lords	8	male	6	drede	5
wyf	7	kynne	6	cursyd	5
shamed	7	herde	6		

Table 12–4 WPs with same first members occurring more than four times

Variations are seen among these most frequent twenty-five types of WPs, like the following examples containing *frende(s)* and *kinge(s)*:

> Whiche ben frendes and kynne vnto Reynard the foxe. (*Reynard* 74/19)
> in payne or / in pouerte. fyndeth but fewe frendes and kynnesmen
> (*Reynard* 105/23–24)
> and also al my frendes and lignage ... shal obeye your commandement and desire
> (*Reynard* 109/31–32)
> and other / of my frendis and alyes Also I shal take somme money
> (*Reynard* 66/16)
> is it kynge or quene / wyf or man (*Reynard* 66/34)
> they sholde make bruyn a kynge and a lorde (*Reynard* 35/35–36)
> how the foxe shal flatre the kynge and queen (*Reynard* 34/22–23)

What is important in leaving an impression among readers, however, is the repetition of the same first members in variant WPs rather than the variations of WPs by themselves.

Among these thirty-five types of WPs occurring more than four times, members of twenty-eight types of WPs derive from the native stock, those of six types from Old French (OF), and those of one type (*scatte*) from Middle Dutch (MD). This clearly shows that OE members predominate among the most frequently used WPs containing the same first members. The OF members of these types of WPs also display one characteristic: all the words were adopted around 1200 in the early ME period, as shown in Table 12–5. This table shows the information on the first citations of these words in the *MED*:

hurte	c1225(?c1200) St.Juliana (Bod 34)
honour	a1225(?a1200) Trin.Hom. (Trin-C B.14.52)
flatre	c1230(?a1200) *Ancr. (Corp-C 402)
male	c1275(?a1200) Lay. Brut (Clg A.9)
traytours	c1225(?c1200) HMaid. (Bod 34)
pardone	c1300 SLeg.Becket (LdMisc 108)

Table 12–5 Chronology of some OF members

However, despite their OF origins, these members used in *Reynard* are thought to be well established in English at the time of Caxton.[7] Therefore, it is clear that the members of WPs most frequently used in *Reynard* were self-evident in meaning to Caxton's contemporaries and were, by themselves, not stylistically elevated, but rather mundane.

From these two analyses in terms of repetition, I have found that the WPs having the same members and member order, and the WPs having the same first members and occurring more than twice, appear very frequently and account for about two-thirds of the WPs in *Reynard*, and that most of them are semantically self-evident, not stylistically elevated by themselves. Thus these features give rise in part to the impression that Caxton's use of WPs is tedious and boring specifically to modern readers.[8]

---

7   This point will be more fully dealt with later in Section 12.3.2.
8   The findings are quite different from those concerning Chaucer's prose, which are discussed by Tani, 'Word Pairs or Doublets' (forthcoming).

12.3. Banal WP Members of OF Origin

To understand the nature of WP members, those consisting specifically of OF words need to be examined. For the purpose, this study analyzes such members in terms of firstly, their word formation, and secondly their chronology, on the basis of the information in the *MED*.

12.3.1. Word formation of WP members of OF origin

Speaking of Chaucerian vocabulary, Burnley (2000:237) stresses the need to classify OF loanwords on the basis of 'their associations and the status conferred by their use'; and he distinguishes by word structure rather than mere etymology between more common OF words and more stylistically elevated: the latter are claimed to be definable by a group of affixes which '[u]ntil the sixteenth century ... were very rarely or never used to form derivatives from English or Scandinavian base forms'. Such affixes include: *-al, per-, in-, -able, -ible, -aunt, -yn, -ive, -ous, -ate, -ion (-auncy, -ent, -ency)*. Using this criterion, the OF members in *Reynard* were analyzed. Among 389 WPs containing OF members, only 28 examples, or merely 3.4 per cent, come into this category:

> wythout grete repentaunce and penaunce (*Reynard* 111/3)
> thise couetouse and rauenous shrewys ben taken vp (*Reynard* 85/21)

This scant use of OF members containing such affixes as help elevate the style attests that the WP members and thus the WPs themselves are self-explanatory and not stylistically elevated. This means the purpose of using WPs in *Reynard* is not to explain or 'gloss' difficult OF members.

12.3.2. Chronology of WP members of OF origin

The chronology of OF loanwords can provide a clue as to how well such words were assimilated into English, though, of course, we will have to be careful in handling this kind of data (as is pointed out by Burnley (1983,

2000)). As regards the chronology of WPs in Caxton in general, Blake (1969:142) points out that 'generally where a doublet occurs it is made up of two words which had been in the language for some time, or were indeed both words of Anglo-Saxon origin'. Therefore, in addition to the examination of word structure, the chronology of all the WP members of French origin has also been analyzed using the first citation data of the *MED*.

The results show that the average year for the first citation of the first members of OF origin is 1283.3, while that of the second members is 1292.9, giving that of both members combined as 1288.4. There is little difference in this respect among WPs consisting of different etymological members. It means that the OF members in *Reynard* had established themselves for nearly 200 years by Caxton's time, and were thus well accommodated in English at the time of publication of *Reynard* in 1481. This confirms Blake's remark, and at the same time what we have seen in the last section, the common or familiar nature of these OF members.

Among them are thirty-one WPs containing OF members whose first citations in the *MED* date later than 1400, such as:

> one may breke his oth and promyse (*Reynard* 72/16–17)
> (*promise* (n): 1410)
> I had for your sake pardoned and forgyue them (*Reynard* 68/4)
> (*pardon* (v): 1430)

Among them, however, there is only one WP containing two such OF members:

> whiche wyth grete facing and bracyng oppresse the poure peple
> (*Reynard* 107/33–34)

The first citations for these members are from 1400 and 1447 respectively. And there are seven WPs consisting of two OF members, in which either of the OF members dates from later than 1400. In these examples, however, the other OF members date from 1150 to 1340 and can be thought to have caused little problem in the interpretation of these words. The following WP with OF technical members could be an exception:

> also alle the herbes and nature of them whiche were <u>viscose or laxatyf</u>
> (*Reynard* 84/29–30) (underlining mine)

But in fact even this example is a literal translation of the MD original:

> alle die cruden die men vinden mocht treckende <u>viscose of laxatiue</u>
> (underlining mine)

In conclusion, examination of the chronology of OF members again attests that these words had been well settled in the language and were familiar to Caxton's contemporaries.

12.4. Etymological Make-up of WPs with Examination of Chronology

As for the etymological makeup of WPs, Ito (1995:289), in the appendix to his Japanese translation of *Caxton's Aesop* (*Aesop*), reports on his research into the etymological makeup of WPs in the work as follows:

> Latinate + Germanic: L. + L.: G. + G. = 2: 1: 1.

To examine this aspect of WPs in *Reynard*, all the members were subjected to an etymological analysis using the information in the *OED2* and *MED*. Examples of major etymological makeups of WPs in *Reynard* include:

> (1) OE + OE
> tho began he to byte and gnawe the grenne in the myddel a sondre
> (*Reynard* 23/10–1)
> whan they haue sorow and shame for theyr olde trespaces
> (*Reynard* 107/25–6)
> (2) OE + OF
> reynart is a shrewe / and felle (*Reynard* 12/29–30)
> hit were good that right and Iustyse were don (*Reynard* 8/25)

(3) OF + OE
And also he is ioconde and glad in his herte (*Reynard* 78/23–4)
I pray and comande alle them (*Reynard* 53/35–6)
(4) OF+ OF
he was so prowde and orguillous (*Reynard* 35/22)
ye be alle betrayed and apechyd ... (*Reynard* 42/31)

The results are summarized in Table 12–6.

Etym of 1st Comp	Etym of 2nd Comp	Num
MD	MD	2
MD	OE	13
MD	OF	7
MD	ON	3
OFlem	OE	1
OE	MD	10
OE	OE	383
OE	MD	2
OE	OF	152
OE	ON	17
OF	MD	1
OF	ON	1
OF	MD	3
OF	OE	126
OF	OF	88
OF	ON	4
ON	OE	13
ON	OF	7
Total		833

Table 12–6 Etymologies and orders of members

According to Table 12–6, the etymological types of WPs are OE + OE > OE + OF > OF + OE > OF + OF in order of descending prevalence, and their ratio is 4.4: 1.7: 1.4: 1. This means that OE + OE WPs are predominant. This also shows a stark contrast to the etymological makeup of WPs in *Aesop*, where Latinate + Germanic WPs, irrespective of the order of the two members, are in a majority.

What, then, does this stark difference result from? Concerning Caxton's translation, Blake (1991:239) points out that 'Caxton's work is a fairly close translation from the Dutch original with occasional words, phrases and clauses inserted or omitted'. Given this observation, we can attribute such a difference to the influence of their originals: *Reynard* is a translation from MD, while *Aesop* is a translation from Julien Macho's *Les subtilles fables de esope*, a Middle French source. *Reynard* contains more OE members since there are a number of OE cognates with MD words, while *Aesop* has more OF members.

What can we say about Caxton's use of WPs from this difference in etymological makeup of WPs between *Reynard* and *Aesop*? Of course, it is certain that Caxton employed a fair number of WPs in both works even if he did not overuse them. Yet it is also true that he was not concerned about the etymological differences in WP members between the two works.[9] This leads us to think that what matters most in Caxton's use of WPs is the very fact of their use, or doubling whatsoever was available to him, irrespective of etymological makeup. Since this rhetorical device was the simplest to handle among the figures of speech, Caxton would have found it easy to take advantage of.

Since the influence of the MD original is quite clear, attention has been paid to WPs containing MD members. Normally when the interpretative

9   This point is also quite different from the use of WPs in the prose works of Chaucer, who clearly distinguishes WPs with members of different etymological makeup, depending on the nature of works, i.e. who was sensitive to shades of meanings of members of WPs. On this point, see A. Tani, 'The Word Pairs in Chaucer's Verse in Comparison with Those in his Prose', in J.O. Askedal, I. Roberts and T. Matsushita (eds.), *Noam Chomsky and Language Descriptions* (Amsterdam and Philadelphia: John Benjamins, 2010): 149–68 and Tani, 'Word Pairs or Doublets' (forthcoming).

use of WPs is discussed, it is for those with OF members. Yet we have seen
that there is little need to use WPs with OF members for an explanation in
Reynard.[10] There is, however, a possibility for such use of WPs in the case
of MD members; for amongst 139 words listed by Blake (1970) as directly
borrowed from the MD original, no fewer than 39 MD words (or 28.06
per cent) are used as WP members:

(1) MD + OE
For I haue so grette <u>scatte</u> and good of syluer and of gold (*Reynard* 34/9–10)
(2) OE + MD
how that his skynne and his flessh was al rawe and <u>thurgh soden</u>
                                                     (*Reynard* 107/2)
(3) OF + MD
whan she sawe his male and <u>palster</u> (*Reynard* 46/21)
(4) MD + MD
he wyste not what to saye <u>buff</u> ne <u>baff</u>   (*Reynard* 99/34)
                                                     (underlining mine)

Given this fact and the rarity of these words in other ME texts, we may
speculate as to such a possibility. In fact, Burnley (1983:148) discusses Chaucer's use as glosses of WPs containing dialectal members when employing
unfamiliar dialectal words for stylistic variations. Unlike Chaucer, who
was ready consciously to exploit dialectal words for stylistic purposes,
however, Caxton is thought to have been uncertain whether his readers
could understand MD words as opposed to OF words. This uncertainty
led him to explain about a quarter of the MD words he directly introduced
by coupling them as WPs.

10   On the so-called 'interpretation theory' of WPs, see Otto Jespersen, *Growth and
     Structure of the English Language.* 9th edn. (Oxford: Basil Blackwell, 1972): 89–90,
     though his claim is not valid at least in respect of Chaucer's prose, as argued by Tani,
     'Word Pairs or Doublets' (forthcoming). See also Tani, 'The Word Pairs in Chaucer's
     Verse', (2010): 149–68 for the great discrepancy between the functions of WPs in
     Chaucer's verse and prose.

12.5. Caxton's Manipulation of the MD Original
Van den Vos Reynaerde in Terms of WPs

In fourteenth- and fifteenth-century Western Europe, a mode of prose writing called 'curial prose/style' was often employed (Burnley 1986). This mode of prose, ultimately derived from legal Latin (Politzer 1961), employed WPs as one of its stylistic features. Both Caxton and the author of the MD original wrote in this tradition. We could expect, then, that prior to Caxton the MD original text would contain a fair number of WPs.

In relation to the translation of *Reynard*, Blake (1991:255–6) points out that Caxton introduced approximately 279 examples of new WPs in an extended sense of WPs,[11] and that Caxton simplified 67 examples of WPs in the original to single words. Blake concludes that Caxton's use of WPs in *Reynard* was 'by no means excessive'. But though Blake gives the total number of WPs added by Caxton and two passages as example for consideration, we cannot be certain how far Caxton's addition of WPs contributed to the frequency of their use more generally.

We should, therefore, revisit the problem of Caxton's adoption of WPs with reference to the MD original. To examine this aspect, Caxton's *Reynard* text has been compared with the MD original in terms of WPs specifically where WPs are used most conspicuously, i.e. in the four chapters with WPs most frequently employed and in the two chapters with WPs least frequently employed. The results are given in Table 12–7.

---

11   This study treats as WPs only those consisting of one-word members for the purpose of etymological analysis. Thus such examples as *by flaterye and fayr wordes* (*Reynard* 34/25) and *ben they take up and rysen* (*Reynard* 82/2) are excluded from consideration. Yet N. Blake, 'Caxton's *Reynard the Fox* and his Dutch Original', in *William Caxton and English Literary Culture* (1991: 231–58) relaxes the definition of WPs to integrate such examples as WPs, like Koskenniemi in *Repetitive Word Pairs* (1968).

capitulo	corr.	add.	red	ch.	# of ME WPs	ME WPs /1000 wds	ME Total wds
0	6	5	1		11	49.8	221
1	1	8			9	48.4	186
42	18	30	5	1	48	32.8	1463
43	15	32	6		47	34.5	1363
19	9	1	5		10	9	1117
20	5	4			9	8.4	1076
capitulo					# of MD WPs	MD WPs /1000 wds	MD Total wds
0					9	46.2	195
1					1	7.6	131
42					26	28.9	901
43					22	13	1692
19					14	12.2	1151
20					5	4.4	1147

Table 12–7 Addition and reduction of WPs by Caxton in comparison
with the MD original

From Table 12–7, it is clear that, though Caxton may have 'far more
restrained' the use of WPs or have 'simplified' WPs in certain places (Blake,
1991:254, 256), we can say for sure, firstly, that Caxton constantly introduced new WPs in almost all the cases except for Capitulo Nineteen, and
secondly that in the proem of the tale (or Capitulo Zero), the frequency of
WPs in the original is as high as in Caxton's translation, showing the same
stylistic features of contemporary Continental and English prose writing
that is influenced by 'curial prose'.

12.5.1. Caxton's attitude to WPs

We have seen how Caxton added and reduced WPs in several capituli. Even though he normally introduced new WPs to his translation, what did Caxton intend by such use? A clue to the answer can be found in the following passage from Cap. 43, where Caxton translates the MD original by using WPs and relevant phrases:

ME	MD
The rightwys peple ben al loste / <u>trouthe and right-wysnes</u> ben <u>exyled and fordriuen</u> / And for them ben abyden wyth vs <u>couetyse / falshede / hate and enuye</u> / Thyse regne now moche in euery contre / For is it <u>in the popes court / the emperours / the kynges dukes or ony other lordes</u> where someuer it be eche man laboureth to put other out <u>fro his worship / offyce and power</u> / for to make hym sylf to clymme hye with lyes / <u>wyth flateryng / with symonye / wyth money / or wyth strengthe and force</u> (*Reynard* 110/18–25)	Die gerechtichede die bliuet al verloren <u>Trouwe ende waerheyt</u> die sijn alle <u>verdreuen</u> Ende daer voer sijn ons ghebleuen <u>ghiericheit loesheit ende nijt</u>. dese hebbent al in hoor berijt. Ende si regneren nv sere opter aerden. ist <u>in des pauwes of in des keysers hof of so</u> waer dat si. elc die pijnt den anderen of te steeken <u>van sijnre eren ende machten</u> om selue te clymmen <u>Mit vordel met simonyen of met gewelt</u> (underlining mine)

This passage clearly demonstrates Caxton's augmentation of WPs in comparison with the original. To be sure, there is one example of total correspondence: ME *trouthe* and *right-wysnes* (< MD *Trouwe ende waerheyt*). But all the other examples underlined are additions or augmentations.

The WP in ME *exyled and fordriuen* is a clear augmentation of the MD single word *verdreuen*. The ME phrase *couetyse / falshede / hate and enuye* is a 'list' adding one more member to the MD triplet *ghiericheit loesheit ende nijt* 'covetousness, falseness and envy'. Furthermore Caxton makes a list in the ME phrase *in the popes court / the emperours / the kynges dukes or ony other lordes* out of the MD WP *in des pauwes of in des keysers hof* 'in the pope's or in the emperor's court'.

As for the ME phrase *fro his worship / offyce and power*, Caxton again makes a triplet out of the MD doublet *van sijnre eren ende machten* 'from his worship and power'. The long list of ME *with lyes / wyth flateryng / with symonye / wyth money / or wyth strengthe and force* is made out of the MD original triplet *Mit vordel met simonyen of met gewelt* 'with advantage, with simony or with force'.

Though some of these phrases can be termed WPs in a wider sense of the expression, these examples clearly show Caxton's strong desire to augment the words or phrases of the original in some way. Specifically, his manipulation of the original triplets to quadruplets or lists demonstrates how strong his desire for amplification was. In our perception, the list breaks the parallelism of doublets or triplet; yet Caxton dared to augment even at the risk of breaking the parallelism of these phrases.

The concept of WPs or doublets is a modern critical concept. The medieval concept that would correspond to it is synonymia. Synonymia, a figure of pathos, is 'the use of several synonyms together to amplify or explain a given subject or term' (Burton, *Sylva Rhetoricae*: s.v. 'synonymia'). As is evident from the preceding discussion, Caxton's use of WPs is more to amplify than to explain. Similarly, the definition of repetition as one of the techniques of amplification by Geoffrey of Vinsauf is the following:

> If you choose an amplified form, proceed first of all by this step: although the meaning is one, let it not come content with one set of apparel. Let it vary its robes and assume different raiment. Let it take up again in other words what has already been said; let it reiterate, in a number of clauses, a single thought. Let one and the same thing be concealed under multiple forms – be varied and yet the same. (Geoffrey of Vinsauf (trans. Nims (1967:24))

Despite the comment by Blake (1991:256) that 'Caxton's use of doublets was by no mean excessive', we must nonetheless admit that Caxton desired to amplify and augment his translation by WPs in a wider sense of the expression.

12.5.2. Relation of WPs with Caxton's audience

In the fifteenth century, as is attested by the emergence of epistolary materials like the *Paston Letters* and the *Cely Letters*, a newly emergent class including the gentry and bourgeoisie became socially prominent. The literary culture of this emerging class may have been limited compared to that of the courtly circle. Yet the rising influence of this class had been felt among people. Caxton aimed his books at such an audience as well as to the nobility (cf. John Paston II's list of books). Therefore, in order to sell more books, Caxton had to be very conscious about the manner and matter of his publications.

Blake (1969:180) argues that, after mentioning the possibility of Caxton's failure to grasp the rhetorical figures present in the original works, the use of WPs was 'the only rhetorical device he knew how to employ'. The findings of the present study support this remark of Blake's. Yet Caxton's incomprehension and his use of WPs as the sole rhetorical figure happened to suit the taste of his wider audience, including the gentry and bourgeoisie. Such social aspirants may have acquired literacy in English but they remained deficient in their knowledge of rhetoric. Nonetheless, they were quite aware of WPs, since people in this class began to write letters in English following the model of chancery letters or *ars dictaminis*, which also made use of WPs.[12] Their familiarity with WPs would presumably have made them welcome Caxton's use of this device, which for them would not have produced the feeling of tediousness that modern readers have when reading his translation of Reynard.

---

12   On the relationship between *ars dictaminis* (strictly, *ars notaria*) and 15th century prose, see M. Richardson, 'The dictamen and its Influence on Fifteenth-century English Prose', *Rhetorica: A Journal of the History of Rhetoric* 2/3 (1984): 207–26. On Chancery English, see John H. Fisher, M. Richardson and J.L. Fisher, *An Anthology of Chancery English* (Knoxville, TN: University of Tennessee Press, 1984), but also M. Benskin 'Some New Perspectives on the Origins of Standard Written English', in J.A. van Leuvensteijn and J.B. Berns (eds.), *Dialect and Standard Language* (Amsterdam: Royal Netherlands Academy of Arts and Sciences, 1992): 71–105.

12.6. Summary and Conclusion

This study has brought out first that Caxton's use of WPs in *Reynard* is not so extensive compared to that of other ME writers like Chaucer, and second that the 'tedious' impression that modern readers get when reading Caxton's works comes from the repeated use of the same or similar WPs, which account for approximately two-thirds of all the WPs.

From the analyses of members of WPs in this work, this study has found first, that OF members of WPs in *Reynard* are not stylistically elevated and second, that these OF words had been well assimilated into the language in Caxton's age. These two observations show that the OF members of WPs in *Reynard* are mostly self-evident in meaning, requiring no need to be explained by the use of WPs, and that the use of an OF member in WPs does not elevate the stylistic value of such WPs.

Caxton indiscriminately or insensitively used WPs with members of different etymological makeup, and his approach to WPs was to take advantage of whatever words were available to him, irrespective of their etymologies, in order to make WPs. In short, what mattered most to Caxton was the use of WPs in itself.

The comparison of *Reynard* with its MD original in several chapters illustrates first that, though there was some variation in his additions, Caxton almost constantly introduced new WPs to his translation, and second, that Caxton's desire was more to augment even at the risk of breaking the symmetry of WPs than simply to construct WPs. This kind of augmentation through WPs happened to suit the taste of the newly emerging readers at whom Caxton targeted his books because this bourgeois class knew at least the use of WPs, a fashionable technique of writing in the age, through chancery letters.

In conclusion, Caxton, who was a businessman, used WPs as ordinary literate English people in the fifteenth century did, and this mode of stylistic elevation met the taste of such people, since it was a stylistic technique well known even to them.

12.7. References

12.7.1. Primary sources

Caxton, William. *The History of Reynard the Fox*. EETS. OS 263, ed. N.F. Blake, London: Oxford University Press, 1970.

Hellinga, W. Gs. ed., *Van den Vos Reynaerde*. I Teksten. Zwolle: N.V. Uitgevers-Maatschappij W.E.J. Tjeek Willink, 1952.

12.7.2. Secondary sources

Bennett, H.S. *Chaucer and the Fifteenth Century*. Oxford: Clarendon Press, 1970.

Benskin, M. 'Some New Perspectives on the Origins of Standard Written English', in J.A. van Leuvensteijn and J.B. Berns (eds.), *Dialect and Standard Language*. Amsterdam: Royal Netherlands Academy of Arts and Sciences, 1992: 71–105.

Blake, N.F. *Caxton and his World*. London: André Deutsch, 1969.

——. 'Caxton's *Reynard the Fox* and his Dutch Original', in *William Caxton and English Literary Culture*. London: The Hambledon Press, 1991: 231–58.

Bornstein, Diane. 'Chaucer's *Tale of Melibee* as an Example of the "Style Clergial"', *Chaucer Review* 12 (1978): 236–54.

Burnley, David. *A Guide to Chaucer's Language*. London: Macmillan Press, 1983.

——. 'Curial Prose in England', *Speculum* 61 (1986): 593–614.

——. 'Language'. in Peter Brown, ed., *A Companion to Chaucer*, Oxford: Blackwell, 2000: 235–50.

Burton, Gideon O. 'synonymia' *Sylvae, Rhetoricae*. 18 Oct 2006, <http://humanities.byu.edu/rhetoric/Figures/S/synonymia.htm> accessed 4 March 2011.

Elliott, Ralph W.V. *Chaucer's English*. London: André Deutsch, 1974.

Fisher, John H., Malcolm Richardson and Jane L. Fisher. *An Anthology of Chancery English*. Knoxville, TN: University of Tennessee Press, 1984.

Geoffrey of Vinsauf. *Poetria Nova of Geoffrey of Vinsauf*, trans. Margaret F. Nims. Toronto: Pontifical Institute of Mediaeval Studies, 1967.

Héraucourt, Will. 'Das Hendiadyoin als Mittel zur Hervorhebung des Werhaften bei Chaucer', *Englische Studien* 73 (1939): 190–201.

Ito, Masayoshi. *Aesop Fables by William Caxton*. (Japanese translation of *Caxton's Aesop*.) Tokyo: Iwanami Book Service Center, 1995.

Jespersen, Otto. *Growth and Structure of the English Language*. 9th edn. Oxford: Basil Blackwell, 1972.

Koskenniemi, Inna. *Repetitive Word Pairs in Old and Early Middle English Prose*. Turku: Turun Yliopisto, 1968.

Malkiel, Yakov. 'Studies in Irreversible Binomials', *Lingua* 8 (1959): 113–60.

Politzer, Robert L. 'Synonymic Repetition in Late Latin and Romance', *Language* 87 (1961): 484–8.

Richardson, Malcolm. 'The *Dictamen* and its Influence on Fifteenth-Century English Prose', *Rhetorica: A Journal of the History of Rhetoric* 2/3 (1984): 207–26.

Tani, Akinobu. '*Thesaurus of Old English* for Early Middle English: An analysis in light of word pairs in the "Katherine Group" lives', in Christian Mair, Reinhard Heuberger in Collaboration with Josef Wallmannsberger, eds. *Corpora and the History of English. Paper Dedicated to Manfred Markus on the Occasion of His Sixty-Fifth Birthday.*). Heidelberg: Carl Winter, Universitätsverlag, 2006: 293–303.

——. 'The Word Pairs in Chaucer's Verse in Comparison with Those in his Prose', in John Ole Askedal, Ian Roberts and Tomonori Matsushita, eds., *Noam Chomsky and Language Descriptions*. Amsterdam and Philadelphia: John Benjamins, 2010: 149–68.

——. 'Word Pairs or Doublets in Chaucer's Prose Works' (forthcoming).

SYLVIA HUOT

13 Senshu University Manuscripts 2 and 3 and the *Roman de la Rose* Manuscript Tradition

13.0. Introduction

The two *Roman de la Rose* manuscripts at Senshu University are typical copies of what is probably the most widely copied poem in medieval French literature.[1] Both manuscripts also have some interesting individual features. In both cases, numerous passages are marked with a 'Nota' sign, which allows us to trace the topics that most interested the scribes or early readers of these books.[2] MS 2 contains a number of scribal errors, many of which were corrected by a medieval hand. This provides visual evidence for medieval concern with the stabilization of the text, as well as identifying particular elements of the text, such as rubrics, that were considered important by medieval owners of these books. In MS 2 it is also possible to distinguish between a moralizing reading supported by illustrations that were originally planned and the marginal annotations entered by the scribe; and a reading more oriented towards Ovidian love teachings

---

1   Guillaume de Lorris and Jean de Meun, *Le Roman de la Rose*, ed. F. Lecoy, 3 vols. (Paris: Champion, 1973–5). All references are to this edition. Translations are my own. On the *Rose* manuscript tradition, see E. Langlois, *Manuscrits du Roman de la Rose: Description et classement* (Lille: Tallandier, and Paris: Champion, 1910); S. Huot, *The Romance of the Rose and Its Medieval Readers: Interpretation, Reception, Manuscript Tradition* (Cambridge, UK: Cambridge University Press, 1993).

2   For a survey of marginal 'Nota' signs in medieval manuscripts, see S. Huot, 'Medieval Readers of the *Roman de la Rose*: The Evidence of Marginal Notations', *Romance Philology* 43 (1990): 400–20. On marginal annotations more generally, see Huot, *Romance of the Rose and Its Medieval Readers*: 40–84.

and social satire, as reflected in the traces left by a medieval reader of the manuscript. In MS 3, finally, marginal annotations point to an educated reader, possibly someone with connections to the University of Paris (see Figures 13–1 and 13–2).

13.1. Manuscript 2

13.1.1. Annotations and emendations

One of the immediately striking features of Senshu MS 2 is the series of corrections entered by a medieval hand. These annotations not only demonstrate a medieval concern with textual accuracy and stability, but also show how the very effort to correct the text could sometimes result in the creation of new variant readings. The correcting hand responded both to lines that made no sense, and to ones that were metrically deficient. In some cases it was a simple matter to supply a missing word, which was obvious from the context:

> 24r: Que chascun chascun // le voit   //*jour* (6775)
> [That everyone, every //, sees her //*day*]

> 42r: Ceste autre riche // nueve   //*reube* (9284)
> [This other rich new //   //*dress*]

In other cases, the scribe copied lines that made grammatical sense, but were metrically irregular. Like most Old French narrative poetry, the *Rose* is composed in octosyllabic couplets, and the corrector attempted to rectify lines that he saw as metrically deficient. Some cases are very straightforward:

> 28r: Bel acueil a esté pris (7220)
> [Fair Welcoming has been captured]

This line has only seven syllables; the corrector easily provided the eighth by adding the word 'sy' at the beginning: 'Sy bel acueil a esté pris' [If Fair Welcoming has been captured]. In fact, this is the correct reading; the line appears like this in all modern editions.

In other cases, however, it is not so obvious why the corrector found fault with a given verse; on examination, it seems that he may have misunderstood the grammatical form of the verbs, mistaking subjunctive for indicative. In one example:

> S'il peust par autre matire (12501)
> [If he can in some other way]

becomes:

> S'il *ne* peust par autre matire (48r)
> [If he can*not* in some other way]

In Lecoy's edition, the line is: 's'il poïst par nule matire' [if he can in no way]. The line made sense and was metrically correct as the scribe wrote it, as long as the verb is recognized as a subjunctive, which has two syllables. The corrector may have seen it as indicative – and thus monosyllabic – and amended the line accordingly. The following case is similar:

> M'ayt diex ne bonnes ne beles (7212)
> [God help me, neither good nor fair]

becomes:

> Sy m'ayt diex ne bonnes ne beles (28r)
> [So help me God, neither good nor fair]

The line is again correct as the scribe wrote it; this is how it appears in the standard editions of the poem. For some reason, the corrector seems to have interpreted the first word as monosyllabic and added the particle 'sy' at the beginning to regularise the meter. Again, he may have seen it as indicative, rather than subjunctive: 'if God helps me', rather than 'God help me'.

In these examples, we can see the care with which a medieval reader studied the text and attempted to correct real or perceived errors. We also see how variant readings are created literally before our eyes, as the correcting hand responds to problematic lines, inventing solutions that may or may not correspond to readings found in other manuscript copies. Perhaps the most interesting point to note here is that there seems to have been some degree of confusion or uncertainty with the grammatical structures of the Old French verses.

One final annotation deserves attention. When Friend is advising the Lover that he must use deception and ruse in order to attain the Rose, he comments that it is perfectly acceptable to deceive those who are, themselves, deceivers:

> 29r: Encontre vezïé, recuit (7322)
>   [Against a trickster, use deception]

A later hand marked the word 'vezïé' [trickster] and in the margin wrote: 'kuviers iestre' [to be deceitful]. For this reader, the word 'vezïé' seems to have been obscure and in need of glossing. This may be yet another indication that the dialect of the thirteenth-century text was not always clear and straightforward for readers of the later Middle Ages.[3]

As is standard in the *Rose* manuscript tradition, the manuscript is supplied with rubrics marking dialogue, indicating changes of speaker.[4] However, this particular scribe was careless with the dialogue: sometimes he left space for rubrics when the speaker changed, but other times he did not. Interestingly, in places where rubrics are lacking we sometimes find marginal annotations marking the changes of speaker (fols. 12r, 33r, 33v). If it was the scribe who made these notes, it is odd that he did not leave space for the rubric; it seems more reasonable to suppose that it was, again, a later annotator, who wanted to provide a more complete demarcation of

---

3   For another example of a *Rose* manuscript in which the marginal annotations suggest
     a fifteenth-century reader's difficulty with the thirteenth-century lexicon, see Huot,
     Romance of the Rose and Its Medieval Readers: 40–6.
4   See S. Huot, *From Song to Book* (Ithaca, NY: Cornell University Press, 1987):
     90–5.

the dialogue in these passages. These notes reflect the importance attached to the rubrication of dialogue, and the desire for a copy of the poem in which changes of speaker are clearly indicated.

13.1.2. The discourse of Reason in Senshu MS 2: A Boethian reading

MS 2 has no miniatures and little decoration. However, there is one coloured ornamental initial in the discourse of Reason, directly following a mutilation of the page that was undoubtedly caused by the removal of a miniature. This illustration would have marked Reason's moralistic diatribe against material wealth, beginning 'A! douces richesces mortex' (fol. 11v, v. 5227) [Oh! Sweet, mortally dangerous wealth]. The illustration would thus have called particular attention to the moral lessons in this part of the poem. One other space was left for a miniature that was never executed; this occurs in the same section of Reason's discourse, at her description of Fortune's house (fol. 16v, v. 5891). This passage is often illustrated, so it would be no surprise to find a miniature here. It was probably supposed to have an ornamental initial like the one that accompanied the missing miniature, but this too was never executed. The original rubricator provided this rubric, a typical one, meant to introduce both the miniature and the passage:

> Ci devise de la maison fortune
> [Here Fortune's house is described]

Since the space remained empty, a later annotator used it to provide a description of the scene that should have been there:

> Et qu'elle senefie. Et parole d'une roche qui est en mer qui se monstre en diverse manieres, une heure oscure, autre clere, autre verde, plaine de flours, autre toute nue sans verdeur, autre luisant comme estoile ou soleil, et puis comme pierre.

> [And what it means. And she speaks of a rock that is in the sea, which appears in different guises, sometimes dark, another time bright, sometimes green and flowery, another time bare with no greenery, sometimes shining like a star or like the sun, and then stony.]

The same hand also filled in a red initial 'U' at the beginning of v. 5891. All this suggests that the original plan was for the manuscript to have two miniatures in the section devoted to Reason, highlighting two aspects of her moralizing discourse: the ultimate worthlessness of the material gifts of Fortune, and the allegorical description of Fortune herself.

The marginal 'Nota' signs provide further evidence for an interest in Reason's moral teachings. 'Nota' signs occur in a great many *Rose* manuscripts, but there is enormous variation in the way they are distributed. Some manuscripts have only a few, while others may have them on nearly every page. Some readers chose to mark moralistic lines or citations of Latin authors; others were drawn to antifeminist and satirical passages; still others concentrated on passages dealing with love and the art of seduction. Sometimes these annotations are entered in the hand of the scribe, and that is the case with this manuscript. There could be two different explanations for this: the scribe might have been reading the text as he went along and marking passages he considered important, but he might also have been dutifully copying the 'Nota' signs along with the text of the book he was working from. In any case, for whatever reason, the manuscript was produced with certain passages highlighted, and marked as particularly noteworthy.

In this manuscript, the 'Nota' signs are clustered in the discourse of Reason. Here is a complete list:

> 6v: Quar bonté faite par priere
>   Est trop malement cher vendue
>   As cuers qui sont de grant value (4682–4)
>   [For a favour done as the result of begging is bought at too high a price, for hearts that are of great worth]
>
>   .I. vaillant homme a grant vergoigne
>   Quant il requiert que l'en li doigne (4685–6)
>   [A valiant man feels great shame when he asks that something be given to him]
>
>   Ne de reproche n'a il garde
>   Car sages hons sa langue garde (4701)
>   [Nor need he worry about reproach, for a wise man holds his tongue]

7r: Or ne puet estre bien amoureus
   Cuer qui n'aimme les gens por preus (4749–50)
   [A heart cannot truly be considered to love, if it does not love people for their worthiness]

8v: Mes li vrai ami les honneurent (4894)
   [But true friends honour them]

9r: Si ne fet pas richesce riche (4945)
   [Riches do not make a person wealthy]

   Que jamés assés n'en aura
   Ja tant aquerre ne saura (4959–60)
   [For he will never have enough; he will never be able to acquire so much]

9v: Car si com dient vostre mestre
   Nus n'est chetis s'i n'el cuide estre (5015–16)
   [As the masters say, no man is unfortunate unless he thinks that he is]

   Tuit cil sont riche en habondance
   Qui cuide avoir soufisance (5033–4)
   [All those who feel that they have enough, are abundantly rich]

14r: Dont di ge que miex vaut amor
   Simplement que ne fet justice,
   Tout voit elle contre malice (5532–4)
   [Therefore I say that love is more valuable, in itself, than justice, even though justice does oppose malice]

In this part of the poem, Reason discusses true friendship, in which a person is honoured not for their wealth or social status, but for their personal qualities; criticizes devotion to material wealth, pointing out that it cannot give spiritual fulfilment or happiness; and notes that for all its value, justice itself would be worth nothing if it was not informed by charitable love. Originally, before the manuscript was mutilated, these marginal signs would have combined with the miniature at v. 5227, to create a visual highlighting of a didactic agenda praising disinterested friendship and Christian charity and condemning the attachment to wealth, social prestige, and other gifts of fickle Fortune; a second miniature, further supporting this thematic programme, was also planned. Most of this material is adapted from the *Consolation of Philosophy*, one of Jean de Meun's most important Latin sources. One could say, indeed, that the manuscript was designed to highlight the Boethian elements in the discourse of Reason.

13.1.3. Bookmarks: Reading the Rose as social satire

An interesting and unusual feature of MS 2 is the vestigial bookmarks that survive on two pages. These mark the beginning of the tirade of the Jealous Husband (fol. 39r), and the death of Foul Mouth (Male Bouche), an allegorical personification of gossip and slander (fol. 46r). This latter passage is also the point where the Old Woman enters the poem. Both passages are important in Jean de Meun's satirical programme. The tirade of the Jealous Husband occurs in the middle of the discourse of Ami, but it stands on its own as a set piece. It describes an enraged husband, berating his wife; it is a powerful antifeminist diatribe, compiling standard medieval arguments about women's lack of moral fibre and the torments of marriage. The death of Foul Mouth is also an important passage in that it marks a real turning point in the narrative quest for the Rose: it is here the Lover learns to adopt a more blatantly hypocritical attitude in his pursuit of the Rose. At this point the focus of the narrative turns to the Old Woman, whose long speech outlines feminine techniques of seduction, and advises young women how to counter male predations with deceptions of their own. The Old Woman's teaching continues and builds on the salacious satire begun in the discourse of Ami and the tirade of the Jealous Husband. Essentially, she preaches exactly the same behaviour that the Jealous Husband condemns. It is therefore no surprise that a reader who chose to mark the Jealous Husband for easy access, would also want to be able to access the discourse of the Old Woman. This would be a reader interested in satirical portrayals of lust, adultery and marital strife, a reader more attracted to the comic and Ovidian aspects of the poem, than to its Boethian philosophy and morality.

13.2. Manuscript 3

The most interesting feature of Senshu MS 3 is its marginal annotation. Occasionally this takes the form of comments, but most often it is a simple 'Nota'; many of these may well have been entered, as in MS 2, by the scribe himself. Whereas MS 2 has only a few Notas, concentrated in the discourse of Reason, MS 3 has a great many, scattered throughout the poem. These annotations are a guide to the interests and preoccupations of the book's late medieval owner. It is clear at first glance that this person was educated. Not only are some of the glosses in Latin; but also, in the annotation of Nature's discussion of free will, the annotator uses Arabic numerals to distinguish the sections of the argument (fols. 106v, 109r). The appearance of Arabic numerals in a late medieval vernacular manuscript is certainly unusual, and suggests a university milieu. Beyond this, the annotator responded to a range of topics, as enumerated below.

13.2.1. Courtly readings

One set of glosses pertains to the 'courtly' depiction of love in Guillaume de Lorris, with an emphasis on the beauty of the love object, the noble suffering of the lover, and the careful game of flirtation, as shown in these examples:

11r   Et li bouton durent tuit frois
A tot le moins .ii. jors ou trois. (1644–5) [*Nota du bouton*]
[And the buds remain fresh for at least two or three days)] [*Note: concerning the bud*]

12r   Ainz doit estre cortois et frans (1937) [ornamental penwork added to initial]
[Thus [a lover] should be courteous and frank]

21r   Et sachez bien, cui l'en ostroie
Le besier, il a de la proie
Le mieuz et le plus avenant. (3387–9)
[And you can be sure, that whoever gets a kiss, he has captured the best and most delightful part of what he wants]

13.2.2. Ovidian and antifeminist readings

The seeming idealism of the above examples contrasts with other passages that were also marked with the 'Nota' sign. Our annotator was attracted to the Ovidian cynicism of characters like Friend and the Old Woman, as these examples show:

> 45v De cels boler n'est pas pechiez
> Qui de boule sunt entechiez.
> Male Bouche si est bolierres. (7322–4)
> [It is no sin to deceive those who are guilty of deception. Foul Mouth is a deceiver]

> 61v Conbien qu'el soit lede clamee,
> Jurt qu'el est plus bele que fee. (9921–2)
> [No matter how ugly she is, swear that she is more beautiful than a fairy]

> 81v S'il sunt mil, a chascun doit dire:
> 'La rose avrez touz seus, biau sire.' (13089–90)
> [Even if there are a thousand men, she should tell each one that he alone will have the rose]

There is also much attention to antifeminist passages. The greatest excitement of all is directed at the Jealous Husband's declaration, marked with both a 'Nota' sign and a large pointing hand:

> 56v Toutes estes, serez et fustes,
> De fet ou de volenté, pustes. (9125–6)
> [You women all are, always have been and always will be, in fact or intention, sluts]

Moreover, a couplet that sometimes appears in this spot in other manuscripts has been entered in the margin: 'Et qui bien vous [encher]cheroyt / [To]utes putains [vo]us trouveroyt' [And anyone who investigated you would find that you are all prostitutes]. In addition, antifeminist lines are picked out wherever else they may occur, for example:

> 58r   Fame ne prise honor ne honte
> Quant riens en la teste li monte. (9383–4)
> [A woman cares nothing for shame or honour when she gets an idea to do something]

The annotator seems to have been particularly concerned with the problem of women who use their sexual charms to extract gifts or payment from men. He marked six passages that touch on that point, for example:

> 28v   Mes ja certes n'iert fame bone
> Qui por dons prendre s'abandone. (4533–4)
> [Certainly, no woman is any good who gives herself in exchange for gifts]

> 51r   N'il n'i a point d'amor, sanz faille,
> En fame qui por don se baille. (8247–8)
> [Nor is there any love, ever, in a woman who gives herself in exchange for gifts]

He also marked passages that portray marriage as a torment for men, because their wives cause them so much suffering, for example:

> 53v   N'est nus qui mariez se sente,
> S'il n'est fols, qu'il ne s'en repente. (8655–6)
> [There is no one who doesn't regret getting married, unless he's a fool]

Overall, these annotations reflect an interest in love not only as virtuous suffering and admiration from afar, but also as calculated seduction. The annotations note both the more innocent and idealistic portrayal of love as refined and patient suffering in an elegant environment, and the more satirical, Ovidian portrayal of love as a constant struggle between the sexes, with men and women each trying to dominate and control the other, in the pursuit of pleasure, personal power and financial gain.

13.2.3. Moral readings

The *Rose* does not only depict the Lover's trajectory from idealistic contemplation of beauty to predatory seduction. It also offers a variety of moral precepts, and these passages also caught the attention of our annotator. For example:

> 27v De fruit avoir ne fet il force,
>   Au deliter sanz plus s'esforce. (4357–8)
>   [A lover is not interested in procreation; his sole interest is pleasure]

> 29v Et loiaus, car riens ne vaudroit
>   Li sens ou leautez faudroit. (4665–6)
>   [A friend is loyal, for a mind lacking in loyalty is worth nothing]

> Mout a vaillanz hom grant vergoigne
> Quant il requiert que l'en li doigne. (4685–6)
> [A valiant man feels great shame when he asks that something be given to him]

The annotator seems to have had a particular interest in the motif of death, and he marked passages touching on this theme no matter what context they appear in. One such passage is when the God of Love laments the death of the Latin elegiac love poets and announces that the two authors of the *Rose* – Guillaume de Lorris and Jean de Meun – are the successors to these poets. He notes that Guillaume will also die before he can finish the poem, but that Jean de Meun will complete it. This passage is very important in modern readings of the poem, because it posits two vernacular poets as the direct successors to the poets of ancient Rome.[5] Our annotator also read this passage attentively, but he was not necessarily interested in theo-

---

5   On the midpoint passage, see D. Hult, *Self-fulfilling Prophecies: Readership and Authority in the First Roman de la Rose* (Ithaca, NY: Cornell University Press, 1985): 10–17; K.D. Uitti, 'From *Clerc* to *Poète*: The Relevance of the *Romance of the Rose* to Machaut's World', in M.P. Cosman and B. Chandler (eds.), *Machaut's World, Annals of the New York Academy of Sciences* 314 (1978): 209–16.

rizing a concept of authorship. The lines that he marked are not the ones that celebrate the work of the Latin poets, the faithful love of Guillaume de Lorris, or the *Rose* itself. Instead, he marked the lines that allude to the death of the Latin poets and Guillaume de Lorris:

> 65r Nous reüssent or bien mestier;
>   Mes chascuns d'aus gist morz porriz. (10494–5)
>   [We could have used their help [the Latin love poets] but they are all dead and decayed now]
>
>   Ci se reposera Guillaumes. (10531)
>   [Here Guillaume will lie in peace]

The focus on death implies a concern with the transience of worldly life, and perhaps an ironic view of the ardent lover whose carefree youth will lead all too soon to old age and death. He also chose to highlight a line, referring to Jean de Meun, which might seem like a trivial moral maxim:

> 65v Car il n'est pas hon qui ne peche,
>   Tourjorz a chascuns quelque teche. (10547–8)
>   [For there is no man who does not sin; everyone has some faults]

Modern readers have paid scant attention to this line. But the medieval reader was trained to react to proverbial sayings and maxims (this one apparently translating *Nemo sine crimine vivit* from the *Disticha Catonis* I. 5) and to look for the moral lesson. Our reader has picked out a sobering lesson about the shadow of sin and the inevitability of death.

The annotator also noted Reason's comments about the perils of Youth, where death is a constant danger:

> 27v Car Jeunece boute home et fame
>   En touz periz de cors et d'ame,
>   Et trop est fort chose a passer
>   Sanz mort ou sanz menbre quasser. (4403–6)
>   [For Youth throws men and women into all kinds of bodily and spiritual danger; and it is very difficult to get through it without death or injury]

And in the discourse of Nature, he focused on a passage in which Nature lists the many possible causes of death. He marked these with a series of seven Notas in the space of less than forty lines:

107r Ou par quelque meschief destruire
       Par leur fez folemant conduire. (16967–8)

       Par glaive a mort, ou par venins,
       Tant ont les queurs faus et chenins. (16973–4)

       Par trop dormir, par trop veillier,
       Trop reposer, trop traveillier. (16975–6)

       Par trop leur qualitez changier (16984)

       Ou par leur coustumes muer (16989)

       Quant soudainement les remuent;
       Maint s'an grievent et maint s'an tuent. (16993–4)

       Don bien se peüssent garder (17003)
       [*Or they are killed by some accident caused by their foolish behaviour*; or by their personal enemies, *who have killed many with the sword or with poison, their hearts are so false*; or by illness, or by unhealthy living, *by too much sleeping or waking, too much rest, too much work*, growing too fat or too lean (for one can go wrong with all those things), by fasting too long, by taking too much pleasure, by too much hardship, too much happiness or too much sorrow, by eating or drinking too much, *by changing their condition*, which is very bad when it is done too suddenly, by being too hot or too cold, which they will eventually regret; *or by changing their habits, which kills many people when they do it too suddenly ... they should be careful not to do that*][6]

Meditation on death is not normally a topic that we associate with the *Romance of the Rose* nowadays, but medieval readers may have approached the poem quite differently. For a moralist, the ever-present danger of death is a very common topic; and for a scholar, the detailed list of the many causes of death might even have some scientific interest.

6   In this example and the following one, lines that are actually marked with 'Nota' signs are in italics; the intervening lines are translated to provide context.

13.2.4. Learned readings

I already noted earlier that the annotator of MS 3 was an educated man, who sometimes used Latin in his annotations. It is no surprise, therefore, that he took an interest in the scientific and philosophical material found in the discourse of Nature. For example, he focused closely on her allusions to a treatise on optics, with particular attention to the advice offered for those who wish to pursue this topic of study:

> 112v Cist fist le livre des *Regarz*:
>   De ce doit cil science avoir
>   Qui veust de l'arc en ciel savoir,
>   *Car de ce doit estre jugierres*
>   Clers naturex et regardierres.
>
> 114r Et sache de geometrie,
>   *Don necessaire est la metrie.* (18006–12)
>   [He wrote the book of *Optics*: anyone who wishes to understand the rainbow should know this science, for a natural scientist and observer *should know about these things*. And he should know geometry, *which must be mastered*]

The annotator also paid careful attention to the long discussion of predestination and free will. He marked the beginning of that section:

> 106v Si dit l'en que les destinees (17029) [*Nota de predestinatione*]
>   [Thus it is said of destinies ...] [Note: concerning predestination]

Our reader placed several Nota signs against lines in which Nature identified the potential problem of reconciling free will with divine foreknowledge; as noted above, he also enumerated the sections of her argument. This kind of annotation is sometimes found in other manuscripts as well, though it is still unusual. It shows that this portion of the text is being subjected to a scholastic study, with an effort to subdivide Nature's somewhat rambling reflections into a logical sequence of arguments.

Finally, it is worth noting that the annotator was attracted to lines that mention the city of Paris. One of the passages marked is a truly offhand allusion, occurring in Wealth's dismissal of anyone who is not sufficiently wealthy to be considered one of her followers:

62r   Nus n'i entre, s'il n'est des miens,
      Tant soit de Paris ne d'Esmiens. (10053–4)
      [No one enters if he is not of my company, even if he is from Paris or
      Amiens]

The other Parisian annotation occurs in the discourse of False Seeming,
and concerns the University of Paris:

73v   L'université, qui lors iere (11795) [*Nota de universtate parisiense*]
      [The University, which then was] [*Note: about the University of Paris*]

One cannot help but wonder if this apparent interest in the University of
Paris is a reflection of the milieu in which MS 3 was originally used.

13.3. Conclusion

This examination allows for a few conclusions concerning both the design
and the reception of the two Senshu *Rose* manuscripts. The scribe of MS
2 was fairly careless; he often omitted words and sometimes even wrote
things that made no sense at all. However, the manuscript was proofread
and corrected by someone who obviously did care about getting the text
right. It is possible that part of the scribe's problem was that the language
of the poem had become slightly archaic; he, like the corrector, may not
always have understood it. Moreover, there seem to be two different patterns of reading reflected in this manuscript. One highlights the poem's
moral content and its affinity with the Boethian *Consolation of Philosophy*;
and one focuses on the satirical passages, with their Ovidian worldliness
and their clerical distrust of marriage. It might well be that the Notas,
like the miniature and the space left for another miniature, derive from
the workshop where this copy was made. The manuscript was produced
with emphasis on the morally edifying teachings of Reason. A subsequent
owner, however, was evidently more interested in the satirical content,
with its antifeminist and anti-marriage tirades and its Ovidian emphasis

on love as a game of power and seduction, and added page markers that would enable him to turn easily to those sections.

The annotations that surround the text in MS 3, in turn, allow us to determine several things about the milieu in which this manuscript was originally used. The use of Latin glosses and Arabic numerals suggests a university environment, or at least a high level of education. This is also supported by the interest in scientific and philosophical topics. The annotator enjoyed the love allegory, but he was not an idealistic reader; he also enjoyed the Ovidian satire and the antifeminist tirades. His interest in arguments against marriage might support the idea that he belonged to a clerical or university milieu. He also had a keen eye for moral maxims, showing that he was trained in medieval reading practices of picking out memorable bits of wisdom. His apparent interest in Paris – and in the University of Paris specifically – offers tantalizing evidence, albeit circumstantial, that the manuscript may have belonged to a resident of that city, perhaps someone affiliated with the University. In all, the two Senshu *Rose* manuscripts afford valuable insights into the varied patterns of reading and reception to which this important and influential poem was subject.

13.4. References

13.4.1. Primary sources

Cato, Dionysius. *Disticha Catonis*, ed. M. Boas & H.J. Botschuyer. Amsterdam: North-Holland, 1952.
Lorris, Guillaume de and Jean de Meun. *Le Roman de la Rose*. ed. F. Lecoy, 3 vols. Paris: Champion, 1973–5.

13.4.2. Secondary sources

Hult, D. *Self-fulfilling Prophecies: Readership and Authority in the First Roman de la Rose*. Ithaca, NY: Cornell University Press, 1985.

Huot, Sylvia. *From Song to Book*. Ithaca, NY: Cornell University Press, 1987.

——. 'Medieval Readers of the *Roman de la Rose*: The Evidence of Marginal Notations', *Romance Philology* 43 (1990): 400–20.

——. *The Romance of the Rose and Its Medieval Readers: Interpretation, Reception, Manuscript Tradition*. Cambridge: Cambridge University Press, 1993.

Langlois, E. *Les Manuscrits du Roman de la Rose: Description et classement*. Lille: Tallandier, and Paris: Champion, 1910.

Uitti, K.D. 'From *Clerc* to *Poète*: The Relevance of the *Romance of the Rose* to Machaut's World', in M.P. Cosman and B. Chandler, eds., *Machaut's World, Annals of the New York Academy of Sciences* 314 (1978): 209–16.

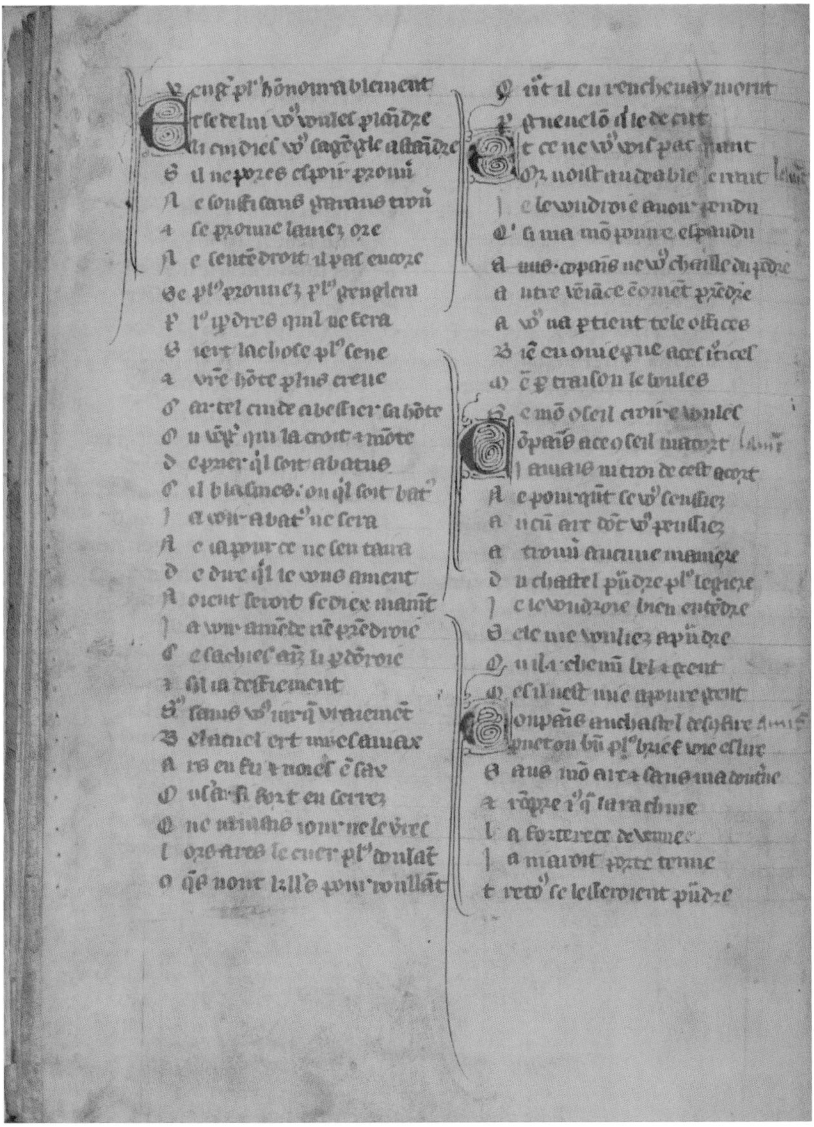

Figure 13–1 *Le Roman de la Rose*, Tokyo: Senshu University Library.
MS 2, fol. 33v. Reprinted with permission.

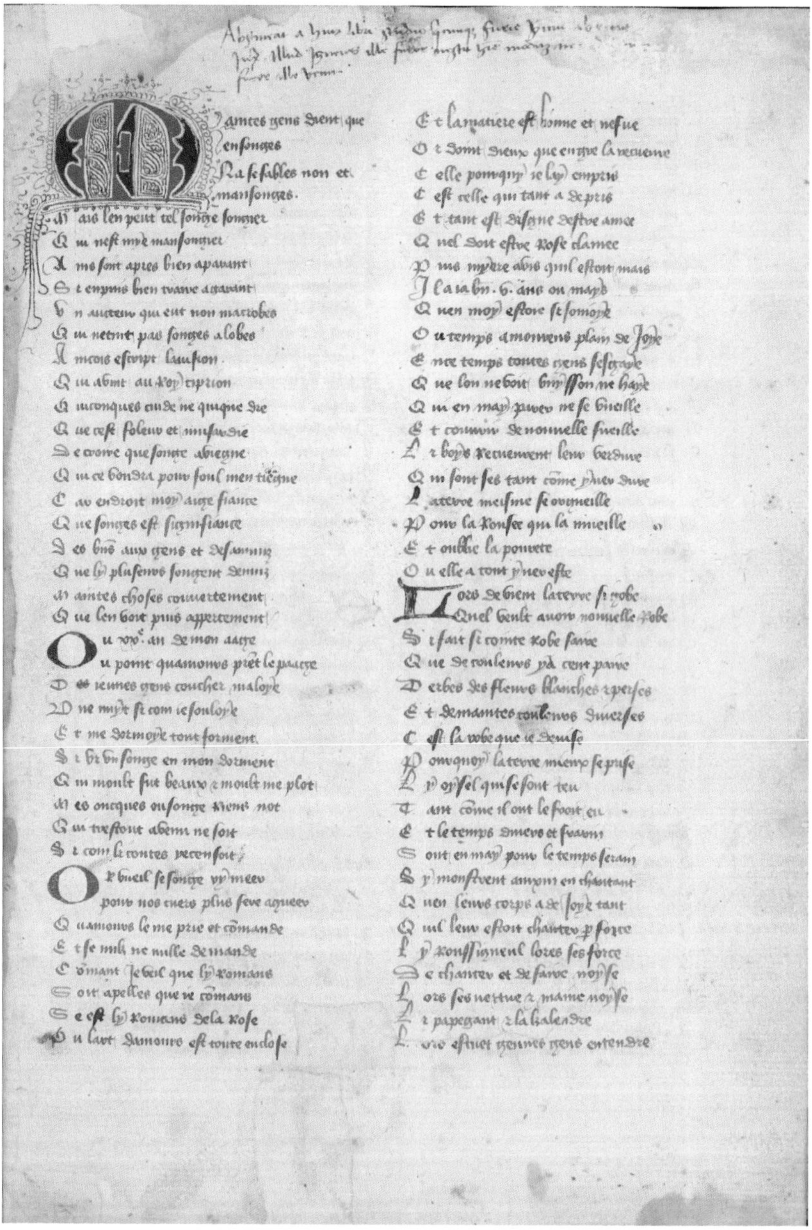

Figure 13–2 *Le Roman de la Rose*, Tokyo: Senshu University Library. MS 3, fol. 1r. Reprinted with permission.

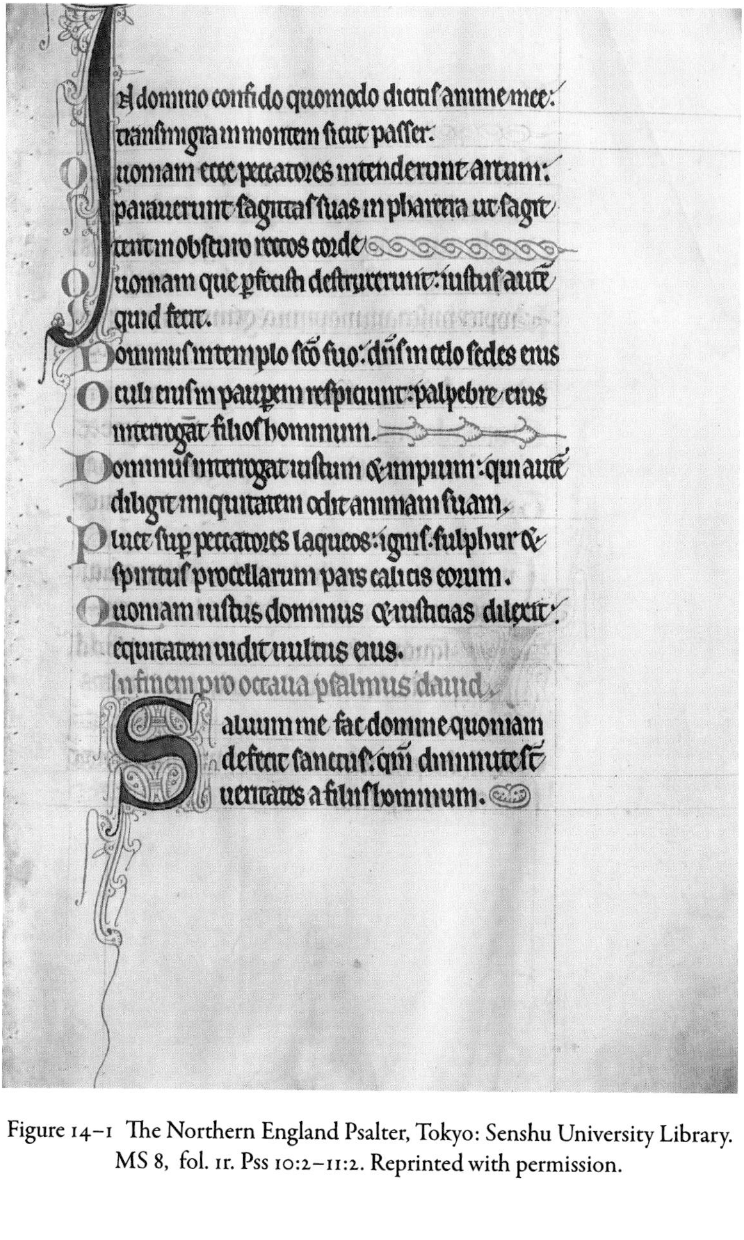

[I]n domino confido quomodo dicitis anime mee:
transmigra in montem sicut passer:
quoniam ecce peccatores intenderunt arcum:
parauerunt sagittas suas in pharetra ut sagit-
tent in obscuro rectos corde
quoniam que perfecisti destruxerunt: iustus autem
quid fecit.
Dominus in templo sancto suo: dominus in celo sedes eius
Oculi eius in pauperem respiciunt: palpebre eius
interrogant filios hominum.
Dominus interrogat iustum & impium: qui autem
diligit iniquitatem odit animam suam.
Pluet super peccatores laqueos: ignis sulphur &
spiritus procellarum pars calicis eorum.
Quoniam iustus dominus & iustitias dilexit:
equitatem uidit uultus eius.
In finem pro octaua psalmus dauid.
Saluum me fac domine quoniam
defecit sanctus: quoniam diminute sunt
ueritates a filiis hominum.

Figure 14-1 The Northern England Psalter, Tokyo: Senshu University Library.
MS 8, fol. 1r. Pss 10:2–11:2. Reprinted with permission.

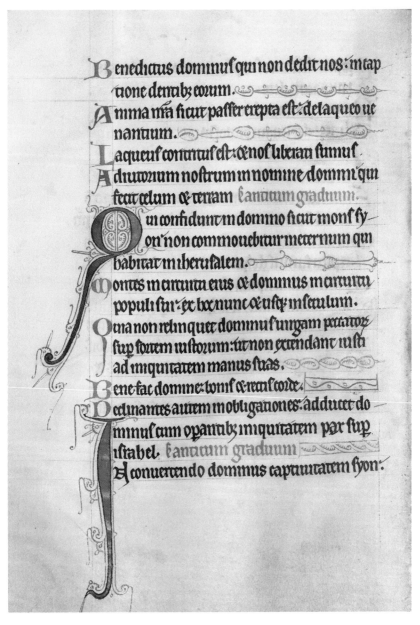

Benedictus dominus qui non dedit nos : in captione dentibz eorum.

Anima nra sicut passer erepta est de laqueo uenantium.

Laqueus contritus est et nos liberati sumus

Adiutorium nostrum in nomine domini qui fecit celum et terram. Sanctum graduum.

Qui confidunt in domino sicut mons syon non commouebitur in eternum qui habitat in iherusalem.

Montes in circuitu eius et dominus in circuitu populi sui ex hoc nunc et usque in seculum.

Quia non relinquet dominus uirgam peccatorum sup sortem iustorum ut non extendant iusti ad iniquitatem manus suas.

Bene fac domine bonis et rectis corde.

Declinantes autem in obligationes adducet dominus cum operantibz iniquitatem pax sup israhel. Sanctum graduum

In conuertendo dominus captiuitatem syon

Figure 14–2 The Northern England Psalter, Tokyo: Senshu University Library.
MS 8, fol. 89v. Pss 123:6–125:1. Reprinted with permission.

PATRICK P. O'NEILL

14 The Senshu Psalter

14.0. Introduction

In the book culture of the medieval West the Bible stood preeminent.
Within the Bible, the Gospels, which conveyed the primary Christian
message of the New Testament, obviously occupied first place. But a close
second in status and frequency of use was an Old Testament book, the collection of 150 Psalms known as the Psalter. There are a number of reasons
why the Psalter received special attention and was so frequently copied in
western Christendom. It enjoyed special status as one of the 'Sapiential' or
'Wisdom' books of the Old Testament. It was also the text used to teach
children (beginning traditionally at the age of seven) how to read and write
Latin, especially in the monasteries where students learned it by heart. And,
most importantly, it was the basic text of the Divine Office, the sequence of
prayers that were sung and recited at fixed hours in a daily liturgical cycle.
The recitation of the Divine Office was originally a monastic and clerical
duty but by the eighth century it was already being embraced by pious laity.[1]
Such Psalters, liturgical or quasi-liturgical, had additional matter besides
their text of the Psalms proper, notably a set of Canticles (hymns taken
mainly from the Old and New Testament), a Litany (a series of interces-
sions) and prayers.[2] It is to this broad category of 'liturgical Psalter' that
the Senshu Psalter (hereafter referred to as 'S') belongs (see Figures 14–1

---

1   For example, King Alfred of Wessex (died 899) observed the daily recitation of the
    Psalms.
2   For an account of the Canticles, see J. Mearns, *The Canticles of the Christian Church
    Eastern and Western in Early Medieval Times* (Cambridge: The University Press,

and 14–2).[3] It contains a text of the *Gallicanum* Psalms with accompanying Canticles and a Litany, and was copied in England in the late twelfth or early thirteenth century. As will be argued below, S was written for lay, rather than monastic or clerical, readers.

14.1. Physical Description

The manuscript is in good physical condition, except for the loss of some thirty leaves. Out of a probable total of 151 leaves,[4] some 120 have survived, most of them well preserved. Average dimensions are 240 × 168mm (written space, 154 × 97mm). The text is written within a rectangular frame (defined in pencil) which provides generous margins. However, it does not appear that the manuscript was formatted for glossing: there are no marginal glosses or annotations.[5] Numerous illuminations in burnished gold, as well as red and blue decoration have all survived remarkably well. Some decoration has been lost at top and bottom, casualties of the binder's knife, and the final quire is blackened and buckled, probably as a result of water damage. The latter damage seems to have occurred after the manuscript received its present binding, as the same damage marks are visible on the end pastedown.

1914); for Litanies, see M. Lapidge (ed.), *Anglo-Saxon Litanies of the Saints*, Henry Bradshaw Society 106 (Woodbridge: Boydell and Brewer, 1991).

3   Now housed at the Library of Senshu University where it is identified as 'MANUSCRIPT PSALTER. ENGLAND C. 1200' (Senshu University Library MS 8).

4   As argued below, section IV.

5   Except for a partially preserved note (sixteenth-century?) in Latin on the top margin of fol. 115, '... petes nct sit'.

14.2. Binding

The binding is described succinctly in the Maggs Catalogue as 'English 16th century blind-stamped calf over wooden boards' (probably oak) with 'roll-stamped borders'.[6] The use of calf (tanned leather) and the blind-tooled binding were both common in the sixteenth century. Such simple binding is associated especially with 'literate clergy, lawyers, other scholars, students and teachers', who had their books bound for personal or professional use and who were found mainly in London and the Cathedral and University towns.[7] Though the leather thongs that held the covers of S closed are missing, the remains of two clasps, a common device of the period (1400–1557), are visible. Also indicative of a sixteenth-century date is the absence of squares; the boards were cut flush with the text-block. The binding is dotted with numerous wormholes. There is no title or identifying words on the binding.

The binder also supplied at the beginning a pastedown and frontispiece, and at the end another pastedown with overlapping to form a partial page. Both were originally bifolia, taken from two different fifteenth-century English breviaries. Given the period in which they were bound into the present manuscript one might surmise that these bifolia were taken from liturgical books which, after the dissolution of the monasteries, had no further use except as binding material. As noted by M.M. Foot, 'The use of both manuscript and printed waste for end-leaves and paste-downs is not uncommon, both in Britain and elsewhere, and vellum manuscript paste-downs are found with especial frequency in Oxford bindings of the end of the fifteenth and the beginning of the sixteenth centuries'.[8] One form of paste-down is '[a] single leaf, folded, sewn through the fold and leaving a stub' – just as in the final end-leaves of S; another form is 'a folded

---

6   *Maggs Bros., Catalogue 1366, European Bulletin no. 23* (London:, 2004–5), 46–7; hereafter referred to as 'Maggs Catalogue'.

7   'Bookbinding 1400–1557' in Lotte Hellinga and J.B. Trapp (eds.), *The Cambridge History of the Book in Britain III (1400–1557)* (Cambridge: Cambridge University Press, 1999): 109–27:120–1.

8   'Bookbinding', 110.

sheet sewn through the fold forming two end leaves, one of which could be pasted down' – again exactly as in the opening endleaves of S. Another binding technique of the sixteenth century evident in S is the insertion of white paper between leaves, which probably served 'to reinforce the spine and hold its shape'.[9] Finally, S shows no evidence of coloured edges, a feature characteristic of leaves of fifteenth- and early sixteenth-century books.[10] Thus, the binding would seem to belong to the sixteenth century, perhaps the first half.

14.3. Foliation and Pagination

None is present, except for three numbers supplied in pencil in a modern hand, '50' (at fol. 29r), '100' (at fols. 72v and 79r), '140' (at fol. 119r). Since these numbers correspond to the present sequence of folios they reveal nothing about the number of missing leaves. They may represent a hypothetical reconstruction of what the manuscript originally had before it lost the batch of leaves at the beginning. Although no formal medieval foliation is present, certain leaves on the lower verso have a catchword entered, which, in effect, marks them as the end of a quire. Such catchwords are visible at the end of quires 1, 2, 5, 8, 9, 11, 13, 14 and 15.

14.4. Physical Collation and Quires

Altogether 120 leaves have survived; the final leaf, although little more than a stub, contains burnished gold illumination on the recto and traces of letters (in the same ink and hand as the main texts) on the verso. In its

9   'Bookbinding', 111.
10 'Bookbinding', 111.

present state S contains sixteen quires and the first folio of another quire, all of which were probably originally quaternions. Judging by the damaged cord (flax or hemp?) of the lower end of the interior spine, the missing first section was removed some time after the manuscript was bound in the sixteenth century. The surviving quires are as follows:

*1⁸ (lacks nos. 2–7) [fol. 1]; 2⁸ [fol. 2–9]; 3⁷ (lacks no. 2) [fols. 10–16]; 4⁶ (lacks nos. 6, 7) [fols. 17–22]; 5⁸ [fols. 23–30]; 6⁷ (lacks no. 3) [fols. 31–37]; 7⁸ [fols. 38–45]; 8⁷ (lacks no. 3) [fols. 46–52]; 9⁸ [fols. 53–60]; 10⁶ (lacks nos. 1, 3) [fols. 61–66]; 11⁸ (nos. 1 and 8 singletons) [67–74]; 12⁷ (lacks no. 1) [fols. 75–81]; 13⁸ [fols. 82–89]; 14⁸ [fols. 90–97]; 15⁸ [fols. 98–105]; 16⁸ [fols. 106–13]; 17⁷ (no. 1 a singleton) [fols. 114–20].

Despite the missing text, it is possible to make a reasonable conjecture as to S's original makeup. The missing text from Pss 1:1 to 10:1 (inclusive) contains 130 verses, which – allowing an average of about twenty verses per leaf – would have covered six and a half leaves. Adding to this the customary introductory matter preceding Psalm 1 and a large illumination for Psalm 1 would account for a full quire.

The present fol. 1 begins with Ps 10:2 and thus appears to be the first folio of the second original quire; significantly, its pricking holes are well defined. Between Ps 12:2 (the end of fol. 1) and Ps 30:7 (the beginning of the surviving fol. 2) some 266 verses (some of them virtual double verses) are missing, which would require at least 14 folios. Special decoration before Psalm 21 (marking the last Psalm for Sunday matins) and Ps 26 (the beginning Psalm for Monday matins) would have added another folio. Thus, the total number of leaves from Pss 10:2 to 30:7 would amount to sixteen, or two full quires.

On the basis of this tentative evidence, it seems that three quires are missing, of which the present fol. 1 is the first leaf of the second quire. If this reconstruction is correct, then the Psalter would originally have had nineteen quires for a total of 151 folios (18x8 + 7).

14.5. Pricking, Ruling and Ink

Pricking marks are visible on the far left margin, twenty holes corresponding to the twenty lines (horizontal) of the main text. A pair of vertical pricks at both the left and right margins served to define the vertical columns (in alternating positions) within which the coloured initials were entered. Ruling is in pencil. Ink is black with a brownish tinge.

14.6. Hair and Flesh

The arrangement for the typical quaternion seems to be as follows:

H/F-F/H-H/F-F/H-H/F-F/H-H/F-F/H. This arrangement gives hair side for the outer leaf at beginning and end with facing hair or flesh alternating for the inner leaves.

14.7. Decoration

The decoration comprises five kinds, each with a distinct function:

1) biblical tituli in red;
2) coloured initial for the first letter of each verse (except the first), alternating between red and blue; this decoration was added after the writing of the main text as evidenced by several instances where the rubricator inserted the wrong initial; e.g., 'Tunc' instead of 'Nunc' (Ps 43:10; fol. 15r);
3) line fillers in red or blue;

4) illuminated initials in burnished gold for the first letter of each psalm. The gold leaf was evidently supplied before the coloured initials, judging by an instance on fol. 51v where coloured 'G(loriosa)' was knocked out of its vertical alignment because of the presence of the foot of the gold initial 'F'.

5) illuminated historiated initials for the first letter of 'important psalms'—none of these have survived, but their presence can be inferred from the offset of an initial of the Holy Trinity (fol. 79), and a trace of green ink in the missing 'C' introducing the Canticles (fol. 105r).

14.8. Contents[11]

A copy of the Psalms in the *Gallicanum* version (fols. 1–104) with twelve accompanying Canticles (fols. 105–117), a Litany (fols. 117–119), and an unidentifiable fragment of text (fol. 120), perhaps prayers. The sequence of texts is as follows:[12]

fol. 1, [Ps 10:2] In Domino confido....[Ps 12:12] in corde meo per diem
fol. 2, [Ps 30:7] odisti obseruantes uanitates....[Ps 30:21a] a conturbatione hominum
fol. 3, [Ps 30:21b] proteges eos....[Ps 31:10] misericordia circumdabit
fol. 4, [Ps 31:11] letamini....[Ps 32:19] et alat eos in fame
fol. 5, [Ps 32:20] anima nostra....[Ps 33:18a] dominus exaudiuit eos
fol. 6, [Ps 33:18b] et ex omnibus....[Ps 34:12] animae meae

11 Not included here are various notes of post-medieval date: the first pastedown has the entry in ink, 'J. Cooke Gauborough (?)' in an eighteenth/nineteenth century hand; the upper right margin of the frontispiece has in pencil in a nineteenth-century (?) hand the entry, '6–0' ('six pounds, zero shillings' ?), possibly the purchase price. On the end pastedown written in ink, the number '133' was entered in an eighteenth-century hand, perhaps a reference to the number of pages then present.

12 Here I provide the opening and closing words of each page. The numbering of the Psalms is that of the Latin Vulgate.

fol. 7,   [Ps 34:13] ego autem....[Ps 35:1] IN FINEM...PSALMUS DAUID
fol. 8,   [Ps 35:2] dixit iniustus....[Ps 36:8] ut maligneris
fol. 9,   [Ps 36:9] quoniam qui....[Ps 36:28] peribit
fol. 10,   [Ps 36:29] iusti autem....[Ps 37:8] in carne mea
fol. 11,   [Ps 38:3] ommutui....[Ps 39:4] in domino
fol. 12,   [Ps 39:5] beatus uir....[Ps 39:18a] sollicitus est mei
fol. 13,   [Ps 39:18b] adiutor meus....[Ps 41:5a] tabernaculi ad-
fol. 14,   [Ps 41:5a] -mirabilis.....[Ps 43:2] in diebus antiquis
fol. 15,   [Ps 43:3] manus tua....[43:21b] et si expan-
fol. 16,   [Ps 43:21b] -dimus manus....[Ps 44:12] adorabunt eum
fol. 17,   [Ps 44:13] et filie Tyri....[Ps 46:2] in uoce exultationis
fol. 18,   [Ps 46:3] quoniam dominus....[Ps 48:2] orbem
fol. 19,   [Ps 48:3] quique terrigene....[Ps 48:21] est illis
fol. 20,   [Ps 49:1] deus deorum....[Ps 49:19a concinnabat dolos
fol. 21,   [Ps 49:19b] sedens aduersus....[Ps 50:17] annun-
fol. 22,   [Ps 53:9b] et super inimicos....[Ps 54:19] erant mecum
fol. 23,   [Ps 54:20] exaudiet deus....[Ps 55:13a] de morte
fol. 24,   [Ps 55:13b] et pedes meos....[Ps 57:5] aures suas
fol. 25,   [Ps 57:6] quae non exaudiet....[Ps 58:12] protector meus
fol. 26,   [Ps 58:13] delictum oris....[Ps 59:12] in uirtutibus nostris
fol. 27,   [Ps 59:13] da nobis....[Ps 61:10] hominum mendaces
fol. 28,   [Ps 61:10] filii hominum (2°)....[Ps 63:6] laqueos dixerunt
fol. 29,   [Ps 63:6] quis uidebitis eos....[Ps 64:12] ubertate
fol. 30,   [Ps 64:13] pinguescent....[Ps 65:18] non exaudiet dominus
fol. 31,   [Ps 65:19] propterea....[Ps 67:10] perfecisti eam
fol. 32,   [Ps 67:11] animalia tua....[Ps 67:29b] hoc quod
fol. 33,   [Ps 68:7] domine uirtutum....[Ps 68:23a] in laqueum
fol. 34,   [Ps 68:23b] et in retributiones....[Ps 69:5a] qui querunt
fol. 35,   [Ps 69:5b] te et dicant....[Ps 70:16] introibo
fol. 36,   [Ps 70:16] in potentias domini....[71:10] offerent reges (2°)
fol. 37,   [Ps 71:10] Arabum et Saba....[Ps 72:9] lingua eorum
fol. 38,   [Ps 72:9] transiuit in terra....[Ps 72:28] predicationes tuas in
fol. 39,   [Ps 72:28] portis filie Syon....[Ps 73:18] nomen tuum
fol. 40,   [Ps 73:19] ne tradas....[Ps 75:4] et bellum
fol. 41,   [Ps 75:5] illuminas tu....[Ps 76:12] mirabilium tuorum
fol. 42,   [Ps 76:13] et meditabor....[Ps 77:9] conuer-
fol. 43,   [Ps 77:9] -<si> sunt in die belli....[Ps 77:28] tabernacula eorum
fol. 44,   [Ps 77:29] et manducauerunt....[Ps 77:47] in pruina
fol. 45,   [Ps 77:48] et tradidit....[Ps 77:65a] dormiens dominus
fol. 46,   [Ps 77:65b] et tanquam potens....[Ps 78:11] posside
fol. 47,   [Ps 78:11] filios mortificatorum....[Ps 79:17] ab increpatione uultus

fol. 48, [Ps 80:15] pro nihilo....[Ps 82:11] stercus terrae
fol. 49, [Ps 82:12] pone principes....[Ps 83:13a] in innocentia
fol. 50, [Ps 83:13b] domine uirtutum....[85:6] inten-
fol. 51, [Ps 85:6] -de uoti....[Ps 87:1] PRO MELECH
fol. 52, [Ps 87:1] AD RESPONDENDUM....[Ps 87:19] notos meos a miseria
fol. 53, [Ps 88:2] misericordias....[Ps 88:20] de plebe mea
fol. 54, [Ps 88:21] inueni Dauid....[Ps 88:42a] transeuntes uiam
fol. 55, [Ps 88:42b] factus est....[Ps 89:9b] defec<i>mus
fol. 56, [Ps 88:9c] anni nostri....[Ps 90:10] tabernaculo tuo
fol. 57, [Ps 90:11] quoniam angelis tuis....[Ps 91:16] iniqui-
fol. 58, [Ps 91:16] -tas in eo....[Ps 93:12b] et de
fol. 59, [Ps 93:12b] lege tua....[Ps 94:7] manus eius
fol. 60, [Ps 94:8] hodie si uocem....[Ps 96:2] sedis eius
fol. 61, [Ps 97:7] mare et plenitudo....[Ps 100:2] domus mee
fol. 62, [Ps 101:14] tu exurgens....[Ps 102:5] renoua-
fol. 63, [Ps 102:5] -bitur ut aquile....[Ps 103:2a] sicut uestimento
fol. 64, [Ps 103:2b] extendens celum....[Ps 103:22b] in cubilibus
fol. 65, [Ps 103: 22b] suis collocabuntur....[Ps 104:8] in mille generationes
fol. 66, [Ps 104:9] quod disposuit....[Ps 104:30] regum ipsorum
fol. 67, [Ps 104:31] dixit et uenit....[Ps 105:5] cum hereditate tua
fol. 68, [Ps 105:6] peccauimus....[Ps 105:25] non exaudierunt
fol. 69, [Ps 105:25] uocem domini....[Ps 105:46] omnium
fol. 70, [Ps 105:46] qui ceperant eos....[Ps 106:17] humiliati sunt
fol. 71, [Ps 106:18] omnem escam....[Ps 106:38] nimis et
fol. 72, [Ps 106:38b] iumenta eorum....[Ps 108:2] apertum est
fol. 73, [Ps 108:37] locuti sunt....[Ps 108:21] propter nomen
fol. 74, [Ps 108:21] tuum quia suauis....[Ps 108:31] animam meam
fol. 75, [Ps 110:10] laudatio eius....[Ps 113:2] potestas eius
fol. 76, [Ps 113:3] mare uidit....[Ps 113:25] neque om-
fol. 77, [Ps 113:25] -nes qui descenderunt....[Ps 116:2] misericordia
fol. 78, [Ps 116:2] eius et ueritas....[Ps 117:22a] edificantes
fol. 79, [Ps 117:22b] hic factus....[Ps 118:13] oris tui
fol. 80, [Ps 118:14] in uia testimoniorum....[Ps 118:34] corde meo
fol. 81, [Ps 118:35] deduc me....[Ps 118:55] legem tuam
fol. 82, [Ps 118:56] haec facta est....[Ps 118:75] iudicia tua et
fol. 83, [Ps 118:75] in ueritate....[Ps 118:94] exquisiui
fol. 84, [Ps 118:95] me exspectauerunt....[Ps 118:115] mandata dei mei
fol. 85, [Ps 118:116] suscipe me....[Ps 118:135] iustificationes tuas
fol. 86, [Ps 118:136] et exitus aquarum....[Ps 118:157] a testi-
fol. 87, [Ps 118:157] -moniis tuis....[Ps 118:176] non sum oblitus
fol. 88, [Ps 119:1] ad dominum....[Ps 121:7] in turribus tuis

fol. 89,   [Ps 121:8] propter fratres....[Ps 125:1a] sion
fol. 90,   [Ps 125:1b] facti sumus....[Ps 127:6] super Israhel
fol. 91,   [Ps 128:1] sepe....[Ps 130:2] anima mea
fol. 92,   [Ps 130:3] speret Israhel....[Ps 131:18] sanctificatio mea
fol. 93,   [Ps 132:1] ecce quam bonum....[Ps 134:8] ad pecus
fol. 94,   [Ps 134:9] et misit....[Ps 135:15] in mari rubro
fol. 95,   [Ps 135:16] qui transduxit....[Ps 137:2b] nomini tuo
fol. 96,   [Ps 137:2c] super misericordia....[Ps 138:12] lumen eius
fol. 97,   [Ps 138:13] quia tu possedisti....[Ps 139:8] obum-
fol. 98,   [Ps 139:8] -brasti super....[Ps 141:2] deprecatus sum
fol. 99,   [Ps 141:3] effundo....[Ps 142:8a] misericordiam tuam
fol. 100, [Ps 142:8b] quia in te....[Ps 143:12] ut s<i>mili-
fol. 101, [Ps 143:12] -tudo templi....[Ps 144:15] tu das
fol. 102, [Ps 144:15] escam....[Ps 146:6] humilians
fol. 103, [Ps 146:6] autem peccatores....[Ps 148:6] non preteribit
fol. 104, [Ps 148:7] laudate dominum....[Ps 150:6] laudet dominum.
fol. 105, CANTICUM YSAIAE PROPHETE [Is 12:1–6] Confitebor tibi...sanctus
          Israhel.
          CANTICUM EZECHIE REGIS [Is 38:10–20] Ego dixi...amaritudo mea
fol. 106, tu autem eruisti...in domo domini.
          CANTICUM ANNE [I Sm 2.1–10] Exultauit cor meum...cornu christi
          sui.
fol. 107, CANTICUM MOYSI SERUI DEI [Ex 15:1–19] Cantemus domino...in
          magnitudine brachii tui
fol. 108, Fiant immobiles...in medio eius.
          CANTICUM ABACUC [Hab 3] Domine audiui...in splendore fulgu-
fol. 109, -rantis haste tue...in psalmis canentem.
          CANTICUM MOYSI [Dt 32:1–44] Audite celi...stulte et insipiens
fol. 110, Numquid non ipse...partes eorum
fol. 111, Dum qui te genuit...amarissimi
fol. 112, Fel draconum...populi sui.
          HIMNUS SANCTI AMBROSII: Te deum laudamus...uniuerse potestates
fol. 113, Tibi Cherubin...non confundar in eternum.
          YMNUS TRIUM PUERORUM [Dn 3:57–89] Benedicite omnia
          opera...benedicite stelle
fol. 114, celi domino...et superexaltatus in secula.
          CANTICUMZACHARIAEPROPHETE[Lc1:68–80]Benedictusdominus
          deus
          Israhel...prophetarum eius
fol. 115, salutem ex inimicis...in uia pacis.

HYMNUS SANCTE MARIE [Lc 1:46–56] Magnificat anima mea...in secula.

CANTICUM SANCTI SIMEONIS [Lc 2:29–33] Nunc dimittis...plebis sue Israhel.

fol. 116, FIDES SANCTI ATHANASI EPISCOPI: Quicumque uult...supradictum est ut

fol. 117, unitas in trinitate...saluus esse non poterit.

[Litany] Kyrie elyson...sancte iohanis baptista

fol. 118, Omnes sancti patriarche...sancte genouesa

fol. 119, Sancte brigida...esto nobis Domine sacerdotes tui Domine.

fol. 120, [stub with initials and a few letters visible, perhaps originally prayers]

Thus, the following portions of the Psalms are missing:

1) Ps 1:1–10:1 (six or seven leaves)
2) 12:3–30:6 (fourteen leaves)
3) 37:9–38:2 (one leaf)
4) 50:17–53:9a (two leaves)
5) 67:29b-68:7 (one leaf)
6) 79:18–80:14 (one leaf)
7) 96:3–97:7 (one leaf)
8) 100:3–101:13 (one leaf)
9) 109:1–110:9 (one leaf)

All but the first two of these lacunae correspond to the loss of individual leaves within the regular quires of eight. That these missing leaves were deliberately cut out is evident from the knife marks visible on the surviving adjacent leaves (for example, fol. 11). At fol. 105 a gaping hole marks the spot which originally had the initial 'C' (of 'Confitebor'), the first letter of the first of the Canticles. A small line of green decoration – a colour otherwise unattested in the rest of the manuscript, where only red and blue are used – suggests that the illumination here was special. The deliberate excision of the illuminated 'C' suggests the explanation for the other missing leaves. Just as the latter marks an important change of text (from Psalms to Canticles), so too with the missing leaves. Nos. 4 (first missing leaf) and 8 coincide with the beginning of Pss 51 and 101, which mark the second and third parts of a tripartite division of the 150 Psalms. This division, common in early medieval Psalters of Insular origin, was usually marked with special illumination. Nos. 3, 4 (one leaf), 5, 6 and 7 contain, respectively, the beginning psalm for the Hour of Matins on Tuesday (Psalm 38), Wednesday

(Psalm 51), Thursday (Psalm 68), Friday (Psalm 80) and Saturday (Psalm 97); while no. 9 marks not only the end of the psalms used for Matins but also the beginning of the weekly sequence of psalms for Vespers. These locations are frequently marked with deluxe decoration in early medieval Psalters such as the so-called Paris Psalter, an English manuscript dated to the mid-eleventh century.[13] The liturgical divisions implied in these missing leaves reflect the Roman Office of the Hours.

14.9. Script

The script is early liturgical Gothic, characterized by the oval aspect of the letters and a spiky quality evident in the top of 't' and in the tops of the ascenders of 'l, h, d'. The feet of the minims are defined, but only in a horizontal direction, in contrast to English scripts from earlier in the twelfth century where the feet are completed with slanting strokes. That the scribe knew other scripts is evident from his occasional use of a triangle-shaped Insular 'a' as a capital letter in the biblical titulus that precedes each psalm in red. And the form of 'misericordias' which he entered in dry-point (with a metal stylus) at the bottom of fol. 52v as a catchword for the next quire shows him employing a sloping, elongated hand such as one finds in twelfth-century English charters. Other catchwords occur on the bottom margins of the folios that end quires 1, 2, 5, 9, 11, 13, 14 and 15 in a somewhat similar hand, though in brown ink. If not entered by the main scribe, they almost certainly belong to someone working with him since their purpose was to facilitate his work as a copyist.

One scribe wrote all the texts. In general the scribe was very competent; mistakes are few and the work seems to have been proofread for errors.

13   See B. Colgrave *et al.* (eds.), *The Paris Psalter (MS. Bibliothèque Nationale Fonds Latin 8824)*, Early English Manuscripts in Facsimile 8 (Copenhagen: Rosenkilde and Bagger, 1958): 14–15.

That consideration and the skillful handling of the layout of texts indicate a scribe who was very familiar with copying Psalters.

14.10. Corrections

Most corrections seem to be contemporary with the text and the work of the main scribe. Erasures are indicated by a punctum below the offending letter or, if necessitated, a series of puncta, one for each letter; by a horizontal stroke through the word, usually in the same red ink that was employed for the coloured initials and the biblical tituli (e.g., fols. 9v, 96r, 99r, 99v, 101r); and by total erasure (e.g., at fol. 1v, four lines corresponding to Ps 11:3–4 were erased, two of them a scribal dittography). Additions are indicated by a comma-like stroke on the line with the addition entered above the main text.

Occasionally alternative readings were supplied; for example, at Ps 46:5, QUEM has a suprascript 'a' above E to give QUAM, a problematic reading as evidenced by the comments of the thirteenth-century biblical scholar, William de Mara. Individual letters sometimes appear on the margins in dry-point; thus, fol. 6r 'ño' adjacent to NO(CENTES) because the scribe stopped at 'NO' to allow space for the titulus; fol. 67r has 'm' twice on the right margin; fol. 67v has a capital 'V' adjacent to a capital (coloured) 'U' in the text; 'ipsi' adjacent to IPSI (fol. 69v). Some corrections were made by a different scribe using a different (brown) ink but a similar hand and thus probably not much later than the main scribe; e.g., 'Te' corrected to 'Me' (Ps 40:13); 'enim' added at Ps 106:17 (fol. 70v).

14.11. Abbreviations

In general, abbreviations are used sparingly. The mark of abbreviation (or contraction) normally appears as a rising tilde located above the abbreviated syllable or, in the case of words, above the central letters. In syllables containing '-l' the abbreviating sign appears as a curved bar through the upper part of that letter.

A. Nomina sacra:
'angełs' for 'angelus';
'bñdix̄' for 'benedixit';
'dñs' for 'dominus'; 'dñi' for 'domini'; 'dñe' for 'domine'; 'dñm' for 'dominum'
'dš' for 'deus'; 'dm̄' for 'deum'; but also 'ds' and 'ds̄' for 'deus';
'eccłia' for 'ecclesia';
'głia(m)' for 'gloria(m)', głiose for 'gloriose' (fol. 107r);
'grīa' for 'gratia';
'isrł' for 'Israhel'; 'isrłite' for 'israhelite';
'miscđia-' for 'misericordia-';
'pr̄em' for 'patrem';
'sc̄a' for 'sancta'; 'scī' for 'sancti'; 'scō' for 'sancto'; 'scs̄' for 'sanctus'; 'scōs' for 'sanctos';
'scōrum' for 'sanctorum';
'scła' for 'secula', 'scłi' for 'seculi';
'xp̄i' for 'christi', 'xp̄m' for 'christum'.

B. Others:
Rising tilde for 'm';
tilde or jagged horizontal stroke for 'n';
'p' with horizontal stroke through descender for 'per' (the normal form);
'p' with backward loop for 'pro';
'7' with stroke through descender for 'et' (the more common form);
'&' for 'et';
'ē' for 'est';
'm̄s' for 'meus';
'ñ' for 'non';
'ñr' for 'noster'; 'nr̄a' for 'nostra'; 'nr̄e' for 'nostre'; 'nr̄o' for 'nostro'; 'nr̄i' for 'nostri';
'nr̄ m' for 'nostrum'; 'nr̄ am' for 'nostram'; 'nr̄ os' for 'nostros'; 'nr̄ as' for 'nostras';
'nr̄is' for 'nostris'; 'nr̄orum' for 'nostrorum';

'oīs' for 'omnis';

'qm̄' for 'quoniam';

'rt̄' for '-runt';

'st̄' for 'sunt';

'uῑa' for 'uestra'; 'uῑe' for 'uestre'; 'uῑm' for 'uestrum'; 'uῑam' for 'uestram';

'ɜ' for final '-us' as in 'derelinquentib-us' (fol. 40r);

A smaller 'ɜ' (on the line) for final '-ue' as in 'usq-ue' (fol. 8r);

a symbol resembling a reversed question mark for final '-um', e.g., 'filior-¿';

'm̄' for '-men-' as in 'testa-men-tum', 'men-datio', 'no-men';

'ū' for '-uer-' as in 'con-uer-tentur';

suprascript '²' for 'ur' as in 'cont-ur-batus' and 'obliuiscant-ur';

suprascript '³' for '-us' as in 'ei-us' and 'annuntiabim-us';

suprascript stroke for 'er' (e.g., 'tram'); and transverse bar through 'b' for '-er' in 'tab-er-nacula' (fol. 48v);

'c' with suprascript 'i' for 'cir-' as in 'cir<cu>ibunt' (fol. 25v);

'm' with suprascript 'i' for 'mihi' (fol. 22v);

'p' with suprascript 'i' for 'pri-' as in 'principum';

'p' with suprascript stroke for 'prae-';

'q' with suprascript 'i' for 'qui' as in 'anti-qui-s' (fol. 14v);

'q' with suprascript 'a' for 'qua-' as in 'appropin-qua-uit' (fol. 23r), 'qua-ndo' (fol 99r), 'qua-m' (fol. 6v); also 'q' with suprascript 'a' and slanted cross bar through the descender for 'quam' (fol. 49v);

Some abbreviations seem to be arbitrary: 'ipo' for 'ipso' (fol. 32v); 'nich' for 'nichil' (fol. 41r), 'oro' for 'oratio' (fol. 98v), 'bened' for 'benedicite' (fol. 114). More highly abbreviated forms were often used when the scribe was stuck for space. For example, 'dd' for 'Dauid' (titulus 54; fol. 22r); 'ītlts' for 'intellectus' (Ps 31:8; fol. 3v); 'p' with the loop ending in suprascript 's' for 'psalmus' (fol. 31r).

14.12. Punctuation

Because the text of the Psalms was already well-defined by the traditional system of dividing each psalm into verses, and marking each of the latter by a coloured initial, the need for punctuation was less pressing. The scribe used only two punctuation marks: a point to mark the end of a verse and a 'tick and point' (inverted semicolon) to mark a division within the verse. These marks, which go back to pre-Conquest England, continued in common use throughout the twelfth century. Noteworthy is the complete absence in S of two new punctuation marks which became common in England during the twelfth century, the 'seven and point' and the 'line', both of which were especially associated with the great monastic centres.[14]

14.13. Text and Textual Affiliations of S

The text of the Psalms is the *Gallicanum*, a Latin translation made by Jerome (*c.* 392) from the Greek Septuagint. Although the version of the Psalms used in Anglo-Saxon England was the *Romanum* (based on an Old Latin Psalter from Rome), already in the late tenth century the *Gallicanum* was becoming dominant in England and after the Norman Conquest became the exclusive Psalter for use in the Divine Office. Given its long history of use in the Western Church it is not surprising that the *Gallicanum* had a complicated textual history with numerous manuscript witnesses. The editors of the Benedictine edition distinguish three main stages in the textual history of the *Gallicanum*: (a) the earliest witnesses, which in general preserve a text closest to the original; (b) the Alcuinian manuscripts of the ninth century which reflect textual changes introduced around the time of the Carolingian reform of the Bible; (c) later manuscripts which reflect, more or less, a revised version of the Psalter produced at Paris in the thirteenth century.[15]

---

14   See N.R. Ker, *English Manuscripts in the Century after the Norman Conquest* (Oxford: Clarendon Press, 1960): 46–9.

15   *Biblia Sacra iuxta latinam vulgatam versionem ad codicum fidem...cura et studio monachorum Abbatiae Pontificiae Sancti Hieronymi in Urbe Ordinis Sancti Benedicti edita. Textus ex interpretatione Sancti Hieronymi: Liber psalmorum*, vol. 10 (Rome: Libreria Editrice Vaticana, 1953): xii.

Broadly speaking, S's text belongs to the Parisian recension, often agreeing with its particular readings as found in the representative manuscripts (VDΩ) used for the Benedictine edition.

For example:[16]

Ps 10: 7, IGNIS, SULPHUR ET SPIRITUS (VDΩ only)] ignis et sulphur et spiritus
Ps 32:16 GIGAS (V²DΩ)] gigans
Ps. 33:16 DIUERTE (VDΩ only)] deuerte
Ps 34:25 DEUORABIMUS (DΩ *et al.*] deuorauimus
Ps 35:9 UOLUPTATIS (VDΩ *et al.*)] uoluntatis
Ps 41:3 FONTEM (DΩ)] fortem
Ps 44:9 MIRRA (VDΩ] murra
Ps 44:13 OMNES DIUITES (VDΩ only)] diuites
Ps 48:3 SIMUL IN UNUM (VDΩ)] in unum
Ps 54:11 DIE AC NOCTE (VDΩ)] die et nocte
Ps 54:17 DOMINUM (VΩ only)] Deum
Ps 62:7 SIC[17] (Ωs)] si
Ps 64:11 INEBRIANS[18] (DΩ only)] inebria
Ps 67:7 DEUS QUI (VDΩ only)] deus
Ps 141:4 ABSCONDERUNT SUPERBI (VDΩ)] absconderunt.[19]

Admittedly, many of these agreements between S and the Paris Recension are less than conclusive in that the readings in question also occur in other (especially Alcuinian) manuscripts. And it must also be noted that S contains a significant element of disagreement with VDΩ either collectively or with its individual representatives, as in Ps 10:8 'Uidit' (omitted in Ω); or Ps 30:20 'in tabernaculo' (VDΩ add 'tuo').

But what is decisively in favour of S's filiation with the Paris Recension is the evidence of its biblical tituli, the headings (in red) which precede

---

16 The reading before the square bracket represents that shared by S and the Paris Recension, the reading after the square bracket is that of the critical text of the *Gallicanum*.

17 However, there is a punctum delens under 'c'.

18 Corrected from 'inebria' in brown ink and a different hand.

19 Curiously, the addition SUPERBI was erased with a red line through it, possibly by the main scribe.

each psalm, giving its authorship, circumstances of composition and musical accompaniment. More than the text proper of the Psalms, these tituli were modified by the Parisian scholars of the twelfth and thirteenth centuries. They not only changed their word order, but more strikingly they added new matter in the form of alternative readings often introduced by 'uel'. This aspect of the Parisian recension is very clearly present in S, as can be seen from the following examples:[20]

> Tit. 36, Psalmus Dauid (VΩ)] ipsi Dauid
> Tit. 40, In finem Psalmus Dauid uel in finem intellectus filii (Ω)] in finem Psalmus Dauid
> Tit. 58, In finem ne corrumpas uel disperdas ut interficeret eum (V)] in finem ne disperdas ut interficeret eum
> Tit. 75 In finem in carminibus canticum ad Assirios Psalmus Asphat (VΩ)] in finem in laudibus psalmus Asaph canticum ad Assyrium.

Not surprisingly, S's readings do not match any one representative manuscript of the Paris recension, sometimes agreeing with one, sometimes with another; overall it is closest to Ωs, a Psalter copied at the Sorbonne in 1270.[21] It appears that S was produced at a centre in touch with recent developments in the text of the Psalms.

14.14. Origin and Date

The Maggs Catalogue suggests that the manuscript was produced in northern England.[22] It notes the presence in the Litany of Oswald, Wilfrid, Cuthbert and John (of Beverley), all Northumbrian saints of the seventh and

---

20   The reading before the square bracket is that of S and any other indicated representatives of the Paris Recension, that after the square brackets represents the critical text of the *Gallicanum*.
21   Paris, Bibliothèque nationale de France, MS Fonds latin 15467.
22   Maggs Catalogue: 47.

eighth centuries whose cults were still thriving in the post-Conquest period. More specifically it proposes Durham as S's place of origin, pointing to similarities of illumination and script, respectively, with two other manuscripts written in the late twelfth century, British Library MSS Additional 35110 and Cotton Claudius E. III. The former manuscript (written before 1195) contains lives of two early Northumbrian saints (Oswald and Cuthbert) and a Life of St Augustine, as well as a reference to the Augustinian priory at Newcastle-on-Tyne;[23] while the latter manuscript contains a work compiled by 1198.[24] Other pieces of evidence in S support a broad date of the late twelfth or early thirteenth century. Its Psalter variants agree closely with the Parisian Recension of the *Gallicanum*, which began circulating about this time. Its use of catchwords (entered at the foot of the verso of the last folio of the preceding quire) without the attending quire signature also suggests a date later in the twelfth-century.[25] On the other hand, its page format of 'writing above top line' highlights a scribal practice which began to die out early in the thirteenth century (in favour of 'below top line' writing).[26]

14.15. Conclusion

The high degree of accuracy evident in the copying of its texts, the professional layout of its contents and the excellent quality of its illuminations all suggest that S was produced by a professional scribe working

23 See *Catalogue of Additions to the Manuscripts in the British Museum in the years 1894–1899* (London: The Trustees of the British Museum, 1901; repr., Oxford: Oxford University Press, 1969): 160–2.
24 See L. Holford-Strevens, *Aulus Gellius: an Antonine Scholar and his Achievement* (rev. edn, Oxford: Oxford University Press, 2003): 15–16 and n. 23.
25 See Ker, *English Manuscripts in the Century after the Norman Conquest* (Oxford: Clarendon Press, 1960): 50.
26 See N.R. Ker, 'From "above top line" to "below top line": a change in scribal practice', *Celtica* 5 (1960): 13–16.

in a scriptorium attached to a religious house, most probably (on other evidence) an Augustinian (or Benedictine) foundation in the north of England. The variant readings in its Psalter text, especially in the tituli, suggest a centre in touch with contemporary Continental developments.[27] Yet despite its origins S was not intended for use in a religious house: the missing illuminated leaves point to a division of the Psalms quite different from the one mandated for the Benedictine Office, which was generally observed in English religious houses of the twelfth and thirteenth centuries. Rather, they point to the *cursus* of the Roman Office, the one that had been observed generally in Anglo-Saxon England until the Benedictine Reform of the late tenth century and which was preserved thereafter among the pious laity. It seems likely then that although written in a religious house, S was intended for a lay person. The absence of glosses and critical signs in S such as might be expected in a Psalter intended for scholarly purposes, accords with this conclusion.[28]

14.16. References

14.16.1. Primary sources

Colgrave, Bertram, *et al.*, eds. *The Paris Psalter (MS. Bibliothèque Nationale Fonds Latin 8824)*, Early English Manuscripts in Facsimile 8. Copenhagen: Rosenkilde and Bagger, 1958.

27   On the intellectual activities of English Augustinian canons in the late twelfth century and their contacts with Continental centres of learning, see R.W. Hunt, 'English Learning in the Late Twelfth Century', *Transactions of the Royal Historical Society*, 4th series, 19 (1936): 19–42: 31–4.

28   I am grateful to Professor Tomonori Matsushita for bringing the Senshu Psalter to my attention and for inviting me to examine it (25–9 June 2007); to Senshu University (Center for Research on Language and Culture, Institute for the Development of Social Intelligence) for financial support; and to the staff of Senshu Library for their help and kindness.

Hieronymus, trans., Libreria Editrice Vaticana, ed. *Biblia Sacra Vetus Vulgata vol. X: Psalmi. Biblia Sacra iuxta latinam vulgatam versionem ad codicum fidem, iussu Pii PP. XI, Pii PP. XII, Ioannis PP. XXIII, Pauli PP. VI, Ioannis Pauli PP. II, cura et studio monachorum Abbatiae Pontificiae Sancti Hieronymi in Urbe Ordinis Sancti Benedicti edita. Textus ex interpretatione Sancti Hieronymi: Liber psalmorum*, vol. X. Rome: Libreria Editrice Vaticana, 1953.

14.16.2. Secondary sources

Hellinga, Lotte and J.B. Trapp, 'Bookbinding 1400–1557', *The Cambridge History of the Book in Britain III (1400–1557)*. Cambridge: Cambridge University Press, 1999: 109–27.

Holford-Strevens, Leofranc. *Aulus Gellius: an Antonine Scholar and his Achievement* (rev. edn). Oxford: Oxford University Press, 2003.

Hunt, R.W. 'English Learning in the Late Twelfth Century', *Transactions of the Royal Historical Society*, 4th series, 19 (1936): 19–42.

Ker, N.R. *English Manuscripts in the Century after the Norman Conquest*. Oxford: Clarendon Press, 1960.

——. 'From "above top line" to "below top line": a change in scribal practice', *Celtica* 5 (1960): 13–16.

Lapidge, Michael ed., *Anglo-Saxon Litanies of the Saints*, Henry Bradshaw Society 106. Woodbridge, Suffolk: Boydell and Brewer, 1991.

Maggs Bros. *Catalogue 1366, European Bulletin no. 23*. London: Maggs Bros, 2004–5.

Mearns, J. *The Canticles of the Christian Church Eastern and Western in Early Medieval Times*. Cambridge: The University Press, 1914.

Notes on Contributors

HELEN BARR is Fellow and Tutor of Lady Margaret Hall, University of Oxford, where she teaches Old and Middle English Language and Shakespeare. Her published work includes critical editions of *The Piers Plowman Tradition* (1993) and *The Digby Poems* (2009). She is the author of *Signes and Sothe: Language in the Piers Plowman Tradition* (1994) and *Socioliterary Practice in Late Medieval England* (2001).

GRAHAM D. CAIE is Professor of English Language and Vice Principal of the University of Glasgow. His research publications are in Old and Middle English Language and Literature, in particular manuscript studies (*Medieval Texts in Context*, co-ed. with Denis Renevey (2008)), editing texts (*The Old English Judgement Day II* (2000), and digitizing manuscripts such as the Middle English *Romaunt of the Rose* (<http://www.memss.arts.gla.ac.uk>).

SYLVIA HUOT is Professor of Medieval French Literature and a Fellow of Pembroke College, University of Cambridge. She has published widely on late medieval French literature, especially the *Roman de la Rose* and the *Roman de Perceforest*. Her most recent book is *Dreams of Lovers and Lies of Poets: Poetry, Knowledge, and Desire in the Roman de la Rose* (2010).

MITSU IDE is Professor of English in the Faculty of Humanities and Social Sciences at Tokyo Metropolitan University. He teaches Old English and the History of English.

MASA IKEGAMI is Professor Emeritus at Keio University, Tokyo. Her research has focused on Middle English pronunciation. She is the author of *Rhyme and Pronunciation: Some Studies of English Rhymes from 'Kyng Alisaunder' to Skelton* (1984) and her recent publications include articles on *The Ashmole Sir Ferumbras, A Gest of Robyn Hode*, John Shirley, Robert Henryson and Shakespeare. She is currently working on final *–e* in later Middle English poems.

AKIYUKI JIMURA is Professor of English Philology, Graduate School of Letters, Hiroshima University. His most recent book is *Studies in Chaucer's Words and his Narratives* (2005). He has been working on textual studies of Chaucer's works in collaboration with Yoshiyuki Nakao and Masatsugu Matsuo and has published several books and articles on Textual Comparison of *The Canterbury Tales* (1995), *Troilus and Criseyde* (1999 and 2009), and on Dream Poetry (2002).

KAZUTOMO KARASAWA, Professor of English Philology at Komazawa University was granted the Young Scholar Award by the English Literary Society of Japan for his article 'The Structure of the *Menologium* and Its Computistical Background', in *Studies in English Literature* 84 (2007). He has recently published 'A Note on the Old English Poem *Menologium* 3b *on ðy eahteoðan dæg*', in *Notes and Queries* 54 (2007), 'A Note on *egesan ne gymeð* in *Beowulf* Line 1757', in *Modern Philology* 106 (2008), and 'Some Problems in the Editions of the *Menologium* with Special Reference to Lines 81a, 184b and 206a', in *Notes and Queries* 56 (2009).

MASATOSHI KAWASAKI, who is Professor of Medieval English literature at Komazawa University in Tokyo, works particularly on the relationship between Chaucer's poetic mind and medieval European tradition. He is the author of *Chaucer's Literary World: 'Game' and its Topography* (1995) and *The Poetry of Chaucer: Medieval European Tradition and its Innovation* (2008). He is now writing an essay on Chaucer's innovative mind and what it might have in common with modern literature.

MASATSUGU MATSUO is Professor Emeritus at Hiroshima University. He works on computer-assisted text processing and is one of the compilers of concordances, rime indices and collation texts of Geoffrey Chaucer's works. He is now preparing collation texts of the Hengwrt and Ellesmere manuscripts of *The Canterbury Tales*. His other publications include *Peace and Conflict Studies: A Theoretical Introduction*.

TOMONORI MATSUSHITA is Professor of Medieval English literature and linguistics at Senshu University and was head of the Center for Research on Language and Culture, Senshu University (2005–9). His main publications are four glossarial concordances to *Piers Plowman* (1998–2010) and four facsimiles of the base manuscripts of *Piers Plowman* (2008–10).

YOSHIYUKI NAKAO is Professor of English Language and Linguistics at Hiroshima University, Japan. He works particularly on ambiguities in Chaucer's language and published *Chaucer no Aimaisei no Kozo* [*The Structure of Chaucer's Ambiguity*] in 2004. He is also a co-editor of *A Comprehensive Textual Collation of Troilus and Criseyde: Corpus Christi College, Cambridge, MS 61 and Windeatt (1990)* published in 2009 and is currently preparing an English version of Nakao (2004).

PATRICK P. O'NEILL is Professor in the Department of English and Comparative Literature at UNC-Chapel Hill and works on Early Medieval Ireland and England. He is the editor of *King Alfred's Old English Prose Translation of the First Fifty Psalms* (2001).

A.V.C. SCHMIDT is Andrew Bradley–James Maxwell Fellow, Senior English Tutor and University C.U.F. lecturer at Balliol College, University of Oxford. He is the editor of *William Langland: Piers Plowman: A Parallel-Text Edition of the A, B, C and Z Versions*, Volume I: Text (1995), and *William Langland: Piers Plowman: A Parallel-Text Edition of the A, B, C and Z Versions*, Volume II: Introduction, Textual Notes, Commentary, Bibliography and Indexical Glossary (2008). Both parts are due to be published in a three-volume revised edition (2011).

AKINOBU TANI is Associate Professor in the Department of Language Studies at Hyogo University of Teacher Education in Kato, Japan. He works particularly on the relationship of word pairs (or doublets/binomials) to genres and styles in Late Middle English prose texts. He is currently preparing a book on word pairs in Late Middle English prose texts.

DAVID WALLACE is Judith Rodin Professor of English at the University of Pennsylvania. He is a former President of the New Chaucer Society

(2004–6) and a Guggenheim Fellow (2009–10). He was awarded the 1998 James Russell Lowell Prize (best book by a member of the Modern Languages Association).

HIROSHI YONEKURA, Professor of English Linguistics in the Graduate School at Hiroshima Jogakuin University, is now President of the Modern English Association in Japan. His publications include *A Rhyme Concordance to the Poetical Works of Geoffrey Chaucer* (1994) and *Studies in English Word Formation: Some Synchronic-Diachronic Problems* (2006). He is currently preparing an article 'Is the Comment Clause observed in Old English?' (included in the book *A Historical Development of the Comment Clause in English*).

Index

Studies in Historical Linguistics

Edited by

DR GRAEME DAVIS, Faculty of Arts, The Open University, UK,

KARL A. BERNHARDT, English Language Consultant with Trinity College London and for the London Chamber of Commerce and Industry International Qualification, and

DR MARK GARNER, School of Language and Literature, University of Aberdeen, UK.

Studies in Historical Linguistics brings together work which utilises the comparative method of language study.

Topics include the examination of language change over time, the genetic classification of language, lexicography, dialectology and etymology. Pronunciation, lexis, morphology and syntax are examined within the framework of historical linguistics. Both synchronic and diachronic approaches are used so that language is examined both at one time and across time.

Historical Linguistics is still a young area of academic study, but it has its foundations in one of the oldest – philology. This series recognises both the seminal importance of philology, and the recent development through the conceptual framework provided by linguistic science.

Vol. 1   Graeme Davis: Comparative Syntax of Old English and Old Icelandic. Linguistic, Literary and Historical Implications. 190 pages. ISBN 3-03910-270-2 / ISBN 0-8204-7199-2

Vol. 2   Graeme Davis (ed.): Dictionary of Surrey English. A New Edition of *A Glossary of Surrey Words* by Granville Leveson Gower with an Introduction by Graeme Davis. 186 pages. ISBN 978-3-03911-081-0